INTRODUCTION TO THE CANADIAN LEGAL SYSTEM

SASHA BAGLAY
University of Ontario Institute of Technology

Toronto

Vice-President, CMPS: Gary Bennett
Editorial Director: Claudine O'Donnell
Senior Acquisitions Editor: Matthew Christian
Marketing Manager: Christine Cozens
Program Manager: Madhu Ranadive
Project Manager: Andrea Falkenberg
Developmental Editor: Cheryl Finch
Production Services: Jogender Taneja/iEnergizer Aptara®, Inc.
Permissions Project Manager: Erica Mojzes
Photo Permissions Research: Candice Velez/QBS
Text Permissions Research: Tom Wilcox/Lumina Datamatics Ltd.
Cover Designer: iEnergizer Aptara®, Inc.
Cover Image: sum1akaJ/Fotolia

Credits and acknowledgments for material borrowed from other sources and reproduced, with permission, in this textbook appear on the appropriate page within the text.

10 9 8 7 6 5 4 3 2 V092 15

Library and Archives Canada Cataloguing in Publication

Baglay, Sasha, 1978–, author
    Introduction to the Canadian legal system / Sasha Baglay,
University of Ontario Institute of Technology.

Includes bibliographical references and index.
ISBN 978-0-13-314285-3 (pbk.)

    1. Law—Canada.   I. Title.

KE444.B27 2015   349.71   C2015-900368-7
KF385.ZA2B27 2015

PEARSON

ISBN 978-0-13-314285-3

Brief Contents

Contents

Part 2   Selected Areas of Law and Critical Perspectives   155

9 Contract Law 202

10 Tort Law   226

Chapters in Pearson Custom Library (online)

Alternative Dispute Resolution and Restorative Justice Initiatives

Preface

This book was inspired by my experience of teaching a first-year Introduction to the Canadian Legal System course at the University of Ontario Institute of Technology (UOIT). The course needed the right balance between substantive law and theory, sophistication and accessibility, and breadth of coverage and depth of analysis, so I wrote the book with these considerations in mind. On the one hand, it is an introductory text intended primarily for first-year university students in disciplines such as law and society, political science, and legal studies. It may also be a useful resource for some second-year university courses as well as college students in law-related programs. On the other hand, the book goes beyond a mere outline of the basics and seeks to help students challenge and question legal rules. It includes a variety of case studies that exemplify the workings of the law and show students the connections between the discussed rules and real life. The writing of this book was an enjoyable learning experience, and I hope the final product will offer a similarly accessible and exciting learning opportunity for you, the reader.

The book is divided into two parts. Part 1 represents a general introduction, covering the systems and sources of law, structure of Canadian government, Canada's courts, theoretical perspectives on the law, and the *Constitution* and the *Charter of Rights and Freedoms*. Part 2 examines six selected areas of law: administrative law, criminal law, contract law, tort law, family law, and human rights in Canada. Each chapter in this part provides not only an outline of substantive law, but also a critical analysis of its selected issues, utilizing theoretical perspectives discussed in Part 1.

In addition to the printed book, the Pearson Custom Library contains two more chapters that can be accessed electronically on the Companion Website; they deal with alternative dispute resolution (ADR) and international law. The ADR chapter describes three main mechanisms of resolving disputes outside of traditional court litigation processes (negotiation, mediation, and arbitration) as well as provides an overview of typologies of conflicts and responses to conflicts—information that helps us to better understand underlying tensions between parties to a dispute and to find more effective ways to address them. The chapter on international law outlines main characteristics of public international law and its difference from domestic law, provides an overview of the United Nations as the main international organization that helps promote peace and interstate cooperation, and briefly reviews three selected areas of international law: the responsibility to protect, prohibition on the use of force in interstate relations, and international criminal law.

Two major themes resonate throughout the book:

1. Principles of liberty, justice, and limited government as guiding values of our legal system. They are reflected and engaged in one way or another in all areas of law. The constitutional structure of our government protects individual liberties and provides

for a range of mechanisms that serve as a check against arbitrary and abusive use of power. The ideas of justice are promoted through the rules of various areas of law: for example, in tort law, through the obligation of wrongdoers to compensate victims for the harm inflicted; in criminal law, through imposition of punishment on offenders; and in administrative law, through the requirements of fairness in government decision making.

2. Pluralism of perspectives and critical analysis. The book emphasizes that there are multiple ways of understanding and analyzing the law: law can be defined in different ways and there may be a variety of views on its underlying values and functions. The book offers students a range of perspectives that can be used for the analysis of legal phenomena. It emphasizes that understanding of the law cannot be separated from its critical analysis: it is not enough to know the content of legal rules; it is necessary to question their underlying rationales, evaluate their perceived objectivity and neutrality, as well as explore the potentially differential impacts of those rules on various groups in society.

As you read the book, you will discover that law does not always provide clear or satisfactory answers; it is a process that evolves under the influence of many factors, including our everyday practices in applying the law, behaving according to it, or challenging rules that we consider unfair or illegitimate. Learning the law is a constant quest, but this is what makes it so exciting. Enjoy the journey!

INSTRUCTOR'S RESOURCES

Instructor's Resource Manual. The Instructor's Resource Manual contains learning objectives, chapter highlights, additional illustrations of key concepts, and discussion questions to aid in lecture preparation.

Test Bank. The Test Bank is available in Word format and includes questions in various formats including multiple choice, true/false, and short answer questions. Each question is accompanied by the correct answer, a page reference to where the answer can be found in the book, and a difficulty ranking of *easy*, *moderate*, or *challenging*.

COURSESMART FOR INSTRUCTORS

CourseSmart goes beyond traditional expectations—providing instant, online access to the textbooks and course materials you need at a lower cost for students. And even as students save money, you can save time and hassle with a digital eTextbook that allows you to search for the most relevant content at the very moment you need it. Whether it's in evaluating textbooks or creating lecture notes to help students with difficult concepts, CourseSmart can make life a little easier.

LEARNING SOLUTIONS MANAGERS

Pearson's Learning Solutions Managers work with faculty and campus course designers to ensure that Pearson technology products, assessment tools, and online course materials are tailored to meet your specific needs. This highly qualified team is dedicated to helping schools take full advantage of a wide range of educational resources, by assisting in the integration of a variety of instructional materials and media formats. Your local Pearson Education sales representative can provide you with more details on this service program.

PEARSON CUSTOM LIBRARY

For enrollments of at least 25 students, you can create your own textbook by choosing the chapters that best suit your own course needs. To begin building your custom text, visit www.pearsoncustomlibrary.com. You may also work with a dedicated Pearson Custom Library editor to create your ideal text—publishing your own original content or mixing and matching Pearson content. Contact your local Pearson Representative to get started.

Acknowledgments

This book project was a bit more challenging and time-consuming than I originally antic-ipated. Nevertheless, it was a wonderful and rewarding experience, in large part due to the support of my family (mom and dad, you are a constant source of love and inspiration) and friends (Lena, thank you for being there to listen to my stressed out ramblings ☺). Thank you, all! Many thanks to my colleagues at UOIT, particularly Rachel Ariss and Thomas McMorrow, for providing very helpful comments on the draft chapters of the book (Tom, I still owe you many, many dinners ☺).

I gratefully acknowledge the assistance of the following reviewers whose comments helped shape the first edition of *Introduction to the Canadian Legal System*: Walter Babicz, University of Northern British Columbia; Graham M. Bennett, University of Waterloo; Leo de Jourdan, Canadore College; Stephen Duggan, Humber College; Greg Flynn, McMaster University; Curtis Fogel, Lakehead University; Mike Gamble, Humber College; Kevin Guest, Seneca College; Melanie Marchand, Georgian College; Craig Stephenson, Conestoga College; Larry White, Seneca College; and Brian Young, Camosun College.

I also appreciate the help of all Pearson Canada staff involved in this project, includ-ing Matthew Christian, Madhu Ranadive, Cheryl Finch, Andrea Falkenberg, and copy editor Laurel Sparrow of Sparrow & Associates.

Sasha Baglay

Chapter 1

What Is Law?

Learning Objectives

After reading this chapter, you should be able to:

- Describe at least five approaches to the definition of law.

- Explain three main functions of law.

- Name three main characteristics of legal rules.

- Describe three main reasons why people obey legal rules.

- Explain the notion of the rule of law.

- Name four ways to classify legal rules.

Chapter Outline

Introduction

What is law? At first blush, it seems to be an easy question: everyone intuitively knows what law is. Yet, on further contemplation, you may discover that there is no one simple answer to it. For centuries, scholars have debated the issue and come up with a variety of responses. In fact, in order to answer "What is law?", we need to examine at least five sub-questions:

- How is law developed and expressed? That is, what form does it take: oral narrations? written documents? ceremonies?
- What are the functions of law in society?
- What values does law reflect and what values should it reflect?
- What are the characteristics of legal rules?
- Why do people obey legal rules?

In this chapter, we will discuss each of the above questions and familiarize ourselves with the concept of the rule of law and various ways to classify legal rules. The ultimate objective of this chapter is to introduce you to various approaches to understanding the law and its forms, functions, and characteristics.

1. HOW IS LAW DEVELOPED AND EXPRESSED?

Read the two descriptions that follow. In your opinion, which one more accurately reflects how law is developed and expressed?

Description 1: Law is a system of rules that are created by a government authority and supported by the enforcement powers of the state. The rules appear in a written form as statutes, regulations, and judicial decisions. Rules are created according to formal, centralized, and strictly prescribed processes. While the general population may have some input into the formation of legal rules, for the most part, it is delegated to specialized bodies: statutes are passed by legislatures; regulations, rules, and policies are developed by various executive departments; and common law rules are developed by courts. Legal rules are arranged in a hierarchy, with the *Constitution* being the supreme law with which all other laws must comply.

Description 2: Law is "the expression of the way to live a good life."[1] It derives from multiple sources: customs; codes and regulations made by chiefs and clan elders; creation stories; and observation of the physical world.[2] Rules are produced in a decentralized manner, often through deliberation and discussion by community members. Such meetings can be formal or informal, ad hoc or highly structured.[3] Law is interrelated with spiritual, political, and other practices of a community. While some rules are written, others are passed through oral narration from generation to generation. Spiritual connection to the land is of great significance to the community. The law's role is to help maintain good relations within the community, with other communities, and with the land and its inhabitants.[4]

Which of the two descriptions provides an accurate characterization of the development and expression of the law? Actually, both of them do. Roughly speaking, description 1 is closer to the system established by the dominant European settler society in Canada—something that many of us are more familiar with. It reflects a state-centred approach to law: law is produced and enforced by government authorities in a highly structured and hierarchical way. Description 2 more closely reflects Aboriginal legal tradition, which represents a deliberative, nonhierarchical, and community-driven process of law creation. Both of these forms of law (descriptions 1 and 2) are present in Canada.

These examples show us that law may be expressed in a variety of ways and should not be understood merely as a system of government-pronounced rules. In fact, in every jurisdiction, various legal regimes exist at the same time: there are centralized rules produced by the state; local customs that developed through habitual long-term practices of a given community; legal traditions of indigenous communities; and rules developed by other nonstate actors such as professional associations, corporate groups, and international bodies. The idea of **legal pluralism** reflects precisely this multiplicity of legal regimes developed by various actors (state and nonstate) and at different sites (local, national, international). (For more on legal pluralism, see Chapter 5.) The Canadian legal system may be better understood through the lens of legal pluralism.

Law is not a mysterious domain reserved exclusively for lawyers and government officials. Each and every one of us can contribute to the development of the law, but in order to do this, we first need to gain a better understanding of its main structure and characteristics—the issues that this book helps to illuminate. Box 1.1 gives some examples of how some writers have described law.

Box 1.1

Examples of Various Definitions of Law

Thomas Aquinas, *Summa Theologica* (1265–1274): "Law . . . is nothing else than an ordinance of reasons for the common good, made by him who has care of the community, and promulgated."

Sir William Blackstone, *Commentaries on the Laws of England* (1765–1769): "Law, in its most general and comprehensive sense, signifies a rule of action; and is applied indiscriminately to all kinds of action. . . . And it is that rule of action, which is prescribed by some superior, and which the inferior is bound to obey."

Black's Law Dictionary (7th edition, 1999): "Law is the regime that orders human activities and relations through systematic application of the force of politically organized society, or through social pressure, backed by force, in such a society."

Paul Schiff Berman, *Global Legal Pluralism: A Jurisprudence of Law beyond Borders* (2012) at 56: Law is "what people view as law. This formulation turns the what-is-law question into a descriptive inquiry concerning which social norms are recognized as authoritative sources of obligation and by whom."

There is no single definition of law. As you can see from the examples in Box 1.1, there are as many definitions as there are theorists. For the purpose of our discussion, it is useful to highlight two ways of characterizing law: a narrow and a broad approach. A narrow approach understands law as a system of prescribed rules. It reflects a more practical orientation of the study of law: we need to know what the rules are in order to identify our rights and obligations, and to know the consequences of our actions and the ways to protect our interests. Much of the discussion in this book is dedicated to this practical information and focuses primarily on the rules created by state authorities.

A broader perspective characterizes law as a process of searching for and formulating principles by which society should operate. It can be viewed as ". . . a social experience that requires us to associate with one another and communicate about how we should best conduct our affairs."[5] Law is not static; it changes and evolves as a result of deliberation and engagement of various actors with the law, including individuals in their everyday activities. Law reflects a particular worldview of a given society and changes along with it. This perspective will be useful for our critical analysis of the law: what objectives does law serve? What should be its objectives? Does it always reflect perspectives of all diverse groups in society? How does it help to ensure legitimacy and accountability of the state and other powerful actors?

2. WHAT ARE THE FUNCTIONS OF THE LAW?

Law performs multiple functions, but we will focus only on the following three:

- establishment and maintenance of order in society;
- promotion of justice and fairness; and
- response to and promotion of social change.

2.1 Order and Regulation

Law establishes rules and parameters of behaviour for individuals, corporations, and the state. It can create incentives to encourage desirable behaviour and impose sanctions to discourage undesirable conduct. Law helps classify human social activities and create rules governing each particular area of those activities.[6] It sets out the scope and limits of state authority. It helps prevent and settle disputes by delineating actors' rights and responsibilities. Law allows us to "speak the same language" in the sense that it creates certain predictable patterns of behaviour: we know what to expect from one another.

The content and underlying rationales of the rules are defined by the nature and worldview of a given society. At a high level of abstraction, we can distinguish two prominent perspectives on society: conflict and consensual. The conflict model relies on the ideas of such philosophers as Thomas Hobbes (1588–1679) and Karl Marx (1818–1883), while the consensual perspective can be identified with the ideas of John Locke (1632–1704), for example.

Hobbes viewed people as selfish and violent. In the "state of nature," an individual's life would be "solitary, poor, nasty, brutish and short."[7] Hence, the purpose of public institutions and the law would be largely coercive in order to restrict the violent nature of human beings. *Marx* also highlighted the oppressive nature of the law, although from a different perspective. He viewed society as consisting of two opposing classes: the bourgeoisie and the proletariat. The bourgeoisie is in the position of power: it holds wealth, controls the means of production, and has political influence. In contrast, the proletariat is in an oppressed position, which the bourgeoisie seeks to exploit in order to gain more from the workers' labour at the lowest cost. In this system, law defined by class division is a tool of oppression in the hands of the rich and powerful bourgeoisie. A Marxist perspective can be applied more broadly to highlight power imbalances and divisions between different groups in society.

In contrast to the conflict perspective, *Locke* viewed society as largely peaceful and cooperative. While individuals do agree to cede some of their freedoms to a central authority, such authority does not take a strongly coercive nature.[8] Law is focused on promoting individual rights and interactions rather than stringently controlling human behaviour.

Of course, the conflict and consensus perspectives reflect two ideal types. Hardly any contemporary society can be viewed as reflecting a model based exclusively on conflict or on consensus. Rather, they are located somewhere on the spectrum between the two extremes, often combining both conflict and consensus dynamics. For example, a large part of the history of interactions between the First Nations and settler communities in Canada can be characterized by conflict and oppression. European settlers employed law, among other means, in order to limit the rights of the First Nations communities and suppress their culture, practices, and traditions (see more on this in Chapters 2 and 3). The lack of consideration of the First Nations' interests provoked challenges and resistance from those communities, which periodically erupted in physical standoffs such as those at Oka and Ipperwash. Since the 1990s, government policy has signalled a shift toward a more consensual approach, emphasizing negotiation and reconciliation. For example, negotiation (as opposed to litigation) is considered a preferred approach to resolving land claims (for more on this, see Chapter 3 and the chapter on alternative dispute resolution and restorative justice on the Companion Website). However, conflicts and tensions still exist for a variety of reasons, including protracted and ineffective land claim resolution processes. Thus, current interactions between the First Nations and settler communities can be characterized by both conflict and cooperation.

2.2 Justice

Law is usually considered instrumental in promoting a just society. However, just as there is no single definition of law, there is no single definition of justice. Justice can be viewed as one of the principles used to regulate human interactions and address conflicts. It can take several forms. Here, we will discuss four forms of justice: distributive, corrective, retributive, and restorative.

Distributive justice refers to rules prescribing how resources and entitlements are to be allocated in a given society. The allocation can be made according to various criteria: equality (each citizen gets an equal share), merit, needs, proportion of one's contribution, or other considerations. The principles of distributive justice can be found in many aspects of law. For example, rules of taxation form part of a system of redistribution of wealth in society. Eligibility criteria for social assistance reflect allocation of supports on the basis of need. Certain rules of contract law (e.g., those that help protect weaker parties from being taken advantage of by more powerful parties) can also be said to help ensure more equal distribution of wealth in society (see Chapter 9).[9]

Corrective justice focuses on remedying inequality that results from wrongdoings or unfair dealings between individual parties. Unlike distributive justice, which deals with issues in society at large, corrective justice is focused on individual interactions. For example, if an individual's property is damaged, the initial equality between the wrongdoer and the victim is lost. A corrective justice approach seeks to restore equality and return the victim to their original position. Corrective justice principles can be found, for example, in tort law (see Chapter 10) and certain aspects of criminal law (e.g., wrongdoers being ordered to pay reparations to victims).

Retributive justice provides a different perspective on how to respond to wrongdoings. It reflects an idea that a wrongdoer should be subject to punishment proportionate to the degree of blameworthiness. The suffering imposed on the wrongdoer is intended to punish and to deter, as well as to advance social objectives such as order, safety, and crime reduction. The ideas of retributive justice are most commonly found in criminal law.

Restorative justice offers yet another approach to addressing wrongdoings. It views an offence as an event that ruins the relationship between a wrongdoer and a victim as well as the relationships within a community. Correspondingly, restorative justice focuses on re-establishing the harmony in these relations through problem solving, dialogue, reconciliation, and forgiveness. The direct communication between the wrongdoer, the victim, and the community is key to the process. Restorative justice is employed in various contexts, including criminal law (e.g., victim–offender mediation, sentencing circles (see the chapter on alternative dispute resolution and restorative justice on the Companion Website)), and national reconciliation in the aftermath of civil wars and widespread human rights abuses.

2.3 Social Change

Law shapes our understanding of what is acceptable, reasonable, and "natural." It influences how we conceive of our rights and interests and ways of pursuing them; how we think of justice and fairness; and where we draw the line between public and private activity.[10] Law is a powerful force that not only establishes parameters for our conduct but also creates a frame of reference for our thinking. Correspondingly, law can play an important role in promoting **social change** (that is, modifications in how individuals interact with each other and the state, how they govern themselves, what values they consider important, and how they organize various activities in public and private spheres).[11]

There is a complex interplay between law and social change. On the one hand, law has to follow changes in society: it reflects society's values and responds to new developments that need a regulatory framework. For example, the expansion of Internet use necessitated legal regulation of various related issues such as privacy, freedom of speech, electronic commerce, and protection from cybercrimes. On the other hand, law can also help promote changes in society. For example, the adoption of federal and provincial human rights codes can be said to contribute to the strengthening of the overall culture of equality and nondiscrimination. In most cases, however, law can be seen as both a result and a cause of social change. For instance, the recognition of same-sex marriage in Canada can be considered to reflect the growing acceptance of same-sex relationships in society. At the same time, such official recognition can also be seen as strengthening the protection of gay rights and promoting further acceptance of same-sex marriage by the wider public.

3. WHAT VALUES DOES LAW REFLECT AND WHAT VALUES SHOULD IT REFLECT?

This issue has been the subject of extensive and ongoing debate. Chapter 5 provides a more detailed overview of various theoretical approaches to understanding the law. In this section, we will only commence the discussion by raising a few questions: how do we determine what values laws should reflect? Are laws neutral and objective?

Natural law and positivism were among the early theoretical approaches to grapple with some of the above issues. **Natural law** theorists argue that there exist objective, identifiable, "natural values" and that it is these values that must be reflected in man-made laws. If laws are inconsistent with natural law principles, such laws are invalid. For example, criminal laws punishing murder can be seen as reflecting a natural law principle that protects the sanctity of human life. We can expect to find natural law principles universally across all societies, cultures, and historic periods. Now, pause for a moment and think: can you identify any values that can be considered natural values?

You may have named such values as liberty, dignity, or inviolability of the individual person and property. Although we can find the reflection and protection of these values in laws of various societies, the understanding of other natural values may vary from society to society. For example, is adultery a crime? Should gay couples be allowed to marry? Is the death penalty permissible? Even within the same society there may be disagreements as to what constitutes a natural value in these cases. For instance, in relation to assisted suicide, what is the core natural value that should be protected: the sanctity of human life (even where the person does not wish to continue living in extreme pain), or the individual right to choose when and how to die?

Positivism provides a different perspective on law. It focuses on what laws actually say as opposed to their consistency with moral or natural law principles. The validity of the law is not tied to morality, but rather depends on whether it was enacted by a legitimate authority according to a prescribed procedure. Thus, a positivist approach to the issue of assisted suicide would be to examine what laws are in place and how they have been enacted.

The twentieth century (particularly, its second half) saw the development of critical scholarship that started to question the neutrality and objectivity of laws. Among these critical approaches are legal realism, critical legal studies, critical race theory, and feminist

Box 1.2

Law and Its Underlying Values: Examples

Different societies may prioritize different values. For example, Western tradition places paramount importance on individualism, autonomy, and equality. Correspondingly, legal rules focus on protecting individual freedoms and creating preconditions for persons to freely pursue their choices in life.[12] The responsibility for bettering oneself rests with the individual. The law does not define what a good life is and is not intended to ensure that everyone has a good life;[13] it only creates preconditions for individuals to pursue their visions of a good life. We can find these principles reflected in many areas of law: individual rights and freedoms in constitutional law, freedom of contract in contract law, various remedies to protect individual interests and property, and the like.

However, not all cultures place the same emphasis on autonomy, equality, and individualism.

For instance, the First Nations legal tradition is more community oriented. Law interwoven with cultural and spiritual practices is seen as a guide for how to live a good life, in harmony with the community and the land. Land itself is considered not merely a resource, but a source of spirituality. It is a part of an interconnected system that is necessary for a community's survival.[14] Control over land is framed not in terms of ownership but rather of trusteeship where the current generation is taking care of the land on behalf of future generations. From this comes the importance of protecting the land from being taken away or being subject to extensive development that can alter a community's way of life. This view often contrasts with Western tradition, which usually views land merely as a resource that can be owned and used for the owner's benefit or general economic development.

studies. The detailed discussion of these approaches is contained in Chapter 5, so here it will suffice to briefly mention only two points. First, these approaches highlight that law must be understood in its broader social context and with the consideration of economic, political, and other factors that influence its content and application. Second, the unequal position of various groups in society impacts their ability to shape the law. Groups that have more power or are more vocal in society have a better chance to have their perspective reflected in legal rules. For example, feminist and critical race theories expose that laws tended to reflect the views and interests of white, middle-class men who dominated legislatures and courts. Thus, in order to identify what values a law reflects, we need to find out how that law came about and what its actual effect on various groups in society is. Box 1.2 gives some examples of law and its underlying values.

4. WHAT ARE THE CHARACTERISTICS OF LEGAL RULES?

In contemporary societies, a variety of rules regulate our conduct but not all of them are legal rules. For example, the rules of etiquette and good manners are not officially prescribed, yet we often feel compelled to follow them. So, what distinguishes legal rules from social norms?

As in relation to other questions discussed in this chapter, there is no universal agreement on characteristics of legal rules. Various theories of law would define somewhat differently what makes a rule legal. For the purpose of our discussion, we will take note of three factors that can help us determine whether a rule is a legal one: how a rule is created; whether it is backed up by a particular authority; and what the "virtues" of legal rules should be.

First, legal rules are created in a particular manner, following a certain process having more or less formality. What process specifically is to be followed depends on a given community and its legal tradition. For example, in Western tradition, norms are created through legislative enactment as well as judicial decision making. In the First Nations communities, they are created through various formal and informal processes, which often involve broad community participation and cultural practices.

Second, legal rules are usually identified with appeal to a particular authority and official recognition of that rule. Some consider that it is the enforcement authority of the state that makes a rule legal. If a legal rule is violated, the offender may be subject to sanctions and/or the victim may turn to authorities to affirm or restore violated rights. In contrast, this is not the case for social norms, for example. However, not everyone agrees that backing by a state authority is an essential element of a legal rule. As briefly mentioned in section 1, legal pluralism recognizes that law may come from both state and nonstate authorities. For example, rules of First Nations communities are not technically backed up by the authority of the state, but they still constitute law and rely on community enforcement.

Third, some theorists identified virtues that legal rules should possess. For example:

- Legal rules should be prospective rather than retroactive. As a matter of fairness, individuals should know the rules in advance in order to be able to make informed decisions about compliance.

- Legal rules should be reasonably constant. On the one hand, laws should not be changed too frequently, but, on the other, they need to be amended from time to time in order to respond to changes in society.

- Legal rules should be intelligible. Individuals should have a reasonably clear idea about what the rule is and what the consequences of a given course of action are.

- Legal rules should be accessible. Individuals should know where to find them and whom to speak to if they have a question about those rules.[15]

5. WHY DO PEOPLE OBEY LEGAL RULES?

Most of the time, people follow legal rules. Why is this so? Is it because they are afraid of being caught and punished? Or because they believe that disobeying the law is morally wrong? Or do they do it out of habit?

All of the above-mentioned reasons may partially explain why people obey legal rules. The threat of sanctions can be a powerful motivator to follow the rules. In fact, the whole of criminal law is based on this presumption. It is often argued that the more severe and the more certain the sanctions are, the more they will deter individuals from violating the rules. However, despite the existence of criminal and other sanctions as well as extensive enforcement mechanisms, some people still break the law. Then the fear of sanctions is not the only reason why people obey or disobey the law.

From a young age, we are socialized into law-abiding conduct. Thus, we can say that some behaviours are attributed to a habit and our internalized understanding of proper conduct. Perhaps most importantly, many feel that we have a moral duty to obey the law. It is a part of being a good citizen. Obeying the law contributes to the overall public good: order and safety in society. But would we feel that we have a moral duty to obey just any law? For example, should we obey a law that is discriminatory and oppressive? One can argue that the basis for the moral duty to obey the law is found in the belief that the existing legal system is fair and just. When individuals feel that they can participate in the rule formation and that their interests are considered, they are more likely to comply with the law even in the absence of coercion. At the same time, individuals may expressly challenge or protest a law and authority that they do not consider legitimate or fair.

6. THE RULE OF LAW

Everyone has heard the expression "the rule of law." It is considered one of the cornerstones of a democratic society. However, what does it mean? Most basically, the **rule of law** means that no one—whether private individual or public official—is above the law. In addition, the rule of law requires the existence of a system of law that creates a normative framework for society and that the relationship between the state and the individual is regulated by law.[16] As some noted, the rule of law is ". . . the glue that binds our society together; it is the social contract by which we agree to live and work together."[17] The rule of law ensures that individuals have "a stable, predictable and ordered society in which to conduct their affairs"[18] and a protection from arbitrary state action[19] (for more on the rule of law, see Chapter 3). It also includes dimensions such as respect for minority rights, reconciliation of Aboriginal and non-Aboriginal interests through negotiation, fair procedural safeguards in the criminal process, and respect for the separation of the executive, legislative, and judicial branches.[20] Courts play an important role in ensuring that law applies equally to everyone and that individuals are protected against unrestricted and arbitrary power of the state. Hence, the respect for courts, their orders, and the administration of justice is an integral component of actual implementation of the rule of law in society. If laws can be disregarded without consequence, the whole legal order can break down. Consider the situation in Box 1.3.

What do we learn from the above discussion? We often seek certainty in law and want to have clear and definitive answers. Of course, legislation and judicial decisions often do provide us with such answers. However, many aspects of both practical application of the law and its theoretical analysis are contested and indeterminate. For example, as the case in Box 1.3 illustrates, courts have not yet definitely and clearly answered the questions with respect to the rule of law in the context of disputes involving competing

Box 1.3

Case Study Illustration: *Henco Industries v Haudenosaunee Six Nations* (2006), 82 OR (3d) 721

Haudenosaunee Six Nations is the First Nations community residing on the lands near the Grand River in Ontario. Their settlement in that location dates back to the eighteenth century when Sir Frederick Haldimand, then governor of Quebec, made a promise that the Six Nations might take possession and settle on these lands (known as the Haldimand Tract). In the centuries to follow, significant portions of this land were taken away by the governments of Ontario and Canada. Since the 1970s, the Six Nations have made multiple claims seeking the return of the lands, and the claims negotiations between the First Nations and federal/provincial governments are ongoing.

In 1992, Henco Industries acquired a parcel of land in the Haldimand Tract near the town of Caledonia and in 2005 decided to build a subdivision there. This parcel of land is among the disputed territories that are subject to the ongoing land

claim process. Having found out about Henco's plans, protesters from the Six Nations occupied the building site seeking to prevent construction on the lands that they consider traditionally theirs. Before we proceed to discuss this case, please attempt to answer the following questions on your own: Whose rights are at stake here and how ought they to be respected? What do you think was the law's response to this situation? What, in your opinion, should the law's response have been? What can this example reveal about the law's forms, functions, values, and characteristics?

What was the law's response to this situation?
Euro-Canadian law provides for various legal measures to protect property and its use. For example, if someone interferes with the owner's rightful use or enjoyment of their property, it is possible to apply for an **injunction**—a court order compelling a certain type of conduct by an individual, a group, or a corporation. In our case, Henco applied for and obtained an injunction against the protesters that directed them to cease occupation of the building site. The Six Nations defied the court order and continued protests.

Disobedience of a court order constitutes contempt of court and can lead to civil and criminal sanctions. The protesters were held in contempt of court and sentenced to 30 days of imprisonment.

What are the underlying values in this case?
In this case, we can observe two sets of perspectives. On the one hand, there is the dominant Euro-Canadian law, according to which the land is subject to ownership and is a resource that is to be used. Thus, the injunction constitutes proper enforcement of Henco's interests.

On the other hand is the Aboriginal perspective on the land. Six Nations see the land in question as

Photo 1.1
A Native protester prepares to raise a Six Nations flag on a barricade at a housing development in Caledonia, Ontario, during unrest in 2006

Nathan Dennette/Canadian Press/AP Images

(continued)

Box 1.3 *(continued)*

traditionally theirs, and they have a particular connection with it. For them, land is not merely a possession or a resource; it is an integral part of a community's lifeworld. Aboriginal communities have their own legal tradition, which requires them to take steps to protect their land and preserve it for future generations. It is this duty to protect the land that motivated the Six Nations to continue protesting the development despite court injunction.[21] They did not see the injunction as legitimate because the dominant Euro-Canadian system did not afford proper consideration to their interests and historic claim to the land in question. The protesters did not even accept the jurisdiction of the courts that ordered the injunctions.[22]

In cases such as *Henco*, we need to look into the underlying cause of the conflict. It cannot be understood without considering the history of treatment of the First Nations in Canada, as well as the extent (or lack) of inclusion of their perspectives in the dominant Euro-Canadian legal system. From our earlier discussion, if individuals or groups do not see law as fair and inclusive, they may resist it and engage in civil disobedience to bring about a change. At the heart of *Henco* and other similar disputes is the discontent of the First Nations peoples with the lack of consideration of their interests and values. Then, holding them in contempt of court may only further alienate them.[23]

The rule of law

The protesters explained that their own First Nations law required them to protect the land.[24] Thus, they were following the law, just not the law of the dominant Euro-Canadian system. What does this mean for our understanding of the rule of law?

In sentencing the protesters for contempt of court, the trial judge acknowledged that the land claims negotiation process has been protracted, allegedly causing the Six Nations injustice, but emphasized that enforcement of court orders was important in order to protect the rule of law[25] (of the dominant system). Whatever the community's

frustration is, a court order must be obeyed and the court must ensure equal application of law to all.[26]

Both First Nations and settler communities have important objectives to advance. For the non-Aboriginal system, ensuring respect for court orders is a legitimate objective that is fundamental to the maintenance of order and respect for the law in society. From the First Nations perspective, the dominant system is questionable because of its limited ability and willingness to offer effective and meaningful resolution of their claims. Further, the First Nations' own legal tradition imposes certain obligations on members, such as the duty to protect the land. How do we reconcile the objectives of the First Nations and the Euro-Canadian systems in the context of the rule of law?

This question is very challenging and has not yet been fully answered by either courts or academics. On appeal, the Court of Appeal for Ontario recognized that the rule of law is not merely about obedience to court orders but includes respect for minority rights and reconciliation of Aboriginal and non-Aboriginal interests.[27] This decision can be considered a step in the right direction, suggesting that the rule of law should not be understood from a single dimension of the dominant Euro-Canadian system but should include consideration of Aboriginal interests. However, some commentators remain skeptical about the potential of the Court of Appeal decision to substantively change understanding of the rule of law.[28] Even if this more inclusive perspective gains ground, its practical implementation may pose challenges: how exactly are courts to take into consideration reconciliation of Aboriginal and non-Aboriginal interests? All of this shows that law is an ongoing and challenging process that encounters new questions and evolves as we engage with it in our everyday lives. In some cases, law does not give us ready-made answers; solutions emerge incrementally through a complex process of discussion, analysis, and contemplation.

perspectives of the First Nations and Euro-Canadian systems. Law is a process and thus it is subject to constant questioning and change. It may be uncomfortable to think of law as ambiguous, changing, and contested, but this is one of the keys to better understanding the law. Law cannot be understood by mechanically learning legal rules alone; it needs to be seen in broader social context—in terms of both being influenced by changes in society and promoting such changes. While, ideally, law should aspire to bring justice and protection to everyone in society, we also need to be aware of law's potential biases and the differential impact that it may have on different groups in society, particularly along gender, class, and race lines.

7. TYPES OF LAW

There are several ways to classify laws: domestic versus international; by subject matter; public versus private; and substantive versus procedural (see Figure 1.1).

7.1 Domestic versus International Law

Domestic or national laws are laws that are produced by a given state and apply to individuals, corporations, and other entities present within that state's territory. For example, anyone in Canadian territory—whether a Canadian citizen or a mere visitor to the country (but not a foreign diplomat[29])—is subject to Canadian domestic law.

International law differs from domestic law in its creation, application, and enforcement. In the international arena, there is no single international parliament to pass laws for all nations. Rather, international law comes from a variety of sources and is created by various actors (states, international organizations, international courts, and tribunals).

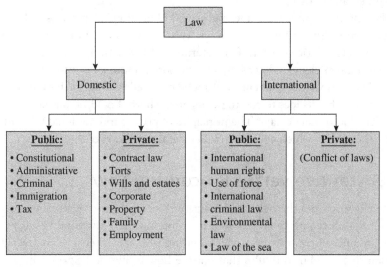

Figure 1.1 Types of law

For the most part, international law is designed to regulate conduct of states rather than individuals. Finally, unlike in the domestic setting, there is no single international authority to enforce international law. For more details on international law, see the chapter on international law on the Companion Website as well as Chapter 12 in this book.

7.2 By Subject Matter

Laws can be distinguished by the types of issues they regulate: torts, family, employment, labour relations, constitutional, administrative, criminal, immigration, and others. We will examine the following selected subject matter areas: criminal, tort, contract, family, administrative, and human rights law (see Chapters 7 to 12).

7.3 Public versus Private Law

Both domestic and international law can be divided into public and private types. In the domestic context, public law deals with collective interests and addresses interactions between the state and individuals as well as society at large. For example, constitutional, administrative, and criminal law are considered public law. In contrast, private law deals with individual interests and regulates private interactions among individuals and/or corporations. For example, contract and tort law are considered private law.

Although, at first sight, the distinction between private and public law seems feasible, there is much debate as to whether it is useful and justified.[30] For example, family law not only deals with private matters within a family, but also has a significant public dimension (e.g., the definition of marriage/cohabitation implies what types of relationships are considered acceptable; child protection provisions allow the state to intervene in dysfunctional families; and so on).

Public international law outlines rights and obligations of states as well as rules of their interaction. Private international law (also called the conflict of laws) does not touch upon state relations but rather determines how national rules deal with cases involving a "foreign element." Let's say an Ecuadorian national is injured while working for a Canadian company in Guatemala. Which laws would determine his entitlements for compensation? If he decides to sue the company, where should he pursue the claim: in Canada, Ecuador, or Guatemala? The principles of private international law will help us determine the rules of which country should govern resolution of this case.

7.4 Substantive versus Procedural Law

Substantive law outlines the rights and obligations of legal persons, while procedural law determines the procedure to be followed in enforcing these rights and obligations. For example, the rules of contract law (which outline who can enter into contracts) constitute substantive law, but the rules that outline how to pursue litigation in the case of contract breach constitute procedural law.

SUMMARY

Law performs a number of important functions in society: it helps establish and maintain order, promotes justice, and can facilitate social change. Law can exist in a variety of forms: written, oral, customary, and others. Despite these different forms, legal rules have some common characteristics: they are developed by a particular authority in a certain prescribed manner; they are backed up by a state or community authority; and they should be prospective, reasonably constant, intelligible, and accessible. Legal rules can be divided according to various criteria: public versus private, substantive versus procedural, domestic versus international, and by subject matter.

While this textbook will deal with law primarily as a system of written rules that are prescribed by the state, law should not be understood so narrowly. It is a social experience in which all of us participate and can contribute to a search for developing a fairer and more just society. The legitimacy and fairness of legal rules is highly important in ensuring individual compliance with them. Individuals can seek to challenge unfair laws in a variety of ways (e.g., protests or litigation) and may even engage in civil disobedience in order to bring about change. Each chapter of this book will not only provide you with an outline of rules for a particular area of law, but also offer some critical perspectives to help you question existing rules and form your own opinion about their fairness and rationality.

Critical Thinking Questions

1. In your opinion, does law serve the interests of all or does it reflect the interests and views of dominant groups or communities in society? Explain and give examples.
2. How would you define law in your own words, based on your understanding of and experience with the legal system?
3. Why is the rule of law important?

Further Readings and Useful Resources

1. Rachel Ariss with John Cutfeet, *Keeping the Land: Kitchenuhmaykoosib Inninuwug, Reconciliation and Canadian Law* (Halifax & Winnipeg: Fernwood Publishing, 2012).
2. George Pavlich, *Law and Society Redefined* (Don Mills: Oxford University Press, 2011).
3. Steven Vago & Adie Nelson, *Law and Society: Canadian Edition* (Toronto: Pearson/Prentice Hall, 2004).

Endnotes

1. Rachel Ariss with John Cutfeet, *Keeping the Land: Kitchenuhmaykoosib Inninuwug, Reconciliation and Canadian Law* (Halifax & Winnipeg: Fernwood Publishing, 2012) at 44.
2. John Borrows, *Canada's Indigenous Constitution* (Toronto: University of Toronto Press, 2010) at 24–36.
3. *Ibid* at 36.

4. Ariss, *supra* note 1 at 42.
5. Borrows, *supra* note 2 at 10.
6. Logan Atkinson & Neil Sargent, *Private Law, Social Life: An Introduction*, 2nd ed (Markham: LexisNexis Canada, 2007) at 2–3.
7. Hobbes, *Leviathan* (1651), Michael Oakshott, ed (Oxford: Basil Blackwell, 1947) at 82.
8. John Locke, *Two Treatises of Government: The Second Treatise* (1690) (Buffalo: Prometheus Books, 1986).
9. See generally, Anthony Townsend Kronman, "Contract Law and Distributive Justice" (1980) 79 Yale LJ 473.
10. Paul Schiff Berman, *Global Legal Pluralism: A Jurisprudence of Law beyond Borders* (Cambridge: Cambridge University Press, 2012) at 100–102.
11. See, for example, Steven Vago & Adie Nelson, *Law and Society: Canadian Edition* (Toronto: Pearson-Prentice Hall, 2004), ch 7.
12. Ariss, *supra* note 1 at 41.
13. *Ibid* at 41.
14. *Ibid* at 44–45.
15. Some of these key characteristics have been identified by Lon Fuller in *The Morality of Law* (New Haven: Yale University Press, 1965), ch 2.
16. *British Columbia v Imperial Tobacco Canada Ltd*, [2005] 2 SCR 473 at para 58.
17. *Platinex Inc v Kitchenuhmaykoosib Inninuwug First Nation*, [2008] OJ No 1014 at para 40.
18. *Reference re Secession of Quebec*, [1998] 2 SCR 217 at 257.
19. *Ibid*.
20. *Henco Industries v Haudenosaunee Six Nations* (2006), 82 OR (3d) 721 at para 142 (CA).
21. Ariss, *supra* note 1 at 83.
22. *Henco Industries v Haudenosaunee Six Nations Confederacy Council* [2006] OJ No 3285 at para 74.
23. Ryan Newell, "Only One Law: Indigenous Land Disputes and the Contested Nature of the Rule of Law" (2013) 11:1 Indigenous LJ 41 at paras 43–45 (Quicklaw).
24. Ariss, *supra* note 1 at 43.
25. *Henco Industries, supra* note 22.
26. *Ibid*.
27. *Henco Industries, supra* note 20 at para 142.
28. Newell, *supra* note 23.
29. While foreign officials are expected to respect and abide by Canadian law, they cannot be prosecuted under Canadian law in case of violation. It will be up to the official's own state to address the violation.
30. See, e.g., Susan Boyd, ed, *Challenging the Public/private Divide: Feminism, Law, and Public Policy* (University of Toronto Press, 1997).

Chapter 2
Systems and Sources of Law

Learning Objectives
After reading this chapter, you should be able to:

- Compare and contrast the main features of six different systems of law.

- Explain the difference between common law and civil law systems.

- Describe Canada's system of law.

- Name two main sources of law in Canada.

- Explain how a body of common law develops.

- Explain the concepts of precedent and stare decisis.

- Name and describe the main stages of the statutory enactment process.

- Explain how to find and cite cases and legislation.

Chapter Outline
Introduction
Part I. Overview of Selected Systems of Law
1. Chthonic Legal Tradition
2. Religious-Based Systems of Law
3. Socialist Systems
4. Common Law System
5. Civil Law System
   5.1 Common Law and Civil Law Compared
6. Mixed Systems
Part II. System of Law in Canada
1. Reception of European Civil and Common Law in Canada
2. First Nations Legal Traditions

Introduction

A **system of law** can be defined as a set of historically rooted beliefs and practices with respect to how the law is formed, its nature and role in society, and organization of the legal system. There are a number of systems of law in the world: chthonic, Islamic, Talmudic, Hindu, socialist, civil law, common law, and others. Each system has its peculiarities. Thus, the knowledge of a system of law in a given country can help us answer practical questions about legal rules as well as better understand the values and ideas they reflect. For example, it tells us what the **sources of law** in a given country are (that is, the authorities, documents, and principles from which legal rules originate), how a body of law develops, and what role courts and other bodies play in creation and application of the law. This chapter primarily focuses on three systems of law that are most relevant to the Canadian context: civil law, common law, and the First Nations (chthonic).

The chapter is divided into three parts. Part I provides a brief overview of several prominent systems of law. Part II describes Canada's system of law. Part III outlines the main sources of law in the Canadian system: legislation and case law. It explains how both of these sources develop, how they interrelate, and how to find, read, and cite them.

Part I. Overview of Selected Systems of Law

There are a number of different systems of law in the world. Among the most well known ones are:

- Chthonic legal tradition;
- Religious-based;

- Civil law;
- Common law; and
- Socialist.[1]

Given that in Canada we find civil law, common law, and the chthonic legal tradition, these are discussed in greater detail than other systems of law.

1. CHTHONIC LEGAL TRADITION

Chthonic legal tradition is the oldest of all and can be said to have as long a history as human-kind itself.[2] "Chthonic" essentially means "centred around the earth and the natural world," which was how early societies conceived of legal rules. By now, chthonic tradition is no longer as prominent as it used to be (often due to being replaced by other systems of law), but it continues to exist across the world and is most commonly found in indigenous communities.

Chthonic legal tradition is notably different from the ways we are currently used to thinking about law. It relies on oral communication rather than the written word. There are no complex institutions to create, administer, and enforce the law. Rather, law formation is a communal process, and no single person or institution has predominant authority over law creation. Law is not considered a separate institution of society but is interwoven with other aspects of community life. There are no formal courts or trials, and disputes are resolved by community-based mechanisms. Some of these mechanisms have found their way into contemporary legal systems as **alternative dispute resolution (ADR)**: a set of mechanisms—including negotiation, mediation, arbitration, and other techniques—that seek to help parties resolve disputes outside courts. Thus, the creation and administration of law is much less structured and institutionalized than in other systems of law.

In chthonic societies, the human is not elevated to the position of dominance over the surrounding environment but rather is seen as a part of it. Hence, living in harmony with and respecting the environment is both necessary for survival of generations and reflective of the community's worldview. The main objective of the law is to provide guidance on how to live in harmony with the land and the environment.

The process of colonization had significant influence on the chthonic legal tradition. In colonized territories where the Western colonizers eventually withdrew (e.g., Africa), no major effort was made to eliminate pre-existing chthonic law. Therefore, local customary laws and practices have been preserved and in some cases explicitly interwoven with imported Western legal traditions, producing mixed systems of law. In contrast, in countries such as Australia and Canada where the colonizers have settled permanently, concerted efforts were made to eliminate and suppress chthonic law of Aboriginal peoples.[3] Part II exemplifies this trend by briefly reviewing the history of the First Nations legal traditions in Canada.

2. RELIGIOUS-BASED SYSTEMS OF LAW

Following chthonic law, other traditions started to emerge that were rooted in the written word and supported by formal institutions for creation and administration of laws. While some systems such as common law and civil law have eventually established themselves within a secular tradition, others have preserved close connection to religious principles.

Religious-based systems of law (such as the Islamic and Talmudic systems) take their root in the word of God—notably, his revelations that have been written down. In such traditions, the sources of law can be broadly broken down into three groups: the revelations from God (such as the Koran or the Torah), commentary on these revelations, and opinions of scholars. The revelations are usually written in the form of verses, songs, prayers, and sayings that are not immediately recognizable as law. They often do not explicitly provide all answers to all situations and so other sources such as commentary and opinions of learned scholars become important.

Talmudic legal tradition of the Jewish people is likely the second oldest system of law after chthonic tradition.[4] The written Torah—God's revelations to Moses in the thirteenth century BCE—is the main source of law. Other sources of law include the Talmud (commentary on the Torah); codes; and written opinions of persons learned in the law.

Talmudic legal tradition can be found anywhere in the world where there is a Jewish population. It is applied by bet din (ecclesiastical courts constituted of three rabbis) that exist in Jewish communities across the world and resolve a variety of private law matters, including contract, commercial, property, and family law.

Islamic law (known as shari'a—"the path to follow") is another example of a religious-based system. The Koran, which contains God's revelations to the prophet Muhammad, is the main source of shari'a. The other sources of law parallel the sources of Talmudic tradition and include: sunna (sayings and acts of the prophet, which explain the Koran); ijma (religiously sanctioned consensus on the interpretation of the Koran and sunna); and qiyas (analogical reasoning).[5] Importantly, there are several schools of thought on Islamic law, which follow different interpretations of shari'a sources. Thus, in order to determine a rule of Islamic law, it is necessary first to identify a school of thought that is to be followed.[6] For example, grounds for divorce may differ from school to school.[7]

Islamic law is practised in a number of countries, although it is often mixed with other systems of law. For example, Saudi Arabia exclusively practises Islamic law, while countries such as Egypt, Algeria, and Tunisia have a combination of Islamic and civil law, and countries such as Bangladesh and Pakistan use Islamic and common law.

3. SOCIALIST SYSTEMS

Socialist systems were established in the twentieth century in a number of countries, including the Soviet Bloc (the USSR and Eastern Europe), Cuba, and Vietnam. They take their inspiration from Marxist theory (recall Chapter 1). Marx (writing in the nineteenth century) viewed society as consisting of two opposing classes: the proletariat and the bourgeoisie. The bourgeoisie holds the power and uses it to oppress and exploit the proletariat. Marx envisioned that the proletariat would ultimately rebel and establish a new communist system in which there would be no classes; everyone would be equal; and everyone would contribute to society according to their ability and receive according to their needs. There would be little need for law or strong state power.

In reality, most socialist states established authoritarian regimes, with the communist party taking control over most aspects of public and private life. Law was used to consolidate the power of the state in order to protect it from internal dissent as well as external threats from capitalist countries. Both legislators and judges were under communist party control and had to conform to the party ideology. The concepts of collective and state property were greatly prominent, while personal ownership was limited and could be used only for satisfaction of personal needs (rather than, for example, entrepreneurial activity). Despite these peculiarities, socialist systems can also be said to follow the civil law tradition: legislation is the main source of law and courts are expected merely to apply the law rather than interpret or create it.

To date, the socialist system has lost much of its importance. After the collapse of the Soviet Union, only a few countries continued to follow it (notably, Vietnam and Cuba).

4. COMMON LAW SYSTEM

The central characteristic of a **common law system** is its reliance on judicial decisions as the primary method of law creation. This is why common law is considered "judge made." The common law tradition can be traced back to England after the Norman conquest of 1066 CE. Prior to the conquest, England was divided into feudal kingdoms and mostly followed a chthonic legal tradition (except during the Roman occupation of the British Isles during 43–410 CE, when Roman civil law tradition was imposed). In the eleventh century, William the Conqueror sought to solidify his power over England through centralization of the legal and political system, including through the establishment of a centralized judiciary.[8]

Initially, judges had no written law to follow and were likely guided by local customs and religious teachings as well as their own notions of justice. However, they gradually departed from applying local customs and started developing common rules for the realm. In the thirteenth century, judicial decisions started being recorded and published in yearbooks. This allowed judges as well as advocates to see what decisions had been made in the past and to rely on them in resolving similar cases at hand. By the seventeenth century, the notion of **precedent** had emerged, in which a decision in an earlier case governed resolution of future similar disputes. Not only was this approach dictated by considerations of fairness (similar cases should be treated alike), but it also allowed for development of a more uniform approach to a given issue.

Common law rules emerged as pragmatic responses to concrete disputes. Their development was determined by the types of cases that came up before the courts and, as a result, the rules emerged incrementally, in a patchwork, ad hoc manner. There was no one centralized authority to produce a single set of rules for a given subject area. Thus, as a regulatory system, common law had a number of weaknesses.

From the point of view of litigants, the common law system also had two major limitations. First, the litigation process was regulated by a rigid system of writs, which outlined *causes of action* (that is, grounds to sue) and procedure to be followed. A *writ* was a type of complaint that had previously been recognized by courts (some 50 types of writs had been recognized by the mid-thirteenth century[9]). A plaintiff needed to obtain a writ in order to be able to sue a defendant. If a plaintiff chose the wrong type of writ, the case would be dismissed. Plaintiffs whose cases did not fit any of the existing writs could not access courts in order to affirm their rights. Second, the remedies under common law were limited. As a rule, a successful plaintiff would obtain an award of damages, however, this remedy would not necessarily be adequate for every situation. For example, a person who had been wrongfully deprived of unique possessions might prefer to receive the possessions back rather than be compensated financially.

In light of the above limitations, some individuals started turning to the king for justice. The king, as the ultimate "fountain of wisdom," could provide a fair remedy where common law courts had failed. Over time, the king delegated the resolution of such cases to his chancellors and eventually the court of chancery emerged. This court developed new types of remedies (e.g., injunctions[10]) seeking to address the rigidity and unfairness of the common law rules. These rules have become known as the **rules of equity**. They took their origin in spiritual ideas of justice and fairness, which were first employed in ecclesiastical courts.[11] For a period of time, courts of equity and common law courts existed in parallel governed by different rules and providing different remedies. In the late nineteenth century, the common law and equity courts were unified and, currently, litigants in Britain and Canada may be able to seek common law and equitable remedies (although the specific remedy would depend on the nature of their case).

5. CIVIL LAW SYSTEM

A **civil law system** developed in continental Europe. In contrast to common law, it relies on codes as the main source of law. Depending on the time period, codes were developed by legislatures, emperors, or prominent scholars, but not courts. These codes aim to create a systematic regulatory framework for a given area of law, and rules are developed from abstract legal principles that are reflected in codes (e.g., a criminal code, a labour law code). There is no concept of precedent and judicial decisions are not considered sources of law.[12] It is presumed that codes provide detailed and comprehensive rules for any type of issue that may come up before courts. Thus, the role of judges is limited to establishing the facts and applying the law to those facts. Judges do not have to look for past decisions as authority to support their judgments.

The civil law system is said to have originated in Rome, and the most notable examples of early codification are the Twelve Tables (a compilation of basic principles on dispute resolution) made around 450 BCE and the Code of Justinian (from the sixth century CE). During their conquests, the Romans exported their law to other territories as far away as Germany and the British Isles. However, with the fall of the Roman Empire in the fourth century, the Roman law receded and previously conquered territories reverted to their old chthonic traditions.

In the eleventh century, Roman law was "rediscovered" in continental Europe as the model to follow. The expansion of trade, urbanization, and centralization of administration created an increasing need for legal knowledge and legal professionals.[13] The first law schools made Roman texts and particularly the Digest of Justinian central to the study of law. These texts also inspired scholars to attempt to codify existing rules and customs in a manner that would provide a clear, uniform approach to a given subject matter.

Civil law can be found in many countries of the world and its spread can be attributed largely to colonization.

5.1 Common Law and Civil Law Compared

The key differences between common law and civil law systems lie in how legal rules develop and the role that different state institutions play in law creation. In a common law system, the development of legal rules is determined by the types and timing of cases that come before courts. For example, in the area of employment, if the only cases that come up before courts are those involving issues of work safety and injuries on the job, then the common law rules will gradually develop "from the ground up" only with respect to these issues. This is, of course, only a fraction of what is involved in employment relations. In contrast, in a civil law system, regulation of employment will be undertaken by means of a code developed by a certain authority other than a court. The work on the code will be started by identifying abstract principles that should govern employment relations (e.g., equality), considering in advance multiple issues that could arise: not only work safety, but also wages, hiring and dismissal, time off work, work hours, and so on. By means of a code, one can implement a detailed and comprehensive regulatory scheme for a given subject matter.

In common law systems, historically, courts have been at the forefront of rule creation. Judicial decisions are prominent sources of law and judges are bound by prior precedents. In contrast, in civil law systems, it is institutions other than courts (e.g., legislatures) that play a central role in law creation. Courts only apply codified rules to specific cases and judges are not required to consult previous decisions on similar issues.

Currently, however, neither common law nor civil law systems exist in pure form. For example, legislation has become an increasingly important source of law in common law countries. At the time when common law started to develop in Britain, Parliament did not exist, however, in the thirteenth century it emerged as a permanent institution.[14] While initially legislating mostly to fill the gaps in common law rules, after the eighteenth century, Parliament acquired a prominent law-making function. The use of legislation as the main means of law creation is linked to industrialization and accelerating pace of social change, which common law (which was developing slowly and haphazardly) could not adequately address. Currently, case law's importance lies mostly in the interpretation of legislation and in filling in gaps not addressed by legislation. It is also not unusual to see that, even in common law jurisdictions, some areas of law have been codified (e.g., Canada's Criminal Code).

In civil law systems, although the idea of precedent does not apply, in practice, previous court decisions may acquire persuasive authority.[15] No single past decision has binding authority for future cases, but once there is sufficient uniformity in previous

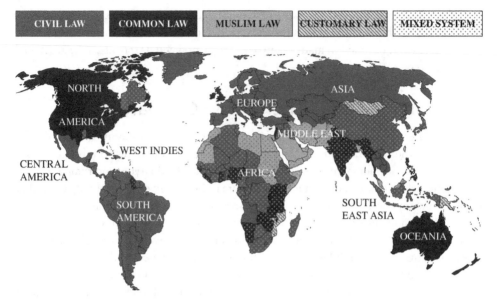

| CIVIL LAW | COMMON LAW | MUSLIM LAW | CUSTOMARY LAW | MIXED SYSTEM |

Figure 2.1 Legal systems of the world

Source: http://www.juriglobe.ca/eng/

case law on a particular issue, it has to be taken into account.[16] This approach is followed, for example, in France, Germany, Italy, and the state of Louisiana in the United States (see Figure 2.1).[17]

6. MIXED SYSTEMS

Mixed systems combine elements of two or more systems of law. They are a result of particular histories of individual countries, including such factors as colonization. Colonizers tended to bring with them their own systems of law, which they either imposed on or mixed with local traditions. For example, colonial powers of continental Europe such as Spain, France, and the Netherlands exported the civil law tradition into many regions of Africa and South America. As a result, such countries have either predominantly civil law (e.g., Mexico, Peru, Brazil) or mixed systems (e.g., Egypt, Libya).[18] Britain brought the common law tradition to its dominions in North America, Australia, and other parts of the world.

Part II. System of Law in Canada

Canada's system of law was shaped under the influence of two major factors: (1) the existence of First Nations populations that have traditionally resided in Canadian territory and developed their own legal traditions; and (2) colonization by English and French explorers who brought civil and common law tradition to Canada.

1. RECEPTION OF EUROPEAN CIVIL AND COMMON LAW IN CANADA

Due to the dominance of French and British settlers in different areas of the country, Canada's system of law comprises both civil law and common law tradition. The civil law system is prevalent in Quebec, which was originally settled by the French, while the British settlers introduced common law to the rest of Canada. Thus, the common law system prevails at the federal level and in all provinces but Quebec.

When control over Quebec was transferred to Britain (following the defeat of France in the Seven Years' War), an attempt was made to assimilate it into the British system. The *Royal Proclamation of 1763* prescribed that English criminal and civil law was to be applied, the territory was to be governed by the British-appointed governor, and Roman Catholics were prohibited from holding government office. However, these assimilationist measures faced resistance and ultimately were unsuccessful. In order to secure order and the allegiance of the people of Quebec, the local law and language were reinstated. The *Quebec Act, 1774* gave official recognition to the Roman Catholic religion and French language, and allowed Quebec to keep its private law rooted in the French tradition.

As a result, Quebec's system of law represents a peculiar combination of civil and common law tradition. Quebec's private law follows French civil tradition, but the province's legal system has also been influenced by the common law in several ways. First, Quebec's public law follows a common law approach. This is due in part to the federal/provincial division of powers under the *Constitution Act, 1867*: matters that are in the jurisdiction of the province are regulated by provincial legislation (and correspondingly reflect the civil tradition), but legislation passed by federal Parliament reflects mostly the common law tradition and applies uniformly across Canada, including Quebec. Second, Quebec's courts are modelled after the British system, including the use of the adversarial system rather than the inquisitorial process of adjudication prevalent in continental Europe.[19] Third, although Quebec judges do not have to follow previous decisions, they tend to refer to past cases to support their findings and, as some suggest, "[i]t is fairly safe to describe the current judicial methodology in Quebec as the de facto use of precedent in decision-making."[20]

2. FIRST NATIONS LEGAL TRADITIONS

Canada is home to many First Nations peoples: Innu, Mi'kmaq, Maliseet, Cree, Montagnais, Anishinabek, Haudenosaunee, Dakota, Lakota, Nakota, Assinaboine, Saulteaux, Blackfoot, Secwepemec, Nlha'kapmx, Salish, Kwakwaka'wakw, Haida, Tsimshian, Gitksan, Tahltan, Gwich'in, Dene, Inuit, Métis, and others.[21] Each of these nations has its particular rules, practices, and traditions. Thus, to say that Canada has a civil or a common law system would be to describe only the dominant systems brought about by European settlers.

The chthonic tradition described in Part I of this chapter is generally applicable to understanding the First Nations traditions in Canada. While there is great variation among First Nations traditions within Canada, they have several key features in common.

First, they give particular significance to the community's connection to the ecosystem and the land; the relationship between the First Nations and the land can be characterized (from a Euro-Canadian perspective) as a trusteeship where the current generation holds the land for the benefit of future generations.[22] The community has collective responsibility to protect the land. It is also recognized that the land should be shared with all other living things such as animals and plants. Law's task is to ensure respect for the land's resources and to promote life in harmony with the Earth and all its inhabitants.[23]

Second, law is intertwined with political, social, and spiritual practices of a community.[24] The nature of rule creation and enforcement is less hierarchical and formalized than in the European legal tradition.[25] The practice and articulation of legal rules involves complex ceremonies such as dances, feasts, and songs, which allow individuals to participate directly in law.[26] There is strong reliance on oral words and storytelling.[27]

Third, indigenous law comes from a variety of sources: teachings about the Creator and creation, observations from nature, proclamations, deliberation, and local custom.[28] Creation stories provide guidance on how to live and avoid conflict. Observations of nature recognize an individual as a part of the ecosystem, including understanding of how human activity may impact nature. Deliberation happens at meetings and gatherings where everyone is allowed to speak and where decisions usually require consensus. Customary law is developed by repetitive practices that are believed to be binding by participants. The approach to dispute resolution, while including punitive measures, often has reconciliation as a primary objective, focusing on negotiation, reparations, and restoration of relations that have been disrupted by the offence in question.[29] Historically, the First Nations communities had no formal courts and disputes were resolved in specially called meetings. Compared to Western legal tradition, First Nations law may appear very nonlegal, but this is so only because we are most familiar with the way law is created and defined by other systems of law—the civil and common law traditions that are dominant in Canada.

Following colonization, there were some instances of interaction between the European settler law and First Nations law, resulting in development of some joint norms or certain recognition of the First Nations norms within the Euro-Canadian system. For example, in *Connolly v Woolrich*, a Cree marriage ceremony that took place in Alberta in 1804 (when Cree law was still the law of that territory) was recognized as valid in Lower Canada.[30]

However, despite some instances of recognition, for the most part European settlers considered First Nations peoples uncivilized and having no law. Not only was settler law imposed on First Nations communities, but it was also used to outlaw Aboriginal practices and assimilate First Nations populations (see Chapter 3 for details). When the First Nations peoples attempted to affirm their rights, they faced challenges in advancing their claims through the dominant European system. Until 1951, they could not freely seek legal assistance or raise money for litigation of their claims. Further, courts trained in the European tradition were often unable to recognize and appreciate the concepts and rules of the First Nations law and culture.[31] Courts tended to characterize the First Nations as objects of the Crown and affirm the superiority of the settler law, with these decisions becoming precedents that further solidified these stereotypes.[32]

More recently, some steps have been taken to recognize Aboriginal rights as well as to incorporate certain elements of the Aboriginal tradition into the dominant legal system. For example, sections 25 and 35 of the *Constitution Act, 1982* recognized Aboriginal and treaty rights and several landmark judicial decisions helped to further strengthen such recognition.[33] For example, *R v Van der Peet*[34] recognized that the interpretation of Aboriginal rights under the *Constitution* has to include the perspectives based in the First Nations' own legal traditions. Case law also recognized that Aboriginal oral history can be accepted at trial as evidence[35] and that First Nations' understanding of the treaties concluded with European settlers could inform the interpretation of those treaties. In the area of criminal justice, sentencing circles and courts specifically for Aboriginal offenders have been introduced in order to provide greater sensitivity to the circumstances of Aboriginal offenders as well as to incorporate the Aboriginal approach to justice. In some communities, courts that bridge European and First Nations traditions have been established (e.g., Cree court in Saskatchewan; Tsuu T'ina Nation court in Alberta[36]). Thus, we can observe increasing interaction between the First Nations and settlers' law and more instances of inclusion of the First Nations perspectives in the dominant system.

However, despite some positive developments, multiple concerns persist, ranging from the general treatment of the First Nations peoples[37] (and particularly the situation on reserves[38]) to disputes over land claims.[39] Some commentators note that even now courts often do not apply indigenous sources of law "because of [their] perceived incompatibility with, or supposed inferiority within, the legal hierarchy."[40] Thus, there remains much work to be done to make the notion of equality of the First Nations and Euro-Canadian legal traditions a reality.[41]

In sum, Canada's system of law can be characterized not as bi-juridical (common law and civil law), but rather as a pluralist system, which encompasses non-Aboriginal as well as various Aboriginal legal traditions. Throughout history, the common law system dominated over the civil law and the First Nations legal traditions. However, it is important to recognize that all three traditions are unique and equal. They do not exist in isolation from each other but constantly develop and influence each other. While, over time, civil law has gained proper recognition, the First Nations legal tradition has not yet.

Part III. Sources of Law in Canada

In this part of the chapter, the discussion is focused on legislation and case law—the two main sources of law in the dominant European legal system in Canada. Other sources of law include customs and conventions (legally recognized practices and usages), the royal prerogative (powers of the Crown that exist historically; e.g., the power to pardon) and scholarly legal writing.

1. LEGISLATION

Legislation is a body of written rules produced by state institutions such as Parliament according to a formally set process. Legislation takes the form of statutes and subordinate legislation. Each is discussed below.

1.1 Statutes

Statutes are enacted by federal and provincial legislative bodies, according to their respective heads of power under the *Constitution Act, 1867*. A statute sets out a framework of regulation for a given subject area or type of activity. All statutes have similar structure: they have a title (a long and a short one) and are divided into parts and sections.

The process of creating a statute starts with drafting and introducing a bill before a legislative body. A bill can seek to bring about a whole new regulatory regime for a given subject area or to amend or repeal an existing statute. The statutory enactment process is described in Chapter 3, Part II, section 1.1.1.

1.2 Subordinate Legislation

Unlike statutes, **subordinate legislation** is passed not by legislatures but by other government bodies to whom legislatures delegated some of their law-making authority. Such authority is given to ministries, departments, agencies, boards, and other government entities under enabling statutes. Subordinate legislation takes the form of regulations, rules, and bylaws. For instance, the *Immigration and Refugee Protection Act* (IRPA) is enabling legislation that authorizes the federal Cabinet to make regulations in relation to immigration and refugee issues[42] and gives the minister of citizenship and immigration the power to issue various instructions.[43]

Subordinate legislation is guided by the principles and objectives of an enabling statute. A statute sets out a regulatory framework, but it is not intended to spell out all the minutiae of multiple requirements, criteria, and procedures. Instead, these details are developed in subordinate legislation. For example, the *IRPA* specifies that a person may immigrate to Canada under economic class "on the basis of their ability to become economically established in Canada."[44] However, the *IRPA* does not define how the ability to become economically established is to be assessed. The factors indicating such ability are outlined in the *Immigration and Refugee Protection Regulations* and include an applicant's education, language ability, work experience, and other factors.[45]

The process of drafting and passing subordinate legislation differs from the statutory enactment process in a number of respects. Subordinate legislation does not go through the three readings and a royal assent. Rather, a proposal for a regulation or other subordinate legislation is developed by a department responsible for a given subject matter. In order to come into effect, it must be approved by an order of the Cabinet or a minister. Prior to approval, the draft of subordinate legislation is usually prepublished in order to inform interested stakeholders and allow them to provide comments on the draft. While this prepublication process allows for some consultation with the wider community, the development and passage of subordinate legislation usually receives less public exposure and debate than bills. Subordinate legislation is usually passed and amended more easily and quickly than statutes.

1.3 Finding and Citing Statutes and Subordinate Legislation

Statutes are published in official sources called "Statutes of Canada" for federal statutes and "Statutes of [Province]" for provincial statutes. These collections are organized in volumes on a yearly basis, containing statutes passed in each given year. Statutes are periodically consolidated in order to incorporate all amendments made to existing statutes over time. The consolidated versions are published in volumes called "Revised Statutes of Canada" and "Revised Statutes of [Province]."

In the past, it was necessary to use hard-copy sources in order to locate a given statute or a regulation. Currently, of course, statutes, regulations, and other legislation can be found online (for example, on the federal Department of Justice website [for federal legislation] or databases such as CanLII or Quicklaw).

All legal sources—including statutes, regulations, and cases—are referenced in a uniform manner. In Canada, the most commonly used legal citation style is the *McGill Guide to Uniform Legal Citation*. The *McGill Guide* provides and explains referencing style for all types of sources: legislation, case law, books, articles, online sources, and so on. In this chapter, we will only review citation for statutes, regulations, and judicial decisions.

All statutes are referenced by title, jurisdiction (federal or of a particular province), year when they were passed, and chapter number in the official publication, such as Statutes of Canada or Statutes of Ontario/Saskatchewan/British Columbia, or the like. Thus, even though we hardly ever use hard copies of official publications, they remain relevant for citation purposes.

Statutes are cited as follows:

Example of a federal statute:

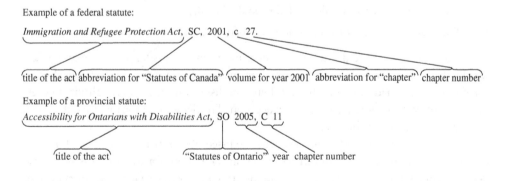

Example of a provincial statute:

Regulations are cited as follows:

Example of federal regulations:

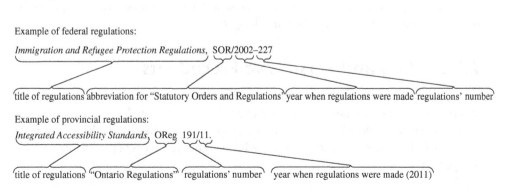

Example of provincial regulations:

2. CASE LAW

Case law (or common law) is a body of judicial decisions produced by courts of a particular country. It is the second major source of law in Canada. Case law is important in at least three respects. First, while most issues are now regulated by legislation, some areas of law are still governed by common law rules (e.g., some defences in criminal law). Second, case law can provide useful interpretation of legislative provisions. Third, due to the rule of precedent, courts rely on past decisions in resolving cases at hand. A lawyer needs to be aware of precedents both favouring and opposing the sought outcome in order to prepare proper arguments and strategy for the case.

2.1 Ratio Decidendi and Obiter Dicta

Each judicial decision can be broken down into key parts:

- Facts;
- History of the case (if we are dealing with a decision of an appellate court) that outlines decision(s) of lower court(s);
- Issues (that is, questions that are to be answered by a court);
- Decision on the case (e.g., did the court decide in favour of the plaintiff or the defendant);
- Reasons for the decision (also called **ratio decidendi**); and
- **Obiter dicta** (or "other things" said in a given decision).

In addition, if we are dealing with a decision from an appellate court where judges usually sit in panels, it is important to note how many judges were on a panel and whether the decision was unanimous or whether there was dissent. If judges were split, it is necessary to identify the majority and minority decision. The decision of the majority of justices dictates the outcome of the case.

Keeping in mind the idea of precedent discussed above, the importance of a given decision lies not in who won and who lost, but in the reasons for the decision—the ratio decidendi or simply "ratio." The ratio contains principles of law that can set direction for resolution of future similar cases. In addition to ratio, judicial decisions contain obiter dicta, that is, comments on law or policy that do not directly impact the decision on the case. Obiter does not have precedential value.

2.2 Binding and Persuasive Precedents

Although any judicial decision can set a precedent, in reality, not all decisions have equal ability to impact future cases. The precedential value of a decision depends on the level of court that made the decision: the higher the court in a court hierarchy, the more impact it will have. To reflect this, our legal system distinguishes two types of precedents: binding and persuasive. (See Figure 2.2.)

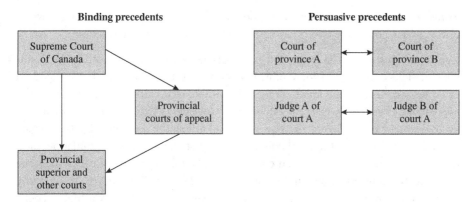

Figure 2.2 Binding and persuasive precedents

Binding precedents are those that must be followed. Precedents of higher courts are binding on lower courts by virtue of the principle of *stare decisis*. **Stare decisis** means "stand by decided matters" and in practice compels lower courts to follow the direction set out by higher courts. For example, decisions of the Supreme Court of Canada are binding on all courts in Canada. In each province, decisions of higher courts (such as, for example, the Court of Appeal) are binding on lower courts in that province. See Box 2.1 for an example.

Box 2.1

Impact of a Binding Precedent: *Childs v Desormeaux*, [2006] 1 SCR 643

Desormeaux attended a "Bring Your Own Booze" party hosted by Courrier and Zimmerman. He drank at the party and was impaired. After leaving the party, he drove his vehicle into oncoming traffic and collided with another car, killing one passenger and seriously injuring three others, including Childs. As a result of the accident, Childs has been paralyzed from the waist down. She sued Desormeaux and the hosts of the party for compensation.

At the time, the law recognized that a negligent driver (like Desormeaux) could be held liable for injuries caused to other drivers and their passengers on the road. It also recognized that bars and restaurants could be held liable for injuries to third parties caused by drunk driving of their patrons.[46] However, it was not clear whether social hosts (such as Courrier and Zimmerman) could be held similarly liable for injuries caused by negligence of their drunken guests. There was no legislation or precedent on the issue. Thus, *Childs v Desormeaux* raised a novel question, which had to be decided by courts. The Supreme Court of Canada eventually concluded that a social host does not owe a duty of care to a person injured by an intoxicated guest (see Chapter 10 for explanation of the duty of care). Had the Court decided differently, our party-hosting practices might have become rather different: hosts would have had a duty to monitor guests' drinking or prevent them from driving. Failing to do so could have led to hosts' tort liability for injuries caused by the drunken driving of their guests.

A *persuasive precedent* is one that a court does not have to follow, but may take into account. A precedent is considered persuasive in the following circumstances:

■ Decisions of justices of the same court have persuasive value for each other. For example, decisions of a judge of the Ontario Superior Court of Justice are not binding on other justices of the same court. Thus, it is possible that, within the same court, the approaches to a specific issue may diverge.[47] However, where possible, courts try to avoid development of divergent approaches and follow the principle of *judicial comity* instead. The principle of judicial comity means that "a substantially similar decision rendered by a judge of . . . [a given court] should be followed [by justices of the same court] in the interest of advancing certainty in the law."[48] However, if diverging approaches within the same court do emerge, they can be settled by a higher court, which will determine which approach is correct.

■ Decisions of courts in one province have only persuasive authority for courts in other provinces. This is so because each province is considered a separate jurisdiction with its own hierarchy of courts. Decisions of, for example, British Columbia courts are not binding on courts in Ontario, but can be used as persuasive authority.

2.3 Researching, Understanding, and Applying Judicial Decisions: *R v Hamilton*, [2004] OJ No 3252

How do the concepts of stare decisis, ratio decidendi, and persuasive and binding decisions work in practice? In preparing to argue a case, a lawyer needs to:

1. Identify main issue(s) in the case at bar (that is, a case at hand).

2. Look for precedents on the issue(s) (both favouring the sought outcome and not).

3. Identify ratios in those precedents.

4. Apply them to the case at bar.

We will expand on this process below.

1. *Identifying main issue(s)*. Issues are questions that must be answered in order to resolve a given case or a legal problem. The issues will depend on a variety of factors such as the subject matter of a case and whether it is an appeal or litigation in the first instance.

2. *Looking for precedents through legal research*. Once the issues are ascertained, a lawyer would research if similar issues have been before the courts and how they have been resolved. The case law research is done using a keyword search of specialized databases such as Quicklaw or CanLII.

An important skill underlying any legal research is knowing how and where judicial decisions are reported. Most, although not all, judicial decisions are reported and published. Thus, you can find their texts either on court websites or in special case report publications and legal databases. Important cases will usually be published in several law-reporting publications.

There are a variety of case law reports that can be classified in the following ways:

- Those that report cases decided by a specific court (e.g., "Supreme Court Reports" which reports only decisions of the Supreme Court of Canada);
- Those that are organized by an area of law (e.g., "Canadian Criminal Cases"); and
- Those that report decisions by courts in a particular province (e.g., "Ontario Judgments").

Like legislation, cases are cited according to a particular format—that of the *McGill Guide*. Any case citation includes the case title, year, and publication source. The title of the case contains the names of the plaintiff and defendant (the plaintiff's name goes first). For example, the *Childs v Desormeaux* case discussed above shows that Childs was the plaintiff and Desormeaux the defendant. Criminal cases are prosecuted on behalf of the Crown and hence always have Rex (king) or Regina (queen) as the plaintiff (abbreviation "R"). All criminal cases are titled "*R v [accused]*."

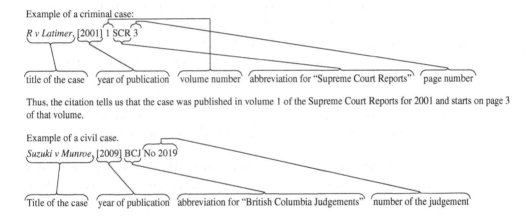

Example of a criminal case:

R v Latimer, [2001] 1 SCR 3

title of the case | year of publication | volume number | abbreviation for "Supreme Court Reports" | page number

Thus, the citation tells us that the case was published in volume 1 of the Supreme Court Reports for 2001 and starts on page 3 of that volume.

Example of a civil case.

Suzuki v Munroe, [2009] BCJ No 2019

Title of the case | year of publication | abbreviation for "British Columbia Judgements" | number of the judgement

3. *Identifying ratios: how to read and understand judicial decisions.* To demonstrate what a judicial decision looks like and help you learn identifying ratios, let's have a look at the Ontario Court of Appeal decision in *R v Hamilton*, [2004] OJ No 3252. Using the provided citation, you can find this case in legal databases such as Quicklaw or CanLII. Read paragraphs 1–4, 6–24, 27–30, 32, 34, 39, 84, 87–88, 90–91, 93–95, 98–104, 107–108, 110, 113–114, 133–134, 136–137, 139, 143, 145–147, 149, and 164–167, and answer the following questions:

   a. Is this a decision of a trial or an appellate court? (See Part I, section 5, in Chapter 4 for discussion of trial and appellate courts.)

   b. What are the facts?

   c. What are the main issue(s)?

d. What did the court decide? (If the decision was given by a panel of judges, was it unanimous or was there a dissent?)

e. What is the reasoning behind the decision (ratio decidendi)?

f. What precedent does this decision set for the future?

Now let's review your answers.

a. *Is this a decision of a trial or an appellate court?* This is a decision of an appellate court: the Ontario Court of Appeal. The case was first heard by the Superior Court of Justice, which imposed a conditional sentence on the two offenders. This sentence was appealed to the Court of Appeal.

b. *What are the facts?* The history and the facts of the case are set out in paragraphs 4 and 6–24. In brief, the two accused—Hamilton and Mason—pleaded guilty to importation of cocaine and received conditional sentences.[49] Both are black single mothers with limited employable skills and in financial need. Although the usual sentence for cocaine importation is imprisonment, the Superior Court ordered conditional sentences (served in the community), reasoning that the marginalized position of the accused due to their race, gender, and poverty mitigated culpability and warranted a more lenient sentence (paragraphs 27–30).

c. *What are the main issue(s)?* Paragraph 32 of the judgment sets out the issue on appeal: is the conditional sentence imposed by the Superior Court appropriate under the circumstances?

d. *What did the Court of Appeal decide?* The case was heard by a panel of three judges: Justices O'Connor, Doherty, and Gillese. The reasons were delivered by Justice Doherty and the other two justices agreed with the reasoning and the ultimate decision. Thus, it was a unanimous decision.

Paragraphs 164–167 outline the outcome of the case. The Court of Appeal concluded that conditional sentences were not appropriate. The fitting sentence would have been 20 months in prison for Hamilton and two years less a day in prison for Mason.[50]

e. *What is the reasoning behind the decision (ratio decidendi)?* Formulating a ratio of a given decision requires some skill and practice. The reasoning of the Court of Appeal is found in paragraphs 84–149 and spans several pages, considering various principles and purposes of sentencing as well as the relevance of social context (such as systemic factors of discrimination and disadvantage) to determining an appropriate sentence. Yet, a ratio would summarize the very gist of those paragraphs in one or two sentences. In short, the Court of Appeal decided that imprisonment is more appropriate because of the serious nature of the offence of drug importation and the importance of sending a denunciatory and deterrent message. According to the Court, the existence of systemic racial and gender bias did not justify conditional sentences: it helped explain the commission of the crimes, but did not detract from their seriousness.

f. *What precedent does this decision set for the future?* The Ontario Court of Appeal is the top court in the provincial judicial hierarchy. Hence, its decisions are binding

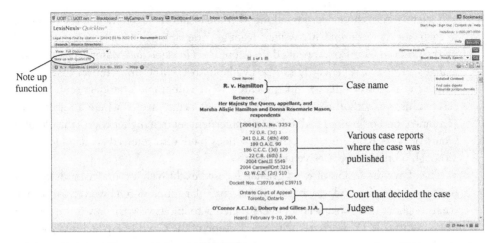

Note up function

Case name

Various case reports where the case was published

Court that decided the case

Judges

Figure 2.3 Screenshot of a Quicklaw window

Source: Quicklaw database, screenshot of case R v Hamilton, [2004] OJ No 3252. Reproduced with permission of LexisNexis Canada Inc. All Rights Reserved.

on all lower courts in Ontario and will have significant impact in the province. Specifically, it will mean that conditional sentences are not appropriate for cocaine importation offences; rather, imprisonment should be imposed. If you have access to Quicklaw, you can use the "Noteup with QuickCITE" function in order to see the cases in which *R v Hamilton* was followed. (See Figure 2.3.)

When you click on "Note up with QuickCITE," you will see the window in Figure 2.4. As you can see, *R v Hamilton* was followed in 15 decisions. If you scroll down, you

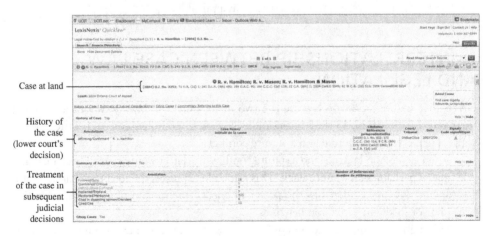

Case at land

History of the case (lower court's decision)

Treatment of the case in subsequent judicial decisions

Figure 2.4 Screenshot of Quicklaw QuickCITE for *R v Hamilton*

Source: Quicklaw database, screenshot of QuickCITE for R v Hamilton, [2004] OJ No 3252. Reproduced with permission of LexisNexis Canada Inc. All Rights Reserved.

will see the list of those decisions along with the location of reference to *R v Hamilton* in each case. For example, *R v White*[51] reads at paragraph 80: "I am bound in this case by the Ontario Court of Appeal's decision in *R v Hamilton and Mason*, that a conditional sentence will generally not be available in cocaine importation cases, even where the importer falls within the category of vulnerable offenders seen in that case." This is exactly the expression of the idea of stare decisis where a lower court (Ontario Court of Justice) had to follow a precedent set by a higher court (the Ontario Court of Appeal). Courts in other provinces have also referred to *R v Hamilton*, although it only has persuasive authority.[52]

The above discussion of *R v Hamilton* focused exclusively on understanding what the court was saying and why it arrived at a particular conclusion. However, as you will see throughout this book, it is not enough merely to know what the law is; we need to assess it critically. Do you agree with the decision of the Court of Appeal? Do you find anything problematic in it? Does it seem to create or rely on certain stereotypes about the accused? We will come back to this case in Chapter 8 (criminal law) and examine it through the lens of feminist and critical race theory. For now, however, please keep in mind that any knowledge and understanding of law cannot be separated from its critical questioning and analysis.

4. *Applying found precedents to the case at bar.* In preparing arguments, a lawyer would seek to rely on precedents that support the sought outcome. However, given that case law is not always uniform in its approach to a given issue, there may also be precedents that undermine the lawyer's intended arguments. Thus, a lawyer may use an important tactic—distinguishing a precedent—in order to avoid the application of those unfavourable precedents to the case at bar. **Distinguishing a precedent** means to argue that there is a significant difference between the precedent and the case at bar and that, as a result, the precedent is inapplicable.

3. INTERRELATIONSHIP BETWEEN CASE LAW AND LEGISLATION

Given that statutes and case law are the two main sources of law, questions arise about their interrelationship: do they harmoniously work to complement each other? What happens if a common law rule and a statute conflict?

When a common law rule and a statute conflict, the latter would prevail because of the principle of **parliamentary supremacy**. This principle expresses the idea that Parliament is the supreme law maker that has the power to enact, amend, and repeal laws, including overriding or modifying common law rules.

Although there may be some conflicts between statutory and common law rules, more often, they work together in a mutually complementary fashion that creates a clear regulatory regime for a given subject matter. In particular, judicial decisions can provide useful interpretation of legislative provisions. This complementarity becomes particularly evident when one seeks to find an answer to a specific legal issue. To illustrate this point, let's take a look at the example in Box 2.2.

Finding an Answer to a Specific Legal Issue

Andrew immigrated to Canada many years ago and is now a Canadian citizen. He has a stepmother who lives abroad. He is looking for ways to help her immigrate to Canada. In order to find out the current rules on immigration, a legal researcher would take the following steps:

1. *Check whether there is a statute that regulates issues of immigration.*
   The relevant statute is the *Immigration and Refugee Protection Act*. Section 12(1) of the *Act* provides: "A foreign national may be selected as a member of the family class on the basis of their relationship as the spouse, common-law partner, child, parent or other prescribed family member of a Canadian citizen or permanent resident." This means that some individuals may be selected for immigration to Canada under the family class if they have a Canadian relative who can act as a sponsor.
   Section 12(1) lists parents among persons that may be sponsored under the family class, but it is silent on the issue of stepparents. It mentions that "other prescribed family member" may also be sponsored, however. Thus, we need to find a definition of "other prescribed family member." The *Act* does not define this concept. Hence, we need to check if the definition is set out in the accompanying *regulations*.

2. *Check out the regulations under the enabling statute.*
   As mentioned above, statutes usually provide only a framework for regulation of a given subject matter, but the details, especially as they concern various requirements and definitions, are usually set out in subordinate legislation.
   Section 117(1) of the *Immigration and Refugee Protection Regulations* that accompany the *Immigration and Refugee Protection Act* lists individuals that may be sponsored under the family class. It includes the sponsor's mother or father, but does not mention stepparents and does not define the words "mother" and "father."

3. *Look for case law that interprets the legislative provision in question.*
   Given that legislation does not provide us with an answer, we need to look for case law to see if an issue similar to Andrew's has come up before the courts and how the courts interpreted s. 117(1) of the *Regulations*, namely whether it includes stepparents.
   A search on Quicklaw reveals that there was indeed a case that dealt with exactly such a question.[53] The Federal Court interpreted s. 117(1) of the *Regulations* and concluded that stepparents were not included in the definition of mother and father and, hence, cannot be sponsored for immigration, unless the stepparent has formally adopted the sponsoring child.
   Thus, the answer to our question is as follows: if Andrew's stepmother formally adopted him, Andrew can apply to sponsor her under the family class as his mother. However, if there is no adoptive relationship between the two, Andrew's stepmother cannot be sponsored to Canada.

SUMMARY

This chapter provided an overview of various systems of law with particular focus on chthonic, civil, and common law traditions, which have the most relevance to the Canadian context. Common law developed as a body of judicial decisions on concrete disputes. It can be said to evolve "from the ground up": decisions on specific cases form the basis for formulating general rules for a given subject matter. In contrast, civil law starts from general legal principles which are embodied in codes or other legislative acts and are then applied to resolution of arising disputes. Both systems rely on the written word and highly structured and institutionalized ways of creating and enforcing law. Unlike in civil and common law, in the chthonic legal tradition of the First Nations, law is usually created through communal deliberation, orally, and often as a part of other cultural practices such as feasts and dances.

All three of these legal traditions are present in Canada. The common law system prevails federally and in all provinces but Quebec and, overall, can be considered the dominant legal tradition in Canada (although as we have seen, legislation now has become one of the main sources of law). Quebec has a largely civil law tradition, but it has also been influenced by the common law system (particularly in the area of public law). Many First Nations communities maintain their own legal practices and some of them have been incorporated into the mainstream system (e.g., specialized First Nations courts). All three systems of law are constantly evolving and influence each other.

While recognizing the presence of both First Nations and Euro-Canadian perspectives in the Canadian legal system, from a practical standpoint, we most frequently encounter two sources of law typical of the European legal tradition: legislation and case law. Each develops in its own particular way, with legislation following an enactment process and case law arising from application of principles of precedent and stare decisis. All legal sources are referenced according to a specialized format—*McGill Guide*—which indicates their date, issuing authority, and publication source.

Critical Thinking Questions

1. Read the following case: *R v NS*, [2012] 3 SCR 726. Which court has rendered this decision? What is the likely precedential value of this decision?

   Identify key elements of the decision:

   a. Facts;

   b. History of the case;

   c. Issues;

   d. Decision of the court (was it unanimous?); and

   e. Ratio.

2. In your opinion, what should be the interrelationship between the First Nations and Euro-Canadian legal traditions?

3. In your opinion, does the principle of precedent and stare decisis make law too rigid and conservative? Explain, applying your knowledge about how the body of case law develops.

4. Read the following case from the British Columbia Court of Appeal: *Casimel v Insurance Corp. of British Columbia* [1994] 2 CNLR 22. How does it help us understand the interaction between the Euro-Canadian and the First Nations systems of law?

Further Readings and Resources

1. John Borrows, *Recovering Canada: The Resurgence of Indigenous Law* (University of Toronto Press, 2002).
2. Patrick Glenn, *Legal Traditions of the World: Sustainable Diversity in Law*, 3rd ed (Oxford: Oxford University Press, 2007).
3. MH Ogilvie, *Historical Introduction to Legal Studies* (Toronto: Carswell, 1982).
4. Theodore Plucknett, *A Concise History of Common Law* (The Lawbook Exchange, 2010).
5. Mo Zhang, "The Socialist Legal System with Chinese Characteristics: China's Discourse for the Rule of Law and a Bitter Experience" (2010) 24 Temple Int'l & Comp LJ 1.

Endnotes

1. H Patrick Glenn, *Legal Traditions of the World: Sustainable Diversity in Law*, 3rd ed (Oxford: Oxford University Press, 2007).
2. *Ibid* at 60.
3. *Ibid* at 80–83.
4. *Ibid* at 93.
5. Steven Vago & Adie Nelson, *Law and Society: Canadian Edition* (Toronto: Prentice Hall, 2004) at 14.
6. Anver M Emon, "Shari'a and the Modern State" in Mark Ellis, ed, *Islamic Law and International Human Rights Law* (Oxford: Oxford University Press, 2013) 52 at 59.
7. Glenn, *supra* note 1 at 197.
8. Ellen Goodman, *The Origins of the Western Legal Tradition: from Thales to the Tudors* (Sydney: Federation Press, 1995) at 227.
9. Glenn, *supra* note 1 at 230.
10. An injunction is an order of court that compels a wrongdoer to abstain from certain actions or to take certain actions.
11. Dale Dewhurst, "Parallel Justice Systems, or a Tale of Two Spiders" in Catherine Bell, ed, *Intercultural Dispute Resolution in Aboriginal Contexts* (Vancouver: UNC Press, 2004) 213 at 225.
12. Rupert Cross & Jim W Harris, *Precedent in English Law*, 4th ed (Oxford: Clarendon Press, 1991) at 10.
13. Goodman, *supra* note 8 at 198–99.
14. *Ibid* at 268.
15. Vincy Fon & Francesco Parisi, "Judicial Precedents in Civil Law Systems: A Dynamic Analysis" (2006) 26 Int'l Rev Law & Econ 519; Mary Garvey Algero, "The Sources of Law and the Value of Precedent: A Comparative and Empirical Study of a Civil Law State in a Common Law Nation" (2005) 65 La L Rev 775.
16. This is called the doctrine of *jurisprudence constante*. Fon & Parisi, *ibid* at 522.
17. Fon & Parisi, *ibid*; M Troper & C Grzegorczyk, "Precedent in France" in D MacCormick & R Summers, eds, *Interpreting Precedents: A Comparative Study* (Dartmouth: Dartmouth Publishing Co, 1997) at 103; Algero, *supra* note 15.
18. "Mixed Legal Systems," online: <http://www.juriglobe.ca/eng/sys-juri/class-poli/sys-mixtes.php>.
19. Rosalie Jukier, "Inside the Judicial Mind: Exploring Judicial Methodology in the Mixed Legal System of Quebec" (2011), online: <http://papers.ssrn.com/sol3/papers.cfm?abstract_id=2002354>.

20. *Ibid* at 6.
21. John Borrows, "Indigenous Legal Traditions in Canada" (2005) 19 Journal of Law & Policy 167 at 175, online: <http://law.wustl.edu/journal/19/p167Borrows.pdf>.
22. John Borrows, *Canada's Indigenous Constitution* (Toronto: University of Toronto Press, 2010) at 246. The discussion is specifically with respect to understanding the relationship to the land in the Anishinabek tradition.
23. Lisa D Chartrand, "Accommodating Indigenous Legal Traditions" (2005) at 7–8, online: <http://www.indigenousbar.ca/pdf/Indigenous%20Legal%20Traditions.pdf>.
24. *Ibid* at 44.
25. See, e.g. Valerie Ruth Napoleon, "Ayook: Gitksan Legal Order, Law, and Legal Theory," PhD thesis (2009) at 9–10, online: <https://dspace.library.uvic.ca:8443/bitstream/handle/1828/1392/napoleon%20dissertation%20April%2026-09.pdf?sequence=1>.
26. *Ibid* at 192.
27. Borrows, "Indigenous Legal Traditions in Canada," *supra* note 21 at 191.
28. Borrows, *Indigenous Constitution*, *supra* note 22, Chapter 2.
29. David Milward, *Aboriginal Justice and the Charter: Realizing a Culturally Sensitive Interpretation of Legal Rights* (Vancouver: UBC Press, 2012) at 7, 10, 23.
30. See John Borrows, *Recovering Canada: The Resurgence of Indigenous Law* (Toronto: University of Toronto Press, 2002); Jeremy Webber, "Relations of Force and Relations of Justice: The Emergence of Normative Community between Colonists and Aboriginal Peoples" (1995) 33 Osgoode Hall LJ 623.
31. Report of the Royal Commission on Aboriginal Peoples (1996), online: <http://www.collectionscanada.gc.ca/webarchives/20071115053257/> or <http://www.ainc-inac.gc.ca/ch/rcap/sg/sgmm_e.html>; D'Arcy Vermette, "Colonialism and the Suppression of Aboriginal Voice" (2008–2009) 40 Ottawa L Rev 225.
32. Vermette, *ibid.*
33. E.g., *Delgamuukw v AG (British Columbia) and Attorney General (Canada)* [1997] 3 SCR 1010. There have also been criticisms of this decision: William F Flanagan, "Piercing the Veil of Real Property Law: *Delgamuukw v. British Columbia*" (1998) 24 Queen's LJ 279; John Borrows, "Sovereignty's Alchemy: An Analysis of *Delgamuukw v. British Columbia*" (1999) 37 Osgoode Hall LJ 537.
34. *R v Van der Peet*, [1996] 2 SCR 507.
35. *Van der Peet*, *ibid*; *Delgamuukw*, *supra* note 33.
36. Borrows, *Indigenous Constitution*, *supra* note 22 at 217.
37. Human Rights Council, Report of the Working Group on the Universal Periodic Review: Canada (2009), online: <http://daccess-dds-ny.un.org/doc/UNDOC/GEN/G09/152/99/PDF/G0915299.pdf?OpenElement>. For issues in the criminal justice system, see, for example: Margot Hurlbert, "*R. v. Moccasin* and the Continued Struggle for Fairness in Aboriginal Sentencing" (2008) 71 Sask L Rev 391; Hadley Friedland, "Different Stories: Aboriginal People, Order, and the Failure of the Criminal Justice System" (2009) 72 Sask L Rev 105.
38. Auditor General of Canada, Status Report 2011, ch 4 "Programs for First Nations on Reserves", online: <http://www.oag-bvg.gc.ca/internet/english/parl_oag_201106_04_e_35372.html>.
39. See, e.g., Rachel Ariss & John Cutfeet, "Mining, Consultation, Reconciliation and Law" (2011) 10:1 Indigenous LJ 1; Amnesty International, "20 Years of Denial of Recommendations Made by the United Nations Human Rights Committee and the Continuing Impact on the Lubicon Cree" (2008), online: <http://www.amnesty.ca/research/reports/canada-20-years-denial-of-recommendations-made-by-the-united-nations-human-rights-c>.

40. John Borrows, "With or Without You: First Nations Law (in Canada)" (1995) 41 McGill LJ 629 at 633. See also Eric H Reiter, "Fact, Narrative, and the Judicial Uses of History: *Delgamuukw* and Beyond" (2010) 8:1 Indigenous LJ 55; Michael Coyle, "Loyalty and Distinctiveness: A New Approach to the Crown's Fiduciary Duty Toward Aboriginal Peoples" (2003) 40 Alta L Rev 841.

41. For inspiration, see John Borrows, "Creating an Indigenous Legal Community" (2005) 50 McGill LJ 153; Borrows, *Indigenous Constitution*, *supra* note 22, Chapters 7 and 8; Mark Ebert, "Feasting Judicial Convergence: Reconciling Legal Perspectives Through the Potlatch Complex" (2013) 18 Appeal 21.

42. *Immigration and Refugee Protection Act*, SC 2001, c 27, s 5(1).

43. *Ibid*, s 87.3(3).

44. *Ibid*, s 12(2).

45. *Immigration and Refugee Protection Regulations*, SOR/2002-227, part 6. The Regulations prescribe several classes for economic immigration—skilled worker, business, Canadian experience class—each with its own criteria.

46. *Stewart v Pettie*, [1995] 1 SCR 131.

47. For example, the meaning of "residence" for the purposes of naturalization under the *Citizenship Act* has received different interpretations by various justices of the Federal Court. Section 5(1) of the *Citizenship Act* provided that in order to be eligible for citizenship by naturalization, an applicant must have accumulated at least three years of residence in Canada in the four-year period immediately preceding the citizenship application. Given that the Act did not define "residence," some justices concluded that "residence" meant physical presence in Canada (*Re Pourghasemi*, (1993), 19 Imm LR (2d) 259), while others gave a more liberal interpretation concluding that it was not necessary to show the exact three years of physical presence in Canada as long as the applicant "regularly, normally or customarily lives" or has "centralized his or her mode of existence" in Canada (*Re Koo* [1993] 1 FC 286). In 2014, Parliament amended the *Citizenship Act*, clarifying that "residence" means physical presence in Canada.

48. *Re Almrei*, 2007 FC 1025 at para 61. See also a more detailed outline in *Bell v Cessna Aircraft Co* [1983] BCJ No 2130 at para 2: "The generally accepted view is that this court is bound to follow a previous decision of the court unless it can be shown that the previous decision was manifestly wrong, or should no longer be followed: for example, (1) the decision failed to consider legislation or binding authorities which would have produced a different result, or (2) the decision, if followed, would result in a severe injustice. The reason generally assigned for this approach is a judicial comity. While doubtless this is a fundamental reason for the approach, I think that an equally fundamental, if not more compelling, reason is the need for certainty in the law, so far as that can be established. Lawyers would be in an intolerable position in advising clients if a division of the court was free to decide an appeal without regard to a previous decision or the principle involved in it."

49. It would include limitations on the liberty of the offender, but in a less severe manner than imprisonment. Among the usual elements of a conditional sentence are: curfew, requirement to keep peace, and enrolment in a treatment program (where applicable).

50. Despite finding that the lower court made an error, the Court of Appeal allowed the two offenders to finish serving their conditional sentences. This was so because by the time the appeal was heard and decided, both offenders have already served close to 17 months of their conditional sentences. It would not have been fair to now impose a new sentence of imprisonment on them.

51. *R v White*, [2010] OJ No 3618.

52. See, e.g., *R v Sidhu*, [2007] BCJ No 1317 at para 39; *R v Ghai*, [2008] AJ No 1448 at para 38.

53. *Canada (Minister of Citizenship and Immigration) v Vong*, [2006] 1 FCR 404.

Chapter 3
Structure of Canadian Government

Learning Objectives

After reading this chapter, you should be able to:

- Name three branches of government and two levels of government in Canada.

- Describe the main functions and composition of each branch of government.

- Explain the impact of minority/majority government on the legislative process.

- Name and explain at least three mechanisms to promote government accountability.

- Define interest groups and outline their impact on the formation of law.

- Explain the meaning of the inherent right of Aboriginal peoples to self-government.

Chapter Outline

Introduction

In Canada, the structure of government is organized along two axes: (1) levels of government: federal and provincial; and (2) branches of government: legislative, executive, and judicial. Each level has exclusive regulatory authority with respect to specific subject matters as outlined in the *Constitution Act, 1867*. Each branch of government also performs distinct functions. However, despite these divisions, levels and branches of government exist in complex interrelationships and work as a system organized by the principles of popular sovereignty, the rule of law, constitutionalism, government accountability, and others. The ultimate objective of this chapter is not only to inform you of the distinct functions of each level and branch of government, but also to allow you to see their joint workings as a system. This understanding will provide you with a better insight into the law and policy formation process as well as the exercise of government accountability. For example, each branch of government can influence formation of the law in different ways: executive departments develop policy proposals and draft bills; the legislature considers bills which, if passed, become law; the judiciary can review whether legislation complies with the *Constitution* and invalidate offending provisions. Further, our system is based on the idea of popular sovereignty and limited government, meaning that there have to be mechanisms that provide a check against arbitrary exercise of power and require ultimate accountability of the government to the people. This is achieved through the principle of the rule of law as well as the powers of a given branch of government that allow it to keep a check on other branches (e.g., the powers of the judiciary to review legislative and executive action, and the ability of the legislature to express no confidence to the executive).

This chapter is in three parts. Part I provides an overview of various classifications of systems of government (e.g., monarchy versus republic, parliamentary versus presidential systems). Part II focuses on the mainstream Euro-Canadian institutions. It explains the composition and functions of each branch of government as well as Canada's federal structure. It also discusses the interaction between branches and levels of government and its impact on the law and policy formation as well as government accountability. Finally, it briefly reviews the role of external pressures from interest groups on the formation of the law. Part III reviews the history of interactions between the First Nations and settler communities in Canada and discusses the policies seeking to implement the inherent right of Aboriginal peoples to self-government.

Part I. Systems of Government

The structure and nature of a given government can be characterized according to various criteria. These classifications allow us to understand the core principles, features, and institutional organization of a given government.

1. DEMOCRACIES VERSUS AUTHORITARIAN AND TOTALITARIAN REGIMES

This classification characterizes the nature and source of authority in a given state.

A *totalitarian regime* is characterized by the presence and imposition of an official ideology, a single-party system, centralized economy, oppressive police, censorship, state-controlled media, and restricted pluralism and participation. Essentially, a governing party and/or individual holds monopoly over political, economic, and military power in society. The state not only controls public life, but also imposes significant restrictions on private lives of citizens.

Authoritarian governments are somewhat less restrictive than totalitarian regimes, but still maintain significant control over public and private life. The power is concentrated in the hands of the few; political life, the economy, and the media are under a significant degree of state control. While some political pluralism may exist, this is so only to the extent allowed by the government. Individual rights are formally observed, but how a person is actually treated may depend on their degree of loyalty to the government.

Democracy can be characterized as rule by the people and a government that is accountable to the people. Democracies are based on principles of popular sovereignty, constitutionalism, accountability of public officials, pluralism, political competition, rule of law, and respect for the rights of minorities (these principles will be explained in Part II).

Given that the ultimate ruling authority in a democracy lies with the people, it is important to create mechanisms for citizens to exercise it. Democracies can take direct and representative form. **Representative democracy** is a system where the population elects representatives who act on its behalf. Thus, regular elections are a necessary feature of representative democracy. For example, Parliament elected by the population is an expression of representative democracy. **Direct democracy** allows the people to be directly involved in government decision making. While direct democracy may have been feasible in small communities, it would be difficult to exercise in contemporary large and complex societies. Thus, today's democracies are organized in a representative form, although some mechanisms of direct democracy can also be employed from time to time. The three main forms of such direct democracy are referendum, recall, and initiative. A *referendum* allows a popular vote on a particular issue. For example, in 1992, Canadians were asked to determine at referendum whether constitutional changes under the *Charlottetown Accord* should be accepted. *Initiatives* are mechanisms that allow groups of individuals to propose new laws or changes to existing laws. A *recall* is a procedure where constituents may recall their representative if they consider that he or she does not adequately represent their interests.

2. REPUBLICS VERSUS MONARCHIES

This classification focuses on whether the head of state is an elected or a hereditary authority. In a monarchy, the state is headed by a hereditary authority—the monarch. In republics, heads of state are elected.

3. PARLIAMENTARY, PRESIDENTIAL, AND MIXED SYSTEMS

This classification characterizes how branches of government are organized and relate to each other.

A *presidential system* is characterized by the **separation of powers** and *a system of checks and balances*. The United States is one of the most well known presidential systems and therefore provides a useful illustration of the aforementioned concepts. Separation of powers means that no official can be a member of more than one branch of government. For example, in the United States, the president and the legislature are elected in separate elections. Members of Congress form the legislative branch, but are not parts of the executive. The president and his or her apparatus are parts of the executive, but have no membership in the legislature. The authority of the cabinet comes from the president, not from the legislature.

The system of **checks and balances** serves to ensure that no one branch can dominate the other two. Each branch has certain powers in relation to the other branches that allow it to "check" against possible abuses of power. For example, the US president can veto a bill passed by Congress. The legislature has the power to impeach the president. The judiciary can review the constitutionality of acts passed by the legislature and actions of the executive.

In a *parliamentary system*, the separation between branches of government is not as clear as in a presidential system. In fact, there is a certain merger between the executive and the legislature. The party that wins the most seats in a parliamentary election gets to form the government and its leader becomes the prime minister. The prime minister and members of the cabinet are simultaneously members of the legislature and parts of the executive. The legislative branch, at least in theory, is considered supreme and, to a significant degree, the authority of the executive comes from the legislature. The government can remain in power only as long as it enjoys the confidence of the legislature.

Mixed systems combine some elements from presidential and parliamentary systems. For example, they usually have a president who is elected by the population, as well as a prime minister and a cabinet that can be dissolved by a vote of no confidence in the legislature.[1]

4. UNITARY VERSUS FEDERAL STATES

This classification describes how a government authority is organized within a state territory, according to various levels of administration: national, regional, and local. In a *unitary system*, a single government controls the entire territory. In a *federal state*, the sovereign authority is divided between the central government and provincial or state governments, with each level of government having its own areas of jurisdiction.

Part II. Structure of Canadian Government

Canada is a democracy, a federation, a constitutional monarchy, and a parliamentary system. This part of the chapter first provides a brief overview of the composition and powers of each branch of government. Then, it examines the interactions among the three branches and their impact on the formation of the law, promotion of government accountability, and other democratic principles. The section also touches upon the role of external actors—interest groups—in the law and policy process.

1. BRANCHES OF GOVERNMENT

Governments are organized around the division of powers into three branches: executive, legislative, and judicial. Each branch performs distinct functions. At the most basic level, their functions can be characterized as follows: the legislative branch passes legislation; the executive branch implements it; and the judicial branch (the courts) adjudicates disputes and oversees legislative and executive action.

Each of the two levels of government in Canada—federal and provincial—is composed of the three branches mentioned above (see Table 3.1). While the functions and composition of the branches at each level are similar, there are also some differences as described below.

Table 3.1 Branches of Government

	Legislative Branch	Executive Branch	Judicial Branch
Federal Level	Parliament: ■ House of Commons (elected) ■ Senate (appointed)	■ Prime minister ■ Cabinet ■ Ministries and departments ■ Governor General	■ Supreme Court of Canada ■ Federal courts ■ Tax court ■ Military courts
Provincial Level	Legislative assembly (elected)	■ Premier ■ Cabinet ■ Ministries and departments ■ Lieutenant governor	Provincial courts

Canadian democracy is built on the following key principles:

- Popular sovereignty (the people as the source of political authority);
- Political equality (all citizens have equal opportunity to influence public policy);
- Pluralism and political competition (there is freedom to establish political parties and these parties have equal opportunity to compete in elections);
- The rule of law (no one is above the law);
- Constitutionalism (all government action must comply with the *Constitution*); and
- Accountability of public officials (existence and use of mechanisms to hold officials responsible for their decisions and actions).

As discussed below, these principles are implemented through various aspects of our structure of government. Not only do they help define interactions among branches and levels of government as well as between the government and the people, but they provide important safeguards against abusive or arbitrary exercise of power. Working together, they seek to ensure practical implementation of the democratic ideal of popular sovereignty and limited government. These principles are behind the current organization of Canadian government.

1.1 Legislative Branch

The legislative branch is composed of Parliament at the federal level and legislative assemblies at the provincial level. Provincial legislative assemblies are unicameral. Parliament is composed of two chambers: the House of Commons and the Senate.

The House of Commons is the lower chamber of Parliament. It is elected by popular vote and consists of 308 members. Each province is allocated a certain number of seats in Parliament in rough proportion to the share of its population within Canada. Elections are one of the means to implement the principles of popular sovereignty, political equality, pluralism, and political competition.

To elect Members of Parliament (MPs), Canada uses the **single member plurality electoral system** (also called "first-past-the-post"). According to this system, the candidate who gains the most votes in a given riding (even if it is less than 50% of votes) wins the seat in the legislature. While this system is easy to use, its main shortcoming is that an elected candidate may not be truly representative of a riding. It also tends to favour established parties and makes it difficult for small parties to gain representation in legislatures. The results of the 2011 federal election vividly illustrate these issues, as shown in Table 3.2.[2]

When voting on various matters in the House, MPs are expected to follow

Photo 3.1 This is the House of Commons chamber.

jiawangkun/Shutterstock

Table 3.2 Results of the 2011 Federal Election

Political Party	Percentage of Votes Received	Percentage of Seats in the House of Commons
Conservative Party of Canada	39.6	54
New Democratic Party	30.6	33
Liberal Party of Canada	18.9	11
Bloc Québécois	6.1	1
Green Party of Canada	3.9	0.3 (the party did get 1 seat)

Source: Electoral Results by Party: 41 General Elections, online: http://www.parl.gc.ca/parlinfo/compilations/electionsandridings/ResultsParty.aspx

strict party discipline, that is, to support their party's position. Each party has a *party whip* who ensures that there are enough party members in the chamber to vote and that members of the party vote according to the position of that party. Failure to vote along party lines may lead to serious consequences, including expulsion from the party caucus. Strict party discipline creates concerns about the interests that MPs represent: can they be considered to represent the interests of their constituents when they vote according to the party line? In some cases, a *free vote* may be allowed where MPs can vote according to their convictions and not follow party discipline.

The Senate is the upper house of Parliament. Its members are appointed by the Governor General on the recommendation of the prime minister. A senator serves until the mandatory retirement age of 75 or until they are removed[3] (see also a reference case on Senate reform in Chapter 4, Box 4.2).

As the main body with the power to pass legislation, Parliament obviously has a defining role in the development of the law. Yearly, it passes a variety of new statutes and amends existing ones to keep legal regulation up to date. Importantly, the legislature has the power to pass statutes that prescribe the authority of the executive (for example, the powers of various departments and ministers are prescribed by legislation). Through these statutes, the legislature can be said to delegate some of its powers to the executive.[4]

Photo 3.2 This is the Senate chamber.

1.1.1 Statutory Enactment Process

Every member of the legislature may introduce bills, but only Cabinet ministers may introduce bills that involve expenditure of money. In federal Parliament, a bill can be introduced in either the House of Commons or the Senate, except for bills that relate to raising revenue or spending public funds, which must be introduced in the House of Commons. As a rule, most bills are started in the House of Commons.

There are several types of bills:

- *Public bills* that concern the public at large. Most bills are public bills.
- *Private bills* that concern only specified individuals or entities and grant them special rights or exemptions.
- *Government bills* that are proposed by the government in power and usually seek to advance that government's policy initiatives and agendas. They are drafted by the Department of Justice on the instructions of the Cabinet and are introduced by a minister responsible for a given subject matter. For example, if a bill concerns immigration, it will be introduced by the minister of citizenship and immigration.
- *Private members' bills* that are introduced by individual MPs who are not Cabinet ministers. These bills receive less time in legislative debates and rarely garner sufficient support to be passed.

Once a bill is introduced, it is assigned a number. Bills introduced in the Senate start with the letter "S," and bills introduced in the House of Commons with the letter "C." Government bills are numbered 1 through 200; private members' bills are numbered 201 through 1000.

The statutory enactment process consists of a number of stages (see below). It is largely the same in federal and provincial legislatures. The only major difference is that provincial legislatures are unicameral, while in federal Parliament a bill must be passed in both the House of Commons and the Senate. This section describes the passage of a government bill in federal Parliament.

The stages of the statutory enactment process are as follows:

1. *Legislative proposal.* Once the draft is approved by the Cabinet, the government House leader recommends for or against its introduction in Parliament.
2. *Introduction and first reading.* A bill is introduced in the House of Commons by a responsible minister. The first reading is mostly a formality as no debate is taking place at this stage. The main objective is to inform MPs that a given bill has been introduced and to allow them to familiarize themselves with that bill.
3. *Second reading.* At this stage, the principle of the bill (but not its individual provisions) is debated. The objectives of legislation are explained and a formal vote takes place. No amendments are made at this stage. If the majority approves the bill in principle, it moves on to the next stage.
4. *Examination by a parliamentary committee.* The bill goes before a specialized committee composed of members of each party. The House of Commons has a number of standing (that is, permanent) committees, but where necessary a committee can also be formed on an ad hoc basis. The committee examines the bill clause by clause and may recommend

amendments. An important feature of this stage is that it allows for input from stakeholders and the public at large. A committee may hold hearings as well as receive written submissions on the bill in question. While the committee is not obligated to follow recommendations outlined in those submissions, it can take them into consideration in deciding on amendments.

5. *Report by the committee and third reading.* The committee reports back to the House of Commons with recommendations for amendments. The House votes on whether to accept or reject the amendments and then the third reading takes place. If the bill is supported, it moves on for consideration in the Senate.

6. *Consideration in the Senate.* The consideration of the bill in the Senate follows the same process as the House of Commons with the three readings and an examination before a committee. If a bill is passed in the Senate without amendment, it moves on to the next stage. However, if the Senate amends the bill, the bill is sent back to the House of Commons, which decides whether to accept or reject the Senate's amendments. If the House of Commons accepts the amendments, the bill is sent back to the Senate while awaiting royal assent. If the House amends or rejects the Senate's amendments, the bill goes back to the Senate, which in turn decides whether to accept what the House has proposed. The communication between the two houses will go back and forth until they agree on the text.

7. *Royal assent and proclamation.* A bill is presented to the Governor General for assent and is proclaimed.

8. *Coming into force.* A bill comes into effect on one of the following days: (a) when it receives royal assent; (b) on a day specified in the bill itself; or (c) on a day or days set by the governor in council (that is, the federal Cabinet). In some cases, different sections of the statute may come into force on different dates (e.g., some on royal assent, while others on the days set by the governor in council or by the bill itself).

The statutory enactment process described above is shown in Figure 3.1.

The texts and status of current as well as past federal bills can be found on the Parliament of Canada website. This is a very useful resource, which also contains parliamentary debates and legislative summaries explaining the content of bills in simple language. An example of a recent bill can be found in Box 3.1.

In addition, the legislature has an important power that allows it to keep the top of the executive in check. According to the **principle of responsible government**, a given government can remain in power only as long as it enjoys the support of the legislature. Once that support is lost, the government falls and, as a rule, a new election is called. A *no confidence vote* can be introduced by a motion on which MPs take a vote. The vote on some bills is automatically considered a vote of (no) confidence. For example, a vote on the annual budget is a vote of (no) confidence at the same time. If the government's budget bill does not garner the support to pass, this is automatically considered an expression of no confidence in the government.

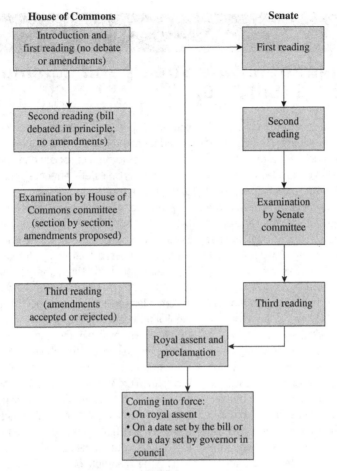

House of Commons   **Senate**

Introduction and first reading (no debate or amendments) → First reading

Second reading (bill debated in principle; no amendments) → Second reading

Examination by House of Commons committee (section by section; amendments proposed) → Examination by Senate committee

Third reading (amendments accepted or rejected) → Third reading

Royal assent and proclamation

Coming into force:
• On royal assent
• On a date set by the bill or
• On a day set by governor in council

Figure 3.1 Statutory enactment process

1.2 Executive Branch

The executive branch is composed of the first minister (prime minister at the federal level and premiers at the provincial level), the Cabinet, and the Queen's representative (Governor General at the federal level and lieutenant governor at the provincial level). The British monarch (or the Crown) is the head of the state. Currently, it is Queen Elizabeth II, who exercises her largely symbolic functions through her representatives in Canada. In addition, the executive embraces various ministries, departments, boards, and administrative tribunals. All department officials are responsible to their respective minister of the Cabinet, who in turn answers to Parliament.

The party that wins the most votes in a parliamentary election gets to form the government and its leader becomes the prime minister. Thus, the outcome of elections defines not only the composition of the House of Commons but also the top of the executive branch. A prime minister is a powerful figure in the political system. Following an election, the prime

Box 3.1

Practical Application: *Safe Streets and Communities Act*, SC 2012, c 1 (Bill C-10)

Bill C-10 is an example of a government bill. Its full title is *An Act to enact the Justice for Victims of Terrorism Act and to amend the State Immunity Act, the Criminal Code, the Controlled Drugs and Substances Act, the Corrections and Conditional Release Act, the Youth Criminal Justice Act, the Immigration and Refugee Protection Act and other Acts.* Its short title is *Safe Streets and Communities Act.* The following link provides the text of the bill and relevant speeches of MPs, as well as shows how the bill progressed through various stages of the legislative process: <http://www.parl.gc.ca/LegisInfo/BillDetails.aspx?Language=E&Mode=1&billId=5120829&View=4>.

Bill C-10 does not introduce an entirely new regulatory scheme for a particular subject matter, but rather seeks to amend existing laws. It is an *omnibus bill* as it seeks to amend not one but several statutes—all of the amendments being linked by the same underlying purpose. For example, Bill C-10 introduces new and increased mandatory minimum sentences for some offences; eliminates availability of conditional sentences (that is, sentences that are served in a community rather than a correctional facility) for certain offences; tightens the rules governing conditional release; and increases periods of eligibility for records of suspension (formerly called "pardons"). The coming into force of various provisions of Bill C-10 was to be set by the order of the governor in council. According to subsequently issued orders, some provisions were to come into force in August 2012, with others in October and November of the same year.[5]

Why were the amendments under Bill C-10 necessary, and what is likely to be their effect? We can glean some answers to these questions from the parliamentary debates. As a rule, you will find a number of different perspectives, of government, opposition parties, and various stakeholders. The

sponsor's speech in Parliament demonstrates the government's rationale: the changes were necessary in order to protect society and combat crime; increased penalties are effective means to deter and sanction criminal behaviour.

A number of stakeholders made submissions on Bill C-10 to both the House of Commons and the Senate committees and a simple Internet search reveals analyses prepared by, for example, the Canadian Bar Association, the Assembly of First Nations, the John Howard Society, and others. Each stakeholder provided its perspective on the bill, highlighting concerns and proposing amendments to the bill. For example, the Canadian Bar Association expressed concern that the bill adopted a punitive approach to criminal behavior rather than focusing on prevention and rehabilitation of offenders.[6] The John Howard Society similarly expressed doubts that the legislation would make communities safer and highlighted the increased pressure that it would put on the justice and corrections systems.[7] The Assembly of First Nations echoed the above concerns, noting that imprisonment is ineffective in controlling or deterring crime and that mandatory minimum sentences would limit the ability of the criminal justice system to flexibly respond to the circumstances of Aboriginal offenders.[8]

Effectively responding to crime is undoubtedly in the public interest. However, there are many different ways to address this issue: by introducing tougher sanctions and allocating more resources to law enforcement; by tackling systemic problems that may contribute to individuals' involvement in crime; by promoting rehabilitation and reintegration of offenders into society; and other measures. As evidenced by Bill C-10, the Harper government took the law and order position, introducing stiffer penalties for some offences and moving away from an earlier trend toward restorative justice.

minister forms the Cabinet (the formal name for the Cabinet is "Governor in Council") and decides which MPs will be appointed ministers. As the head of government, the prime minister provides political leadership and represents Canada nationally and internationally. Many formal powers of the Governor General are exercised on the advice of the prime minister, and it is rare for the Governor General not to follow that advice. For example, the prime minister recommends who should be appointed to the Senate and to the Supreme Court of Canada.

When a particular party has the majority of seats in the House of Commons, it is said to have a **majority government**. In such a case, not only can it be certain that the House will pass government bills, but it also does not have to worry about losing the confidence of the legislature. Effectively, a majority government has significant control over both the House of Commons and the executive branch. A majority government is able to advance its agenda more rigorously and with few modifications from the opposition. In a **minority government**, the governing party has more seats in the House than any other party, but falls short of 50% plus one seat. In that case, the governing party will need to negotiate with one or several other parties and possibly compromise on certain points in order to gain support for government bills (see Box 3.2). Correspondingly, the content of government bills may change to reflect not only the minority government's vision but also that of opposition parties.

The executive is involved in the formation of the law in a variety of ways. First, it has powers that relate directly to the development of legislation: executive departments draft

Box 3.2

Minority versus Majority Government: Refugee Reform Legislation

The Conservative party has been the governing party since 2006. However, it won majority only in May 2011. Some government bills that had little chance of being passed during minority government have subsequently succeeded under the majority government. For instance, the Conservative government initiated many changes to the immigration and refugee determination system. In particular, it argued that the Canadian refugee system was subject to abuse and therefore tougher measures were necessary to create disincentives for nongenuine claimants seeking asylum in Canada.[9] In October 2010, the government introduced Bill C-49, *Preventing Human Smugglers from Abusing Canada's Immigration System Act*. While the title of the bill suggested that it targeted human smugglers, in reality, it also proposed a number of mea-

sures that would negatively impact some refugee claimants.[10] For example, Bill C-49 provided that some refugee claimants would be subject to mandatory 12-month detention.

A number of advocacy groups voiced major concerns about the bill and mounted campaigns, including lobbying MPs not to support this bill. Eventually, all opposition parties publicly stated that they would not support the bill. Given that the Conservative government had minority, the bill could not have been passed without some support from the opposition and, thus, was abandoned.

In 2012, the Conservative majority introduced Bill C-31, *Protecting Canada's Immigration System Act*, which incorporated many aspects of Bill C-49. The bill was passed (despite ongoing advocacy campaigns against it) and has now become law.

government bills and ministers introduce them in the legislature. Second, the party in power defines what is in the "national interest" and reflects this vision in proposed legislation (see Box 3.1) as well as in various policies and other initiatives. Third, the executive (through its various ministries and departments) develops and adopts subordinate legislation. Fourth, the executive's power to select candidates for judicial appointment and the Senate can indirectly influence the content of developing legal norms and their application. For example, a governing party may be inclined to appoint individuals who are aligned with that party's position and correspondingly are more likely to support the government's bills and decisions.

1.3 Judicial Branch

The judicial branch is composed of federally and provincially created courts, which are described in detail in Chapter 4. For the purpose of discussion in this chapter, it is important to know that the judicial branch performs the following key functions: adjudicates disputes; interprets legislation; reviews actions of the executive and statutes passed by the legislature for compliance with the *Constitution*; and reviews administrative decision making for compliance with the principles of administrative law. Thus, it can play an important role in oversight of legislative and executive action and the implementation of principles of the rule of law and constitutionalism.

2. INTERACTION BETWEEN BRANCHES OF GOVERNMENT

Although each branch has its distinct functions, they do not act in isolation. Our system of government can be properly understood only when we see how the three branches interrelate with each other. First, the formation of the law is directly and indirectly influenced by such interactions. Second, not only is each branch expected to observe the rule of law and constitutionalism, but it also has certain powers that are designed to keep a check on other branches. These mechanisms are key to the implementation of the principle of government accountability.

2.1 Impact on the Formation of the Law

Although legislatures are key in shaping the law, as you already know, other branches also participate in this process directly and indirectly. Executive departments play a role in developing policy, drafting bills that are subsequently considered by the legislature, and developing and passing subordinate legislation. Through review of legislation, courts can invalidate provisions that are unconstitutional, subsequently triggering re-examination of a respective regulatory regime. This section briefly notes the dynamics between courts and legislatures, as well as between courts and the executive, that can help you see the formation of the law in a larger political context. Law making is not merely a technical process of following the stages of an enactment process. It is influenced by multiple factors within the legislative branch itself (e.g., minority versus majority government) as well as external factors such as constitutional review, pressure from interest groups, and considerations of federalism.

Constitutional review (that is, when courts examine constitutionality of legislation) is one of the factors that may trigger changes in the law. If a court declares a particular statute of no force and effect, the legislature is prompted to consider how to respond to the court's ruling. Several options are open to it: (a) pass a new law, which takes into consideration guidance from the court's decision; (b) take no action; or (c) enact a new law that effectively overrides the judicial decision in question. Box 3.3 provides an example that can help you understand the judicial–legislative interaction. In addition, Part II of Chapter 6 contains further discussion of judicial–legislative dialogue. For the purpose of our current discussion, two points are important. First, a judicial decision can provide useful guidance to the legislature with respect to the redesign of the invalidated provisions. Second, legislative regimes such as those ultimately developed in tobacco advertising (Box 3.3) can be seen as a result of input from both legislative and judicial branches.

Box 3.3

Regulation of Tobacco Advertising: Judicial–Legislative Dialogue? (*RJR-MacDonald Inc v Canada (Attorney General)*, [1995] 3 SCR 199 and *Canada (Attorney General) v JTI-Macdonald Corp*, [2007] 2 SCR 610)

In 1988, Parliament passed legislation that prohibited all advertising and promotion of tobacco products, subject to some exceptions, and required tobacco manufacturers to print unattributed health warnings on the packages of all tobacco products. This legislation could have had a very serious impact on the profitability of tobacco companies: they would have incurred significant expenses to alter their packages and would have been very restricted in advertising their products. A group of tobacco companies challenged the validity of this legislation, arguing that it violated their freedom of expression under the *Charter*. It is interesting to note that companies used a public interest argument (the importance of freedom of expression) to advance essentially their commercial interests. The Supreme Court found the provisions unconstitutional.[11] The majority of the Court noted that the legislation was seeking to advance an important objective—to discourage individuals from tobacco use—but there was no direct scientific evidence that advertising bans lead to a decrease in tobacco consumption. Thus, there was no rational connection between the law's objective and the means used to achieve it.

In response to the Court's decision, Parliament enacted new legislation that did not fully ban advertising but nevertheless imposed some limitations on it. It permitted information and brand-preference advertising, but forbade lifestyle advertising and promotion, advertising appealing to young persons, and false or misleading advertising. Tobacco companies challenged this new legislation. However, this time, the Supreme Court found that the restrictions on freedom of expression were justifiable and the legislation was upheld.[12]

This example can be seen as two branches engaging in a metaphorical "dialogue" in search of a regulatory regime that properly balances various objectives (although not everyone will necessarily agree with such characterization—see Chapter 6 for details).

The judiciary also has the power to review actions of the executive for compliance with the *Constitution* and administrative law principles. In some cases, such judicial oversight may lead to significant changes in government practices and policies. For example, in the area of criminal law, landmark court decisions mandated greater disclosure of information by the Crown to the defence[13] and an obligation on the police not only to inform a detainee of the right to counsel but also to facilitate access to counsel.[14] Thus, review by courts can trigger revisions of laws as well as executive practices, and is an important means to implement the principles of government accountability, the rule of law, and constitutionalism.

The judiciary is independent and must make decisions impartially and in accordance with the law. However, as we will see in Chapter 5 on theoretical perspectives, judges' backgrounds and values may have an impact on how they decide cases. For example, if judges are conservative, they may be more likely to uphold existing laws and it may be more difficult to use litigation to achieve social change. Thus, by making decisions on judicial appointments (see Chapter 4 for details), the executive can have some (albeit indirect) influence on judicial decision making. While the importance of political connections has decreased since the 1980s, it still has some role in the appointment process.[15] The party in power may be inclined to prefer candidates who are either more closely aligned with its position or have had some connections to that party. For example, it has been noted that the Harper government has placed more emphasis on ideology of candidates for judicial appointment, preferring individuals with socially conservative and law and order views.[16] Given the length of judicial tenure, the appointment choices of a given governing party may have a long-lasting impact, one that extends beyond the period of that party's stay in power.

The executive may have a more direct impact on the development of case law by participating in litigation. Whenever a government decision or a piece of legislation is challenged, a government authority represented by lawyers of the Department of Justice becomes a party to a case. Government lawyers may influence outcomes of cases by advancing arguments and explaining government rationales behind the chosen policy options if such arguments persuade the court to uphold a given law or policy.

2.2 Government Accountability

The ultimate governing authority rests with the people, but how does this authority flow to various branches of government, and how can the people ensure that the government does not abuse or overstep the delegated authority? In brief, the current system implements these ideas in the following way. Popular sovereignty is exercised most notably through elections to federal and provincial legislatures. Through this mechanism, the public delegates its ruling authority to the legislature. The legislature, in turn, delegates some of its authority to the executive as well as holds the executive accountable through the principle of responsible government and other mechanisms discussed below. The legislature itself is accountable to the people: if a governing party has not lived up to its promises, voters can express their displeasure at polls and elect a new party to power.

As you have seen, our system allows for significant concentration of power within the executive. The legislature is dominated by the government in power, which is in turn controlled by the prime minister and Cabinet ministers. On the one hand, the concentration of power clearly assigns responsibility for laws and policies to the governing party.[17] On the other hand, it raises concerns of *democratic deficit*—a situation where legislature has little real power and is dominated by the governing party.[18] Our system has several mechanisms designed to allow the legislature to keep a check on the prime minister and the Cabinet: the principle of responsible government, the question period, general opposition, and debates on the Speech from the Throne and annual budget.

During *daily question period*, the prime minister and ministers are expected to be present in the House of Commons to provide answers to MPs on various issues. Each minister is responsible for everything that goes on in their department and is expected to answer any related questions. The Speech from the Throne and annual budget indicate the government's legislative and economic direction and are followed by debates in the House where MPs can question proposed measures. The *Speech from the Throne*, which opens each new session of Parliament, outlines what legislation the government has planned for that session. The budget sets out revenue generating and borrowing measures that the government plans to introduce and outlines the general state of the country's finances and economy.

There are, however, concerns that the above mechanisms are relatively weak and do not facilitate real accountability of the executive. For example, a majority government would not lose the confidence of the legislature due to strict party discipline. The debates and question period in the House are often considered largely symbolic, with each party trying to score political points rather than promoting real accountability for executive decisions. Further, there is relatively little diversity of parties within Parliament, as the single member plurality system favours larger and more established parties. Some argue that a number of changes are necessary to help address democratic deficit: (1) a move away from strict party discipline; (2) electoral reform to introduce a proportionate representation system (where a party would have a number of seats in the legislature proportionate to the number of votes it received); (3) senate reform to ensure that senators are elected and more independent; and (4) development of greater citizen engagement.[19]

In addition to the above mechanisms, the principles of the rule of law and constitutionalism impose important constraints on actions of all three branches of government. The rule of law means that everyone is equal and no one—whether a private citizen or a public official—is above the law. The exercise of public power must have a source in law and all state officials must act in accordance with the law rather than on the basis of their wishes and desires. As a subset of the rule of law, the principle of **constitutionalism** dictates that all government action must be compliant with the *Constitution*. The rule of law and constitutionalism reflect the idea of limited government and help protect individuals against arbitrariness of state power.[20] Courts play a very important oversight role that helps ensure compliance with the rule of law and constitutionalism.

3. FEDERALISM: THE INTERACTION BETWEEN LEVELS OF GOVERNMENT

Federalism is one of the key factors in Canada's constitutional and political life. It reflects the division of sovereignty between two levels of government: federal and provincial. In the words of the Supreme Court, "[f]ederalism was a legal response to the underlying political and cultural realities that existed at Confederation and continue to exist today."[21] It helped create unity among regions, while also respecting their diversity.

Under the *Constitution Act, 1867*, some subject matters are reserved for exclusive regulation by the provinces (e.g., property and civil rights, hospitals, and the medical profession): this allows each province the flexibility to develop a regime that is most suitable to its unique context. Other powers are reserved exclusively to the federal government (e.g., criminal law, banking, and aeronautics), allowing for uniform regulation of matters of national concern across the whole of Canada. In a few areas (e.g., immigration), the *Constitution* gives the two levels of government shared responsibility (see Chapter 6 for more).

In federations, the interactions between levels of government can develop in a variety of ways. In the Canadian context, the following six models of federalism are most relevant:

- Independent governments—each level of government has its exclusive authority and operates independently;

- Consultation—the two levels of government exchange information and discuss issues before they take their independent action;

- Coordination—the two levels of government not only consult but also develop mutually acceptable policies that each level subsequently implements in its area of jurisdiction;

- Collaboration—both levels of government work as equals in order to develop major policies;

- Joint decision making—both levels of government develop a policy and both must approve any changes to it; and

- Competitive federalism—each level of government seeks to maximize its autonomy and areas of influence.[22]

Each of the above models not only has been observed in Canada at a particular point in time, but is also present today. Overall, we can see gradual progression from independent governments during early Confederation to greater coordination and collaboration between the two levels.[23] However, the degree of cooperation varies depending on the subject matter. For example, currently, federal and provincial governments act collaboratively in the areas of healthcare and postsecondary education; they exercise joint decision making with respect to pension plans, but in areas of unemployment insurance and climate change they still act as independent bodies.[24] It is also not uncommon to see a competitive side of Canadian federalism, where each level seeks to assert and expand its jurisdiction. For example, Quebec's strong interest in preserving its unique identity led it to seek more extensive powers than other provinces.[25] In addition, if one level of government considers that the other acted outside of its constitutional powers, it can challenge the validity of that action in courts (see Box 3.4). If such challenges are successful, they can lead to changes in respective federal or provincial laws.

Even areas reserved exclusively to either level of government usually require some consultation or cooperation between the two levels. As the Supreme Court stated, "[a] federal state depends for its very existence on a just and workable balance between the central and provincial levels of government."[26] Among the most important mechanisms of intergovernmental consultation are conferences and meetings of first ministers (the prime minister and premiers); meetings of federal and provincial ministers and public servants; and interprovincial meetings (without the participation of the federal government).[27] During the meetings, federal and provincial executives may negotiate agreements on specific issues, resolve disputes, and coordinate various policy and implementational measures. As you can see, all of these mechanisms give the leading role to federal and provincial executives, and so Canadian federalism is characterized as **executive federalism**. Some academics have argued that Canada's executive federalism undermines democracy, as most intergovernmental negotiations take place behind closed doors and without citizen participation.[28] There are no mechanisms specifically created to ensure transparency and accountability in dealings between levels of government. In addition, the growing trend of federal and provincial governments settling disputes informally limits the oversight role of courts, exacerbating existing concerns.[29]

Thus, federalism is another important factor that needs to be taken into account in understanding the law and policy formation, as well as issues of government accountability.

Box 3.4

Provinces as Challengers of Federal Laws: Firearms Registration

In 1995, Parliament amended the *Firearms Act*, which required holders of all firearms to obtain licences and register their guns. The legislation was partially a response to the 1989 massacre at École Polytechnique in Montreal and was considered an important step in making the country safer. However, this change inspired much criticism among a rural population that commonly owns guns and hunts. Several provinces (e.g., Alberta, Newfoundland and Labrador, Ontario) opposed the federal government's decision to create a gun registry and stated that they would not prosecute individuals who do not register their guns.[30] Alberta referred constitutional questions to the provincial Court of Appeal to determine whether Parliament had the power to enact the provisions in question. The case ultimately ended up before the Supreme Court, which upheld the provisions as constitutional.[31]

In 2012, the federal government moved to abolish the long-gun registry. Bill C-19 provided for the destruction of all accumulated records on firearms which were neither prohibited nor restricted. Quebec

(continued)

Box 3.4   *(continued)*

strongly opposed this move, arguing that gun registration is important to preventing occurrences such as the Montreal massacre. The province turned to courts to prevent the destruction of the records as it wanted to use them in a new provincial registry. Quebec's argument succeeded at the trial level, but was reversed on appeal.[32] The province filed a further appeal with the Supreme Court of Canada and the outcome remains to be seen.

This example demonstrates that provinces and the federal government may have different interests and different positions on a given issue. Further, there may be differences among provinces in their reaction to a given federal law: some may support it, while others may oppose it. Where provinces disagree with a federal law, they may seek to challenge it in courts and, if successful, this may lead to changes in federal laws.

4. EXTERNAL PRESSURES: INTEREST GROUPS

In addition to the dynamics between branches and levels of government, the law and policy process is often subject to pressures from participants outside government structures, most notably interest groups. **Interest groups** can be defined as groups of individuals or organizations that share a common set of goals and have joined together to persuade a government authority to adopt a policy, law, or decision that will help protect or advance the interest of a given group. Interest groups are usually characterized by the following: they have a formal organizational structure; they articulate and aggregate interests; they act within the political system to influence policy; and they seek to influence regulatory structures rather than exercise government power themselves.[33] Interest groups can be of several types: self-interest groups (advance interests of their members), public interest groups (advance the public good), and sectoral groups (represent specific sectors of society).[34] There are hundreds of interest groups in Canada: over 2000 business associations, some 1000 environmental groups, approximately 500 organizations representing agricultural interests, and several hundred women's associations and groups focusing on Aboriginal issues.[35] Box 3.5 provides an example of an interest group.

Box 3.5

Example of an Interest Group: Women's Legal Education and Action Fund (LEAF)

Having started as a grassroots organization, LEAF was officially incorporated in 1985 and since then has become an active and influential player in the promotion of women's rights and equality. LEAF employs a variety of strategies: research, education campaigns, submissions to parliamentary committees, and litigation. It has intervened in over 150 cases spanning various areas of law, including family, criminal, freedom of expression, and many others.[36] In fact, it is one of the most frequent nongovernmental interveners before the Supreme Court.[37] For example, in 2013, LEAF intervened in *Quebec v A* (discussed in Chapter 11)—a family law case that asked the Supreme Court to decide whether exclusion of common-law unions from spousal support and property division regimes under the *Quebec Civil Code* was unconstitutional.[38] LEAF submitted that such exclusion was discriminatory as it provided for differential treatment of married and unmarried partners. In 2011, LEAF intervened in a criminal case—*R v JA*[39]—which dealt with the interpretation of consent in the context of sexual assault. In this case, the accused and the complainant experimented with erotic choking and unconsciousness. In the course of sexual relations, the accused began to choke the complainant, rendering her unconscious for approximately three minutes during which he engaged in sexual activity with her. The accused argued that the complainant consented in advance to the sexual activity that might take place while she was unconscious. LEAF argued that there can be no advance consent, that consent should be interpreted as active and contemporaneous with the sexual activity in question, and hence that consent can be validly given only by a conscious person.

It is difficult to confirm definitively how much influence interveners' arguments have on courts. Some studies suggest that LEAF's submissions had at least some impact on the Supreme Court decisions,[40] although the success varies by policy field.[41] In *Quebec v A*, the Supreme Court found that exclusion of common-law couples from the provisions under the *Quebec Civil Code* was not discriminatory. In *R v JA*, the Court adopted the interpretation of consent urged by LEAF (although some academics question whether the Court's conclusion is a direct result of LEAF's arguments).[42]

For more on LEAF, see <www.leaf.ca>.

In order to advance their agendas, interest groups employ various tactics, including lobbying, litigation, public education, protests, and others. We will briefly discuss lobbying and litigation as two of the most common strategies.

4.1 Lobbying

Lobbying is "any form of direct or indirect communication with government that is designed to influence public policy."[43] It is focused primarily on the legislative and policy process. Given that most legislation is usually initiated by the government in power, interest groups may target the Cabinet and individual ministers as well as civil servants who are involved in the drafting of law and policy proposals.

In addition to attempting to influence the initial stages of law or policy development, interest groups can seek to provide their input after a bill has been introduced in legislature, notably at the committee stage.

Interest groups may also attempt to persuade MPs to vote for or against a particular piece of legislation. They may lobby MPs directly as well as organize media and awareness campaigns to create a critical mass of public opinion and thereby influence the MPs. For example, in the fall of 2010, the Canadian Council for Refugees (CCR), an umbrella organization advocating on behalf of refugees in Canada, conducted a "take action" campaign against Bill C-49. The CCR arranged expert panels that discussed the content and implications of Bill C-49, an online campaign, as well as other activities that sought to persuade constituents to lobby their MPs not to support the bill. Ultimately, all opposition parties announced that they would not support the bill. While the decision of opposition parties cannot be attributed solely to the CCR campaign, the campaign focused considerable attention on the issue and possibly contributed to the parties' stance.

4.2 Litigation

Unlike political lobbying, which is concentrated on the legislative process and attempts to mould the law at the creation stage, litigation seeks to challenge laws already in force. Interest groups can participate in litigation in one of two ways:

- By launching a case
- By seeking **intervener** status, which allows individuals and organizations that are not parties to a given case to provide legal arguments to the court on the issues in question. By providing their perspectives, interveners help mitigate one of the limitations of the adversarial process—its narrow focus on the positions of the two parties to the case. Interest groups have intervened in many landmark cases, including on abortion, Aboriginal rights, and assisted suicide.

Litigation can be both an empowering and a constraining force in promoting social change.[44] On the one hand, activist groups can use it to challenge current injustices and inequalities. On the other hand, litigation can also be used by powerful groups either to preserve the status quo (e.g., the tobacco advertising case in Box 3.3) or to defend a government policy. In addition, individual companies may use strategic litigation against public participation (SLAPP) to impede actions of private activist groups that interfere with their operations (recall the *Henco* case from Chapter 1).[45] As a part of SLAPP, a company may seek injunctions against protesters or file defamation suits if activist groups make certain statements that affect the company's reputation.[46] The primary objective of a SLAPP lawsuit is not to win a case, but to silence or intimidate an activist group. Such lawsuits force activist groups to divert their attention and resources from public campaigns to the defence litigation.

Part III. Aboriginal Self-Government

The above discussion focused only on the mainstream institutions established by the European settlers in Canada. But what about the government of the First Nations communities? They had their own ways of government prior to colonization. Has this way of government been preserved, was it altered due to colonization, or has it been completely subsumed into the mainstream institutions? This section will provide a very brief overview of the treatment of the First Nations communities following European settlement, as well as current initiatives and struggles to implement the inherent right of Aboriginal peoples to self-government.

1. BRIEF HISTORIC OVERVIEW

The 1996 report of the Royal Commission on Aboriginal Peoples provided a detailed account of the history of interaction between the First Nations and settler populations in Canada. This interaction has evolved in several stages from infrequent and relatively peaceful contacts during the early settlement, to the policies of displacement and assimilation, and finally, to attempts at reconciliation in the second half of the twentieth century.[47] During the period from 1600 to the 1750s, the increased interaction between the settlers and the First Nations often took the shape of economic and military alliances. As the European settlement expanded, the colonizers acquired greater power to impose their will on the First Nations. Growing economic activity in agriculture and industry required access to new, vaster areas of land to which the First Nations were seen as a barrier.[48] Treaties signed between the British government and various First Nations communities during 1871–1923 provided for surrender of large tracts of land in exchange for cash payments and other "benefits." In reality, however, the treaties often forced on the Aboriginal people a system of reserves in remote areas, which were often devoid of resources and put the native populations at a significant disadvantage.

The First Nations were viewed as inferior, incapable of progressive development and thus, an impediment to the establishment of civilized life in Canada.[49] They therefore had to be assimilated into the mainstream society and educated about the proper way of living. For example, it was an offence for an Aboriginal person to be found "in a state of intoxication" on reserve. In addition, the operation of pool rooms, dance halls, and other places of amusement on reserves was strictly regulated to ensure that Aboriginal peoples learned to be industrious and did not waste too much time on leisure and entertainment. During 1884–1951, traditional ceremonies and practices such as potlatch and the Tamanawas dance were prohibited and criminalized. Beginning in the 1870s and continuing until 1996, Aboriginal children were taken into residential schools where they were forbidden to speak their languages or to engage in traditional practices.[50]

First Nations' self-government and other opportunities for political participation were limited. Historically, Aboriginal people were treated mostly as objects of governance rather than as its active participants, and since the late nineteenth century, many aspects of Aboriginal life were put under the control of the federal government. On reserves, traditional tribal leaders were not allowed to exercise their powers and instead a European-style elective system was imposed. Band councils had limited powers and some of their decisions could be overridden by the Indian agents appointed by the government. Such agents controlled most local administrative, financial, and judicial matters. Aboriginal people did not have the right to vote in federal elections until 1960.

The *Constitution Act, 1867* does not refer to Aboriginal self-government and recognizes only two levels of government: federal and provincial. This effectively left no official space for the First Nations to engage at the intergovernmental level as equal partners with federal and provincial governments. Neither had they specified representation in formal institutions such as federal Parliament, the Cabinet, or the Supreme Court.[51]

It was not until the 1970s that the treatment of the First Nations populations started coming into the spotlight of government and public debate. An important stepping stone in the affirmation of Aboriginal rights was the Supreme Court's decision in *Calder*[52] (1973), which recognized the existence of the **Aboriginal title**—the right to land and to the use of that land for a variety of activities, whether connected to distinct Aboriginal traditions or not.[53] It stems from Aboriginal peoples' occupation of the land prior to the European settlement and does not require government recognition in order to exist. In 1982, the *Charter* recognized and affirmed Aboriginal and treaty rights of Aboriginal peoples. During the negotiation of constitutional changes under the Charlottetown Accord in the early 1990s (see Chapter 6), the issue of Aboriginal self-government occupied significant place and the Accord proposed to entrench the inherent right to self-government. Although the Accord never came into force, in 1995, the federal government recognized the inherent right of Aboriginal communities to self-government as an existing Aboriginal right and adopted a policy regarding the implementation of that right.[54] In its 1996 report, the Royal Commission on Aboriginal Peoples called for the recognition of Aboriginal self-government as a third-order government in Canada. Certain progress in this area has been made but many issues remain.

2. INHERENT RIGHT OF ABORIGINAL PEOPLES TO SELF-GOVERNMENT AND ITS IMPLEMENTATION

In general terms, *self-government* refers to a given community's ability to decide on vital issues of its life and direct its future. For First Nations communities, self-government is an important means to preserve their unique cultures, identities, traditions, and languages, and reflect these in governing institutions. In addition to self-government in their territories, it is important to facilitate broader participation of the First Nations in the mainstream institutions.[55]

Canada is home to some 40–60 Aboriginal nations with distinct traditions, languages, and history.[56] They constitute approximately 4.3% of the total Canadian population,[57] and have different visions of self-government depending on their unique circumstances and needs (see Table 3.3). Self-government may take the following forms:

- Sovereignty and self-government based on the recognition of inherent indigenous authority to make laws over their territory;

- Self-administration and self-management when indigenous communities do not exercise their inherent authority, but derive powers from settler legislation; or

- Co-management and joint management, which most commonly take place in the context of mining or oil, gas, or other exploration on Aboriginal lands. The lands are managed by the federal or provincial government, but it has a duty to consult with Aboriginal communities with respect to any land development projects.[58]

The **inherent right to self-government** means that it exists independently, by virtue of First Nations' traditional settlement in Canada. This right cannot be granted or taken away by dominant Euro-Canadian institutions. Rather, it should be affirmed and realized through negotiation and cooperation between the First Nations and settler communities.

Currently, Aboriginal self-government can be developed as a part of negotiation of comprehensive land claims, as well as through other initiatives such as incremental expansion of Aboriginal communities' management over various matters. The issues of Aboriginal title and self-government are closely connected, and self-government agreements are often negotiated together with the resolution of land claims. This is so because

Table 3.3 Number and Distribution of Aboriginal Peoples in Canada

Provinces and Territories	Aboriginal Identity Population	Percent Distribution	Aboriginal Identity Population as a Percentage of the Total Population
Canada	1 400 685	100.0	4.3
Newfoundland and Labrador	35 800	2.6	7.1
Prince Edward Island	2 230	0.2	1.6
Nova Scotia	33 845	2.4	3.7
New Brunswick	22 615	1.6	3.1
Quebec	141 915	10.1	1.8
Ontario	301 425	21.5	2.4
Manitoba	195 900	14.0	16.7
Saskatchewan	157 740	11.3	15.6
Alberta	220 695	15.8	6.2
British Columbia	232 290	16.6	5.4
Yukon	7 705	0.6	23.1
Northwest Territories	21 160	1.5	51.9
Nunavut	27 360	2.0	86.3

Source: Statistics Canada, National Household Survey, 2011, online: http://www12.statcan.gc.ca/nhs-enm/2011/as-sa/99-011-x/2011001/tbl/tbl02-eng.cfm

Aboriginal title is a right that is to be exercised collectively, and therefore requires the existence of mechanisms for communities to decide collectively on how to manage the land. Further, given that Aboriginal communities have a particular connection to the land that defines their way of life, practices, and traditions, the ability to decide for themselves how to use the land is of crucial importance.

The federal policy on the implementation of Aboriginal self-government rests on several key principles. First, Aboriginal self-government is to be exercised in accordance with the *Constitution* and the *Charter*. Second, the matters that may be subject to negotiation are those internal to the Aboriginal group and can include such issues as establishment of governing structures; Aboriginal language, culture, and religion; education; health; marriage, adoption, and child welfare; administration/enforcement of Aboriginal laws; policing; land and natural resource management; hunting, fishing, and trapping on Aboriginal lands; and others. Third, some issues cannot be subject to negotiation, namely powers related to Canadian sovereignty, defence, and external relations, and a number of other national interest powers (e.g., regulation of currency, aeronautics, navigation). Fourth, given the great diversity of Aboriginal communities, negotiated arrangements are to be tailored to the unique circumstances of each community rather than take a "one-size-fits-all" form of self-government.[59]

When self-government arrangements are negotiated in conjunction with the resolution of land claims, they are governed by the *Comprehensive Land Claims Policy*. This policy applies to cases where a given community has not concluded a treaty with the Crown in the past and asserts its claims to land on the basis of traditional use and occupancy and unextinguished Aboriginal title.[60] These claims are considered comprehensive because there is no treaty in place and a claim is made to resolve multiple issues by means of a new treaty.

Under the *Comprehensive Land Claims Policy*, the negotiation process is started by an Aboriginal community submitting a statement of claim. The federal government accepts the claim if the community can demonstrate that: it has occupied and used the territory since time immemorial; the territory is currently used for traditional purposes; and the title has not been extinguished by another treaty. The next step is for all parties—the federal government, provincial government, and an Aboriginal community—to develop a framework agreement that outlines the issues to be negotiated. When parties reach an agreement on substantive issues, they conclude an agreement in principle and then a final agreement[61] (also see the chapter on alternative dispute resolution and restorative justice on the Companion Website).

Since 1973, 26 comprehensive land claim and self-government agreements, covering over 40% of Canada's land mass, have been negotiated and brought into effect.[62] Among them are the James Bay and Northern Quebec Agreement, the Nunavut Land Claims Agreement, the Yukon First Nations Land Claims Settlement, the Nisga'a Final Agreement, and others. For example, the Nisga'a Agreement provided for the establishment of a Nisga'a central government and village governments; outlined Nisga'a law making powers over matters such as culture and language, public works, regulation of traffic and transportation, land use, and solemnization of marriages; and provided ownership of specified lands in the Nass River Valley, harvesting rights, resource rights, and financial compensation.

The government policy on Aboriginal self-government and negotiation of comprehensive land claims has been criticized and rejected by a number of Aboriginal communities.[63] While providing for recognition of self-government, the policy sets strict parameters on what is and is not negotiable. It also seems to implicitly suggest that Aboriginal self-government can be developed only through the federal government's recognition—a position that contradicts the notion of the inherent nature of Aboriginal self-government. In relation to land claims in particular, the Aboriginal peoples and Canadian government seem to seek different objectives. The Canadian government negotiates in order to achieve certainty regarding lands and resources, while Aboriginal communities seek recognition of their inherent rights and also see the process as a precondition for reconciliation.[64] Another significant concern of comprehensive land claims agreements is that they usually provide for release or surrender clauses whereby Aboriginal peoples cannot claim in the future any rights that are not outlined in the agreement. This means that Aboriginal peoples may be relinquishing some of their rights—and reducing their traditional territories—in order to achieve a final settlement of a land claim.[65] While some communities have negotiated self-government arrangements under this policy, concerns around it can partially explain the reluctance of other communities to engage in negotiations with the government.

SUMMARY

In Canada, governing structures are organized along two major dimensions: (1) division of areas of jurisdiction between federal and provincial governments; and (2) within each level of government, division of authority into three branches: legislative, executive, and judicial. Each branch has a particular function: the legislature passes laws, the executive implements them, and the judiciary resolves disputes and oversees legislative and judicial action for compliance with the *Constitution* and other principles. In parliamentary systems such as Canada's, there is a certain merger between the executive and the legislative branch. The party that gets the most seats in a parliamentary election gets to form the government, and its leader becomes the prime minister. The prime minister and the Cabinet are members of both the legislature and the executive. In addition, the executive has a role to play in the legislative process: it drafts government bills and has the power to pass subordinate legislation. Further, various administrative tribunals (which are part of the executive) have the power to adjudicate disputes, thereby performing a function similar to courts.

The three branches of government interact in complex ways that both influence the formation of the law and the exercise of government accountability. For example, mechanisms such as the vote of no confidence, daily question period, and debates of the budget and the Speech from the Throne seek to provide for scrutiny of the executive by the legislature. Further, each branch of government must comply with the rule of law: its actions must be authorized by law and it must not overstep the boundaries prescribed by the law. Constitutional and judicial review by courts plays an important role in ensuring such compliance.

Any discussion of the system of government in Canada needs to take account of Aboriginal self-government as well as initiatives seeking to provide for greater participation of the First Nations populations in the mainstream institutions. First Nations communities have the inherent right to self-government. This right exists by virtue of their traditional settlement in Canada and cannot be granted or withheld by the Euro-Canadian authorities. In 1995, the federal government adopted a policy on the implementation of this right. However, the implementation process, especially when it also involves resolution of land claims, has been subject to criticism and many challenging issues remain.

Critical Thinking Questions

1. Find a bill that is currently before Parliament and has been examined by a parliamentary committee, or a bill that was recently passed. Identify the subject matter of the bill and the reasons for its proposal. Is this a government bill or a private member's bill? Is this a private or a public bill? What are the objectives of this bill? Find out which interest groups made submissions at the committee stage and compare their comments on the bill with the sponsor's speech. After reading perspectives from both sides, what is your opinion on the bill? For a list of bills, see http://www.parl.gc.ca/LegisInfo/Home.aspx?Language=E&Mode=1&ParliamentSession=41-2. (An interesting bill to examine is Bill C-24, *Strengthening Canadian Citizenship Act*, which was passed by Parliament in June 2014.)

2. Examine the *Canada (Attorney General) v Bedford* [2013] SCC 72 case, recently decided by the Supreme Court of Canada. Were there interveners in this case? Pick any one or two interveners, research what kind of organization they are (what interests do they advance?) and what their positions on the case were.

3. Using the *Bedford* case mentioned in Question 2, find out what the legislative response to the decision was (hint: have a look at Bill C-36 introduced in Parliament in June 2014). In your opinion, does the bill take into consideration the Court's guidance from the *Bedford* decision? How does this case inform your understanding of interaction among the executive, legislative, and judicial branches in formation of the law?

Further Readings and Useful Resources

1. Herman Bakvis & Grace Skogstad, *Canadian Federalism: Performance, Effectiveness, and Legitimacy*, 3rd ed (Oxford University Press, 2012).

2. Louis Knafla & Haijo Westra, *Aboriginal Title and Indigenous People* (UBC Press, 2010).

3. Mintz et al, *Democracy, Diversity, and Good Government: An Introduction to Politics in Canada* (Toronto: Pearson Canada, 2011).

4. Joan Grace & Byron Sheldrick, eds, *Canadian Politics: Democracy and Dissent*, (Toronto: Pearson Canada, 2006).

Endnotes

1. For a detailed discussion, see Matthew Søberg Shugart, "Semi-Presidential Systems: Dual Executive and Mixed Authority Patterns" (2005) 3 *French Politics* 323.
2. Elections Canada, "Official Voting Results: Forty-first General Election 2011, Table 9: Percentage of Valid Votes by Political Affiliation," online: <http://www.elections.ca/scripts/ovr2011/default.html>.
3. Under s. 31 of the *Constitution Act, 1867*, among the grounds for removal are: failure to attend two consecutive sessions of the Parliament; being declared bankrupt or insolvent; and being convicted of certain offences (e.g., treason).
4. David Elliott, *Introduction to Public Law: Readings on the State, the Administrative Process, and Basic Values*, 6th ed (Concord: Captus Press, 2007) at 127.
5. *Safe Streets and Communities Act*, Order Fixing Various Dates as the Day on which Certain Sections of the Act Come into Force, P.C. 2012-841 June 19, 2012, SI/2012-48, July 4, 2012.
6. Canadian Bar Association, "Submission on Bill C-10 *Safe Streets and Communities Act*" (2011), online: <http://www.cba.org/cba/submissions/PDF/11-45-eng.pdf>.
7. The John Howard Society of Canada, "Submission to the Senate Committee on Legal and Constitutional Affairs on *Safe Streets and Communities Act*: Bill C-10" (2012), online: <http://www.johnhoward.ca/media/Submission%20Bill%20C-10%20Senate.pdf>.
8. Assembly of First Nations, "Submission: Bill C-10 *Safe Streets and Communities Act*" (2011), online: <http://www.afn.ca/uploads/files/parliamentary/billc-10.pdf>.
9. See speeches in Parliament related to Bill C-49: <http://www.parl.gc.ca/HousePublications/Publication.aspx?Pub=Hansard&Doc=89&Parl=40&Ses=3&Language=E&Mode=1#int-3432590>.

10. A refugee claimant is a person who has fled his or her country of origin due to persecution, risk to life, or risk of torture, and who is seeking protection in another state.

11. *RJR-MacDonald Inc v Canada (Attorney General)*, [1995] 3 SCR 199.

12. *Canada (Attorney General) v JTI-Macdonald Corp*, [2007] 2 SCR 610.

13. *R v Stinchcombe*, [1991] 3 SCR 326.

14. *R v Bartle* [1994], 92 CCC (3d) 289 (SCC); *R v Brydges* [1990], 53 CCC (3d) 330 (SCC).

15. Lori Hausegger et al, "Exploring the Links Between Party and Appointment: Canadian Federal Judicial Appointments from 1989 to 2003" (2010) 43 *Canadian Journal of Political Science* 633. The authors found that 17.2% of judges appointed between 1989 and 2003 had major connections to the party that appointed them (compared to 24.2% for appointments made between 1984 and 1988).

16. Troy Riddell, Lori Hausegger & Matthew Hennigar, "Federal Judicial Selection: Examining the Harper Appointments and Reforms" (2009) JPPL 495 at 509.

17. Jonathan Malloy, "Is There a Democratic Deficit in Canadian Legislatures and Executives?" in Joan Grace & Byron Sheldrick, eds, *Canadian Politics: Democracy and Dissent* (Toronto: Pearson Canada, 2006) 61 at 78–79.

18. *Ibid*.

19. *Ibid* at 79–81.

20. For a detailed discussion, see Allan C Hutchison & Patrick Monahan, "Democracy and the Rule of Law" in Allan C Hutchinson & Patrick Monahan, eds, *The Rule of Law: Ideal or Ideology?* (Toronto: Carswell, 1987) 119.

21. *Reference re Secession of Quebec* [1998] 2 SCR 217 at para 43.

22. Herman Bakvis & Grace Skogstad, "Canadian Federalism: Performance, Effectiveness, and Legitimacy" in Herman Bakvis & Grace Skogstad, *Canadian Federalism: Performance, Effectiveness, and Legitimacy*, 3rd ed (Oxford University Press, 2012) 2 at 4–6.

23. For discussion of various models, see Bakvis & Skogstad, *ibid*, at 4–11. For the discussion of the historic development of Canadian federalism, see Carolyn Johns, "Federalism and Intergovernmental Relations" in Joan Grace & Byron Sheldrick, eds, *Canadian Politics: Democracy and Dissent* (Toronto: Pearson Canada, 2006) 85.

24. See Grace Skogstad & Herman Bakvis, "Conclusion: Taking Stock of Canadian Federalism" in Bakvis & Skogstad, *supra* note 22 at 340–345.

25. For example, since the 1970s, Quebec had a say in selection of immigrants destined for the province—an authority that other provinces did not have.

26. *Reference re Firearms Act (Canada)*, [2000] 1 SCR 783 at 812.

27. Bakvis & Skogstad, *supra* note 22 at 7.

28. Donald Smiley, "An Outsider's Observations of Federal–Provincial Relations among Consenting Adults" (1979) at 105–106.

29. See generally Gerald Baier, "The Courts, the Constitution, and Dispute Resolution" in Bakvis & Skogstad, *supra* note 22, 79.

30. Matthew Hennigar, "Exploring Complex Judicial–Executive Interaction: Federal Government Concessions in *Charter* of Rights Cases" (2010) 43:4 *Canadian Journal of Political Science* 821 at 828.

31. *Reference re Firearms Act*, *supra* note 26.

32. *Canada (Attorney General) v Quebec (Attorney General)*, [2013] QJ No 6676.

33. A Paul Pross, "Pressure Groups: Adaptive Instruments of Political Communication" in A Paul Pross, ed, *Pressure Groups Behavior in Canadian Politics* (Whitby: McGraw-Hill Ryerson, 1975).

34. Eric Mintz, Livianna Tossutti, & Christopher Dunn, *Democracy, Diversity, and Good Government: An Introduction to Politics in Canada* (Toronto: Pearson Canada, 2011).

35. Stephen Brooks, *Canadian Democracy: An Introduction*, 6th ed (Toronto: Oxford University Press, 2009) at 325.

36. LEAF, "Making a Difference," online: http://leaf.ca/about-leaf/making-a-difference.

37. FL Morton & Avril Allen, "Feminists and the Courts: Measuring Success in Interest Group Litigation in Canada" (2001) 34:1 Canadian Journal of Political Science 55 at 56.

38. *Quebec (Attorney General) v A*, 2013 SCC 5.

39. *R v JA*, 2011 SCC 28.

40. Lauri Hausegger, "The Effectiveness of Interest Group Litigation: An Assessment of LEAF's Participation in Supreme Court Cases" (unpublished MA thesis, University of Calgary, 1994) cited in Morton & Allen, *supra* note 37 at 57.

41. Morton & Allen, *supra* note 37.

42. Richard Jochelson & Kirsten Kramar, "Essentialism Makes for Strange Bedmates: The Supreme Court Case of JA and the Intervention of LEAF" (2012) 30 Windsor YB Access Just 77.

43. Brooks, *supra* note 35 at 346.

44. Byron Sheldrick, *Perils and Possibilities: Social Activism and the Law* (Halifax: Fernwood, 2004) at 10.

45. *Ibid* at 49–52.

46. See, for example, Alberto R Salazar, "Consumer Counter-Advertising law and Corporate Social Responsibility" (2010) 58:4 *Buffalo L Rev* 977.

47. *Royal Commission Report on Aboriginal Peoples* (1996), online: <http://www.ainc-inac.gc.ca/ch/rcap/index_e.html>.

48. *Ibid*.

49. *Ibid*.

50. A detailed account of the system may be found in the report of the Royal Commission on Aboriginal Peoples, *ibid*.

51. See generally Martin Papillon, "Canadian Federalism and the Emerging Mosaic of Aboriginal Multilevel Governance" in Bakvis & Skogstad, *supra* note 22 at 287–88.

52. *Calder v Attorney General of British Columbia* [1973] SCR 313.

53. *Delgamuukw v British Columbia* [1997] 2 SCR 1010 at 1080–1081.

54. "The Government of Canada's Approach to Implementation of the Inherent Right and the Negotiation of Aboriginal Self-Government," online: <http://www.aadnc-aandc.gc.ca/eng/1100100031843/1100100031844>.

55. Papillon, *supra* note 51 at 293–94.

56. *Royal Commission Report*, *supra* note 47.

57. Statistics Canada, "Aboriginal Peoples in Canada: First Nations People, Métis and Inuit (2011)," online: <http://www12.statcan.gc.ca/nhs-enm/2011/as-sa/99-011-x/99-011-x2011001-eng.cfm>.

58. See Shin Imai, "Indigenous Self-Determination and the State" in Benjamin J Richardson, Shin Imai & Kent McNeil, eds, *Indigenous Peoples and the Law: Comparative and Critical Perspectives* (Oxford: Hart Publishing, 2009) 285.

59. "The Government of Canada's Approach to Implementation of the Inherent Right and the Negotiation of Aboriginal Self-Government," *supra* note 54.

60. Jill Wherrett, "Aboriginal Self-government" (1999), online: <http://www.parl.gc.ca/Content/LOP/researchpublications/962-e.htm>.

61. Aboriginal Affairs and Northern Development Canada, "Comprehensive Claims," online: <http://www.aadnc-aandc.gc.ca/eng/1100100030577/1100100030578>; Indian and Northern Affairs Canada, "Resolving Aboriginal Claims: A Practical Guide to Canadian Experiences" (2003) at 13–15, online: <http://www.collectionscanada.gc.ca/webarchives/20071115132640/> or <http://www.ainc-inac.gc.ca/pr/pub/rul/rul1_e.pdf>.

62. Aboriginal Affairs and Northern Development Canada, "General Briefing Note on Canada's Self-government and Comprehensive Land Claims Policies and the Status of Negotiations," online: <http://www.aadnc-aandc.gc.ca/eng/1373385502190/1373385561540>.

63. David C Nahwegahbow, "Recognition of Inherent Rights through Legislative Initiatives" paper prepared for a conference hosted by Indigenous Bar Association (Toronto, October 18, 2002) at 13, online: <http://www.indigenousbar.ca/pdf/Recognition%20of%20Inherent%20Rights%20Through%20Legislative%20Initiatives.pdf>.

64. Jennifer E Dalton, "Aboriginal Title and Self-government in Canada: What Is the True Scope of Comprehensive Land Claims Agreements?" (2006) 22 WRLSI 29.

65. *Ibid.*

Chapter 4
Canada's Courts

Learning Objectives

After reading this chapter, you should be able to:

- Explain which level of government has the power to create courts and appoint judges.

- Name three levels of provincial courts in Canada.

- Describe the difference between a trial court and an appellate court.

- Name and describe three key features of a court system.

- Explain the difference between an adversarial and an inquisitorial system.

- Outline main steps in the judicial appointment process.

- Name and explain at least five ethical principles of judicial conduct.

- Name and explain at least five initiatives to facilitate access to justice.

- Identify and explain at least two major limitations of the adversarial process.

Chapter Outline

Introduction

Part I. Substantive Issues

1. Power to Establish Courts and Appoint Judges
2. Functions of Courts
    2.1 Resolving Disputes
    2.2 Interpreting Legislation
    Box 4.1 Practical Application: What Does "at the time of application" Mean?
    2.3 Overseeing Administrative Decision Making
    2.4 Reviewing Constitutionality of Government Actions and/or Legislation
    Box 4.2 Example of a Reference Case: *Reference re Senate Reform*, 2014 SCC 32
3. Jurisdiction of Courts
4. Participants in Litigation
5. Structure of Canadian Courts
    5.1 Provincial Court System: Ontario
        5.1.1 Ontario Court of Justice

Introduction

Imagine the following situation. You loaned your friend $3000 on the condition that she repay it within a month. A month has passed and your friend has not repaid the loan. You have asked her multiple times for the money back. She keeps feeding you promises but does not pay back and tries to avoid you altogether. You consider going to court to collect the debt, but you have unanswered questions: Which court do you go to? What are the proceedings like? Do you have to be represented by a lawyer? We will discuss these issues in this chapter. As you can see, they are important not only from an academic standpoint but also from a practical perspective. Even if you will never need to be involved in a court system, it is useful to have at least basic knowledge of it.

    Part I of this chapter provides an overview of substantive issues such as the structure and functions of courts, the main features and participants of a court process, and the judicial appointments process. Part II discusses the experiences of individuals in the litigation process, highlighting some of the existing barriers and challenges. In particular, it focuses on two selected issues: (1) access to justice (what are some of the barriers faced by individuals in accessing courts, and how are they overcome?); and (2) the adversarial system, vulnerable witnesses, and the discovery of the truth (does the adversarial process pose particular challenges for vulnerable witnesses [e.g., children, victims of sexual assault]?).

Part I. Substantive Issues

1. POWER TO ESTABLISH COURTS AND APPOINT JUDGES

In order to understand the organization of courts in Canada, one needs to know which level of government has the following powers:

■ to create courts;

■ to prescribe procedure before courts; and

■ to appoint judges.

Canada's federal structure has definitive impact on the organization of courts. The *Constitution Act, 1867* allocates the powers between the two levels of government in the following manner:

■ *Creation of courts.* Under s. 92(14), provinces have exclusive jurisdiction over the administration of justice in each province. Thus, each province has the power to create its own system of courts. This provision allows the preservation of court systems that were established in the provinces prior to Confederation. It also explains the differences across provinces in the titles of courts and their jurisdiction.

  However, provinces are not the sole authorities that can create courts. Under s. 101, the federal government also has the power to establish certain types of courts, namely a "General Court of Appeal for Canada, and ... any additional Courts for the better Administration of the Laws of Canada." This power was used to set up the Supreme Court of Canada, the Federal Courts, the Tax Court, and military courts.

■ *Procedure before courts.* As the extension of the power to administer justice in a province, provinces can prescribe procedure before provincially created courts. However, this power is limited to the realm of civil procedure. Criminal procedure is prescribed by the federal government as part of its exclusive jurisdiction over criminal law.

■ *Power to appoint judges.* Both levels of government have the power to appoint judges to certain types of courts. Provincial governments appoint judges to the lowest level of provincial courts. The federal government appoints justices of all other provincial courts (superior courts and courts of appeal) as well as to federally created courts.

2. FUNCTIONS OF COURTS

Generally, courts can be said to perform the following functions: resolving disputes, interpreting legislation, overseeing administrative decision making, and reviewing constitutionality of legislation and/or government action.

2.1 Resolving Disputes

Courts resolve disputes in a variety of areas of law (e.g., contract, torts, employment, family) and involving various parties (individuals, businesses, and the state). In this process, courts have to determine whether a breach of a legal right has occurred and, if it has, what remedy would be appropriate.

2.2 Interpreting Legislation

While we expect legislation to clearly outline applicable rules, when it comes to their practical application, it may appear that some provisions are either unclear or may be understood in several different ways (see Box 4.1). In case of such ambiguity, courts can determine how a given provision is to be interpreted.

Box 4.1

Practical Application: What Does "at the time of application" Mean?

What can possibly be unclear about the phrase "at the time of application"? Most of us will likely say that the answer is simple: it is the time when you submit your application and documents for processing. However, as you will see from the case described below, there may indeed be at least two ways of understanding this phrase. This is where courts' role in interpreting legislation acquires great practical significance.

dela Fuente applied for immigration to Canada in 1992. In her application, she stated that she was single. Several months later, her application was approved and she became a permanent resident. Two weeks prior to arrival in Canada, dela Fuente got married but did not inform immigration authorities about that. In 2002, she applied to sponsor her husband for immigration to Canada, but was refused because she had not declared him at the time of her application for permanent residence. dela Fuente challenged the refusal before the Federal Court, bringing up the issue of how "at the time of application" should be interpreted.

There is usually a lag of several months or even years between the time when a person submits application for immigration and when he or she becomes a permanent resident. If "at the time of application" means the moment when the application is filed, then dela Fuente should not be precluded from sponsoring her husband as she was not married at the time. However, if "at the time of application" is interpreted as a continuing process that starts with lodging an application and completes with obtaining permanent residence, then she would not be able to sponsor her husband.

The Federal Court dealt with a number of cases similar to dela Fuente's and different judges adopted different interpretations of the phrase. Some concluded that it means a continuing process until a person becomes a permanent resident,[1] while others took it to mean the time when an application was submitted.[2] The issue of competing interpretations was finally resolved by the Federal Court of Appeal[3] which sided with the "continuing process" approach.

Historically, three main approaches to statutory interpretation have been developed:

a. *Plain meaning rule*. Provisions are to be interpreted literally, with their words being given plain and obvious meaning.

b. *Golden rule*. This approach not only looks at the literal meaning of the words, but also puts them into broader context so as to avoid any absurdity or inconsistency in interpretation.

c. *Parliamentary intention*. This approach suggests that courts should interpret statutes according to the intention of the legislature that passed them.

The modern approach to statutory interpretation combines all three of the above rules and can be summarized as follows: ". . . [T]he words of an Act are to be read in their entire context and in their grammatical and ordinary sense harmoniously with the scheme of the Act, the object of the Act, and the intention of Parliament."[4]

2.3 Overseeing Administrative Decision Making

Government officials and administrative tribunals/agencies make thousands of decisions on a daily basis that can have crucial impact on individuals (e.g., decisions on applications for benefits, various licences and permits, immigration to Canada, and the like). Courts have the power to review such administrative decisions to check whether they have been made fairly, without bias, and according to the law (see Chapter 7).

2.4 Reviewing Constitutionality of Government Actions and/or Legislation

The questions of constitutionality can arise in three major contexts:

a. *Jurisdictional disputes*. Such disputes raise questions as to whether a given level of government acted within its powers under the *Constitution Act, 1867*. As discussed in more detail in Chapter 6, the Act allocates most subject matters to exclusive jurisdiction of either federal or provincial governments. If one level of government takes action in the area exclusively reserved for another level, such action will be considered unconstitutional and of no force and effect. For example, the *Constitution Act, 1867* gives exclusive jurisdiction over criminal law to the federal government. If a province enacts a criminal law, such law can be challenged on jurisdictional grounds and would be recognized as being beyond provincial powers (this is called **ultra vires**) and hence invalid (for more, see Chapter 6, Box 6.2).

b. *Charter cases*. *Charter* cases question whether legislation and/or government action infringes a *Charter* right. For example, if a certain law unduly limits a *Charter* right, an affected individual may challenge such law in court. If a court decides that such limitation is unjustifiable, the law will be declared of no force and effect (for more on the *Charter* and *Charter* litigation, see Chapter 6).

Box 4.2

Example of a Reference Case: *Reference re Senate Reform*, 2014 SCC 32

As you will recall from Chapter 3, the Senate is currently an appointed body where senators serve until the age of 75 or until retirement/removal. There have been several calls for Senate reform, and one such recent attempt is federal Bill C-7.

In June 2011, the federal government introduced Bill C-7, which proposed a nine-year, nonrenewable term for senators and a process of consultative elections for the selection of senatorial nominees. Bill C-7 would have followed a regular statutory enactment process and would have become law if passed by Parliament. However, according to the *Constitution Act, 1982*, changes to the powers or selection of the Senate require approval of both federal and provincial legislatures (see Chapter 6 for discussion of amending formulas). Yet the federal government insisted that it could proceed with such changes unilaterally. The controversy on whether provincial approval was required resulted in two reference cases. The Quebec government asked the Quebec Court of Appeal whether, under the *Constitution*, the approval of the provinces was necessary in order to make the changes proposed by Bill C-7. Similarly, the federal government referred a set of questions to the Supreme Court of Canada asking whether Parliament had the unilateral authority to make the proposed changes. The Quebec Court of Appeal concluded that, had Bill C-7 been adopted, it would have been unconstitutional without the agreement of the majority of the provinces.[5] The Supreme Court also concluded that Parliament could not unilaterally make the proposed changes without approval by the majority of the provinces.[6] This clearly indicated that the federal government should not unilaterally proceed with Bill C-7.

c. *Reference cases*. The Supreme Court of Canada and provincial Courts of Appeal have the power to hear reference cases. Unlike the first two types of cases, reference cases do not arise out of a specific dispute. Rather, in a reference case, a federal or provincial government asks a court's opinion on the interpretation or constitutionality of a particular legislation or action. (See Box 4.2.)

As seen from the above description of judicial functions, courts have an important supervisory role over the executive and legislative branches of government. Such oversight is of great significance in ensuring the democratic and accountable nature of government and the rule of law.

3. JURISDICTION OF COURTS

As you will see in subsequent sections, there are several levels of courts both federally and provincially. When a dispute arises, how do we know which court to go to? This question is answered by the concept of a court's **jurisdiction**—that is, the scope of authority to deal with certain types of cases. Jurisdiction essentially reflects an idea of "division of labour" among various courts.

The scope of a court's jurisdiction can be outlined in several ways:

- By subject matter (e.g., civil, criminal, family law)
- Geographically (that is, a court can hear only cases that occurred in a particular territory—for example, a case that occurred in Ontario should be heard before Ontario courts); or
- Defined in monetary terms (e.g., disputes for amounts above or below a certain sum)

For example, recalling the scenario from the introduction, if you wish to enforce the repayment of your loan and both you and your friend are located in Ontario, you will have to file a claim with the Ontario Superior Court of Justice, Small Claims division. This court has jurisdiction over civil actions (subject matter jurisdiction) for amounts not exceeding $25 000 (jurisdiction defined in monetary terms).

As a rule, a court's jurisdiction is prescribed by legislation (e.g., the Ontario *Courts of Justice Act*, RSO 1990, c C.43 prescribes jurisdiction of each level of Ontario courts), but some courts also have inherent jurisdiction (see below).

4. PARTICIPANTS IN LITIGATION

Before we proceed to examine the structure and jurisdiction of various courts, it is useful to briefly outline the main participants in a litigation process and their roles.

Cases fall into two major types: civil and criminal. Both of them are resolved following the adversarial model of adjudication (see the description in section 6.3 of this chapter) and parties are usually represented by lawyers (although they may also choose to represent themselves). It is the task of the parties and their lawyers to collect and present evidence as well as to make arguments to support their respective cases. Lawyers are to protect and advance the interests of their clients but they must not mislead the court and cannot knowingly present false evidence. Trial can be conducted by a judge alone or by a judge and jury. In Canada, trials by judge and jury are more common in criminal rather than civil cases.

In civil litigation, the main participants are the *plaintiff* (the person who launches the lawsuit) and the *defendant* along with their lawyers and the judge. In the criminal context, the main participants are the Crown prosecutor, the *accused* and his or her counsel, and the *victim*. Criminal cases are prosecuted on behalf of the state, which is represented by *Crown prosecutors*. The Crown prosecutors have a number of powers that include deciding whether to carry on a prosecution, whether to proceed by summary conviction or indictment (in the case of hybrid offences), and whether to reduce or drop the charge; of course, they are also responsible for presenting evidence and arguments at trial. Importantly, the prosecutor's task is not to obtain a conviction, but to ensure that justice is done; the prosecutor must act fairly and must not succumb to public or political pressures. The *victim's role* is rather limited: victims usually appear as witnesses at trial and may submit victim impact statements at the sentencing stage.

5. STRUCTURE OF CANADIAN COURTS

Courts are organized in a hierarchy. Broadly speaking, all courts can be divided into trial courts and appellate courts. *Trial courts* are where a case is litigated for the first time. These courts establish the facts of the case and decide how a dispute should be resolved.

A decision of a trial court can be appealed to a court higher up in the judicial hierarchy—an *appellate court*. Either party in both civil and criminal cases can file an appeal. The party that launches the appeal is called an **appellant** and the other party is called a *respondent*. In some cases, a party may appeal as of right and in others a leave to appeal may be required. A **leave to appeal** is permission from a court to have a case heard, and it is a case management tool that allows courts to weed out cases that seem to have little merit.

Appellate courts do not hear a given case anew, but rather review the decision of a lower court to determine whether its findings were correct and reasonable. The review is conducted on the basis of a transcript of a lower court hearing as well as arguments submitted by the parties. As a rule, appellate courts would not interfere in the lower court's findings of fact or credibility unless such findings were unreasonable. Most frequently, arguments on appeal focus mainly on the meaning and application of case law or legislation to the case at hand. An appellate court usually may make one of the following decisions: (a) uphold the lower court's decision (that is, let that decision stand); (b) overturn the lower court's decision and order a new trial; or (c) substitute a lower court's decision with its own.

Canadian courts are organized in a federal but unified system (see Figure 4.1). Each province or territory has its own system of courts and, in addition, there is a system of federally created courts. Canada's court system is unified in the sense that provincial

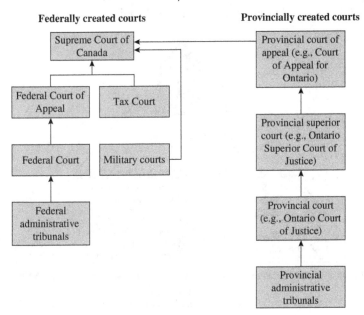

Figure 4.1 System of courts

courts can adjudicate matters involving both provincial and federal laws and the Supreme Court of Canada can also rule on both federal and provincial matters. This is in contrast to, for example, the United States, where state courts adjudicate only matters of state law while matters involving federal laws are heard in federal courts.

The sections below discuss first the system of provincial courts and then the powers and composition of federal courts.

5.1 Provincial Court System: Ontario

Each provincial system usually has three levels of courts, as shown in Figure 4.2. Although there may be some variation in their titles and jurisdictions, there is significant commonality across provinces. In this section, we will use Ontario as an example.

5.1.1 Ontario Court of Justice

The Ontario Court of Justice is the lowest in the provincial hierarchy, and its jurisdiction is established by statute. It is a trial court that hears criminal cases, cases of young offenders, and some family law cases. In the area of family law, the court deals with child protection, adoption, custody, access, child support, and spousal support. However, it cannot hear cases regarding divorce or division of matrimonial property as those are reserved for another level of court—the Superior Court of Justice. In the area of criminal law, the Ontario Court of Justice usually tries less serious offences, namely, all summary conviction offences, some indictable offences (for a definition of summary and indictable offences, see Chapter 8), and offences under provincial legislation (e.g., the *Highway Traffic Act* or the *Occupational Health and Safety Act*). This court also determines issues of bail, conducts preliminary inquiries, and makes decisions on search and arrest warrants.

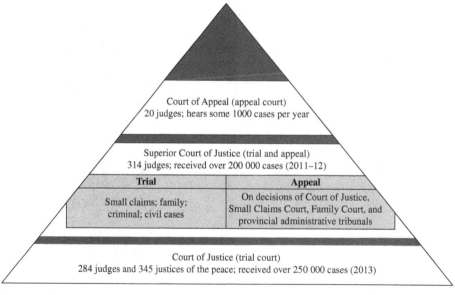

Figure 4.2 Courts in Ontario

The court has 284 provincially appointed judges and 345 justices of the peace and sits in close to 200 locations in Ontario.[7] In 2013, it received over 229 000 criminal cases and over 22 000 family cases.[8]

5.1.2 Superior Court of Justice

The Superior Court of Justice has two types of jurisdiction: statutory jurisdiction, which is prescribed by a provincial law, and inherent jurisdiction, which stems from the common law tradition. *Inherent jurisdiction* means that this court may hear any matter that is not specifically assigned to another level of court. The existence of inherent jurisdiction is an important safeguard of access to justice.

The Superior Court hears criminal, civil, and family cases. This court can hear all civil matters in the province (e.g., commercial disputes, cases of personal injury, bankruptcy, and wills and estates). In the area of criminal law, the court has the power to try any indictable offence under the *Criminal Code*, but usually deals with the most serious offences. Some offences (e.g., murder and treason) can be tried only in the Superior Court. In addition, it can hear criminal cases where an accused has chosen a trial by judge and jury, as well as hear appeals on summary conviction cases decided by the Ontario Court of Justice. In the family law context, the Superior Court has exclusive jurisdiction over divorce and division of property; it can also deal with issues of spousal support, custody, access, and child support that arise in the context of divorce (for more on family law, see Chapter 11).

Unlike in the Ontario Court of Justice, where hearings are always conducted by a single judge, in the Superior Court cases can be decided either by judge alone or by judge and jury.

The Superior Court has three specialized branches:

- *Small Claims Court.* The Small Claims Court is geared toward self-represented parties and speedier, more informal resolution of cases. It hears civil actions for amounts not exceeding $25 000. Thus, for example, if your friend does not repay your $3000 loan, you can file a claim against her in the Small Claims Court.

- *Family Court.* In Ontario, the jurisdiction over family matters is divided between the Superior Court of Justice and the Ontario Court of Justice. Both of these courts can hear cases involving child and spousal support, child custody, and access. There are, however, two areas in which each level of court has exclusive jurisdiction: the Superior Court presides over divorce and division of property cases, and the Ontario Court of Justice over child protection and adoption cases. In 17 of the 50 Superior Court locations, this split jurisdiction has been unified under the Family Court branch of the Superior Court. All family matters can be heard in such unified Family Court branches.

- *Divisional Court.* The Divisional Court is an appellate branch of the Superior Court. It hears appeals from the Small Claims Court, the Family Court, and provincial administrative tribunals. Cases are usually heard by a panel of three judges.

The Superior Court has 314 federally appointed judges and sits in 52 locations across Ontario.[9] Between April 1, 2011, and March 31, 2012, 3921 criminal proceedings, 81 465 civil proceedings, 66 394 small claims cases, and 57 021 family proceedings were commenced in this court.[10]

5.1.3 Court of Appeal for Ontario

This court is the highest in the province. It is an appellate court that hears appeals from decisions of the Ontario Court of Justice and the Superior Court of Justice. Cases are heard by panels of three or five judges. The court has 20 federally appointed full-time judges and is located in Toronto. It hears over 1000 cases per year.[11]

5.1.4 Specialized Courts

In addition to the described three major levels of courts, provinces established a number of specialized courts, including mental health courts, drug treatment courts, domestic violence courts, and courts for Aboriginal offenders. They are also known as *problem solving courts* as they seek to address underlying causes and/or contributing factors leading to crime within particular groups in the population. Many of these courts apply *diversion*—an initiative that keeps offenders out of the criminal justice system and instead redirects them into a specific, more appropriate option (such as a drug treatment program, mental health system, or restorative justice initiative). The main objective of diversion is to give individuals proper supports and/or treatment that would help them avoid repeatedly ending up in the criminal justice system.

Mental health courts are designed to deal with offenders who have mental illness, and seek to provide support and treatment that would minimize their chances of repeatedly appearing before courts for minor offences. The first mental health court was established in Toronto in 1998. It is staffed with specially trained Crown counsel, duty counsel, a psychiatrist, and mental health social workers. When an individual is directed into the diversion program, the court mental health worker links the accused with relevant treatment options, housing, and community support programs. The charges against the accused are stayed (halted) after he or she has been successfully integrated with appropriate community supports.

Drug treatment courts deal with nonviolent, drug-dependent offenders. Like with mental health courts, the emphasis is on providing treatment and supports to the accused instead of incarceration. Such diversion is usually available to those who plead guilty and agree to participate in a closely monitored treatment program. Drug treatment courts exist in major metropolitan areas such as Toronto, Vancouver, Ottawa, and others.

Domestic violence courts deal with matters involving domestic violence and abuse. The specific designs and functions of these courts vary somewhat across provinces. For example, in Nova Scotia, such courts provide offenders with access to educational and therapeutic programs to help them change their behaviour and prevent future violence. Ontario has the only integrated domestic family violence court in Canada that allows family law matters and criminal law charges related to domestic violence to be heard before a single judge on the same day (instead of appearing before different courts and judges). The court also employs a community resource coordinator who can help parties find resources and services to assist them with their problems.

Finally, there are so called **Gladue courts** that were established following the Supreme Court decision in R v Gladue,[12] which recognized that particular circumstances of Aboriginal offenders are to be taken into account in sentencing. Gladue courts are staffed with specially trained judges and take a restorative justice approach to sentencing (see the chapter on restorative justice on the Companion Website). A court case worker is assigned to produce a "Gladue report" on the life circumstances of each Aboriginal offender appearing before the court and to make recommendations for sentencing. Gladue courts have been implemented most extensively in Ontario.[13]

5.2 Federal Courts

The federally created courts include the Federal Courts, the Tax Court, courts martial, and the Court Martial Appeal Court of Canada.

The Federal Courts consist of the Federal Court and the Federal Court of Appeal. Their jurisdiction is prescribed by statute and includes dealing with such matters as intellectual property, immigration, citizenship, appeals on decisions of federal boards, commissions and tribunals, and other issues. Decisions of the Federal Court can be appealed to the Federal Court of Appeal. While the Federal Courts are located in Ottawa, their judges travel on circuit to major Canadian cities in order to hear cases. The Tax Court focuses on issues of federal taxation and federal benefits, while military courts deal with issues of military law.

5.2.1 The Supreme Court of Canada

The Supreme Court of Canada was established in 1875. However, until 1949, it was not the highest court of appeal in Canada. Its decisions could be further appealed to the Judicial Committee of the Privy Council in the UK.

The Supreme Court is composed of nine justices. They are appointed on the basis of geographic representation: three from Ontario, three from Quebec, one from British Columbia, one from the Prairies (Alberta, Manitoba, and Saskatchewan), and one from the Atlantic provinces (New Brunswick, Newfoundland and Labrador, Prince Edward Island, and Nova Scotia). Women have been represented on the court since 1982 (the first woman appointed to the Court was Bertha Wilson). Racial minorities or First Nations have not been represented on the Supreme Court to date.

The Supreme Court hears appeals on decisions of provincial courts of appeal and federal courts. For most cases, there is no automatic right to appeal[14] and appellants must first seek a leave to appeal.

Photo 4.1 The Supreme Court building in Ottawa sits on a bluff high above the Ottawa River, west of the Parliament buildings.

aiok/Shutterstock

The Court considers between 500 and 600 applications for leave to appeal each year,[15] and only about 10–12% of such applications are granted.[16]

The Supreme Court sits in three sessions annually, with each lasting for three months. The Court usually hears approximately 70 appeals per year.[17] In 2013, 27% of all appeals related to criminal law, followed by *Charter* issues and issues of civil procedure.[18] Table 4.1 presents a summary of case statistics for the Supreme Court of Canada for 2003–2013.

Table 4.1 Supreme Court of Canada: Case Statistics, 2003–2013

	2003	2004	2005	2006	2007	2008	2009	2010	2011	2012	2013
Complete applications for leave to appeal						Cases filed					
Notices of appeal as of right	550	568	544	506	602	528	542	488	557	548	491
Applications for leave	12	12	16	7	16	18	14	24	12	15	18
Submitted to the Court	609	559	575	477	629	509	518	465	541	557	529
Granted (pending)	75	83	65	55	69	51	59	55	69	69(2)	46(57)
Percentage granted	12	15	11	12	11	10	11	12	13	12*	9*
Appeals heard											
Total number	82	83	93	80	53	82	72	65	70	78	75
As of right	16	13	13	13	10	16	12	15	19	15	12
By leave	66	70	80	67	43	66	60	50	51	63	63
Hearing days	56	61	62	56	46	60	55	51	60	65	65
Appeal judgments											
Total number	81	78	89	79	58	74	70	69	71	83	78
Delivered from the bench	19	16	17	4	2	5	2	4	8	8	9
Delivered after being reserved	62	62	72	75	56	69	68	65	63	75	69
Unanimous	62	57	65	63	36	56	44	52	53	60	53
Split	19	21	24	16	22	18	26	17	18	23	25
Percentage of unanimous judgments	76	73	73	80	62	76	63	75	75	72	68
Appeals standing for judgment at the end of each year	25	32	35	35	30	38	40	36	35	30	27
Average time lapses (in months)											
Between filing of application for leave and decision on application for leave	3.9	3.7	3.7	3.4	3.5	3.2	3.2	3.4	4.1	4.4	3.3
Between date leave granted (or date notice of appeal as of right filed) and hearing	10.5	9.4	9.1	7.7	9.0	8.9	7.6	7.7	8.7	9.0	8.2
Between hearing and judgment	5.1	4.0	5.2	5.9	6.6	4.8	7.4	7.7	6.2	6.3	6.2

All applications for leave, appeals and judgments are counted by individual file number.

*This percentage may change once all pending leave applications are decided.

Source: Supreme Court of Canada, online: http://www.scc-csc.gc.ca/case-dossier/stat/sum-som-eng.aspx

The Court is located in Ottawa and litigants are expected to travel there to present their cases, although they may also be allowed to participate from remote locations by videoconference. As a general rule, a hearing of an appeal is allocated two hours.[19] Cases can be heard by a panel of nine, seven, and five judges.

Decisions of the Court may be delivered right away or *reserved* (that is, the Court provides a written decision at a later date). Most frequently, Supreme Court decisions are reserved and a judgement is released, on average, six months after the hearing took place.[20]

6. KEY FEATURES OF THE COURT SYSTEM

The court system in Canada is characterized by the following key features:

- Open court;
- Formality and decorum; and
- Adversarial system.

6.1 Open Court

As a rule, court hearings are open to the public, which means that almost anyone can enter courtrooms and watch the proceedings. The principle of open court is important for at least two reasons. First, it serves an educational purpose, allowing the public to see how justice is administered and to gain a better understanding of the court process. Second, it provides a safeguard against unfairness and arbitrariness: if hearings were held behind closed doors, it would be hard to know whether the rights of the parties were observed, and whether courts were acting in accordance with the law. This openness, in turn, helps promote confidence in the court system and is a hallmark of a democratic society.[21]

There are, however, some limitations on the principle of open court. First, witnesses can be excluded from the courtroom in order to ensure that their testimony is not affected by the testimony of others or other information presented at trial. Second, a court may order the exclusion of all or any members of the public from the courtroom where this is "in the interest of public morals, the maintenance of order or the proper administration of justice or is necessary to prevent injury to international relations or national defence or national security."[22] Finally, there are special limitations on the principle of open court in the cases of young offenders.[23]

Related to the principle of open court is the freedom of the press. As a rule, the press can observe and report on court proceedings. However, there may be some circumstances when the freedom of the press has to be limited.[24]

6.2 Formality and Decorum

The procedures before courts are highly formalized. Judges and counsel wear special attire. The court must be addressed in a particular manner (e.g., "Your Honour"). These formalities and decorum are said to uphold the respect for and prestige of the court, and to create a dignified atmosphere.[25] Laypeople may find these formalities strange or difficult to follow. Thus, while formality and decorum are intended to promote respect for the court, they may also be intimidating and confusing for unrepresented litigants.

6.3 Adversarial System

While Canada, the United States, and the United Kingdom use an adversarial system of justice, other countries follow inquisitorial systems. The key difference between the two systems lies in the roles of the judge and the parties in the examination of the case and relevant evidence.

In an **adversarial system**, the collection and presentation of evidence is in the hands of the parties to a case. They collect documents, question and cross-examine witnesses, conduct research, and present supporting case law. Witnesses' oral testimony and their cross-examination by opposing counsel are key parts of the fact-finding process. The adversarial system is often described as a battle between the two parties, with each presenting different versions of the event in question and advancing contrasting arguments. The judge plays the role of an impartial arbiter, controlling the overall process, hearing all evidence, deciding on its admissibility, and making a final decision on a case. In trials by judge and jury, the judge explains the law and provides other instructions to the jury, but does not make a decision on liability: it is the task of the jury to determine the facts of the case and make a decision on conviction or acquittal (in a criminal process) or civil liability (in a civil case).

An **inquisitorial system**, in contrast, involves the participation of a judge in the investigation and collection of evidence as well as questioning of witnesses. The examination of evidence is often conducted on the basis of a written record and oral testimony is not as key to the process as in an adversarial system. While parties may question witnesses, there is no cross-examination.[26] Trials by a jury are not very common. Given that the collection of evidence is driven not by the parties but by the court, it may produce a more complete record of what has happened. This is contrasted with the adversarial system, where the party that has the most persuasive arguments and/or more able legal counsel has a better chance of winning.[27]

Importantly, neither inquisitorial nor adversarial systems exist in a pure form, but rather are ideal types that allow us to distinguish different models of adjudication. In the contemporary world, most systems employ a certain combination of inquisitorial and adversarial techniques, although they often more strongly gravitate toward one end of the spectrum.

7. JUDICIAL APPOINTMENTS

Judges in Canada are appointed by the executive: judges of the lowest provincial courts (such as the Ontario Court of Justice) are appointed by provincial governments, and judges of provincial superior courts, provincial courts of appeal, and federally established courts are appointed by the federal government.

In the past, the judicial appointment process was not very transparent and raised concerns that it was highly influenced by political patronage.[28] In response to these concerns, a number of changes have been made since the 1980s. Currently, candidates are screened by independent committees that assist the executive in identifying qualified candidates. The minimum requirement for candidates for provincial appointments is usually to have been a member of the bar for a period of time ranging from five years (e.g., in Manitoba and Prince Edward Island) to 10 years (e.g., in Saskatchewan and Ontario).[29] For federally appointed justices, the minimum requirement is 10 years.[30] In addition, such factors as professional excellence, skills, community awareness, and personal characteristics are considered (see also the discussion in Chapter 5 on representation of women and minorities in the Canadian judiciary). Studies show that since independent committees were established, the number of judges with party connections has gone down. However, political connections still play a role, and the percentage of appointees with political connections varies by province.[31]

7.1 Appointments to Lowest Provincial Courts

For provincial appointments, screening and selection of candidates is done with the assistance of independent committees[32] that are composed of legal professionals and laypersons. In Ontario, for example, the Judicial Appointments Advisory Committee (JAAC) consists of 13 members: two judges, three lawyers, seven laypersons appointed by the attorney general, and one member appointed by the Judicial Council.[33] Members are appointed for a three-year term and can be reappointed.[34]

The powers of the committees differ somewhat depending on the province, but they usually screen candidates and provide a list of recommendations to provincial ministers of justice.[35] The appointment decision rests with the executive. For example, in Ontario, the screening process consists of the following stages. First, the JAAC reviews all applications and conducts reference checks and confidential inquiries with court officials, lawyers, law associations, and community and social service organizations. Then, the committee determines which candidates should be interviewed. Candidates are evaluated on the following criteria: professional excellence, community awareness, personal characteristics (e.g., ethics, patience, punctuality, integrity, fairness, compassion), and demographics (the judiciary should be reasonably representative of the population it serves).[36] Following the interviews, the committee prepares a ranked short list and submits it to the attorney general of Ontario. The attorney general must select a candidate for the appointment from that list.

7.2 Appointments to Provincial Superior Courts and Federally Created Courts

Candidates wishing to apply for a position as a judge of a superior court of a province/territory or of the Federal Court, the Federal Court of Appeal, or the Tax Court must apply to the Commissioner for Federal Judicial Affairs Canada. The commissioner coordinates the application process. However, actual evaluation of candidates is conducted by independent judicial advisory committees that are established in each province (note that these committees are different from the ones evaluating candidates for provincially appointed judgeship). As a rule, there is one committee in each province or territory but, because of their larger populations, Ontario has three and Quebec has two. Each committee consists of eight members: one representative of the provincial/territorial law society; one from the provincial/territorial branch of the Canadian Bar Association;

one judge; one nominee of the provincial attorney general; one nominee of the law enforcement community; and three laypersons.

The committees evaluate candidates on such criteria as professional competence, experience, personal characteristics, and diversity. The committees also undertake consultations with both the legal and the nonlegal community in respect of each applicant. The committees rank candidates as either "recommended" or "unable to recommend" for appointment and provide these recommendations to the federal minister of justice. The minister then makes recommendations to the federal Cabinet.

7.3 Appointments to the Supreme Court of Canada

The minimum requirement for candidates for the Supreme Court is that they have been either a judge of a superior court or a member of at least 10 years' standing of the bar of a province or territory. Given that the Court must be representative of Canada's regions, a judge who steps down must be replaced by a judge from the same region.

The appointment process is different than for other federal judges. The minister of justice usually identifies potential candidates and then consults with the the chief justice of the Supreme Court of Canada, the chief justices, the attorney general, and senior members of the Canadian Bar Association and the law society(ies) of the region with the vacancy. Then a list of candidates is reviewed by a selection panel that consists of five members of Parliament. The selection panel assesses the candidates and provides an unranked short list of three to the prime minister and to the minister of justice. The prime minister and the minister of justice select a nominee from that list. Since 2006, the selected nominee appears for a public hearing before an ad hoc parliamentary committee prior to confirmation for appointment.

7.4 Judicial Ethics

Once appointed, justices are expected to conduct themselves with the highest degree of integrity and professionalism, and several mechanisms exist to ensure that they do. First, codes of ethics set out key principles of judicial behaviour. Second, special complaints procedures exist to investigate and reprimand judicial misconduct. Third, judges have various opportunities for professional development. Central to these mechanisms are federal and provincial judicial councils, which have been established under federal and provincial legislation to improve quality of judicial service, provide continuing education, review complaints of judicial misconduct, and promote discussion and consensus among council members on various issues involving the administration of justice.

The Canadian Judicial Council (CJC) as well as provincial judicial councils developed sets of ethical principles for judges. For example, the CJC outlined the following principles for federally appointed judges:

- *Independence.* Judges must make decisions independently and not be subject to any external pressure. Among institutional mechanisms to support judicial independence are the security of tenure, financial security, administrative autonomy, and immunity from civil liability for judicial acts.

- *Integrity*. Judges are to ensure that "their conduct is above reproach in the view of reasonable, fair minded and informed persons."[37]

- *Diligence*. Judges must perform their duties diligently, including taking steps to maintain and enhance their professional skills and complete judicial tasks promptly.

- *Equality*. Judges must treat all persons without discrimination. They should strive to become aware of and understand differences arising from such factors as gender, race, culture, ethnic background, sexual orientation, or disability.

- *Impartiality*. Impartiality presupposes the absence of bias and neutrality with respect to the outcome of a dispute. Judges' political affiliations or close dealings with interest groups or potential litigants may give rise to concerns about impartiality. Thus, while judges can participate in civic and religious activities, they should refrain from membership in political parties, should not give legal or investment advice, and should avoid involvement in any activity or association that could reflect on their impartiality.[38]

Similar principles were outlined by provincial judicial councils. For example, the principles of judicial office in Ontario include: striving for impartiality and objectivity; following the law; endeavouring to maintain order and decorum in court; exercising duties with diligence and in the spirit of collegiality; maintaining professional competence in the law; avoiding any conflict of interest; not abusing the power of the judicial office; and other principles.[39]

7.5 Judicial Misconduct

Judges usually hold office until they retire or until they reach a certain age (e.g., 75 for all federally appointed judges). A judge may also be removed from office or temporarily suspended due to misconduct. Cases of judicial misconduct are dealt with by the CJC for federally appointed justices and by provincial judicial councils for provincially appointed justices.

It is important to distinguish allegations of misconduct from appeals on judicial decisions. If a party disagrees with a judge's decision on a case and considers that the judge made a mistake, the proper avenue to pursue is an appeal to a higher court. Even if the higher court finds that the judge erred, this does not constitute judicial misconduct and the overturning of the judge's decision by the higher court is not a form of reprimand. However, if a party to a case or any member of the public feels that a judge violated ethical principles, then a complaint of misconduct can be made. For example, if a judge makes sexist, racist, or disparaging remarks to persons appearing in court, this can be grounds for a complaint about judicial misconduct.

A complaint against a federally appointed judge is dealt with in the following way. The CJC conducts an investigation, informs the judge in question of the complaint, and gives him or her an opportunity to respond. If the complaint is not resolved at that stage, it is handed over to a review panel for further study. The panel may close the file with an expression of concern or recommend counselling for the judge. However, if the case is particularly serious, the review panel may move the case to an inquiry committee. The committee can conduct its own investigation and hold a public hearing at which the judge and the complainant can give evidence. The inquiry committee then prepares a report and submits it for discussion by the full CJC. The council decides whether to recommend that the minister of justice remove the judge from office. If removal is recommended, Parliament has to approve such removal and the governor general must accept Parliament's request for removal. Only in relatively few cases has removal been recommended, and even in those cases Parliament has never had to take a vote since the judges in question chose to retire prior to the vote.

A similar procedure exists for complaints against provincially appointed judges (e.g., through the Ontario Judicial Council[40]). A vote in the legislature is not usually necessary in order to remove a judge (however, Ontario, for example, does require such a vote[41]).

Removal is not the only sanction available. For example, a judge can be reprimanded and instructed not to repeat the conduct or be suspended with or without pay.

8. ADMINISTRATIVE TRIBUNALS

In addition to courts, there exist a variety of provincial and federal administrative tribunals that specialize in hearing particular types of disputes. For example, provincial labour relations boards mediate and adjudicate labour disputes. Provincial human rights tribunals (see Chapter 12) examine complaints of alleged discrimination under provincial human rights legislation. The federal Immigration and Refugee Board hears claims for refugee protection and various immigration matters.

Tribunals are often more informal than courts and are intended for speedier and more accessible dispute resolution, including for self-represented claimants.

Part II. Critical Perspectives

Scholars have addressed a variety of critical issues related to the court system and judicial decision making. Many of them concentrate on institutional issues such as the judicial appointment process, the nature of judicial decision making, judicial activism, and interaction between the judiciary and other branches of government. Some of these issues are discussed in other chapters of this book. For example, Chapter 5 reviews critical theoretical perspectives on judicial decision making, and Chapter 6 discusses judicial activism in the post-*Charter* era. While these issues are important and are a useful measure of a court system and process, they paint only a partial picture. A given court system is to be evaluated not only in respect of its capacity to deal with cases fairly and efficiently but also from the perspective of persons appearing before courts: litigants and witnesses. Thus, in this section, we will discuss two sets of questions that focus on the experience of individuals in the court system:

- *Access to justice.* Are courts accessible to everyone? What barriers do litigants face, especially those from marginalized groups? How are these barriers overcome? What are other avenues (besides courts) for individuals to protect their rights?

- *Adversarial system, vulnerable witnesses, and discovery of the truth.* Does the adversarial system facilitate discovering the truth about an event in question? Does the adversarial process pose particular challenges for vulnerable witnesses (e.g., children, or victims of sexual assault)?

1. ACCESS TO JUSTICE

In theory, everyone has the right to turn to the courts in order to protect their interests. However, is this also the case in practice? Individuals may face many barriers in pursuing a legal action, including lack of information about their rights, prohibitively high costs of litigation, and intimidation or confusion about the law and the legal process. Addressing such barriers is important for a variety of reasons. If individuals have limited or no ability to access courts, they will be unable to affirm their rights, causing some injustices to go unremedied and reinforcing distrust and disillusionment in the judicial system, particularly among groups that are already disadvantaged and disproportionately absent from legislatures, the judiciary, and the legal profession.[42]

It is increasingly apparent that an effective and meaningful justice system needs not only to provide an institutional structure within which individuals can advance their claims, but also to address barriers that may hamper individuals' ability to pursue such claims. The latter issue has been the subject of a growing number of access to justice initiatives.

Access to justice can be defined as "effective right of an individual to advance in appropriate *fora* legitimate legal claims or defences against claims by others."[43] Initially, access to justice was understood as access to courts and lawyers. Access to justice initiatives concentrated on provision of legal aid, pro bono representation, and expanding opportunities for individuals to participate directly in legal processes without resorting to expensive legal representation (e.g., by establishment of small claims courts, which allow self-represented litigation).[44]

The affordability of legal assistance has always been a primary concern around access to justice. **Legal aid** systems were established to allow low-income individuals access to legal advice free of charge. In most provinces, this is achieved through two channels: (a) private lawyers who are paid set fees by a legal aid agency for providing services to eligible individuals; and (b) legal aid clinics with full-time salaried lawyers who provide legal services on matters of primary concern for low-income people.[45] While legal aid is an important mechanism of access to justice, it does not fully address issues of affordability. First, the scope of coverage has been reduced in some provinces, making legal aid available primarily for criminal rather than civil matters. Second, recent studies have found that it is the middle-income families who are least likely to use lawyers,[46] since their income is above the threshold established to qualify for legal aid but is too low to allow them to hire legal counsel at their own expense.

While the cost of legal services is a factor in individual decisions about seeking legal advice, and it is generally documented that lawyer use increases with income,[47] income is not the only factor. In fact, whether someone seeks legal advice is based less on demographic and socioeconomic factors and more on the nature of the problem (e.g., criminal law, family law, wills and estates, and real estate issues are significant for individuals of all income groups).[48] Another influential factor is whether individuals interpret a situation as a legal problem or whether they see it as a social or moral issue or a matter of bad luck.[49] Low- and moderate-income individuals may be more likely to take no legal action because they consider that the overall balance of power in society is unfavourable to them.[50] Awareness of legal rights is another important factor in individual decisions to use legal services.[51]

Thus, access to justice initiatives need to take a comprehensive approach, addressing not only affordability of lawyers but also rights awareness, education, and empowerment. This progression is evident in the five "waves" of access to justice initiatives in Canada:

a. 1960s: access to lawyers and courts;

b. 1970s: institutional redesign to enhance procedural fairness, streamline access to remedies, eliminate problems of bureaucracy, create agencies other than courts to deal with civil disputes more efficiently (e.g., human rights commissions, worker compensation boards);

c. 1980s: "demystifying law," which included the plain language movement and development of alternative dispute resolution (ADR) mechanisms and restorative justice initiatives;

d. 1990s: development of new mechanisms that help avoid conflicts and improve involvement of the public in law making; and

e. Currently: empowering individuals through law, and devising mechanisms to overcome disempowerment and disengagement felt by citizens.[52]

Thus, currently, some of the main elements of the access to justice system are legal aid, public legal education and information, ADR, public interest advocacy, pro bono services, and court reforms aimed at increased accessibility, increased efficiency, and simplified procedures.[53] While the past decades saw notable development and diversification of access to justice initiatives, more recently, significant concerns have arisen due to cuts to government funding, limited availability of legal aid for civil matters, tightened eligibility criteria, and other restrictions.[54]

2. ADVERSARIAL SYSTEM, VULNERABLE WITNESSES, AND DISCOVERY OF THE TRUTH

The adversarial process is an integral part of our legal system, and while it possesses many strengths, we also have to be aware of its limitations. In the past few decades, increasing attention has been paid to two issues: (1) Does the adversarial process facilitate discovery of the truth? and (2) Is it well equipped to deal sensitively with vulnerable witnesses?

2.1 Does the Adversarial Process Facilitate Discovery of the Truth?

Since the 1980s, there has been increasing discussion about the ability of the adversarial process to fulfill a truth-seeking function.[55] Such concerns arose due to several features of the adversarial system. First, the process is party-driven and represents a "battle" between two parties who each seek to win. Each party is interested in presenting evidence and arguments that support its desired outcome, while at the same time probing and attempting to undermine the evidence and arguments of the opposing side. It is the task of a lawyer to mould the client's story into the most credible narrative, which may include making choices about what is said and what is not said and how material is presented. As some noted, "[t]he purpose of shaping and refining these narratives is to win the case for the client, not to find the truth. Perhaps the truth is not forgotten, but it can be easily neglected."[56] The party's success in creating a persuasive narrative can be significantly dependent on the competence of their counsel. In turn, as we saw in the preceding section, the affordability and quality of legal advice are often linked to the party's resources. Where the resources of the two parties are unequal (especially if one party cannot afford a lawyer), the "battle" takes place on an uneven playing field and can raise concerns of fairness.

Second, the rules of evidence impose restrictions on the information that can be considered by decision makers. In order to be admitted at trial, evidence must be relevant and reliable. For example, if a witness is not believed, their testimony will not form part of the information considered by the decision maker and of the "truth" discovered in the process. As we will see below, credibility assessment is highly challenging and, in some cases, individuals who are telling the truth may nevertheless face difficulties being believed. As a result, concerns exist that the truth in an adversarial justice model represents whatever is left over "after we remove . . . all those things that the parties choose not to adduce, all things that are unavailable, all things that are rendered inadmissible . . ., all things that are found unpersuasive, all things that are found to be untrue and all things that, though potentially true, are fundamentally unfair."[57] Of course, this does not mean that the adversarial process can never lead to the discovery of the truth, but we need to be aware of its potential limitations.

2.2 Is the Adversarial Process Well Equipped to Deal Sensitively with Vulnerable Witnesses?

Discuss the following scenario:

> Andrea experienced repeated sexual abuse in her childhood. She now wants to bring the perpetrator to justice. She is the main witness in the case and much is riding on her testimony: if she is not believed, her case will likely be dismissed. The court process was explained to her in general terms but she is still rather confused about it. It has been many years since the abuse took place, but she still gets very stressed out whenever she talks about it. What kinds of challenges is she likely to face while giving testimony in court?

As you have probably already identified, some of the challenges that Andrea is likely to face are being intimidated by the court process,[58] being uncomfortable testifying about a traumatic and deeply personal event such as sexual assault, and having difficulty recounting details given the passage of time and past trauma. There is a concern that she may be retraumatized as a result of having to relive the experience through testimony. Is the adversarial process sensitive to vulnerable witnesses to ensure that they are not retraumatized? Would Andrea's credibility be questioned if, due to trauma, she was unable to provide a coherent and detailed account of the sexual abuse?

Witnesses play an important role at trial, but until recently little attention was paid to their experiences in the courtroom. Traditionally, the focus of (especially criminal) proceedings was on protecting the rights of the accused. The public nature of the trial, the right of the accused to face the accusers, and the cross-examination of witnesses are important safeguards of fairness and accuracy of the process. However, they may also increase stress on victims and impact their ability to communicate effectively and accurately.[59] For example, cross-examination is considered one of the central means to test reliability of witness testimony and to uncover inconsistencies, errors, and lies. While it is a legitimate and integral part of an adversarial process, intrusive questioning may intimidate and retraumatize witnesses, especially vulnerable ones such as children, persons with disabilities, or victims of sexual assault or other abuse. In Andrea's case, she (apart from the abuser) is likely the only witness of the abuse. Thus, undermining her credibility is the best defence strategy in order to collapse the case. In advancing the interests of their clients, it was not uncommon for defence counsel to question witnesses aggressively in order to confuse and upset them and in turn undermine their credibility. Counsel can use complex questions that are beyond the command of a child or a witness with an intellectual disability that in turn could reduce their comprehension and ability to respond accurately.[60] They may demand only short "yes" or "no" answers without allowing a witness to elaborate.[61] Even counsel's tone of voice, gestures, and facial expressions may be manipulated to unnerve the witness. Repeated and misleading questions may distort a witness's memory of events, particularly in children who may be more susceptible to suggestive questioning.[62] All of these techniques are likely not only to retraumatize witnesses but also to reduce the accuracy of their testimony and, in turn, hamper the fact finding process.[63] Over the past few decades, various jurisdictions have started implementing measures to protect vulnerable witnesses. These measures typically include allowing children to testify behind a screen (so that they do not see the offender); using recorded video interviews; testifying via video link (which protects the witness from facing the defendant or being intimidated during testimony); and excluding the public from parts of a hearing.[64]

Another complex issue is how decision makers determine if a witness is telling the truth. Assessing credibility is a challenging task. Credibility is a ". . . complex intermingling of impressions that emerge after watching and listening to witnesses and attempting to reconcile the various versions of events."[65] Credibility assessments often rely on factors such as consistency, coherency, witnesses' ability to provide details and recall time and place, the presence of supporting evidence, and witnesses' demeanour. While these considerations can be useful, scientific studies caution that no factor can reliably and definitively determine whether a person is lying.[66] Studies also reveal that credibility assessments can be influenced by verbal and nonverbal clues given by witnesses. For example, witnesses who speak more confidently, maintain more relaxed posture, and make frequent contact with the audience are usually perceived as more credible and trustworthy.[67] Witnesses' demeanour and emotional expressions may also impact credibility assessment. An "appropriate" amount of emotion expressed by a witness increases the perception of their credibility.[68] Those who do not conform to a stereotype of a "real" victim may face greater difficulty being believed.[69] For example, victims of sexual assault may be expected to show emotions and may be less likely to be believed if they don't.[70]

Not all witnesses are able to live up to the standard of these markers of credibility, even though they are telling the truth. Interviews with sexual assault victims demonstrated that they tended to suppress their emotions because they believed that a courtroom requires neutral and controlled testimony.[71] Past trauma can cause memory loss, confusion, and suppression of memories. Thus, if Andrea in our discussion scenario has difficulty providing details or if there is some inconsistency in her testimony, this should not be automatically considered an indication of a lie.[72] Rather, her testimony must be understood in its context: Andrea may not be able to recall everything accurately and coherently due to the psychological trauma as well as the time that has passed since the assault.

Various studies have evaluated the ability of laypersons and legal/law enforcement professionals to determine credibility accurately, and overall, lie detection accuracy rates are usually rather low.[73] However, there have been some conflicting findings regarding the ability of professionals to detect lies. Some studies have shown that professionals such as police detectives and judges are hardly any better at lie detection than laypersons,[74] while others have suggested that judges usually do significantly better than laypersons in credibility assessments, possibly due to their knowledge and experience as well as a better ability to filter relevant from irrelevant information.[75] Analysis of judicial decisions has also demonstrated that judges are aware of various issues involving vulnerable witnesses.[76]

There is no one magic formula for assessing credibility. However, the growing body of academic research on credibility assessment does help us become more aware of the pitfalls and challenges of the process. Scientific research on lie detection is an important factor in promoting such awareness. For example, judges have shifted away from relying on demeanour in credibility assessments toward a more nuanced analysis that gives greater consideration to other factors such as plausibility.[77] As one judge noted, judges should rely on their knowledge and experience in the world to assess plausibility, but they should also be open to accepting that highly unusual things do occur and should not be dismissed outright.[78] Self-awareness of possible biases is also an important factor in ensuring open mindedness and fairness of decision makers.

SUMMARY

Courts perform four key functions: resolving disputes, interpreting legislation, overseeing administrative decision making, and reviewing constitutionality of legislation and/or government action. Both federal and provincial governments have the power to create certain types of courts and appoint judges. Each province has its own system of courts that usually comprises three levels: provincial court, superior court, and court of appeal. Each court has a particular jurisdiction—that is, a scope of authority that defines what cases a given court can hear. Jurisdiction can be defined geographically, by subject matter, and in monetary terms. In addition, courts are divided into trial and appellate courts. Trial courts hear cases for the first time, while appellate courts have the power to review lower courts' decisions to determine if an error has been made. Both at trial and on appeal, the court process is based on three key principles: open court; formality and decorum; and adversarial procedure.

Provincial governments have the power to appoint justices to the provincial court. The federal government can establish federal courts and appoint justices to provincial superior courts and courts of appeal as well as the federally created courts. The screening and evaluation of candidates for judicial office is conducted by independent committees on the basis of such factors as professional qualifications, personal qualities, and diversity, but the ultimate decision on appointment rests with the executive. Once appointed, judges are expected to act in accordance with the principles of independence, impartiality, equality, diligence, and integrity. Allegations of judicial misconduct can be examined according to special complaints procedures by federal and provincial judicial councils. The findings of misconduct may result in reprimand, suspension, or removal from office.

Critical Thinking Questions

1. A judge of a provincial court is asked by a friend for some legal advice. The judge not only provides the legal advice but also appears in court to represent the friend's interests in pending litigation. Does this represent a case of judicial misconduct? If it does, what ethical principles has the judge violated?

   In order to answer the question, you may find it useful to consult ethical principles outlined by the Canadian Judicial Council or provincial judicial councils. See, for example, <http://www.cjc-ccm.gc.ca/cmslib/general/news_pub_judicialconduct_Principles_en.pdf> (CJC) and <http://www.ontariocourts.ca/ocj/ojc/principles-of-judicial-office/> (Ontario).

2. Is the current process of appointment to the Supreme Court of Canada problematic in any way? If it is, why and how? How would you change the process?

3. Should judges be appointed by the executive or elected by the population? Research various approaches to judicial appointments in different jurisdictions and identify strengths and weaknesses of each approach.

Further Readings and Useful Resources

1. Laverne Jacobs & Sasha Baglay, eds, *The Nature of Inquisitorial Processes in Administrative Regimes: Global Perspectives* (Surrey: Ashgate, 2013).

2. Heather MacIvor, *Canadian Politics and Government in the Charter Era*, 2nd ed (Oxford University Press, 2013).

3. Richard D Schneider, Hy Bloom & Mark Heerema, *Mental Health Courts: Decriminalizing the Mentally Ill* (Toronto: Irwin Law, 2007).

Endnotes

1. *Dave v Canada (Minister of Citizenship and Immigration)*, [2005] FJC No 686; *Tallon v Canada (Minister of Citizenship and Immigration)* [2005] FCJ No 1288; *De Guzman v Canada (Minister of Citizenship and Immigration)*, [2005] 2 FCR 162.

2. *dela Fuente v Canada (Minister of Citizenship and Immigration)*, [2005] FCJ No 1219; *Tauseef v Canada (MCI)*, [2005] FCJ No 1516; *Beauvais v Canada (Minister of Citizenship and Immigration)* [2005] FCJ No 1713.

3. *dela Fuente v Canada (Minister of Citizenship and Immigration)*, [2006] FCJ No 774 (FCA).

4. EA Driedger, *Construction of Statutes*, 2nd ed (1983) at 87 cited in *Barrie Public Utilities v Canadian Cable Television Assn* [2003] SCJ No 27 at para 20.

5. *Projet de loi fédéral relatif au Sénat (Re)*, [2013] JQ no 7771.

6. *Reference re Senate Reform*, 2014 SCC 32.

7. Ministry of the Attorney General, "Courts Annual Report 2012–13" at 31, online: <http://www.attorneygeneral.jus.gov.on.ca/english/about/pubs/courts_annual_12/>.

8. Ontario Courts, "Introduction to Ontario's Courts," online: <http://www.ontariocourts.ca/ocj/general-public/introduction-to-ontario-courts/>; Ontario Courts, "Offence Based Statistics: All Criminal Cases," online: <http://www.ontariocourts.ca/ocj/files/stats/crim/2013/2013-Q4-Offence-Based-Criminal.pdf>; Ontario Courts, "Family Cases," online: <http://www.ontariocourts.ca/ocj/files/stats/fam/2013/2013-Q4-OCJ-Family-RDP.pdf>.

9. "Courts Annual Report 2012–13", *supra* note 7 at 31.

10. Ontario Courts, "The Superior Court of Justice: Mapping the Way Forward" (2010–2012) at 22–23, 27, online: <http://www.ontariocourts.ca/scj/en/reports/>.

11. Ontario Courts, "About the Court," online: <http://www.ontariocourts.ca/coa/en/>.

12. *R v Gladue* [1999] 1 SCR 688.

13. Don Clairmont, "The Development of an Aboriginal Criminal Justice System: the Case of Elsipogtog" (2013) 64 UNBLJ 160 at para 7 (Quicklaw).

14. There is an automatic right to appeal in criminal cases where there was a dissent on a point of law in a provincial court of appeal.

15. Supreme Court of Canada, "Role of the Court," online: <http://www.scc-csc.gc.ca/court-cour/role-eng.aspx>.

16. Supreme Court of Canada, "Summary 2003 to 2013," online: <http://www.scc-csc.gc.ca/case-dossier/stat/sum-som-eng.aspx>.

17. *Ibid.*

18. Supreme Court of Canada, "Appeals Heard 2013: Type," online: <http://www.scc-csc.gc.ca/case-dossier/stat/cat3-eng.aspx>.

19. Supreme Court of Canada, "Role of the Court," online: <http://www.scc-csc.gc.ca/court-cour/role-eng.aspx>.

20. Supreme Court of Canada, "Summary 2003 to 2013," online: <http://www.scc-csc.gc.ca/case-dossier/stat/sum-som-eng.aspx>.

21. *Re Vancouver Sun*, [2004] 2 SCR 332 at paras 23 & 25.

22. *Criminal Code*, RSC 1985, c C-46, s 286(1).

23. The *Youth Criminal Justice Act* provides for a possibility of in camera hearings in cases involving young offenders. A judge may exclude any person from all or part of the proceedings if she considers that any information presented to the court would be seriously injurious or seriously prejudicial to the young offender, a witness, or a victim in the proceedings, or if "it would be in the interest of public morals, the maintenance of order or the proper administration of justice." *Youth Criminal Justice Act*, SC 2002, c 1, s 132. In addition, the *Youth Criminal Justice Act* provides for a ban (with some exceptions) on publishing the name or other information that would identify a young offender, his/her victim, or witness in the proceedings (ss 110, 111 of the *Act*).

24. The test is as follows: (1) Is such an order necessary in order to prevent a serious risk to the proper administration of justice because reasonable alternative measures will not prevent the risk; and (2) Do the salutary effects of the order outweigh the deleterious effects on the rights and interests of the parties and the public, including the effects on the right to free expression, the right of the accused to a fair and public trial, and the efficacy of the administration of justice? *R v Mentuck* [2001] 3 SCR 442 at para 32.

25. Gerald Gall, *The Canadian Legal System*, 5th ed (Carswell, 2004) at 135.

26. *Ibid* at 8–10.

27. See Laverne Jacobs & Sasha Baglay, "Introduction" in Laverne Jacobs and Sasha Baglay, eds, *The Nature of Inquisitorial Processes in Administrative Regimes: Global Perspectives* (Surrey: Ashgate, 2013) 1 at 7–8.

28. For example, Russell and Ziegel found that 47.4% of judicial appointees between 1984 and 1988 had some connection to the party that appointed them. Peter H Russell & Jacob S Ziegel, "Federal Judicial Appointments: An Appraisal of the First Mulroney Government's Appointments and the New Judicial Advisory Committees" (1991) 41:1 U f T LJ 4.

29. *Provincial Court Act*, CCSM, c C275, s 3(2); *Provincial Court Act*, RSPEI 1988, c P-25, s 2(2); *Provincial Court Act*, SS 1998, c P-30.11; *Courts of Justice Act*, RSO 1990, c C.43, s 43(10).

30. *Judges Act*, RSC 1985, c J-1, s 3.

31. For example, in Nova Scotia the percentage went down from 41.7% to 22.9%; in Newfoundland and Labrador, it went down from 33.3% to 18.5%. However, in New Brunswick, Saskatchewan, and Manitoba, the percentage of appointees with major political connections remained relatively high. Lori Hausegger et al., "Exploring the Links between Party and Appointment: Canadian Federal Judicial Appointments from 1989 to 2003" (2010) 43 Canadian Journal of Political Science 633.
    Although the number of appointees with ties to the appointing party went down, some connection still continues to exist. For example, 30% of appointees between 1988 and 2003 had donated money to the appointing party. Troy Riddell, Lori Hausegger & Matthew Hennigar, "Federal Judicial Appointments: A Look at Patronage in Federal Appointments since 1988" (2008) 58 U f T LJ 3. Close to 13% of appointees during 2006–2008 had donated to the appointing party. Troy Riddell, Lori Hausegger & Matthew Hennigar, "Federal Judicial Selection: Examining Harper Appointments and Reform" (2009) 2 Journal of Parliamentary and Political Law 495 at 505.

32. In some provinces, it is the provincial judicial council that conducts screening of applicants (e.g., Saskatchewan, Alberta, Newfoundland and Labrador).

33. *Courts of Justice Act*, RSO 1990, c C.43, s 43(2).

34. *Ibid*, s 43(4).

35. See generally, Peter McCormick, "Selecting Trial Court Judges: A Comparison of Contemporary Practices" (2010), online: <www.cepnj.gouv.qc.ca/etudes-des-experts.html?eID=tx_rtgfiles>.

36. Ontario Courts, "JAAS Annual Report: 2011" at 11–12, online: <http://www.ontariocourts.ca/ocj/jaac/annual-report/>.

37. Canadian Judicial Council, "Ethical Principles for Judges" at 13, online: <http://www.cjc-ccm.gc.ca/cmslib/general/news_pub_judicialconduct_Principles_en.pdf>.

38. *Ibid*.

39. Ontario Courts, "Principles of Judicial Office," online: <http://www.ontariocourts.ca/ocj/ojc/principles-of-judicial-office/>.

40. Ontario Courts, "Ontario Judicial Council," online: <http://www.ontariocourts.ca/ocj/ojc/>.

41. *Courts of Justice Act*, RSO 1990, c C.43, s 43(10).

42. Constance Blackhouse, "What Is Access to Justice?" in Julia Bass et al., eds, *Access to Justice for a New Century: The Way Forward* (Toronto: Law Society of Upper Canada, 2005) 113 at 122–123.

43. Michael Trebilcock, Anthony Duggan & Lorne Sossin, "Introduction" in Michael Trebilcock, Anthony Duggan & Lorne Sossin, eds, *Middle Income Access to Justice* (Toronto: University of Toronto Press, 2012) 3.

44. Patricia Hughes, "Law Commission and Access to Justice: What Justice Should We Be Talking about?" (2008) 46 Osgoode Hall LJ 773 at para 7; Seana C McGuire & Roderick A Macdonald,

"Small Claims Court Cant" (1996) 34 Osgoode Hall LJ 509; Deborah Rhode, *Access to Justice* (Oxford University Press, 2004) at 20.

45. RJ Gathercole, "Legal Services and the Poor" in Robert G Evans & Michael J Trebilcock, eds, *Lawyers and the Consumer Interest: Regulating the Market for Legal Services* (Toronto: Butterworths, 1982) at 417.

46. Pascoe Pleasence & Nigel J Balmer, "Caught in the Middle: Justiciable Problems and the Use of Lawyers" in Trebilcock, Duggan & Sossin, *supra* note 43, 27 at 54.

47. *Ibid.*

48. Jamie Baxter, Michael Trebilcock & Albert Yoon, "The Ontario Civil Legal Needs Project: A Comparative Analysis of the 2009 Survey Data" in Trebilcock, Duggan & Sossin, *supra* note 43, 55 at 85.

49. Rebecca L Sandefur, "Money Isn't Everything: Understanding Moderate Income Households' Use of Lawyers' Services" in Trebilcock, Duggan & Sossin, *supra* note 43, 222 at 222, 236.

50. Pleasence & Balmer, *supra* note 46 at 49.

51. *Ibid.*

52. Roderick Macdonald, "Access to Justice in Canada Today: Scope, Scale and Ambitions" in Julia Bass et al., eds, *Access to Justice for a New Century: The Way Forward* (Toronto: Law Society of Upper Canada, 2005) 19 at 20–23.

53. Ab Currie, "Some Aspects of Access to Justice in Canada" in *Expanding Horizons: Rethinking Access to Justice in Canada: Proceedings of a National Symposium* (Department of Justice Canada, 2000) at 41–44, online: <http://www.justice.gc.ca/eng/rp-pr/csj-sjc/jsp-sjp/op00_2-po00_2/op00_2.pdf>. See also Lucinda Vandervort, "Access to Justice and Public Interest in the Administration of Justice" (2012) 63 UNB LJ 125 for other suggestions on the change to the judicial process and Faisal Bhabha, "Institutionalizing Access-to-Justice: Judicial, Legislative and Grassroots Dimensions" (2007) Queen's LJ 139 for suggestions for a more multifaceted and coordinated approach to access to justice.

54. See, for example, Melina Buckley, "Moving forward on Legal Aid: Research on Needs and Innovative Approaches" (2010), online: <http://www.cba.org/cba/Advocacy/PDF/CBA%20Legal%20Aid%20Renewal%20Paper.pdf>; Richard Devlin, "Breach of Contract?: The New Economy, Access to Justice and the Ethical Responsibilities of the Legal Profession" (2002) 25 Dalhousie LJ 335. In 2005, the Canadian Bar Association launched a court challenge, arguing that the inadequacies in the provision of legal aid amounted to breaches of the *Charter*, the *Constitution*, and international human rights instruments. However, the challenge was unsuccessful. *Canadian Bar Assn v British Columbia* [2008] BCJ No 350.

55. See, for example, Carrie Menkel-Meadow, "The Trouble with the Adversary System in a Postmodern, Multicultural World" (1996) 38 Wm & Mary L Rev 5; David Luban, *Lawyers and Justice: An Ethical Study* (Princeton: Princeton University Press, 1988).

56. Ray Finkelstein, "The Adversarial System and the Search for Truth" (2011) 37:1 Monash University Law Review 135.

57. Jula Hughes, "Home Truths about Truth Commission Processes: How Victim-Centered Truth and Perpetrator-Focused Adversarial Processes Mutually Challenge Assumptions of Justice and Truth" in Laverne Jacobs & Sasha Baglay, eds, *The Nature of Inquisitorial Processes in Administrative Regimes: Global Perspectives* (Ashgate, 2013) 271 at 281

58. For example, interviews with witnesses in sexual violence cases show that the ability to speak in court empowered them, but many also felt intimidated by the court process. Cheryl Regehr et al., "Victims of Sexual Violence in the Canadian Criminal Courts" (2008) 3 Victims and Offenders 99.

59. Louise Ellison, *The Adversarial Process and the Vulnerable Witness* (Oxford: Oxford University Press, 2001) at 20–21.

60. *Ibid* at 94–98; Janine Benedet & Isabel Grant, "Hearing Sexual Assault Complaints of Women with Mental Disabilities: Evidentiary and Procedural Issues" (2007) 52 McGill LJ 515.

61. *Ibid* at 98–100.

62. For example, Nicholas Bala et al, "Judicial Assessment of the Credibility of Child Witnesses" (2005) 42 Alberta L Rev 995 at para 13–14 (Quicklaw).

63. Ellison, *supra* note 59 at 31.

64. *Ibid* at 40–46; Jenny McEawn, "The Testimony of Vulnerable Victims and Witnesses in Criminal Proceedings in the European Union" (2009) 10 ERA Forum 369.

65. *R v Gagnon* [2006] 1 SCR 621 at para 20.

66. For example, Nicholas Bala et al., "Judicial Assessment of the Credibility of Child Witnesses" (2005) 42 Alberta L Rev 995 at para 22 (Quicklaw).

67. MT Boccaccini, "What Do We Really Know about Witness Preparation?" (2002) 20 Behavioural Sciences and the Law 161.

68. JM Golding et al, "Big Girls Don't Cry: The Effect of Child Witness Demeanor on Juror Decisions in a Child Sexual Abuse Trial" (2003) 27 Child Abuse & Neglect 1311; RL Wiener et al, "Emotion and the Law: A Framework for Inquiry" (2006) 30 Law Hum Behav 231.

69. Melanie Randall, "Sexual Assault Law, Credibility, and "Ideal Victims": Consent, Resistance, and Victim Blaming" (2010) 22 Canadian Journal of Women and the Law 397; Geir Kaugmann et al, "The Importance of Being Earnest: Displayed Emotions and Witness Credibility" (2003) 17 Appl Cognit Psychol 21.

70. Tasha A Menaker & Robert J Cramer, "The Victim as Witness: Strategies for Increasing Credibility among Rape Victim-Witness in Court" (2012) 12 Journal of Forensic Psychology Practice 424.

71. A Konradi, "'I Don't Have to Be Afraid of You': Rape Survivors' Emotion Management in Court" (1999) 22 Symbolic Interaction 45.

72. See also Deborah A Connolly & Heather L Price, "Judicial Decision-Making in Timely and Delayed Prosecutions of Child Sexual Abuse in Canada: A Study of Honesty and Cognitive Ability in Assessment of Credibility" (2010) 16 Psych Pub Pol & L 177 for discussion of credibility assessment in historic sexual abuse cases and differences in the assessment of credibility of child and adult victims/witnesses.

73. Amina Memon, Aldert Vrij & Ray Bull, *Psychology and Law: Truthfulness, Accuracy and Credibility*, (London: McGraw-Hill, 1998) at 32–53; GTG Seniuk & JC Yuille, *Fact Finding and the Judiciary* (Saskatoon: Commonwealth of Learning, 1996).

74. Charles F Bond & Bella M DePaulo, "Individual Differences in Judging Deception: Accuracy and Bias" (2008) 134 Psychological Bulletin 477; Charles F Bond & Bella M DePaulo, "Accuracy of Deception Judgments" (2006) 10 Personality and Social Psychology Review 214; Memon, Vrij & Bull, *supra* note 73 at 49.

75. For example, Nicholas Bala et al., "Judicial Assessment of the Credibility of Child Witnesses" (2005) 42 Alberta L Rev 995; Ellen Wessle et al, "Credibility of the Emotional Witness: A Study of Ratings by Court Judges" (2006) 30 Law Hum Behav 221.

76. Deborah Connolly et al., "Judging the Credibility of Historic Child Sexual Abuse Complaints: How Judges Describe Their Decisions" (2009) 15:2 Psych Pub Pol & L 102.

77. Honourable Justice Lynn Smith, "The Ring of Truth, the Clang of Lies: Assessing Credibility in the Courtroom" (2012) 63 UNB LJ 10 at para 57, 71–78 (Quicklaw).

78. *Ibid.*

Chapter 5
Theoretical Perspectives

Learning Objectives

After reading this chapter, you should be able to:

- Name and describe key points of seven major theoretical perspectives on law.

- Understand the relevance of theoretical perspectives to everyday life.

- Apply discussed theoretical perspectives to analysis of concrete cases.

Chapter Outline

Introduction

In students' minds, theory is often associated with something very complex, boring, abstract, and disconnected from practical reality. While theories can be highly abstract, they have important practical relevance as they can help us see general patterns in law and society, identify problems, and offer ideas for change. Knowing these theories will give you a choice of perspectives to use in both academic work and assessment of everyday events. In fact, theory and scholarly work can be useful in crafting policy and legislation as well as in supporting litigation and advocacy efforts.

As we already saw in Chapter 1, theorists and practitioners have long laboured to answer such questions as, "What should law's values be?" and "What does a just society look like?" These questions are not purely theoretical, but constantly emerge in our daily lives. They are embedded in legislative and public debates, and they are raised when we engage with government and private actors in the course of employment, leisure, or other activities. For example, if a landlord refused to rent you an apartment because of your race or disability, you would feel this to be grossly unjust. How does the law respond to situations like these? Does it offer an avenue of recourse for you, or does it side with the landlord? Or, if a provincial government prescribes a minimum wage of $11 per hour, is this fair? Is it enough to support a decent standard of living? Or does it drive costs of production too high up and impede business development?

There is a variety of theoretical perspectives on law. We cannot review all of them and will concentrate only on a select few:

- Natural law;
- Positivism;
- Legal realism;
- Critical legal studies;
- Critical race theory;
- Feminist studies; and
- Legal pluralism.

This chapter has two objectives: (1) to make you familiar with key points of the above theoretical perspectives; and (2) to help you see the link between theory and practice. The chapter highlights only key points of each theory and does not represent comprehensive discussion of any particular theory or theorist.

1. NATURAL LAW

Natural law and positivism reflect two different ways of evaluating whether a given law is valid. Natural law does so by focusing on consistency of laws with higher moral values, while positivism concentrates on whether a law was enacted by a proper authority and whether a prescribed procedure was followed.

Law often gives us direction on the way we ought to behave. Thus, there is inevitably a strong link between law and moral principles. Natural law theorists consider that there are some natural, higher order values (e.g., justice, right to life) that exist independently of the human made system. These values should be the starting point for all human laws, and the validity of those laws is determined by their consistency with higher order values. For example, various basic rights protected in domestic constitutions can be considered expressions of natural law values. Similarly, international human rights and prosecution of international crimes (such as crimes against humanity and war crimes) can be said to reflect the ideas of natural law.[1]

Natural law theory has a long history and can be traced back to Greek philosophers such as Plato (427–347 BCE) and Aristotle (384–323 BCE). Plato is generally considered the founder of political philosophy: in his work, *The Republic*, he discussed how a just human society should be structured. He considered that a just society is a natural condition of any civilized community, and that what is just can be determined by the use of reason and logic. Plato spoke of justice as both an individual and a societal virtue. According to him, a just individual is one who keeps in balance and harmony the three basic elements of the body: appetite (satisfaction of basic needs as well as security and pleasure), spirit, and reason. By analogy to a human body, a society should be organized in three classes: craftsmen who provide necessities of life; guardians who protect the society (they represent spirit); and rulers–philosophers who are trained to reign wisely (they represent reason). When these three classes work harmoniously together, social consciousness and justice can be achieved. Thus, Plato's idea of justice is based on specialization (division of tasks among different classes), hierarchy, and viewing an individual as a part of a collective.

The ideas of harmony and justice also have resonance in the works of Plato's student Aristotle. He considered that every individual has a unique, naturally assigned purpose in life, and that people who follow their natural predispositions flourish. A just society is one that creates the necessary conditions for human flourishing. Aristotle discussed the notions of distributive and corrective justice. As we discussed in Chapter 1, distributive justice promotes proportional equality in which all receive a share of resources according to their merits under a given criterion, while corrective justice refers to a moral obligation of a wrongdoer to rectify the harm caused to a victim. When a wrong is done, original equality between the wrongdoer and the victim is lost and needs to be restored. The principles of both distributive and corrective justice can be found in many aspects of contemporary laws (recall Chapter 1).

The ideas of Greek philosophers have been further developed by Christian scholars such as St. Thomas Aquinas (1225–1274 CE), building a link between the natural law theory and religious values. Aquinas argued that God gives all human beings moral values and the capacity to reason, which helps them grasp these eternal moral values. He also posited that laws should be made for the common good, and that laws not in the common good and created by an abusive ruler lack the moral authority to be obeyed.

Box 5.1 considers how natural law might apply to assisted suicide.

Prominent contemporary natural law theorists such as Lon Fuller (1902–1978) present the relationship between law and morality as a way of doing things rather than as pure abstract principles. Fuller focused on the law making process, offering eight principles on which it should be based:

1. Laws must be general rules that apply to everyone.
2. Laws need to be passed following a transparent process that allows individuals to learn about this new law.
3. Laws should not be retroactive.

Box 5.1

Assisted Suicide: Can Natural Law Provide Us with a Guiding Value?

The idea of natural law presupposes that we can objectively know what is right and what is wrong, and can easily identify key moral principles. However, is this really the case? For example, natural law would not give us a clear answer to such longstanding and divisive issues as assisted suicide and abortion. As you probably know, helping someone to die (even if the person is terminally ill and asked for such assistance) is an offence under the Canadian *Criminal Code*. In the 1990s, Sue Rodriguez launched a challenge to this *Criminal Code* provision, arguing that it violated her *Charter* rights. She had amyotrophic lateral sclerosis—an incurable illness that would gradually eliminate her ability to move, speak, swallow, and breathe without assistance. Rodriguez did not wish to die as long as she had the capacity to enjoy life, but once she lost that capacity, she wanted to be able to terminate her life, at the time of her choosing, with the assistance of a physician. A number of organizations inter-

vened in the case, providing submissions both in favour of and against the provision in question. Although the arguments of Rodriguez and the interveners were framed in reference to the *Charter*, in their essence, they invoked natural law values. The Supreme Court upheld the provision, concluding that the protection of the sanctity of human life was of paramount importance.

While the decision has settled the law for now, another similar challenge is making its way to the Supreme Court. In 2011, Kay Carter and Gloria Taylor, two women with incurable progressive degenerative diseases, argued that the prohibition on assisted suicide was unconstitutional.[2] The case has not yet been decided by the Supreme Court. So what should the law be, and what is the "natural" higher value in this case: the right of the person to choose when and how to die, or the protection of human life (even where a person does not wish to live)?

4. Laws should be clear and understood by the population.

5. Laws should not be contradictory.

6. Laws should not make impossible demands that individuals cannot comply with.

7. Laws should be reasonably constant.

8. There should be an alignment between the pronounced laws and government action.[3]

The observation of the above principles helps achieve "internal morality" of the law, which is a necessary precondition for its validity. Thus, unlike earlier natural law theorists, he sought natural values not in external higher norms, but in law's own internally coherent and morally defensible practices. Although these principles have been identified in theoretical writing, they in fact constitute essential practical criteria for determining the validity of laws, and some of them can even be used as grounds to challenge laws in court. For example, in *Canada (Attorney General) v Whaling*,[4] the Supreme Court considered whether retrospective elimination of accelerated parole review (APR) (which could result in early release of an inmate) was constitutional. Whaling was convicted at the time when

APR was available and he would have been eligible for early day parole under it. However, Parliament passed a law that eliminated the review and, with it, the possibility of earlier release; the law applied retroactively, including to Whaling's case. The Supreme Court concluded that the law violated his rights under s. 11(h) of the *Charter* (not to be punished again for committed offences) and was invalid.

2. POSITIVISM

Positivism, which has a more recent history, developed partially as a challenge to the natural law position. Positivism insists on the study of law as a distinct discipline, according to its internal logic rather than external standards like morality. As John Austin (one of the prominent positivist scholars) noted, "[t]he existence of law is one thing; its merit or demerit is another."[5] Morality should not be used as the standard to evaluate law's validity. While this idea may not seem so revolutionary now, at the time of its conception some 250 years ago, calls for separation of law into a distinct area of study constituted a significantly new development. Positivism is associated with the work of such scholars as Jeremy Bentham (1748–1832), John Austin (1790–1859), Hans Kelsen (1881–1973), and H.L.A. Hart (1907–1992).

Positivism seeks to understand the nature of law by focusing on its internal organization and reasoning. The validity of a law depends on considerations internal to the legal field itself: whether a law was passed by a legitimate authority following a prescribed procedure. The focus is not on what a law ought to be, but on what it is. Thus, for example, on the issue of assisted suicide, positivists would ask what the current law is and whether it was enacted by a valid authority and according to a prescribed procedure. If it was, then it constitutes a valid law.

Why are proper authority and procedure so important that they can be determinants of a valid law? Because both of them have important implications for the content and clarity of the law. For example, if an authority is abusive and unrestricted, it may choose to enact tyrannical laws (we can find many historic as well as contemporary examples of this). Further, if a law does not provide enough clarity, it cannot serve as a fair and effective guide for human behaviour. Bentham, for example, criticized precedent (which was the main source of law in Britain until the eighteenth century) as unclear, made in a nontransparent manner, and not allowing individuals to know rules in advance. As you recall from Chapter 2, common law is reactionary and in novel cases establishes rules (including imposing liability or sanctions) after certain conduct has occurred. Bentham wrote: "They [judges] won't tell a man beforehand what it is he *should not do*—they won't so much as allow of his being told: they lie by till he has done something which they say he should not *have done*, and then they hang him for it."[6] He advocated for the development of codified rules by legislatures that left little room for uncertainty and discretion of decision makers, as well as allowed individuals to know in advance prohibited conduct and its consequences.

Later theorists such as Austin identified four characteristics of positive law: (1) it is produced by a sovereign; (2) it takes the form of a command; (3) it is accompanied by a sanction; and (4) it facilitates a habit of obedience from subjects. These characteristics are closely related to contemporary ideas of the rule of law where all authority must have a

Box 5.2

Natural Law versus Positivism: Hart–Fuller Debate

To illustrate the difference between positivist and natural law approaches, we can use the famous debate between two scholars: H.L.A. Hart (positivist) and Lon Fuller (natural law theorist). Both analyzed the same case that had arisen in Germany during World War II but provided different assessments of it.

In the case, a wife who wanted to get rid of her husband reported to the authorities that he had made critical remarks against Hitler. At the time, it was an offence to speak against the Third Reich. The man was tried and sentenced to death. However, eventually he was sent to fight in the war instead. After the war, the woman was prosecuted under the 1871 German *Criminal Code* for illegally depriving her husband of freedom.

She argued that what she had done was not illegal as, at the time in question, her husband's conduct was a crime according to the Nazi law. The court nevertheless found her guilty.

This decision can be seen as reflecting a natural law position: the Nazi law, while validly enacted, contradicted the most basic principles of justice and hence could not be considered valid. Thus, a natural law theorist such as Fuller endorsed the German court's decision as correct. In contrast, Hart, from a positivist perspective, argued that the decision was erroneous: the Nazi law was properly enacted and thus was valid, despite the fact that it ran contrary to moral principles. In his opinion, the law's morality or immorality is beside the point in deciding on the woman's criminal responsibility.

source in law and must act according to it. Furthering these ideas, Kelsen defined law as a system of norms arranged in a hierarchy with a basic norm as the foundation of the whole legal system. We can consider domestic constitutions as expressions of such basic norms. That is why Kelsen considered that any rule made in accordance with the constitution cannot be considered nonvalid, regardless of whether it is just or unjust. This view, however, also recognizes that the basic norm is relative to a given society and may alter as a result of a regime change (e.g., this happened in the former Soviet republics when they transitioned from totalitarian to democratic regimes and adopted new constitutions).

Boxes 5.2 and 5.3 consider these ideas more fully.

Box 5.3

Connecting Theory and Practice: Representative Democracy, Individual Liberty, and the Rule of Law

As you recall from Chapter 3, Canada is built on such principles as representative democracy, respect for individual liberty, and the rule of law. The origins of these and other principles of government can be traced back to the writings of various philosophers. The examples below illustrate this point.

Representative democracy. Early theorists such as Hobbes and Locke (recall Chapter 1) conceived of governing authority as a creature of a so called "social contract." A social contract is an agreement of individuals in society to limit some of their rights and delegate some of their powers to a central authority, which would promote peace and stability in a society for the benefit of all. Hobbes considered that an absolute sovereign would be necessary in order to help control inherently selfish and violent human nature. Locke, in contrast, viewed people as largely peaceful and cooperative and supported the notion of a limited sovereign. The important idea stemming from social contract is that government exists by the consent of the people. Particularly in Locke's view, where a government fails to work in the public good, it can be challenged and replaced. These ideas are mirrored in contemporary principles of representative democracy.

Separation of powers and the rule of law. The writings of Baron de Montesquieu (1689–1755) and Albert Dicey (1835–1922) had profound impact on organization of governments. Montesquieu is the author of the idea of separation of powers among three branches: executive, judicial, and legislative. This idea was famously adopted in the United States following its declaration of independence, and by now has become a common way of arranging division of government authority across the world. Dicey's *Law of the Constitution* became one of the most influential writings on public law in the common law world. For example, he developed the foundation for the contemporary idea of the rule of law. His concept rested on three principles: (1) everyone is subject to the law and equal before law; (2) arbitrary and discretionary authority is inconsistent with the rule of law; and (3) individual rights are to be protected through common law rules rather than bills of rights, which can be vague and unenforceable. Both the separation of powers (with appropriate checks and balances) and the rule of law serve as important safeguards for protection of individual liberty.

3. LEGAL REALISM

Unlike positivism, which focused on law as a discrete discipline, **legal realism** and other critical approaches, which developed in the twentieth century, emphasize the importance of analyzing law in the broader social, economic, and political context. Legal realism emerged in the 1920s and focused particularly on judicial decision making. Some of the prominent representatives of this school of thought have been lawyers and judges. For example, Oliver Wendell Holmes (1841–1935) was a law professor and a judge of the Supreme Court of the United States. Other prominent representatives of this movement include Karl Llewellyn (1893–1962) and Jerome Frank (1889–1957).

Legal realists contend that there is a difference between what judges claim to be the reasons for their decision and what those reasons really are. In effect, they suggest that legal principles and reasons given by judges are just a façade that masks nonlegal factors that actually motivated such decisions. Realists claim that, while legal rules and principles play a role, judges react primarily to the facts of the case and other nonlegal considerations. Legal rules are resorted to as a post facto justification for an outcome that a judge considers fair under the circumstances. Some suggested that a judge's personality is the main factor explaining how a judge decides a case. Others say that socioeconomic, political, and other considerations are at play. Consequently, there are no predetermined outcomes in law: good lawyers can successfully argue either side of the case and the outcome largely depends on the predispositions of the judge who decides it. Legal rules and principles can be interpreted in a variety of ways, and judges can select an interpretation that better aligns with their views. In order to be able to predict how judges would decide a given case, we need to understand the impact of extralegal factors and recognize that law is developed and applied in a context of social, cultural, and institutional practices.

In fact, judges themselves recognize the impossibility of completely separating themselves from their opinions, values, experiences, and assumptions.[7] A study of the Canadian Supreme Court during the period of 1949–2000 found certain correlations between judicial outcomes and personal attributes of judges. For example, it showed that judges' political preferences had an impact on their decision making.[8] Regionalism also seemed to play a certain role: Quebec judges tended to be more conservative in cases involving individual rights, while judges from Ontario were more liberal. See Box 5.4 for an example.

Box 5.4

Sauvé v Canada (Chief Electoral Officer), [2002] 3 SCR 519

This case is discussed in detail in Chapter 6, Box 6.8. In brief, the Supreme Court had to decide whether it was a violation of the *Charter* to deny the right to vote to inmates who were serving a sentence of two years or more. The judges were split four to five on the outcome. They had heard exactly the same arguments and considered exactly the same provisions, but arrived at very different conclusions (see Table 5.1). The government argued that the prohibition was a justifiable limit on the *Charter* right to vote as it sought to enhance civic responsibility and respect for the rule of law as well as impose additional punishment.

Table 5.1 Majority versus Minority Reasoning in *Sauvé v Canada (Chief Electoral Officer),* [2002] 3 SCR 519

Majority	Minority
■ Denial of the right to vote is likely to undermine respect for the law and democracy.	■ Disenfranchisement serves to deliver a message that serious criminal activity will not be tolerated.
■ Denial of the right to vote on the basis of moral unworthiness is inconsistent with the respect for the dignity of every person.	■ Denial of the right to vote can contribute to the rehabilitation of prisoners.
■ There is no evidence to support the claim that disenfranchisement deters crime or rehabilitates criminals.	■ There is no empirical evidence, but common sense and logic dictate that denial of the right to vote promotes civic responsibility and the rule of law.

The majority found the government's arguments unpersuasive and declared the prohibition unconstitutional, while the minority upheld the government position. One can argue that the different positions of the minority and majority of the Court stem from particular beliefs and predispositions of different justices.

4. CRITICAL PERSPECTIVES

In this section, we continue our critical examination of the law. Building on legal realism, critical studies take the analysis further, seeing law as a part of a power structure. Various theorists focus on various dimensions of power: feminists consider those that stem from gender dynamics; critical race theorists concentrate on race inequalities; and critical legal studies theorists look at institutional practices and mainstream discourse that portray hierarchical organization of society as natural and fair.

4.1 Critical Legal Studies

The **critical legal studies** (CLS) movement emerged in the United States in the 1970s. It has been led by younger, leftist academics who wanted to draw attention to racial and wealth inequalities and their impact on the law. CLS has roots in legal realism and Marxist scholarship (recall Chapters 1 and 2). Like legal realism, it views law as interconnected with political, economic, and other issues, as well as impacted by personal beliefs of lawyers and judges. Correspondingly, CLS adopts an interdisciplinary approach to the analysis of the law, drawing on politics, philosophy, linguistics, and other disciplines. From Marxist theory, CLS has drawn the idea of societal division and a view that law is a tool in the hands of the powerful.

CLS questions the neutrality and objectivity of law. While law may seem neutral and fair, in reality, it reflects dominant values and the interests of more powerful groups in society. It legitimates the status quo and perpetuates inequalities in society. Societies are organized in hierarchies along class, race, and gender lines that perpetuate the marginalization of the powerless. Further, mainstream rhetoric and practices are used to shape the views of the population in such ways that they accept the existing state of affairs as natural, or at least believe that there are no realistic alternatives to it. For example, various symbols and rituals of the legal processes (e.g., a judge in official robes whose seat is elevated over everyone else in the courtroom) seek to instill the idea that persons in power deserve to be there. Legal training and law schools reproduce hierarchies and inequalities, which eventually feed into the practice of law that is organized along the same lines of hierarchy and domination.[9] Law professes the ideas of justice and equality, but in reality does little to realize them. Even if inequalities and injustices are addressed in some cases, this is done on an individual basis, without addressing structural issues.[10] CLS scholars seek to raise the consciousness of the population by exposing inequalities and the role of the mainstream in perpetrating them.

CLS questions the idea that law is a clear and coherent system. It highlights law's *indeterminacy*, which means that law is subject to any number of possible interpretations and does not have a predetermined answer to a given question. Rather, the case may be decided either way, depending on which line of authority is used or how facts are interpreted. Thus, law is a manipulative device that can be used to rationalize and justify a wide range of possible outcomes.[11]

4.2 Critical Race Theory

The **critical race theory** movement is "a collection of activists and scholars interested in studying and transforming the relationship among race, racism, and power."[12] It is closely connected to CLS, sharing with it the position that law is not neutral but rather a force that is able to exclude and subjugate certain populations. Critical race scholarship emerged in the mid-1970s, partially as a response to concerns that the advancements of the 1960s civil rights era had started to stall, and the first conference of critical race scholars took place in 1989 in Madison, Wisconsin. Critical race theory draws on ideas of CLS, radical feminism, and the civil rights movement. Among prominent representatives of this movement are Richard Delgado, Derrick Bell, Alan Freeman, and Kimberlé Williams Crenshaw.

Critical race theory is based on several key foundations. First, race is seen as a social construction rather than a biological reality. Race is used to create certain images and categorizations of persons as more or less intelligent, reliable, hardworking, and so on. These images and stereotypes in turn lead to the creation of racial hierarchies with groups at the top (whites) obtaining greater benefits and privileges. Racial distinctions are in turn used to rationalize the mistreatment and subjugation of one group by another on the basis of perceived inferiority. For example, residential schools in Canada—as well as other oppressive practices against the First Nations—were justified by the need to educate those "backward" and "inferior" populations. Second, despite the rhetoric of equality and nondiscrimination in contemporary societies, racism is seen as a systemic factor and an endemic presence. Third, law reflects racial biases and tends to perpetrate racist practices. Chapter 10 (torts) illustrates the impact of racial stereotypes on calculation of damages, leading to lower awards to minority plaintiffs.

In analyzing issues of discrimination, critical race theorists rely on the idea of intersectionality, "the examination of race, sex, class, national origin, and sexual orientation, and how their combination plays out in various settings."[13] It highlights that a combination of several marginalized identities (e.g., being black and a woman) can lead to compound disadvantage. Intersectionality presents a more nuanced picture of reality and appreciates that individual experiences differ greatly even within the same group. For example, while all minority populations may face racism, a minority individual with a disability may face additional disadvantage. In Chapter 8 (criminal law), we will discuss whether and how the understanding of compound disadvantage resulting from an accused's race, gender, and class may inform determination of appropriate sentence.

Critical race theory advocates an activist approach to promoting change, and one of the tools that critical race scholars employ is storytelling. Storytelling shares with an audience an individual's experiences in the system in order to help the listeners understand

and relate to those experiences. It helps make the majority aware of the unique perspective of minority individuals, which might be unfamiliar. In addition, it gives voice to those who have often been excluded from debate and the law making process.

4.3 Feminist Theory

Feminist theory specifically focuses on the position of women in society. Feminist scholarship has been most prominent since the 1970s, although the origins of the movement can be traced back to the late nineteenth century. In questioning the objectivity and neutrality of the law, **feminist theory** exposes its male-dominated nature. Chapters 10 (torts) and 11 (family law) provide various examples of such male-centred rules.

The dominance of the male perspective in law can be explained by the fact that major law creating bodies such as legislatures and courts (as well as the legal profession) have generally been dominated by men. The concept of precedent also tended to perpetuate the status quo, which was more reflective of male perspective. Not only was the female perspective not recognized as valuable, but women had no voice in the law creation process. Although we see growing representation of women in the legal profession, courts, and legislative bodies, they still often constitute a minority (see Box 5.5).

Box 5.5

Critical Perspective: Diversity in Canadian Judiciary and Legislature

Critical race and feminist theory highlight issues of power, systemic oppression, and social constructions of race and gender roles. They expose that law is a reflection of power dynamics: it embodies the view of those who have the power within the state and/or can influence policy and the legislative process. In light of this, it is important to consider the representation of women and minorities in the branches of government as well as in the political arena generally. Such representation is important not only as a matter of fairness, but also as a way to enrich the perspectives of law and policy making bodies. For example, feminist scholarship argues that, as judges or policy makers, women may bring in new ways of understanding and addressing various issues. They can also serve as role models, showing that women have a place in the traditionally male-dominated fields.[14] In fact, studies have demonstrated that the presence of women in legislatures has an impact on policy, particularly in the areas of child support, domestic abuse, and foreign aid.[15] Similar findings have been made with respect to the impact of representation of racial and sexual minorities.[16] The judiciary, too, has to be inclusive and representative of various perspectives if it is truly to exercise justice in a diverse society like Canada.[17] Judges' diverse experiences and backgrounds help ensure that they have a better understanding of persons appearing before them and appreciate various social, cultural, and other factors involved in a case.[18]

(continued)

Box 5.5   *(continued)*

Women constitute roughly half of Canada's population,[19] and visible minorities are approximately 16% of the population (with more than half of them living in Ontario).[20] Yet, of all federally appointed judges in Canada, only about 34% are women (Table 5.2), and no nationwide data is even collected on the rate at which visible minorities apply and are being appointed to the bench.[21] There are some locally focused studies, however. For example, in the Greater Toronto Area (GTA),

only 8.3% of judges are visible minorities.[22] In the Court of Appeal for Ontario, only 4.2% of judges are visible minorities.[23] The first Aboriginal judge was appointed to an appellate court only in 2004, and the first black judge in 2012.[24] Since 2009, the federal government has appointed just three nonwhite judges, out of nearly 200 first-time judges named to the bench.[25]

The situation is similarly dismal for the representation of women and minorities in the halls of

Table 5.2 Women Judges Appointed to Federal and Provincial Courts as of July 1, 2014

Canada					
Court	Total Number of Judges in Office	Supernumeraries	Grand Total	Total Number of Women Judges	Number of Current Vacancies
Supreme Court	9	0	9	3	0
Federal Court of Appeal	8	4	12	4	5
Federal Court	33	6	39	12	0
Tax Court of Canada	21	2	23	6	1

	Court	Total Number of Judges in Office	Super-numeraries	Grand Total	Total Number of Women Judges	Number of Current Vacancies
Alberta	Court of Appeal	14	5	19	8	0
	Queen's Bench	63	18	81	35	0
British Columbia	Court of Appeal	15	6	21	10	0
	Supreme Court	89	21	110	38	0
Manitoba	Court of Appeal	6	4	10	4	2
	Queen's Bench Trial	21	7	28	8	1
	Queen's Bench Family	13	3	16	8	0

	Court	Total Number of Judges in Office	Super-numeraries	Grand Total	Total Number of Women Judges	Number of Current Vacancies
New Brunswick	Court of Appeal	6	2	8	2	0
	Queen's Bench Trial	15	6	21	3	2
	Queen's Bench Family	8	2	10	6	0
Newfoundland and Labrador	Appeal Division	6	2	8	2	0
	Trial Division	20	9	29	9	1
Northwest Territories	Supreme Court	4	0	4	4	0
Nova Scotia	Court of Appeal	8	2	10	3	0
	Supreme Court	26	9	35	10	0
	Family Division	9	2	11	6	0
Nunavut	Court of Justice	6	0	6	2	0
Ontario	Court of Appeal	19	7	26	12	3
	Superior Court of Justice	196	80	276	85	16
	Family Court	30	7	37	18	0
Prince Edward Island	Appeal Division	3	0	3	1	0
	Trial Division	5	0	5	2	0
Quebec	Court of Appeal	20	9	29	8	1
	Superior Court	141	45	186	61	4
Saskatchewan	Court of Appeal	7	2	9	2	0
	Queen's Bench	32	9	41	11	1
Yukon	Supreme Court	2	0	2	0	0
TOTAL		**855**	**269**	**1124**	**383**	**37**

Source: Adapted from Office of the Commissioner of Federal Judicial Affairs, online: http://www.fja.gc.ca/appointments-nominations/judges-juges-eng.html#ab

government. For example, in Parliament in 2014, there were 77 women out of 308 members in the House of Commons (25%),[26] and 38 women out of 105 members in the Senate (36%).[27] There were 28 visible minority MPs in Parliament (9.1%).[28] See Tables 5.3, 5.4, and 5.5, below.

(continued)

Box 5.5   (continued)

Table 5.3 Visible Minority MPs, 1993–2011

	1993	1997	2000	2004	2006	2008	2011
All visible minority MPs							
Number	13	19	17	22	24	21	28
Percent	4.4	6.3	5.6	7.1	7.8	6.8	9.1
Percent of visible minorities in population	9.4	11.2	13.4	14.9	16.2	17.3	19.1
Ratio of vis. min. MP % to pop. %	0.47	0.56	0.42	0.48	0.48	0.39	0.48
By party*							
BQ	–	–	–	9.1	16.7	14.3	3.6
CPC	7.7	26.3	29.4	31.8	25.0	38.1	42.9
Lib	92.3	68.4	70.6	59.1	54.2	42.9	7.1
NDP	–	5.3	–	–	4.2	4.8	46.4
(N)	(13)	(19)	(17)	(22)	(24)	(21)	(28)

*Column percentages.

Source: For 1993–2008 data, see Jerome H. Black, "Visible Minority Candidates and MPs: An Update Based on the 2008 Federal Election," *Canadian Parliamentary Review*. Vol. 34, No. 1, 2011, pp. 30–34. MP data for 2011 assembled by author; for the 2011 census estimate, see text.

Table 5.4 Women in the Canadian House of Commons since 1984

Year	Total Number of Seats	Seats Held by Women	Proportion of Seats Held by Women
1984	282	27	9.6
1988	295	39	13.2
1993	295	53	18.0
1997	301	62	20.6
2000	301	62	20.6
2004	308	65	21.1
2006	308	64	20.8
2008	308	68	22.1

Source: Julie Cool, "Women in Parliament", Publication No 05-62E (2010), online: http://www.parl.gc.ca/content/lop/researchpublications/prb0562-e.htm

Table 5.5 Women in Provincial and Territorial Legislatures (2014)

Federal Representation*

Political Party	Number of Women in Caucus	Percent
Conservative Party of Canada	28/161	17%
New Democratic Party of Canada	38/100	38%
Liberal Party of Canada	9/36	25%
Bloc Québécois	0/4	0%
Green Party of Canada	1/2	50%
Independents	1/3	33%

Representation in Provincial and Territorial Legislatures

Province	Number of Women in Legislature	Percent
Northwest Territories	2/19	10.5%
New Brunswick	7/55	13%
Nunavut	3/21	14%
Newfoundland and Labrador	7/48	14.5%
Saskatchewan	11/58	19%
Prince Edward Island	6/27	22%
Alberta	23/87	26%
Manitoba	15/57	26%
Nova Scotia	14/51	27%
Quebec	35/125	28%
Yukon	6/18	33%
Ontario	38/107	35.5%
British Columbia	31/85	36%

Women in Municipal Governments Across Canada

Position	Percent in Councils
Mayors	16%
City Councillors	26%

*There are two seats vacant in the House of Commons.

Source: Equal Voice, "Fundamental Facts: Elected Women in Canada by the Numbers" (as of June 2014), online: http://www.equalvoice.ca/assets/file/Fundamental%20Facts%20-%20Elected%20Women%20in%20Canada%20by%20the%20Numbers%281%29.pdf

Several waves of feminists have sought to draw attention to women's issues and improve their position in society. The first wave in the late nineteenth and early twentieth centuries focused on women's access to education, women's right to vote, and elimination of women's subordination in the family sphere. The second wave during the 1960s and 1970s raised issues with respect to birth control and sexual expression as well as many other areas of life, calling for structural and systemic reforms. Third wave feminism focused on recognizing the multiplicity of women's experiences, paying attention to the particular circumstances of immigrant women, lesbians, and ethnic minorities. Using intersectionality, third wave feminism highlighted the multiplicity of women's identities and the importance of personal narratives and multiple voices in understanding women's experiences.

Currently, the feminist movement and related scholarship are diverse, comprising a range of perspectives: liberal, radical, socialist, cultural, and others. While all of them share an underlying concern with patriarchy, they differ in their main issue focus and strategies for change. For example, *liberal feminism* emphasizes the idea of individual rights, equality, and individual choice. Individuals are viewed as autonomous, rational, equal beings, and liberal feminists concentrate on ensuring that women are given the same opportunities as men. They focus on promoting representation of women in government, equal pay legislation, and the education of women and girls. In fighting for change, liberal feminists seek to work within the existing institutional system. In contrast, *radical feminists* view existing institutions as patriarchal and advocate for a dramatic change. They highlight that relations in society are permeated by gender inequalities that result in oppression of women. Scholars such as Catherine MacKinnon find the root of women's domination in society's constructions of sex and sexuality. Women are portrayed as sex symbols and violence against them is normalized; sexual violation is the expression of women's subordinate status. Chapter 8 (criminal law) provides an example of the use of liberal and radical feminist scholarship in litigation challenging Canada's prostitution-related laws (*Bedford v Canada* case). At trial, both parties called feminist scholars as expert witnesses to help inform the court about relative advantages and disadvantages of criminalization of sex work.

5. LEGAL PLURALISM

In this book, we mostly speak of law as a unified system that is created and administered by state institutions. This traditional perspective sees courts and legislatures as the main sources of authority and law formation. While this is true, does such a description paint a full picture of the law? Think, for example, of the existence of both European and First Nations legal traditions in Canada: they represent different worldviews and different expressions of the law (recall Chapter 1). Further, in addition to national laws, there is a body of international law that governs interstate relations but can also impact domestic law. We also observe multiple instances where nonstate actors (e.g., corporations, communities) develop regulatory rules for particular areas of activity (for example, the International Accounting Standards Board sets standards for financial reporting in the industry). What does all of this mean for our understanding of the law?

Legal pluralism, which emerged in the 1970s, acknowledges the existence of multiple legal regimes at the same time in the same space and produced by various actors. It recognizes that there may be multiple sources of authority and hence multiple sites at which law is produced (which go beyond just courts and legislatures). The main challenge for pluralists is in defining what law is: can any rule be considered law? In the traditional understanding (which is the one that is predominantly used in this textbook), law is made up of rules that are produced and enforced by the state. Pluralist theory adopts a more expansive understanding of the law, which includes rules produced and enforced by state as well as nonstate actors.[29]

History shows that pluralism of legal systems and orders has long existed. For example, in the medieval period (from the fifth to the fifteenth century) activities were regulated by multiple coexisting and overlapping rules (local customs, codes, feudal law, canon law of the Roman Catholic Church, and others), and a judge could apply these various bodies of law depending on the case at hand.[30] There was no single unified system of legal rules. With the emergence of the nation–state, centralization processes began, giving rise to the traditional notion of the law as mentioned above. However, the colonization period, which peaked in the nineteenth century, propelled pluralist systems in colonized territories: on the one hand, local law continued to exist, and on the other, new and distinct rules were introduced by the colonizers.[31] In the twentieth century, the development of global networks and markets, international organizations, multinational corporations, and supranational entities (such as the European Union) expanded the production of rules beyond the nation–state. For example, multinational corporations develop codes of conduct that apply to their activities worldwide; international courts and tribunals contribute to evolution of international law; and various international organizations play a role in developing rules for their members as well as particular areas of activity (labour relations, trade, and the like). Within states themselves, various nonstate actors (professional associations, religious organizations, corporations, tribes, or ethnic communities) produce rules regulating various activities. These multiple regimes may coexist well or may clash and conflict. For example, the *Henco Industries v Haudenosaunee Six Nations* case discussed in Chapter 1 demonstrates the conflicting Euro-Canadian and First Nations perspectives on land title.

Legal pluralism may not necessarily be the most relevant lens through which to examine each and every area of law, but much depends on the jurisdiction. For example, it may come into play where a given area is regulated by state law as well as local custom and/or religious norms. In contrast, where an area is regulated exclusively by state-made rules, legal pluralism will be of little assistance. Perhaps most usefully, the legal pluralism lens is employed in the area of international law where there is traditionally no centralized authority for the production of the law, and various organizations, groups of states, and even associations of nonstate actors such as NGOs and corporations play a role in producing rules. Legal pluralism is also fitting for more insightful understanding of systems of law in countries like Canada where several legal traditions are present.

While legal pluralism may not apply immediately to many of the issues discussed in this book, its underlying idea of being aware of the possibility of multiple regimes and perspectives offers a useful way to approach any issue. At a minimum, we should question whether there is only one set of rules that applies to a given situation, and be aware of multiple ways in which the circumstances may be dealt with and analyzed.

SUMMARY

In this chapter, we examined key points of seven theoretical perspectives: (1) natural law, (2) positivism, (3) legal realism, and (4) legal pluralism, as well as three critical perspectives—(5) critical legal studies, (6) feminist, and (7) critical race theory. Natural law and positivism offer ways of determining the validity of laws: natural law on the basis of its consistency with higher moral values, and positivism by asking whether a law was enacted by a proper authority and according to a prescribed procedure. Legal realism and the critical perspectives analyze law in its political, social, and economic context, also noting that the content and application of legal norms may be influenced by the backgrounds and values of policy and decision makers. Thus, law is not neutral and has a tendency to reinforce the existing status quo, including hierarchies within society. The critical legal studies, feminist, and critical race theory perspectives take an activist approach, seeking not only to expose societal inequalities and the law's biases, but also to facilitate change. Their ideas have long influenced various aspects of laws and policies. Finally, legal pluralism makes us aware of the fact that rules can emanate not only from the state, but also from nonstate authorities. In some cases, we may have several (at times, conflicting) legal regimes in place. Legal pluralism promotes a more expansive understanding of the law and its various forms.

The discussed theoretical perspectives can help you gain greater insight into current laws and policies and the forces driving them. Not every theory would be suitable for analysis of a specific situation, so you will need to choose carefully those that have greatest relevance to the analyzed issue. What is important is your awareness of these different perspectives and ability to identify those best suited for the case at hand.

Critical Thinking Questions

1. Do you agree with the legal pluralists' view that law is not one unified system administered by the state, but is rather a system of uncoordinated, overlapping, and potentially contradictory bodies of law? In your opinion, is this view of the law problematic or challenging in any way?

2. Which of the discussed theoretical approaches aligns most closely with your view of law and society? Why?

3. Can you think of an example where any of the discussed theoretical approaches have motivated actual changes in law? Describe the example and explain how a given theoretical approach can be connected to the change in question.

Further Readings and Useful Resources

1. George Pavlich, *Law and Society Redefined* (Don Mills: Oxford University Pre
2. Richard Delgado and Jean Stefancic, *Critical Race Theory: An Introduction* York University Press, 2001).

Endnotes

1. Raymond Wacks, *Understanding Jurisprudence: An Introduction to Legal Theory* (Oxford; Oxford University Press, 2012) at 22.
2. In 2012, the B.C. Supreme Court held that the *Criminal Code* provisions against assisted suicide violate individual rights of the terminally ill. However, the B.C. Court of Appeal overturned the decision, relying on the precedent set in *Rodriguez v British Columbia (Attorney General)* [1993] 3 SCR 519. The case is currently on appeal to the Supreme Court of Canada.
3. LL Fuller, *The Morality of Law* (New Haven: Yale University Press, 1969) at 38–39.
4. *Canada (Attorney General) v Whaling*, [2014] SCJ No 20.
5. John Austin, *The Province of Jurisprudence Determined*, WE Rumble, ed (Cambridge: Cambridge University Press, 1994) at 157.
6. Jeremy Bentham, "Truth *versus* Ashhurst: or, Law as It Is, Contrasted with What It Is Said to Be" (1792) in *The Works of Jeremy Bentham*, published under the superintendence of his executor, John Bowring, vol V (Edinburgh: London, Simpkin, Marshall, 1843) 231 at 235.
7. See, e.g., Rosalie S Abella, "The Dynamic Nature of Equality" in S Martin & K Mahoney, eds, *Equality and Judicial Neutrality* (Toronto: Carswell, 1987) 3 at 8–9; Hon Justice Nemetz, "The Concept of an Independent Judiciary" (1986) 20 UBC L Rev 286 at 290.
8. Donald R Songer & Susan W Johnson, "Judicial Decision Making in the Supreme Court of Canada: Updating the Personal Attributes Model" (2007) 40:4 Can J Pol Sci 911.
9. Duncan Kennedy, "Legal Education and Reproduction of Hierarchy" (1982) 32 Journal of Legal Education 591; Duncan Kennedy & P Carrington, *Legal Education and the Reproduction of Hierarchy: A Polemic against the System* (New York: New York University Press, 2004).
10. P Gabel & P Harris, "Building Power and Breaking Images: Critical Legal Theory and the Practice of Law" (1983) 11 NYU Rev L Soc Change 369; J Boyle, *Critical Legal Studies* (New York: New York University Press, 1992).
11. Alan C Hutchison & Patrick Monahan, "Law, Politics, and the Critical Legal Scholars: The Unfolding Drama of American Legal Thought" (1984) 36 Stan L Rev 199 at 206.
12. Richard Delgado & Jean Stefancic, *Critical Race Theory: An Introduction* (New York: New York University Press, 2001) at 2.
13. *Ibid* at 51.
14. Hon Bertha Wilson. "Will Women Judges Really Make a Difference?" (1990) 28:3 Osgoode Hall LJ 517–22.
15. Michele L Swers, "Understanding the Policy Impact of Electing Women: Evidence from Research on Congress and State Legislatures" (2001) 34:2 Political Sci & Pol 217; LH Bryne, "Feminists in Power: Women Cabinet Ministers in the New Democratic Party (NDP) Government of Ontario, 1990–1995" (1997) 25:3 Policy Standards J 601; M Breuning, "Women's Representation and Development Assistance: A Cross-National Study" (2001) 23:3 Women & Politics 35.

16. Kathleen A Bratton & Kerry L Haynie, "Agenda Setting and Legislative Success in State Legislatures: The Effects of Gender and Race" (1999) 61:3 Journal of Politics 658; DP Haider-Markel et al., "Minority Group Interests and Political Representation: Gay Elected Officials in the Policy Process" (2000) 62:2 Journal of Politics 568.

17. Sabrina Lyon & Lorne Sossin, "Data and Diversity in the Canadian Justice Community" (2014) 10:5 Osgoode Hall Law School Legal Studies Research Paper Series, paper No 12/2014 at 6.

18. Richard Devlin, Wayne MacKay & Natasha Kim, "Reducing Democratic Deficit: Representation, Diversity and Canadian Judiciary, or towards a Triple P Judiciary" (2000) 38 Alberta L Rev 734; Sonia N Lawrence, "Cultural (In) Sensitivity: The Dangers of a Simplistic Approach to Culture in Courtroom" (2001) 12 Can J Women & L 107.

19. Statistics Canada, "Female Population", online: <http://www.statcan.gc.ca/pub/89-503-x/2010001/article/11475-eng.htm>.

20. Statistics Canada, "Visible Minority Population, by Province and Territory (2006 Census)", online: <http://www.statcan.gc.ca/tables-tableaux/sum-som/l01/cst01/demo52a-eng.htm>.

21. Lyon & Sossin, *supra* note 17 at 3.

22. Diversity Institute, "DiverseCity Counts 3: A snapshot of Diverse Leadership in the GTA" (2011) at 26, online: <http://www.ryerson.ca/content/dam/diversity/AODAforms/Publication/Special/Counts_2011%20AODA.pdf>.

23. *Ibid* at 27.

24. Lyon & Sossin, *supra* note 17 at 3–4.

25. Sean Fine, "Tories Chastised for Lack of Racial Diversity in Judicial Appointments," *The Globe and Mail* (10 April, 2014).

26. "Current Members of Parliament," online: <http://www.parl.gc.ca/parliamentarians/en/members>.

27. "Women in the Senate," online: <http://www.parl.gc.ca/SenatorsMembers/Senate/SenatorsBiography/isenator.asp?sortord=W&Language=E>.

28. Jerome Black, "Racial Diversity in the 2011 Federal Election: Visible Minority Candidates and MPs" (2013) 36:3 Canadian Parliamentary Review 21.

29. Brian Z Tamanaha, "Understanding Legal Pluralism: Past to Present, Local to Global" (2008) 30 Sydney L Rev 375 at 390–96.

30. *Ibid* at 377.

31. *Ibid* at 381–86.

Chapter 6

The *Constitution* and the *Charter of Rights and Freedoms*

Learning Objectives

After reading this chapter, you should be able to:

- Name two main elements of the Canadian *Constitution*.

- Describe the difference between a constitution and an ordinary statute.

- Name and explain at least five rights enshrined in the *Charter of Rights and Freedoms*.

- Describe two situations in which *Charter* rights may be justifiably limited.

- Compare and contrast remedies for violations of *Charter* rights.

- Outline and explain various perspectives on the impact of the *Charter* on the Canadian legal system.

Chapter Outline

Introduction

In Chapter 3, we examined the structure of Canadian government, but we have not discussed in detail the the legal framework in which the government operates: the *Constitution*. This chapter will discuss the main elements of the Canadian *Constitution* with particular focus on the *Charter of Rights and Freedoms*. The *Charter* not only is one of the most important legal documents in Canada, but, according to opinion polls, is also one of the key symbols of national identity.[1] What is the *Charter* and why is it so important? This chapter will discuss a number of cases to demonstrate the practical importance of the *Charter*, as well as provide an overview of scholarly debates on its impact on the Canadian legal system.

Part I. Substantive Law

1. WHAT IS A CONSTITUTION?

A constitution is the fundamental law of a given country. It outlines the structure of government and its powers; it also usually includes a bill of individual rights and freedoms. Constitutions are important for both practical and symbolic reasons: they define the organization of the state and the nature of a political system, prescribe the boundaries of state action, reflect values and aspirations of a given community, and help foster unity and a sense of national identity.

Due to their importance, constitutions enjoy special status compared to other legal documents. First, a constitution is the supreme law of the land and all other laws must be consistent with it. Laws that conflict with the constitution can be declared of no force and effect. Second, constitutions can be amended only by special procedures, usually more complex than for ordinary statutes. Such procedures seek to prevent arbitrary changes and to ensure that amendments result from serious deliberation and enjoy substantial support.

What does a constitution look like? A constitution may take the form of a single written document or may comprise several documents as well as unwritten constitutional conventions and principles. Constitutional conventions are unwritten rules that have arisen as a result of past practices (e.g., the principle of responsible government is a constitutional convention). Some constitutions have developed over time and consist of several documents reflecting such gradual development. An example of this is the United Kingdom's constitution, which consists of constitutional conventions as well as such documents as the *Magna Carta* (1215), the *Petition of Rights* (1628), and others. Other constitutions have come about following a dramatic regime change (e.g., from totalitarianism to democracy), seeking to lay foundations for a new system. For instance, the constitutions of former republics of the Soviet Union are products of such dramatic changes.

Before continuing to the substantive discussion of this chapter, consider the following questions: If you were to create a new constitution for a country, what would you include in that constitution? What principles would it be built on? Why?

2. CANADA'S *CONSTITUTION:* AN OVERVIEW

According to the preamble of the *Constitution Act, 1867*, Canada is to have "a Constitution similar in Principle to that of the United Kingdom." Thus, the Canadian *Constitution* consists of several documents as well as constitutional conventions originating from the British tradition. In addition, the Supreme Court has recognized such unwritten constitutional principles as federalism; democracy; constitutionalism and the rule of law; and respect for minorities.[2]

The two most important elements of Canada's *Constitution* are:

- The *British North America Act, 1867* (later renamed the *Constitution Act, 1867*);
- The *Constitution Act, 1982*, which includes the *Charter of Rights and Freedoms*.[3]

This structure of the *Constitution* is reflective of Canada's history and of the gradual acquisition of independence from Britain. The *Constitution Act, 1867* created a new entity—the Dominion of Canada—composed of four provinces: Nova Scotia, New Brunswick, Ontario, and Quebec. It outlined the structure of government for this new entity, but did not create an independent country. Rather, Canada was a British colony with a substantial degree of self-government. Only in 1931 did Canada gain independence under the *Statute of Westminster*. However, the power to amend Canada's *Constitution* remained with the British Parliament.

In 1980, Pierre Elliott Trudeau pledged to patriate (bring home) the *Constitution* and implement a charter of rights. Trudeau's plan to unilaterally request changes to the *Constitution*, without seeking the approval of the provinces, was met with significant opposition.[4] However, an agreement was finally reached and in December 1981, the British Parliament passed the *Canada Act*, which removed the power of the British Parliament to amend Canada's *Constitution*. The *Act* was proclaimed by Queen Elizabeth II on April 17, 1982, completing the process of patriation. This marked one of the most significant moments in Canadian constitutional history. After 1982, two major attempts for constitutional reform have been made, but they have not been successful (see the discussion in section 3).

2.1 Constitution Act, 1867

The *Constitution Act, 1867* founded the political and economic union of the four provinces and outlined the basic organization of the new entity. It established the federal system and set out the composition and powers of the three branches of government. The *Act* also reflected the idea that Canada was a compact of the French and the English, providing for protection of minority language and religious education rights. It did not acknowledge the presence of Aboriginal peoples, however, except to mention that the federal government has jurisdiction over "Indians and lands reserved for Indians."

In Chapter 3, we described the two levels of government. However, we have not examined how exactly the powers are distributed between the federal and provincial governments. The *Constitution Act, 1867* allocates the powers between levels of government in the following manner (see Box 6.1):

■ *Exclusive federal jurisdiction.* Some subject matters can be regulated by federal Parliament only. They are listed in section 91.

■ *Exclusive provincial jurisdiction.* Section 92 lists subject areas reserved for exclusive regulation by the provinces. The division between exclusive federal and provincial jurisdiction explains why in some areas we have legal rules that apply universally across Canada, while in others there are differences across provinces.

■ *Concurrent (shared) jurisdiction.* Agriculture and immigration (section 95) are matters of concurrent jurisdiction, meaning that both the federal government and provinces have the power to legislate in these areas: the former for the whole of Canada, and the latter within provincial territory. However, in case of a conflict between a federal and a provincial law, the federal law prevails.

Box 6.1

Sections 91 and 92 of the *Constitution Act, 1867*

Powers of the Parliament

Legislative Authority of Parliament of Canada

91. It shall be lawful for the Queen, by and with the Advice and Consent of the Senate and House of Commons, to make Laws for the Peace, Order, and good Government of Canada, in relation to all Matters not coming within the Classes of Subjects by this Act assigned exclusively to the Legislatures of the Provinces; and for greater Certainty, but not so as to restrict the Generality of the foregoing Terms of this Section, it is hereby declared that (notwithstanding anything in this Act) the exclusive Legislative Authority of the Parliament of Canada extends to all Matters coming within the Classes of Subjects next hereinafter enumerated; that is to say,

1. Repealed.
1A. The Public Debt and Property.
2. The Regulation of Trade and Commerce.
2A. Unemployment insurance.
3. The raising of Money by any Mode or System of Taxation.
4. The borrowing of Money on the Public Credit.
5. Postal Service.
6. The Census and Statistics.
7. Militia, Military and Naval Service, and Defence.
8. The fixing of and providing for the Salaries and Allowances of Civil and other Officers of the Government of Canada.
9. Beacons, Buoys, Lighthouses, and Sable Island.
10. Navigation and Shipping.
11. Quarantine and the Establishment and Maintenance of Marine Hospitals.
12. Sea Coast and Inland Fisheries.
13. Ferries between a Province and any British or Foreign Country or between Two Provinces.
14. Currency and Coinage.
15. Banking, Incorporation of Banks, and the Issue of Paper Money.
16. Savings Banks.
17. Weights and Measures.
18. Bills of Exchange and Promissory Notes.
19. Interest.
20. Legal Tender.
21. Bankruptcy and Insolvency.
22. Patents of Invention and Discovery.
23. Copyrights.
24. Indians, and Lands reserved for the Indians.
25. Naturalization and Aliens.
26. Marriage and Divorce.
27. The Criminal Law, except the Constitution of Courts of Criminal Jurisdiction, but including the Procedure in Criminal Matters.
28. The Establishment, Maintenance, and Management of Penitentiaries.
29. Such Classes of Subjects as are expressly excepted in the Enumeration of the Classes of Subjects by this Act assigned exclusively to the Legislatures of the Provinces.

And any Matter coming within any of the Classes of Subjects enumerated in this Section shall not be deemed to come within the Class of Matters of a local or private Nature comprised in the Enumeration of the Classes of Subjects by this Act assigned exclusively to the Legislatures of the Provinces.

(continued)

Box 6.1 *(continued)*

Exclusive Powers of Provincial Legislatures

Subjects of Exclusive Provincial Legislation

92. In each Province the Legislature may exclusively make Laws in relation to Matters coming within the Classes of Subjects next hereinafter enumerated; that is to say,

1. Repealed.

2. Direct Taxation within the Province in order to the raising of a Revenue for Provincial Purposes.

3. The borrowing of Money on the sole Credit of the Province.

4. The Establishment and Tenure of Provincial Offices and the Appointment and Payment of Provincial Officers.

5. The Management and Sale of the Public Lands belonging to the Province and of the Timber and Wood thereon.

6. The Establishment, Maintenance, and Management of Public and Reformatory Prisons in and for the Province.

7. The Establishment, Maintenance, and Management of Hospitals, Asylums, Charities, and Eleemosynary Institutions in and for the Province, other than Marine Hospitals.

8. Municipal Institutions in the Province.

9. Shop, Saloon, Tavern, Auctioneer, and other Licences in order to the raising of a Revenue for Provincial, Local, or Municipal Purposes.

10. Local Works and Undertakings other than such as are of the following Classes:

a. Lines of Steam or other Ships, Railways, Canals, Telegraphs, and other Works and Undertakings connecting the Province with any other or others of the Provinces, or extending beyond the Limits of the Province:

b. Lines of Steam Ships between the Province and any British or Foreign Country:

c. Such Works as, although wholly situate within the Province, are before or after their Execution declared by the Parliament of Canada to be for the general Advantage of Canada or for the Advantage of Two or more of the Provinces.

11. The Incorporation of Companies with Provincial Objects.

12. The Solemnization of Marriage in the Province.

13. Property and Civil Rights in the Province.

14. The Administration of Justice in the Province, including the Constitution, Maintenance, and Organization of Provincial Courts, both of Civil and of Criminal Jurisdiction, and including Procedure in Civil Matters in those Courts.

15. The Imposition of Punishment by Fine, Penalty, or Imprisonment for enforcing any Law of the Province made in relation to any Matter coming within any of the Classes of Subjects enumerated in this Section.

16. Generally all Matters of a merely local or private Nature in the Province.

■ *Peace, order, and good government (POGG)*. Section 91 provides that Parliament can "make Laws for the Peace, Order, and good Government of Canada." The POGG power encompasses three areas:

    a. residual power—it includes matters that are not specifically allocated to either federal or provincial government;

b. emergency power—in case of emergency, it allows Parliament to intrude temporarily into provincial jurisdiction in order to take measures necessary to address the emergency; and

c. matters of national concern—it usually applies to new issues that have not been contemplated at the time of Confederation and that have nationwide importance (e.g., regulation of atomic energy).

Importantly, the meaning of the *Constitution Act, 1867* is not frozen in the time of its adoption. For example, "postal service" and "banking" currently encompass many activities that neither existed nor could have even been contemplated in 1867. The *Constitution* is viewed as a "living tree" whose meaning evolves to correspond to the changing realities.

While the *Constitution* seems to neatly distinguish areas of federal and provincial jurisdiction, in reality, defining whether a matter falls under federal or provincial heads of power may be a challenging task. In fact, a sizable number of cases have required courts to resolve such jurisdictional questions (see Box 6.2).

Box 6.2

Controversies Over Federal/Provincial Jurisdiction: *R v Morgentaler*, [1993] 3 SCR 463

In 1988, the Supreme Court determined that s. 251 of the *Criminal Code,* which limited access to abortions, was unconstitutional. Thus, it was no longer an offence under the *Criminal Code* to obtain or perform an abortion at a private clinic such as the one run by Morgentaler.

In 1989, Morgentaler announced his intention to establish a private abortion clinic in Halifax. Shortly after that announcement, Nova Scotia adopted the *Medical Services Act* and an accompanying regulation, which mandated performance of certain medical procedures (including abortion) in hospitals and made it an offence to perform them outside hospitals.

Despite this, Morgentaler opened a private clinic in Nova Scotia and performed a number of abortions. He was charged with an offence under the *Medical Services Act.* At trial, Morgentaler did not deny that he performed the abortions, but argued that the *Act* and regulation were unconstitutional.

He contended that the *Act* and regulation constituted matters of criminal law and that the province had no power to pass them because criminal law falls under exclusive federal jurisdiction. The province, however, argued that it had the power to pass the *Act* and the regulation under such provincial head of power as the establishment, maintenance, and management of hospitals. In your opinion, how are the *Act* and the regulation to be characterized: are they criminal law, or do they relate to the regulation of hospitals?

The Supreme Court was called upon to resolve the above question and concluded that the *Medical Services Act* and the regulation were criminal law and hence outside of the powers of the province (ultra vires).[5] In arriving at that conclusion, the Court looked not merely at the words of the legislation, but at its true nature: what was its real purpose and practical effect?

(continued)

Box 6.2   *(continued)*

Officially, the purpose of the *Act* was "to prohibit the privatization of the provision of certain medical services in order to maintain a single high-quality health-care delivery system for all Nova Scotians." However, in reality, the legislation approached the issue of abortion not from the viewpoint of healthcare policy, but from the viewpoint of public wrongs and crime. The debates before the Nova Scotia legislative assembly revealed that there was general opposition to free-standing abortion clinics in Nova Scotia and that members of the legislature wanted to find a way to prohibit Morgentaler's clinic in particular. Abortions were perceived as socially undesirable, and Morgentaler clinics as a public evil. Thus, in substance, Nova Scotia legislation attempted to impose certain standards of morality—a function performed by criminal law and an area where provinces have no legislative power.

This decision is illustrative of the importance of critical analysis in law generally: It is not enough to look at the face value and the words of legislation; we need to uncover its true meaning and effect.

2.2 Constitution Act, 1982

The *Constitution Act, 1982* added new elements to the Canadian *Constitution*. First, it entrenched the *Charter of Rights and Freedoms*. Second, it declared the *Constitution* to be the supreme law of the land. Third, it recognized and affirmed Aboriginal and treaty rights of Indian, Inuit, and Métis people. Fourth, it prescribed rules by which the *Constitution* could be amended.

The *Constitution Act, 1867* contained no amending formulas, but once Canada gained the power to amend its own constitution, it became necessary to prescribe such rules. Depending on the type of the change intended, a different formula is to be used. These formulas are:

- *Section 38 of the* Constitution Act, 1982: a majority of federal Parliament and a majority of at least two-thirds of the legislative assemblies in the provinces that make up at least 50% of Canada's population. This formula is to be used if amendment is sought for such matters as the powers and composition of the Senate (recall the Senate reference case in Chapter 4, Box 4.2), representation of each province in the House of Commons and the Senate, and establishment of a new province.

- *Section 41*: a majority of federal Parliament and a majority of each province. This formula is used for amendments concerning the office of the Queen or of the governor general or lieutenant governors, and the composition of the Supreme Court.

- *Section 43*: a majority of federal Parliament and a majority of province(s) affected by the change. This formula is used in such matters as alteration of provincial boundaries and amendments to provisions relating to the use of English or French within a province.

- *Section 44:* federal Parliament alone (in relation to, for example, the federal executive, the Senate, or the House of Commons).
- *Section 45:* provincial legislature alone (in relation to matters that concern a province alone).

3. ATTEMPTS FOR FURTHER CONSTITUTIONAL REFORM

Quebec did not accept the patriation arrangements and, as a result, the reform was seen as incomplete. Further, First Nations communities were not provided with an opportunity to participate fully in the constitutional negotiations. Hence, two major attempts at constitutional reform—the *Meech Lake Accord* (1987) and the *Charlottetown Accord* (1992)—were undertaken to remedy these deficiencies.

3.1 Meech Lake Accord (1987)

The Quebec government outlined a number of conditions under which it was willing to accept the *Constitution Act, 1982*. They included: recognition of Quebec as a distinct society; greater powers for Quebec to control immigration into the province; Quebec's input into nomination of the justices of the Supreme Court of Canada; financial compensation for opting out of new federal programs in the area of provincial jurisdiction; and veto power in relation to constitutional amendments affecting Quebec.

At Meech Lake, the first ministers (the prime minister and premiers of all provinces) agreed to these conditions and approved the Accord. Some of the mentioned provisions— reasonable compensation for opting out of new federal programs, and a provincial role in nomination of Supreme Court justices—extended the power of not only Quebec but also the other provinces. The Accord essentially responded to the demands of Quebec but did not consider First Nations' concerns. Another significant shortcoming of the Meech Lake process was its secret and elitist nature. The negotiations were conducted behind closed doors, by first ministers only, and without public participation or input from stakeholders.

In order to come into effect, the Accord had to be approved by the federal Parliament and all provincial legislatures within three years. Two provinces—Newfoundland and Manitoba—failed to ratify the Accord by the prescribed deadline.

3.2 Charlottetown Accord (1992)

The second attempt at constitutional reform sought to avoid the shortcomings of Meech Lake by providing a more inclusive and participatory process. The government's proposal for constitutional reform was referred to the Special Joint Committee of the House of Commons and the Senate, which travelled across Canada seeking feedback. It received 3000 submissions and heard testimony of 700 individuals. Provinces and territories also created opportunities for public discussion of the proposal. Following these public consultations, representatives of the federal and provincial governments as well as First Nations leaders engaged in a series of negotiations on constitutional amendments.

The Charlottetown Accord proposed more extensive changes than Meech Lake. The key ones included:

- Recognition of the inherent Aboriginal right to self-government within Canada

- Recognition of Quebec as a distinct society;

- A Canada clause, which outlined such Canadian values as democracy, parliamentary federalism, rule of law, equality, and respect for individual and collective human rights;

- A commitment to preservation and development of Canada's social and economic union with such objectives as full employment, a reasonable standard of living for all Canadians, and sustainable and equitable development;

- Senate reform: creation of an elected senate with equal representation by all provinces; and

- Greater powers for provincial governments in selected areas.

The Accord was put to a vote by national referendum, but failed to gather the necessary support.[6] Hence, like the Meech Lake Accord, it did not come into effect. This closed a chapter in a series of major attempts at constitutional reform.

4. THE *CHARTER OF RIGHTS AND FREEDOMS*

The entrenchment of a charter of rights in the *Constitution* signified stronger protection of individual rights and, as you will see, has had a notable impact on the Canadian legal system. Of course, the common law allowed for protection of certain individual rights (e.g., the right to a fair trial, the right to detention review, freedom of religion). However, such protections were weaker and more limited than a constitutionally entrenched bill of rights.

Photo 6.1 Canada's *Charter of Rights and Freedoms* is fundamental to law and government in this country.

Thomson Reuters

The first step toward the creation of a charter of rights was taken in 1960 with the adoption of the *Canadian Bill of Rights*. It enshrined many rights similar to those later found in the *Charter*. However, the *Bill of Rights* was not part of the *Constitution*, but rather an ordinary statute, which could be easily amended. Furthermore, it applied to the federal government but not to provincial governments. These features of the *Bill of Rights* constituted significant limitations on its ability to become a strong protector of individual rights. Hence, a further step was taken to create the *Charter of Rights* and include it in the *Constitution*.

In order to understand the scope and significance of the *Charter*, four issues need to be examined:

- What rights are protected by the *Charter*?
- Is it possible to limit *Charter* rights? If yes, under what circumstances?
- What type of interaction does the *Charter* apply to (e.g., interactions among individuals, or between individuals and state authorities)?
- What remedies are available if *Charter* rights are violated?

The *Charter* contains 34 sections and can be roughly divided into four main components:

- list of rights and freedoms as well as other guarantees and protections (sections 2–23, 25–29);
- scope of *Charter* application (section 32);
- permissible limitations on *Charter* rights (sections 1 and 33); and
- remedies (section 24).

4.1 Charter Rights

Please read s. 1–15 of the *Charter* (reproduced in Box 6.3) and answer the following questions:

- Who can claim *Charter* rights: Canadian citizens only, or anyone in Canada regardless of citizenship or immigration status?
- Can *Charter* rights be limited?

Box 6.3

Sections 1–15 of the *Charter of Rights and Freedoms*

1. The *Canadian Charter of Rights and Freedoms* guarantees the rights and freedoms set out in it subject only to such reasonable limits prescribed by law as can be demonstrably justified in a free and democratic society.

Fundamental Freedoms

Fundamental freedoms

2. Everyone has the following fundamental freedoms:

(a) freedom of conscience and religion;

(b) freedom of thought, belief, opinion and expression, including freedom of the press and other media of communication;

(c) freedom of peaceful assembly; and

(d) freedom of association.

Democratic Rights

Democratic rights of citizens

3. Every citizen of Canada has the right to vote in an election of members of the House of

(continued)

Box 6.3   *(continued)*

Commons or of a legislative assembly and to be qualified for membership therein.

Maximum duration of legislative bodies

4. (1) No House of Commons and no legislative assembly shall continue for longer than five years from the date fixed for the return of the writs at a general election of its members.

Continuation in special circumstances

(2) In time of real or apprehended war, invasion or insurrection, a House of Commons may be continued by Parliament and a legislative assembly may be continued by the legislature beyond five years if such continuation is not opposed by the votes of more than one-third of the members of the House of Commons or the legislative assembly, as the case may be.

Annual sitting of legislative bodies

5. There shall be a sitting of Parliament and of each legislature at least once every twelve months.

Mobility Rights

Mobility of citizens

6. (1) Every citizen of Canada has the right to enter, remain in and leave Canada.

Rights to move and gain livelihood

(2) Every citizen of Canada and every person who has the status of a permanent resident of Canada has the right

(a) to move to and take up residence in any province; and

(b) to pursue the gaining of a livelihood in any province.

Limitation

(3) The rights specified in subsection (2) are subject to

(a) any laws or practices of general application in force in a province other than those that discriminate among persons primarily on the basis of province of present or previous residence; and

(b) any laws providing for reasonable residency requirements as a qualification for the receipt of publicly provided social services.

Affirmative action programs

(4) Subsections (2) and (3) do not preclude any law, program or activity that has as its object the amelioration in a province of conditions of individuals in that province who are socially or economically disadvantaged if the rate of employment in that province is below the rate of employment in Canada.

Legal Rights

Life, liberty and security of person

7. Everyone has the right to life, liberty and security of the person and the right not to be deprived thereof except in accordance with the principles of fundamental justice.

Search or seizure

8. Everyone has the right to be secure against unreasonable search or seizure.

Detention or imprisonment

9. Everyone has the right not to be arbitrarily detained or imprisoned.

Arrest or detention

10. Everyone has the right on arrest or detention

(a) to be informed promptly of the reasons therefor;

(b) to retain and instruct counsel without delay and to be informed of that right; and

(c) to have the validity of the detention determined by way of habeas corpus and to be released if the detention is not lawful.

Proceedings in criminal and penal matters

11. Any person charged with an offence has the right

(a) to be informed without unreasonable delay of the specific offence;

(b) to be tried within a reasonable time;

(c) not to be compelled to be a witness in proceedings against that person in respect of the offence;

(d) to be presumed innocent until proven guilty according to law in a fair and public hearing by an independent and impartial tribunal;

(e) not to be denied reasonable bail without just cause;

(f) except in the case of an offence under military law tried before a military tribunal, to the benefit of trial by jury where the maximum punishment for the offence is imprisonment for five years or a more severe punishment;

(g) not to be found guilty on account of any act or omission unless, at the time of the act or omission, it constituted an offence under Canadian or international law or was criminal according to the general principles of law recognized by the community of nations;

(h) if finally acquitted of the offence, not to be tried for it again and, if finally found guilty and punished for the offence, not to be tried or punished for it again; and

(i) if found guilty of the offence and if the punishment for the offence has been varied between the time of commission and the time of sentencing, to the benefit of the lesser punishment.

Treatment or punishment

12. Everyone has the right not to be subjected to any cruel and unusual treatment or punishment.

Self-crimination

13. A witness who testifies in any proceedings has the right not to have any incriminating evidence so given used to incriminate that witness in any other proceedings, except in a prosecution for perjury or for the giving of contradictory evidence.

Interpreter

14. A party or witness in any proceedings who does not understand or speak the language in which the proceedings are conducted or who is deaf has the right to the assistance of an interpreter.

Equality Rights

Equality before and under law and equal protection and benefit of law

15. (1) Every individual is equal before and under the law and has the right to the equal protection and equal benefit of the law without discrimination and, in particular, without discrimination based on race, national or ethnic origin, colour, religion, sex, age or mental or physical disability.

Affirmative action programs

(2) Subsection (1) does not preclude any law, program or activity that has as its object the amelioration of conditions of disadvantaged individuals or groups including those that are disadvantaged because of race, national or ethnic origin, colour, religion, sex, age or mental or physical disability.

As you can see, the *Charter* rights are grouped into the following categories:

- Fundamental freedoms (section 2);
- Democratic rights (section 3);
- Mobility rights (section 6);
- Legal rights (sections 7–14); and
- Equality rights (section 15).

Most *Charter* rights apply to "everyone" and "any person/every individual," which includes both Canadian citizens and noncitizens in Canada. Only two rights are reserved exclusively for citizens: democratic rights and the right to enter, remain in, and leave Canada.

Although the language of the *Charter* seems clear, on a closer look, at least two major questions may arise: (1) What is the meaning and scope of each right? and (2) If two *Charter* rights conflict, how are we to resolve such a conflict?

4.1.1 What is the Meaning and Scope of Each Right?

While we cannot discuss all *Charter* rights in this section, let's have a look at a few selected issues:

a. *What does freedom of expression under s. 2(b) mean? Does it include only political expression, or does it cover commercial advertising? Do corporations enjoy freedom of expression?*
You will not find answers to the above questions in the *Charter* itself and courts have been instrumental in interpreting *Charter* provisions. The freedom of expression is considered to cover such areas as political expression, commercial expression (e.g., advertising[7]), issues of public access to certain information/proceedings, censorship/obscenity, and others. It encompasses verbal as well as nonverbal expression such as picketing[8] and postering on public property.[9] Further, the freedom of expression includes not only the right to say something, but also the right to say nothing or the right not to say certain things.[10] Freedoms under s. 2 apply to both natural persons and corporations.

b. *What does the liberty and security of person under s. 7 mean? What are the principles of fundamental justice?*
Section 7 is one of the most interesting sections that has been invoked in multiple contexts, including criminal law, immigration, medical treatment, child protection, and others. However, the section itself does not provide a definition of "life, liberty and security of person" or of the "principles of fundamental justice." Thus, courts, particularly the Supreme Court of Canada, have played an important interpretive role (Box 6.4).

Liberty interest includes not only freedom from physical restraint, but also autonomy in making fundamental life choices.[11] The *security of person* extends to both bodily and psychological integrity.[12] Serious state-imposed psychological stress can constitute a breach of the security of person.[13] For example, this may occur where a state interferes in the person's ability to control her physical or psychological integrity by prohibiting abortion or assisted suicide.[14]

Box 6.4

Is a Fetus Considered a "Human Being" and Does it Have the Right to Life?

This question was considered by the Supreme Court in *Tremblay v Daigle*.[15] The couple cohabited for several months but then broke up. At the time of the breakup, Daigle was pregnant. She decided to have an abortion, but Tremblay obtained a court injunction preventing her from proceeding with abortion. The Quebec Superior Court concluded that, under the Quebec *Charter*, a fetus constituted a human being and enjoyed the right to life. This decision was upheld by the Quebec Court of Appeal. Daigle appealed to the Supreme Court.

The Supreme Court concluded that a fetus was not considered a "human being" and hence could not enjoy the right to life. The Quebec *Charter* did not contain a definition of a "human being" and the Court did not find that the framers of the *Charter* had an intention to consider the rights and status of a fetus. The Court also noted that Anglo-Canadian jurisprudence similarly did not consider a fetus a human being: in order to enjoy rights, a fetus must have been born alive.

To establish a violation of s. 7, an applicant must demonstrate that: (1) there has been or could be a deprivation of the right to life, liberty, or security of the person; and (2) the deprivation was not or would not be in accordance with the principles of fundamental justice.[16]

The **principles of fundamental justice** are "to be found in the basic tenets and principles not only of our judicial process but also of the other components of our legal system."[17] In order to be considered a principle of fundamental justice: (a) it must be a legal principle; (b) there must be sufficient consensus that this principle is fundamental to the society's notion of justice; and (c) the principle must be capable of being clearly formulated and applied to cases at hand.[18]

There is no one single list of these principles; rather, they are defined contextually, depending on the process in question and interests at stake.[19] For example, in the context of detention, the principles of fundamental justice require the state to accord a fair judicial process to detainees, including a hearing and the right to know the case against oneself and to answer that case.[20] In the context of criminal prosecution, the requirement of a guilty mind is a fundamental principle of justice.

c. *What does "a right to counsel" mean? Does it entail only being informed of a right to counsel, or is there an obligation on the authorities to provide information about available legal services as well as give a person a meaningful opportunity to consult a lawyer?*
Courts determined that the right to counsel has two components:

- *Informational.* This component requires not only that the detainee be advised about the right to counsel, but also that the police inform the detainee of the existence of legal aid and duty counsel[21] as well as of legal services available 24 hours a day.[22]

- *Implementational.* This component requires that the detainee be given an opportunity to exercise the right to counsel: once the detainee indicates a desire to speak to a lawyer, the police must abstain from questioning until the detainee has had a reasonable opportunity to consult a lawyer.[23] The underlying purpose of s. 10(*b*) is to provide an individual with legal advice so that he understands his rights, including the right to silence, and that he can make an informed choice as to whether to cooperate with the police investigation.[24]

The police are to give a detainee an additional opportunity to consult a lawyer if there is a significant change in the circumstances (e.g., new charges are contemplated).[25] However, s. 10(*b*) does not require that defence counsel be present throughout an interrogation.[26]

d. *When can search and seizure be considered unreasonable?*

Section 8 protects an individual's private space from state interference. One's privacy includes personal, territorial (privacy of one's home), and informational aspects. Section 8 nevertheless allows for searches that are authorized by a reasonable law and carried out in a reasonable manner (Box 6.5).[27] What is reasonable will depend on the circumstances, including the place where the search has occurred; whether the subject matter was in public view; and whether the police technique was intrusive. A search is usually considered unreasonable if it is performed without a warrant.[28]

As you can see from the above examples, courts have played a very significant role in giving meaning to the provisions of the *Charter*. On the one hand, they often not only provided the necessary clarity, but also affirmed and expanded protections under the *Charter*. On the other hand, concerns have been raised that by doing so courts have taken

---

Box 6.5

R v Tessling, [2004] 3 SCR 432: Does Flying a Forward-Looking Infrared (FLIR) Camera Over One's House Amount to Search and Violation of One's Privacy?

The police received a tip that Tessling was growing marijuana in his house. The police then flew an airplane with a FLIR camera over Tessling's home and recorded the heat pattern, which suggested that there was a grow-op in the house. A warrant was obtained on the basis of the heat image and subsequently a large amount of marijuana was found in Tessling's house. He was charged and convicted. Tessling argued that the use of a FLIR camera amounted to a search and, since this was done without a warrant, constituted a violation of his rights under s. 8. The Supreme Court disagreed and found no violation. It determined that the use of FLIR technology does not amount to a search. Further, a FLIR camera shows only heat distribution, without revealing any intimate details of a person's lifestyle, and, thus, does not intrude on a person's privacy.

over the legislative role and/or expanded some rights to an extent that may impede enforcement action. Part II of this chapter will review various opinions on the role of courts in the *Charter* era.

4.1.2 Reconciling Competing Rights

It is not uncommon for situations to arise where two *Charter* rights are at stake and are creating a potential conflict. How are we to resolve such conflicts? Can and should we give priority to one right over the other?

It is generally accepted that there is no hierarchy of *Charter* rights and that all rights are equally important. In case of a conflict, an attempt should be made to strike a balance that respects both rights. However, it is equally recognized that an individual's rights may be limited by the rights and freedoms of others.[29] The case of NS in Box 6.6 provides a useful illustration of the balancing of two competing rights.

Box 6.6

Reconciling Competing Rights: *R v NS*, [2012] SCJ No 72

A female named NS filed a sexual assault complaint against two of her relatives. At a preliminary inquiry, due to NS's religious beliefs, she wished to testify wearing a niqab, which covers her face, except for the eyes. The accused, however, asked the court to order her to testify without the niqab. Defence counsel argued that nonverbal clues such as facial expressions are important in order to test NS's credibility. Allowing a witness to wear a niqab would compromise the accused person's right to a fair trial.

This case involves a potential conflict between two rights: the witness's right to freedom of religion, and the accused's right to a fair trial. In your opinion, what order should the judge make: order NS to remove her niqab, or allow her to testify wearing a niqab? Why?

The Supreme Court examined the NS case and provided guidance on how to resolve the potential conflict between the two rights. The Court did not design one hard and fast rule in relation to the NS scenario, either always requiring the face to be revealed or always allowing it to be covered. Rather, the Court outlined a test that would help to balance the two rights with an attempt to find an acceptable compromise. The test involves the following stages:

a. Does an individual hold a sincere religious belief? Would requiring the witness to remove the niqab interfere with her religious freedom?

b. Would permitting the witness to wear the niqab create a serious risk to the fairness of trial?

c. Is there a way to accommodate both rights and avoid the conflict between them? ·

d. If no accommodation is possible, do the benefits of requiring the witness to remove the niqab outweigh the injurious effects of doing so?

(continued)

Box 6.6   (continued)

This test would be applied in each individual case and the outcome would depend on the circumstances. For example, where evidence is uncontested, the inability to see the witness's face would not interfere with the fairness of trial, and a witness may be allowed to testify wearing a face covering.

After the Supreme Court outlined the four-part test, the NS case went back to the Ontario Court of Justice. The Court of Justice applied the test to the case and came to the following conclusion:[30]

a. NS holds a strong and sincere belief that her religion requires her to wear a niqab in the presence of men who are not her relatives.

b. Permitting NS to testify wearing a niqab will impair defence counsel's ability to assess her demeanour as well as the ability of the decision maker to assess her credibility.

c. There is no way to accommodate both rights. It is not possible to accommodate NS by excluding men from the courtroom as this would violate the principle of open court and

the freedom of the press. Further, all accused are entitled to counsel of choice, be they male or female.

d. The judge acknowledged that the effects of requiring NS to remove the niqab would be felt on both a personal and societal level. On a personal level, it would exacerbate NS's stress of testifying. On a societal level, this precedent might create disincentives for persons in position similar to NS's from turning to the justice system. However, on the other side of the equation are the interests of the accused, who face a possibility of long incarceration if convicted. If a niqab impedes effective cross-examination of NS and assessment of her credibility, this may increase the risk of a wrongful conviction.

Overall, the court concluded that NS could not be permitted to testify wearing a niqab, as this would create a serious risk to fair trial: she is the key witness for the prosecution and her credibility is an issue.

4.2 Limitations on *Charter* Rights

Charter rights are not absolute, which means that they may be subject to limitations. The *Charter* outlines two types of circumstances when the government may impose some restrictions on *Charter* rights:

■ Under section 1 of the *Charter*; and

■ Under section 33 (the notwithstanding clause).

4.2.1 Section 1

Section 1 of the *Charter* reads: "The *Canadian Charter of Rights and Freedoms* guarantees the rights and freedoms set out in it subject only to such reasonable limits prescribed by law as can be demonstrably justified in a free and democratic society."

This section recognizes that there may be compelling public objectives necessitating limitations on individual rights. For example, freedom of expression is important, but if it is used to promote hate propaganda, substantial harm to society may result. Thus, a provision of the *Criminal Code*, which makes it an offence to willfully promote hatred against an identifiable group, is a justifiable limitation on the freedom of expression.[31]

This does not mean, however, that any limitation that the government chooses to impose would be justified under s. 1. Persons affected by limiting legislation may challenge it before courts, which will then determine whether a given limitation constitutes a reasonable limit under s. 1.

Section 1 does not provide any specific definition of what constitutes a reasonable limit or how it is to be determined. Hence, courts developed a test that assists in the application of s. 1. The test was set out in the case of Oakes (hence it is also called the **Oakes test**[32]). As shown in Figure 6.1, it includes the following stages:

1. What is the law's objective? Is it pressing and substantial?
2. Is the legislation rationally connected to the objective?
3. Does the legislation impair a *Charter* right as little as possible?
4. Is there proportionality between the effects of the limitation and the objective sought by that limitation?

If the answers to all four questions are "yes," then the limitation on the right in question is considered saved under s. 1 and hence will remain in effect. In contrast, if one of the above questions is answered in the negative, the infringement will be considered unjustifiable. We will examine the application of this test in the *Sauvé* case in Box 6.8.

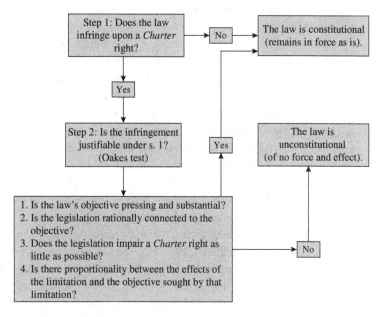

Figure 6.1 Section 1 analysis (*Oakes* test)

4.2.2 Section 33

The second possible way to impose limitations on *Charter* rights is found in section 33, the so called **notwithstanding clause**. This clause allows federal Parliament and provincial legislatures to enact laws that infringe upon *Charter* rights and declare that those laws will operate notwithstanding the provisions of the *Charter*. This effectively immunizes a given law from judicial scrutiny. However, there are some limits on the application of the notwithstanding clause:

- It cannot be invoked in relation to rights listed in sections 3–6 of the *Charter*.

- The notwithstanding clause is valid only for a five-year term (although it may be renewed).

While some circumstances may warrant the invocation of the notwithstanding clause, there is a concern that its use may undermine the confidence of the population in the democratic nature of legislatures. This likely explains why s. 33 is rarely used.[33]

4.3 Application of the *Charter*

Section 32(1) of the *Charter* reads:

> This Charter applies
>
> (a) to the Parliament and government of Canada in respect of all matters within the authority of Parliament including all matters relating to the Yukon Territory and Northwest Territories; and
> (b) to the legislature and government of each province in respect of all matters within the authority of the legislature of each province.

This means that the *Charter* applies to interactions between government and individuals only; it does not apply to private interactions between individuals or corporations. Thus, for example, an employee who has been discriminated against by a private company cannot launch a *Charter* challenge against the company. Such violation can, however, be addressed under a different regime—provincial human rights codes (see Chapter 12).

Some cases may very clearly involve a government authority (e.g., when the police interact with an accused, or when a legislative body passes a law). Thus, there is no doubt that the *Charter* applies. However, some agencies are not formally part of the government, yet exercise important public functions (e.g., hospitals). Does the *Charter* apply to them?

Case law established that *Charter* application can extend to entities that are controlled by the government, implement government programs, exercise government functions, or derive powers from the state. For example, although hospitals are independent from the government in their day-to-day operations, they act as agents for the government in providing medical services. Hence, the *Charter* applies to hospitals.[34] The *Charter* also applies to colleges, as they are established by the government to implement government policy and their operation is directed by the government.[35] In contrast, universities are neither implementing a government program nor acting in a governmental capacity and, thus, the *Charter* does not apply to them.[36] In sum, in order to determine whether the *Charter* applies to a given entity, it is necessary to examine not only whether it performs a public function, but also the nature and scope of government control over that entity.

4.4 Remedies Under the *Charter*

It is expected that government authorities act in accordance with the *Charter*. However, *Charter* infringements still occur, and usually fall into one of two categories:

a. *Legislation infringes upon* Charter *rights* (e.g., a law that prohibits inmates from voting is an infringement on s. 3 rights of the *Charter*—see the *Sauvé* case in Box 6.8). A person affected by such legislation may seek to have it declared unconstitutional. In examining the constitutionality of legislation, courts utilize the *Oakes* test to determine whether the infringement may be justified under s. 1 of the *Charter*.

b. *Actions of government authorities violate* Charter *rights* (e.g., the police do not observe a detainee's right to counsel). Here the legislation empowering the authority to act is not subject to a challenge and is valid; it is how the government authority is exercising its powers that is in question.

Sections 24 and 52 of the *Charter* outline remedies that may be available when *Charter* rights have been unjustifiably infringed. Section 52 is used when the validity of legislation is challenged, while section 24 provides for remedies when government's action violates the *Charter*.

Section 24 provides:

(1) Anyone whose rights or freedoms, as guaranteed by this Charter, have been infringed or denied may apply to a court of competent jurisdiction to obtain such remedy as the court considers appropriate and just in the circumstances.

(2) Where, in proceedings under subsection (1), a court concludes that evidence was obtained in a manner that infringed or denied any rights or freedoms guaranteed by this Charter, the evidence shall be excluded if it is established that, having regard to all the circumstances, the admission of it in the proceedings would bring the administration of justice into disrepute.

An "appropriate and just" remedy under s. 24(1) may include the award of damages, an injunction (compelling a particular type of behaviour), or a declaration that the individual's rights have been violated. Section 24(2) provides for a very specific remedy in the form of exclusion of evidence, which is most frequently invoked in the criminal law context (see Box 6.7).

Section 52 proclaims that the *Constitution* is the supreme law of the land and that any law inconsistent with the *Constitution* is of no force and effect. If a law cannot be saved under s. 1, it will be declared invalid. Depending on the case at hand, the remedy under s. 52 may take several forms:

a. *Striking down legislation.* In this case, a whole piece of legislation is invalidated.

b. *Severing offending provisions from legislation.* Some provisions offending the *Charter* may be struck down, but the rest of the legislation will remain in effect as long as it can operate in a coherent manner without the invalidated provisions. For example, when the Supreme Court invalidated s. 251 of the *Criminal Code* in the 1988 *Morgentaler* case, the rest of the *Code* remained in effect.

Box 6.7

Practical Application: Exclusion of Evidence Under s. 24(2)

Andrew is suspected of murder and is taken to a police station at 10:00 A.M. and continuously questioned until 7:00 P.M. Although Andrew states that he wishes to remain silent and wishes to speak to a lawyer, the police do not give him access to counsel and continue their questioning. Andrew eventually confesses and tells the police where he hid the murder weapon. The weapon is recovered and is presented as evidence at trial along with Andrew's confession. Andrew can argue that both the confession and the murder weapon have been obtained in violation of his right to silence and the right to counsel and seek their exclusion from evidence. When evidence is excluded, it means that it will not be presented at trial.

The exclusion of evidence is not automatic and it will be up to a court to decide whether in a given case the evidence should be excluded. In making a decision, a court must consider three factors: (1) the seriousness of the *Charter*-infringing state conduct, (2) the impact of the breach on the *Charter*-protected interests of the accused, and (3) society's interest in the adjudication of the case on its merits.[37]

Given the serious nature of the violations in our example, it is likely that a court would order exclusion of the confession and of the murder weapon from trial. The exclusion of this key evidence may significantly undermine the prosecution's case and may even lead to acquittal. Thus, this remedy sends a strong message that convictions are not to be obtained at all costs and can help promote more *Charter*-compliant conduct by the police in the future.

c. *Reading in.* Reading in means that a court adds a certain requirement to invalid legislation in order to make it compliant with the *Charter*. This option is used when legislation is underinclusive and does not extend protection to certain groups, therefore leading to *Charter* violation. For example, in *Vriend v Alberta*, Vriend was fired from his teaching job because he was gay. At the time, the Alberta *Human Rights, Citizenship and Multiculturalism Act* did not provide protection against discrimination on the basis of sexual orientation. Instead of invalidating the *Act*, the Supreme Court chose to read in sexual orientation as a ground of protection under the *Act*.

d. *Reading down.* By reading a provision down, a court gives legislation more restrictive interpretation in order to achieve *Charter* compliance. This remedy is fitting when legislation is overly broad.

e. *Declaration of invalidity and its temporary suspension.* A court declares certain legislation or a portion of it invalid, but suspends the effect of this declaration for a period of time. This keeps the invalid legislation in effect in order to allow legislature to change the law and bring it in compliance with the *Charter*. For example, if the Supreme Court were to strike down criminal law provisions on homicide and the decision were to be effective immediately, this would create a gap in criminal law.

No one could be charged with homicide until a new law was enacted, which, as you recall from Chapter 3, can take some time. A declaration of invalidity allows such temporary gaps in regulation to be avoided.

f. *Constitutional exemption.* This remedy exempts an individual from application of valid legislation. It is rarely used and may be warranted only in exceptional circumstances.

Prior to reading about the case in Box 6.8, consider the following question: should inmates be allowed to vote? If yes, why? If not, why?

Box 6.8

Practical Application: *Sauvé v Canada (Chief Electoral Officer)*, [2002] 3 SCR 519

Various arguments are advanced for and against prohibiting inmates from voting. The supporters of the prohibition reason that inmates violated the social contract to comply with the law and cannot be trusted with the responsibility to vote. The opponents of the prohibition emphasize the importance of rehabilitating offenders and view voting as one of the means to assist their reintegration into society. Approaches across jurisdictions vary. For example, Brazil, India, Portugal, the United Kingdom, and Venezuela do not allow inmates to vote. In Belgium and the Philippines, disenfranchisement extends past the duration of a prison sentence and, in some cases, can be for life. In contrast, Germany, Namibia, and Sweden do not prohibit voting by inmates. In France, Japan, and Spain, only some inmates are prohibited from voting, depending on the crime committed.[38]

Canada's approach to inmates' voting has changed over time, in large part due to *Charter* litigation. The 1985 *Canada Elections Act* disqualified from voting "every person undergoing punishment as an inmate in any penal institution for the commission of any offence." In 1992, this provision was challenged by Richard Sauvé, a former member of the Satan's Choice Motorcycle Club, who was serving a life sentence in prison

(*Sauvé* 1).The Supreme Court held that such prohibition violated s. 3 of the *Charter* and was not saved under s. 1.[39]

In 1993, the *Canada Elections Act* was amended: it no longer contained a full prohibition on voting, but barred inmates from voting if they had been sentenced to two years or more of imprisonment. The law was challenged again (*Sauvé* 2).[40] The Supreme Court was split on the issue: five justices (the majority) found that the limitation on voting rights was unconstitutional and could not be saved under s. 1, while four justices (the minority) agreed with the government's position.

In order to decide the case, the Court had to answer two questions. Below is the outline of the majority's conclusions on these two questions:

1. **Does the *Canada Elections Act* infringe on a Charter right?**
   Section 51(e) of the *Canada Elections Act* limits inmates' right to vote and, thus, constitutes an infringement on the right to vote under s. 3 of the *Charter*.

2. **Is the infringement justified under s. 1 of the *Charter*?**
   This question is answered using the *Oakes* test and consists of the following stages:

(continued)

Box 6.8   *(continued)*

a. *What is the law's objective? Is it pressing and substantial?*

The government stated that the objectives of the prohibition were: (1) to enhance civic responsibility and respect for the rule of law; and (2) to impose additional punishment.

The majority of the Court found these objectives vague and symbolic. The first objective could be asserted with respect to virtually every criminal law and many noncriminal measures. It was also unclear why additional punishment was required for the offenders serving two or more years in prison.

Overall, the majority had difficulty finding that the law was directed at a pressing and substantial objective. This would have been enough for the Court to declare the provision unconstitutional, but the majority decided to proceed to the next stages of the test.

b. *Is the legislation rationally connected to the objectives?*

In other words, will denying inmates the right to vote enhance respect for the law and impose legitimate punishment? The government advanced three arguments: (i) the prohibition sends an "educative message" about the importance of respect for the law; (ii) allowing penitentiary inmates to vote "demeans" the political system; (iii) disenfranchisement is a legitimate form of punishment.

The majority did not find these arguments persuasive. First, it reasoned that people respect the law because they see it as made by and on behalf of citizens. Then, disenfranchisement would undermine rather than strengthen the respect for the law. Second, the majority reasoned that the idea that some people are not morally worthy to vote contradicts the principles of dignity of every person, equality, inclusiveness, and citizen participation, on which Canadian democracy is built. Third, the majority noted that there was no evidence that disenfranchisement deters crime or rehabilitates criminals. Hence, the majority concluded that the government failed to demonstrate a rational connection.

c. *Does the legislation impair a right as little as possible?*

The prohibition applied to all persons serving sentences of two years or more and, thus, caught individuals who have committed relatively minor crimes and who could not be said to have broken their ties to society. Thus, the legislation did not impair as little as possible the right to vote.

d. *Is there proportionality between the effects of the limitation and the objective sought by that limitation?*

The majority concluded that the negative effects of denying citizens the right to vote would greatly outweigh the benefits of the prohibition. The limitation on the right to vote undermined the goals of rehabilitation and integration. It also undermined the major principles of the Canadian political system: the right to political expression and participation, equal worth of all individuals, and respect for all under the law. The prohibition was more likely to erode respect for the rule of law than to enhance it. It also had a disproportionate impact on Aboriginal peoples, given their overrepresentation in penitentiaries. Hence, the proportionality requirement has not been met.

The majority's overall conclusion was that the infringement on the right to vote was not saved under s. 1 and, as a result, the provision in question was unconstitutional and of no force and effect. Consequently, federal inmates currently enjoy the right to vote.

5. IMPACT OF THE *CHARTER*

As can be gleaned from the above discussion, the *Charter* has had a significant impact on the legal system. First, it strengthened rights protections and the role of citizens in government. While certain individual rights have been long recognized at common law, they did not enjoy constitutional status. The concept of *Charter* rights brought to the fore the importance of citizens in governance of society. Prior to that, government was seen mostly as a process of interaction between federal and provincial levels where citizens played a limited role. Further, the *Charter* helped previously marginalized groups such as women and First Nations fight for greater participation in political life and affirm their rights.[41]

Second, the *Charter* expanded the power of courts to scrutinize legislation and government action. Prior to the *Charter*, courts could review legislation, but only on limited jurisdictional grounds, namely checking whether a given level of government was acting within its head of power under s. 91 or 92 of the *Constitution Act, 1867*. This limited nature of review and limited protection that it provided for individual rights is well illustrated by the case *R v Quong-Wing* in Box 6.9.

Third, the *Charter* as well as *Charter* litigation changed the conduct of government authorities. In the legislative process, for example, all bills are now checked for

---

Box 6.9

Limited Nature of Judicial Review Prior to the *Charter*: *R v Quong-Wing* (1914), 49 SCR 440

At the turn of the twentieth century, several provinces enacted legislation that imposed various discriminatory restrictions on persons of Chinese descent, including in employment and voting.[42] For example, a Saskatchewan statute prohibited Chinese men from employing white women and girls, so as, it was said, to protect the morals of white women and girls. The validity of this statute was challenged by Quong-Wing, a naturalized Canadian of Chinese descent who was convicted for violating the prohibition.

Quong-Wing argued that the subject matter of the statute was outside the area of provincial jurisdiction and hence the provincial law was invalid. The central question for the court was whether the statute dealt with the issue related to "aliens and naturalization" (federal jurisdiction) or constituted an issue of "property and

civil rights" (provincial jurisdiction). As noted by Justice Davies: "The question on this appeal is not one as to the policy or justice of the Act in question, but solely as to the power of the provincial legislature to pass it. . . . Once I find its subject-matter is not within the power of the Dominion Parliament and is within that of the provincial legislature, I cannot inquire into its policy or justice or into the motives which prompted its passage."[43]

This statement vividly demonstrates the limitations of judicial review under the *Constitution Act, 1867*: the sole question is the subject matter of the legislation; the issue of discrimination or violation of individual rights does not even enter the judicial debate. In contrast, the *Charter*, which is focused on protection of individual rights, allows them to be brought to the centre stage of litigation.

Charter compliance. The Department of Justice plays a central role in this and provides advice to federal departments on whether their policy proposals are consistent with the *Charter*. In addition, *Charter* litigation often created additional incentives for government authorities to ensure that they observed individual rights. In some cases, such litigation led to changes in agencies' practices and procedures.

Part II. Critical Perspectives

It is hard to deny that the *Charter* has had multiple impacts on our legal system. However, opinions diverge on the nature of such impacts and on whether they have been positive or negative. In this brief section, we cannot provide an exhaustive review of the extensive literature on the subject, but we will briefly discuss three of the most hotly debated topics:

- How has the *Charter* influenced political life in Canada?
- Who has benefited from *Charter* challenges the most?
- Has the *Charter* brought about positive changes overall?

1. HOW HAS THE *CHARTER* INFLUENCED POLITICAL LIFE IN CANADA?

The *Charter* has influenced all three branches of government. It informs the decisions of legislators on how to balance various competing objectives and imposes certain limitations on their policy choices. The executive must ensure that it exercises its powers in accordance with the *Charter*. The *Charter* has extended the ability of courts to subject legislation and government action to scrutiny and, by virtue of that, to impact the content and direction of legal and policy regulation.

The most extensive debates have developed with respect to the judicial role in policy making and the interaction between legislatures and courts in this context of *Charter* challenges. Given that the Supreme Court has the strongest ability to influence policy, a great deal of scholarship is dedicated particularly to this court and its interaction with the federal Parliament.

1.1 Judicial Role in Policy Making

In the past decades, the Supreme Court has examined many controversial issues (e.g., abortion, prisoners' right to vote, collective bargaining, Sunday closing of retail stores) that often resulted in changes to regulatory regimes in respective areas. The Court has also increased the use of such remedies as reading in or reading down legislation, which allowed it to essentially amend the language of the law.[44] Thus, it is considered that the Supreme Court is no longer merely adjudicating disputes, but has become a policy making institution.[45] Some critics say that the *Charter* has led to the judicialization of politics, or "the greater participation by the judiciary in fundamental policy debates that occur when courts determine the constitutionality of public policy by their consistency with rights and freedoms."[46]

Why is courts' increasing policy making role a cause for concern? It is traditionally considered that policy making falls within the domain of the legislature and the executive. Democracy requires that key decisions (such as choices of regulatory regimes for specific subject matters) be made by elected representatives in a transparent process that allows for input from stakeholders and the public. Hence, the shift of decision making to nonelected judges who are not accountable to the general public is considered to undermine the democratic process. Judicial decisions are made in private: we do not see the debates between judges and cannot easily identify to what extent judges are guided by legal principles as opposed to personal preferences. Further, litigation does not allow for public debate of relevant issues.[47] Only opinions of parties to—and interveners in—a case are heard.[48] In contrast, a legislative process is open to input from various stakeholders (think of the committee stage of the statutory enactment process). A legislative process is also thought to be better geared toward considering various interests and finding a compromise. In contrast, litigation is a zero-sum game: there is a winner and a loser; there is no middle ground. Finally, when the litigation route is pursued, important questions of policy are often transformed into technical legal issues that are inaccessible to most of the general public.

While critics suggest that the policy making role of courts under the *Charter* undermines Canadian democracy, others argue that this is not necessarily so. For example, the legislative process does not guarantee that all interests will be heard and taken into account. As you recall from Chapter 3, if a party holds a majority in both houses of Parliament, it may pass proposed legislation without much change or compromise. Further, courts do not necessarily choose to take a policy making role, but often have to step in where legislatures have not properly protected *Charter* interests. [49] Finally, some authors suggest that, instead of debating whether courts should play a policy making role, we need to face the reality: courts have already been transformed from primarily adjudicative to policy making bodies.[50] Thus, the question is not whether courts should play a policy making role, but how they perform that role, including whether they make good policy.[51]

1.2 Interaction between Legislatures and Courts in the Context of *Charter* Challenges

As discussed in Chapter 3, traditionally our system has been characterized by parliamentary supremacy in which Parliament is the supreme law maker. However, this notion has come under question in the context of *Charter* litigation. When a law is declared unconstitutional, the legislature may enact a new law on the same subject, but must be mindful of judicial pronouncements that invalidated preceding legislation. In some cases, the legislature may take no action at all. This effectively poses a question: who has the last word on a given subject—legislatures or the Supreme Court? In fact, some authors have suggested that the judicial review under the *Charter* may promote judicial supremacy where the Supreme Court has the last word on various controversial issues.[52] Others say that even where a legislature took some action, courts essentially dictated the content of new legislation.[53]

Perhaps a more helpful way to examine judicial–legislative interaction is not in terms of competition for supremacy but as a dialogue between the two branches whereby both are contributing to the promotion of *Charter* values.[54] Peter Hogg and Allison Bushell introduced an influential idea of "dialogue" (which was subsequently invoked by the Supreme Court itself).[55] By dialogue they meant that a Supreme Court decision on a given issue does not necessarily put an end to debates, and there is usually room for legislatures to respond to that decision.[56] At least three avenues are open for the legislature:

a. It may pass a new law or modify an existing law, taking into consideration guidance provided in a relevant judicial decision. For example, recall the tobacco advertising case discussed in Chapter 3 (Box 3.3). After a complete ban on tobacco advertising was found unconstitutional by the Supreme Court, Parliament passed a new law that took into consideration the Supreme Court's decision: it allowed information and brand-preference advertising, but banned lifestyle advertising, advertising to the young, and false and misleading advertising.[57]

b. The legislature may take no action or may be unable to agree on the action to be taken. For example, following the 1988 *Morgentaler* decision, Parliament could have enacted a new *Criminal Code* provision with lesser restrictions on abortion, yet it was unable to do so. In 1989, a bill was introduced, but it was never passed.

c. The legislature may choose to pass a new law that overrides a judicial decision and may invoke the notwithstanding clause to immunize the new law from further judicial scrutiny. This course of action is used rather rarely, usually when Parliament strongly disagrees with the judicial approach and considers it in the public interest to override it (see, for example, *R v Daviault* in Chapter 8, Box 8.4).

As we can see from the above, a judicial decision is usually not the last word on a given issue and the legislatures can revise or reject effects of judicial decisions. Legislatures and the judiciary have a shared responsibility to find a regulatory approach that complies with *Charter* values.[58] Parliament has initial responsibility to ensure *Charter* compliance at the legislative stage. If litigants make a persuasive case that that responsibility has not been fulfilled, then courts have the obligation to step in to invalidate noncompliant legislation.[59]

2. WHO HAS BENEFITED FROM *CHARTER* CHALLENGES THE MOST?

As discussed in Chapter 3, various interest groups resort to litigation, including on the basis of the *Charter*, in order to pursue their own or public interest objectives. For example, the tobacco advertising case (Chapter 3, Box 3.3) exemplifies corporations challenging legislation that is considered to undermine their business interests (although they used a public interest argument to advance their private interests). Groups such as LEAF (recall Chapter 3, Box 3.5) consistently participate as interveners in various cases involving women's rights and equality.

What has been the effect of interest groups on *Charter* litigation? Opinions on the issue diverge. Critics argue that interest groups are trying to bypass the democratic process and achieve through courts what they could not do through legislatures.[60] Some claim that *Charter* litigation has been used primarily by left-leaning interest groups.[61] Others contend that *Charter* litigation has legitimized neoconservative policies and exacerbated societal inequalities.[62]

However, ultimately, the answer is not black and white: both left- and right-leaning interest groups have had their successes and failures in *Charter* litigation. While interest groups can and do have an impact on legal regulation, their influence should not be overstated.[63] There are procedural and financial barriers to their ability to pursue litigation frequently. Further, while the *Charter* can be a useful policy tool, it does not guarantee the sought outcome. Thus, we need to pay attention to which interest groups launched challenges and/or intervened in cases and for what reasons they did so, but we should not be too quick to conclude that *Charter* litigation is hijacked by interest groups.

3. HAS THE *CHARTER* BROUGHT ABOUT POSITIVE CHANGES OVERALL?

There is no one simple answer to this question. Overall, we have seen refinement and enhancement of individual rights and protections in many subject areas. However, such advancement has not been even across all fields. For example, while there have been gains in relation to reproductive rights and violence against women, litigation to address socioeconomic disparities has been largely unsuccessful.[64] Even in the area that has perhaps been most dramatically influenced by the *Charter*—criminal justice—the reviews are mixed. On the one hand, *Charter* litigation can be said to have enhanced the rights of the accused at every stage of the criminal process and helped promote more *Charter* compliant conduct by the authorities. On the other hand, the strengthening of the rights of the accused has been criticized for making police work and prosecution more difficult. The cases *R v Stinchcombe* and *R v Askov* provide good illustrations of these points.

The *Stinchcombe* decision[65] established that, by virtue of s. 7 of the *Charter*, the Crown has a legal duty to disclose all relevant information to the defence. Prior to *Stinchcombe*, this duty was not extensively recognized under common law: the prosecutor had the discretion to decide what material to disclose. Prosecutors could use the strategy of ambush by bringing new information at trial that was unknown to the defence. On the one hand, the decision strengthened the rights of the accused and helped defence counsel to be better prepared. On the other hand, the duty to disclose evidence to the defence has led to lengthier and more costly trials.[66]

In *R v Askov*,[67] the Supreme Court affirmed the right to trial within a reasonable time under s. 11(b) of the *Charter*. It found that the 34-month delay between the laying of charges and the holding of a trial was unreasonable. The Court concluded that staying (halting) of charges against the accused was a proper remedy for violation of s. 11(b) rights. On the one hand, the *Askov* decision resulted in some 50 000 prosecutions being stayed[68] and those individuals never being tried for their alleged criminal acts. On the other hand, the decision highlighted the injustice stemming from delays and affirmed the importance of addressing the delays in the criminal justice system. It motivated the government to allocate more resources to the administration of justice, including building more courthouses, appointing more judges, and making other changes to ensure timely trials.

Finally, we need to be aware that the *Charter* is only a tool that is as useful as the skills and knowledge of the actors involved in specific cases. For example, as Alan Young notes in the context of criminal justice, in an adversarial process where most of the work is left in the hands of the parties, a lot is riding on how competent, knowledgeable, and responsible counsel are.[69] It is they (and particularly counsel for the accused) who help to effectively invoke and assert constitutional protections.

SUMMARY

A constitution is a fundamental law of a country, which outlines the structure and principles of government as well as gives protection to individual rights. The Canadian *Constitution* consists of two major parts: the *Constitution Act, 1867* and the *Constitution Act, 1982*. The *Constitution Act, 1867* outlines the composition of the branches of government as well as the division of jurisdiction between federal and provincial governments. Some powers are reserved exclusively to federal Parliament; others, to provinces; and yet others are under shared jurisdiction. The *Constitution Act, 1982* contains the amending formulas and the *Charter of Rights and Freedoms*. The *Charter* enshrines the following categories of rights: fundamental freedoms, democratic rights, mobility rights, legal rights, and equality rights. While these rights enjoy supreme protection, they are not absolute—that is, they may be subject to limitations under s. 1 and s. 33.

The adoption of the *Charter* has increased the ability of courts to subject government action to scrutiny. Where legislation or government action infringes upon *Charter* rights, individuals and organizations can launch a constitutional challenge and it will be for courts to determine if such infringement is justifiable. In order to determine if an infringement can be saved under s. 1 of the *Charter*, courts employ the *Oakes* test, which looks into the objectives of the legislation in question and the means chosen to achieve them. If courts find a violation, they can order a remedy under sections 24 and 52. Section 24 of the *Charter* is used where government action violated the *Charter*, and it allows courts to order any remedy that would be "appropriate and just" in the circumstances; it also allows for exclusion of evidence that was improperly obtained. Section 52 is employed when legislation is subject to a *Charter* challenge, and it includes the following remedies: striking down legislation, severing an offending provision, reading in, reading down, declaration of invalidity, and constitutional exemption.

As numerous examples in this chapter demonstrate, the *Charter* has had a major impact on the Canadian legal system. However, opinions diverge on whether this impact has been positive and who has benefited from it the most. The issue of the *Charter*'s impact is likely to remain hotly debated for many years to come.

Critical Thinking Questions

1. In Canada, assisted suicide is criminalized. Does this prohibition violate s. 7 (right to life, liberty, and security of person)? Explain, keeping in mind the interpretation of the right to life, liberty and security of person described in this chapter. Find any recent cases that dealt with assisted suicide: did courts find prohibition of assisted suicide to be a justifiable limitation on s. 7 rights?

2. Polygamy is an offence under the *Criminal Code*. Does this provision contravene the right to freedom of religion under the *Charter*? Apply the *Oakes* test to the analysis of this question. Find out if any recent cases examined the constitutionality of polygamy under the *Charter*.

3. Is the *Charter* relevant to your everyday life? Explain.

4. In your opinion, has the *Charter* given courts too much power to scrutinize and invalidate government legislation and actions? Explain your answer by reference to any of the cases or critical perspectives discussed in this chapter.

Further Readings and Resources

1. James Kelly and Christopher Manfredi, eds, *Contested Constitutionalism: Reflections on the Canadian Charter of Rights and Freedoms* (Vancouver: UBC Press, 2009).

2. Janet L Hiebert, *Charter Conflicts: What Is Parliament's Role?* (Montreal: McGill-Queen's University Press, 2002).

3. Heather McIvor, *Canadian Politics and Government in the Charter Era* (Toronto: Thompson Nelson, 2006).

4. Kent Roach, *The Supreme Court on Trial: Judicial Activism and Democratic Dialogue* (Toronto: Irwin law, 2001).

5. Faisal Bhabha, "*R. v. N.S.*: What Is Fair in a Trial? The Supreme Court of Canada's Divided Opinion on the Niqab in the Courtroom" (2013) 50:4 Alta L Rev 871.

Endnotes

1. Environics Institute, "Focus Canada 2010" at 17, online: <http://www.environicsinstitute.org/uploads/institute-projects/pdf-focuscanada2010.pdf>.
2. *Reference re Secession of Quebec*, [1998] 2 SCR 217.
3. In addition to these acts, the *Constitution* includes other acts and orders listed in the Schedule to the *Constitution Act, 1982* as well as other historic texts and such common law principles as the royal prerogative.
4. Several reference cases were launched before provincial courts of appeal as well as the Supreme Court of Canada, asking whether the proposed reforms were constitutional. See, for example, *Reference Re Amendment of the Constitution of Canada* (1981), 125 DLR (3d) 1 (SCC).
5. *R v Morgentaler*, [1993] 3 SCR 463.
6. For discussion of the Accord and referendum, see Kenneth McRoberts and Patrick Monahan, eds, *The Charlottetown Accord, the Referendum, and the Future of Canada* (Toronto: University of Toronto Press, 1993).
7. See *Ford v Quebec (Attorney General)*, [1988] 2 SCR 712; *Irwin Toy Ltd v Quebec (Attorney General)*, [1989] 1 SCR 927.
8. *Weisfeld v Canada (Minister of Public Works)* (1994), 116 DLR (4th) 232.

9. *Ramsden v Peterborough (City)* (1993), 15 OR (3d) 548 (SCC).
10. *Slaight Communications Inc v Davidson*, [1989] 1 SCR 1038 at 1080.
11. *Blencoe v British Columbia (Human Rights Commission)*, [2000] SCJ No 43 at para 49.
12. *R v Morgentaler*, [1988] 1 SCR 30 at 55–56.
13. *Rodriguez v British Columbia (Attorney General)*, [1993] 3 SCR 519 at 587.
14. *R v Morgentaler*, *supra* note 12, *Rodriguez*, *ibid*.
15. *Tremblay v Daigle*, [1989] 2 SCR 530.
16. Test originally set out in *R v Beare*, [1988] 2 SCR 387 at 401.
17. *Re BC Motor Vehicle Act*, [1985] 2 SCR 486 at 503.
18. *R v Malmo-Levine*, [2003] 3 SCR 571 at para 113.
19. *R v Lyons*, [1987] 2 SCR 309 at 361; *Chiarelli v Canada (Minister of Employment and Immigration)* [1992] 1 SCR 711 at 743–44; *Charkaoui v. Canada (Citizenship and Immigration)*, [2007] 1 SCR 350 at para 20; *Kindler v Canada (Minister of Justice)*, [1991] SCJ No 63 at 848; *R v Wholesale Travel Group Inc.*, [1991] 3 SCR 154 at 226.
20. *Charkaoui, ibid* at para 29.
21. *R v Brydges* (1990), 53 CCC (3d) 330 (SCC).
22. *R v Bartle* (1994), 92 CCC (3d) 289 (SCC).
23. The detained must be reasonably diligent in exercising the right to counsel. *R v Tremblay* [1987] 2 SCR 435 at 439; *R v Black*, [1989] 2 SCR 138 at 154–55.
24. *R v Hebert*, [1990] 2 SCR 151 at 176–77.
25. *R v Sinclair*, [2010] 2 SCR 310.
26. *Ibid*.
27. *R v Caslake*, [1998] 1 SCR 51; *R v Collins*, [1987] 1 SCR 265.
28. *R v Golden*, [2001] 3 SCR 679 83 at paras 90–92.
29. *Trinity Western University v British Columbia College of Teachers*, [2001] 1 SCR 772 at para 29.
30. *R v MS* [2013] OJ No 1855.
31. *R v Keegstra* [1990] SCJ No 131.
32. The title of the test stems from the name of the case—*R v Oakes*, [1986] SCJ No 7—where this test was spelled out for the first time. Oakes was charged with possession of narcotics for the purpose of trafficking. Under s. 8 of the *Narcotic Control Act*, a person found in possession of narcotics was presumed to have them for the purpose of trafficking. It was then up to the accused to prove that the possession was not for the purpose of trafficking. The accused argued that s. 8 of the *Narcotic Control Act* violated the presumption of innocence under the *Charter*. The prosecution argued that this legislation was justified by the objective of combating drug trafficking. The Supreme Court, however, agreed with the accused and found s. 8 of no force in effect. In analyzing the provision, the court invoked s. 1 of the *Charter* and spelled out the test. It found that there was no rational connection between the fact of possession and presumption of trafficking: being in possession of a drug does not automatically translate into trafficking.
33. One of the notable examples is the decision of the Quebec legislature to add notwithstanding clauses to all its statutes following the proclamation of the *Constitution Act, 1982*. The effect of those clauses was that the relevant sections of the *Charter* did not apply to Quebec laws. Section 33 was also invoked by other provinces (Saskatchewan in 1986 in relation to public service back-to-work legislation, and Alberta in 2000 in relation to legislation that limited marriages of same-sex couples).
34. *Eldridge v British Columbia (Attorney General)*, [1997] 3 SCR 624.
35. *Douglas/Kwantlen Faculty Assn v Douglas College*, [1990] 3 SCR 570.

36. *McKinney v University of Guelph*, [1990] 3 SCR 229.
37. *R v Grant*, [2009] SCJ No 32.
38. Andre Blais, Louis Massicotte, & Antoine Yoshinaka, "Deciding Who Has the Right to Vote: A Comparative Analysis of Election Laws" (2001) 20 Electoral Studies 41.
39. *Sauvé v Canada (Attorney General)*, [1993] 2 SCR 438.
40. [2002] SCJ No 66.
41. See generally, Alan C Cairns, "The Barriers to Constitutional Renewal in Canada: The Role of Constitutional Culture," reproduced in David W Elliott, *Introduction to Public Law*, 6th ed (Toronto: Captus Press, 2003) at 206 – 213.
42. This provincial legislation produced a string of litigation with respect to constitutional division of powers over immigration, naturalization, and aliens. See, e.g., *Union Colliery Co of BC v Bryden*, [1899] CCS No 40; *Re British Columbia Provincial Elections Act, 1897* [1902] JCJ No 3; *Re Act to validate and confirm orders in council and provisions relating to the employment of persons on Crown property (British Columbia)* (1922), 63 SCR 293; *Brooks-Bidlake and Whittall v British Columbia (Attorney General)*, [1923] JCJ No 3.
43. *R v Quong-Wing* (1914), 49 SCR 440 (QL).
44. James Kelly & Christopher Manfredi, "Should We Cheer? Contested Constitutionalism and the Canadian Charter of Rights and Freedoms" in James Kelly & Christopher Manfredi, eds, *Contested Constitutionalism: Reflections on the Canadian Charter of Rights and Freedoms* (Vancouver: UBC Press, 2009) 3 at 7–8, 10.
45. Christopher Manfredi & Antonia Maioni, "Judicializing Health Policy: Unexpected Lessons and an Inconvenient Truth" in James Kelly & Christopher Manfredi, eds, *Contested Constitutionalism, ibid*, 129.
46. James Kelly & Christopher Manfredi, "Should We Cheer?", *supra* note 44 at 4.
47. Andrew Petter, "Legalise This: The Chartering of Canadian Politics" in James Kelly & Christopher Manfredi, eds, *Contested Constitutionalism, supra* note 44, 33.
48. Christopher Manfredi & Antonia Maioni, "Judicializing Health Policy" *supra* note 45 at 142.
49. Kent Roach, "The Role of Litigation and the Charter in Interest Advocacy" in F Leslie Seidle, ed, *Equity and Community: The Charter, Interest Advocacy and Representation* (Montreal: Institute for Research on Public Policy, 1993) 159; Byron Sheldrick, *Perils and Possibilities: Social Activism and the Law* (Halifax: Fernwood Publishing, 2004) at 14.
50. Heather McIvor, *Canadian Politics and Government in the Charter Era* (Toronto: Thompson Nelson, 2006) at 92.
51. *Ibid*.
52. Mark Tushnet, "Judicial Activism on Restraint in a Section 33 World" (2003) 53 UfT LJ 89; Christopher Mandredi, *Judicial Power and the Charter: Canada and the Paradox of Liberal Constitutionalism*, 2nd ed (Don Mills: Oxford University Press, 2001).
53. FL Morton, "Dialogue or Monologue?" (1999) Policy Options 23.
54. Peter W Hogg & Allison A Bushell, "The Charter Dialogue between Courts and Legislatures (or Perhaps the Charter of Rights Isn't Such a Bad Thing After All)" (1997) 35 Osgoode Hall LJ 75; Peter W Hogg, Allison A Bushell Thornton & Wade K Wright, "Charter Dialogue Revisited—Or "Much Ado about Metaphors" (2007) 45 Osgoode Hall LJ 1; Kent Roach, "Dialogic Judicial Review and Its Critics" (2004) 23 SC L Rev 49 at 55-56; McIvor, *supra* note 50 at 149.
It should be noted that although the idea of dialogue has become rather influential in characterizing the interaction between Parliament and the Supreme Court, it has also been criticized

on a number of grounds. See, for example, FL Morton, "Dialogue or Monologue?" in Paul Howe & Peter H Russell, eds, *Judicial Power and Canadian Democracy* (Montreal and Kingston: McGill-Queen's University Press, 2001) 111; Christopher P Manfredi & James B Kelly, "Six Degrees of Dialogue: A Response to Hogg and Bushell" (1999) 37 Osgoode Hall LJ 153; Grant Huscroft, "Rationalizing Judicial Power: The Mischief of Dialogue Theory" in James Kelly & Christopher Manfredi, eds, *Contested Constitutionalism, supra* note 44 at 59–60.

55. *R v Hall,* [2002] 3 SCR 309; *R v Mills,* [1999] 3 SCR 668.

56. Kim Campbell, "Parliament's Role in Protecting the Rights and Freedoms of Canadians" in Philip Bryden, Steven Davis & John Russell, eds, *Protecting Rights and Freedoms: Essays on the Charter's Place in Canada's Political, Legal, and Intellectual Life* (Toronto: University of Toronto Press, 1994) 23 at 27.

57. This new law has been challenged again, but this time the Supreme Court has upheld its validity. *Canada (Attorney General) v JTI-Macdonald Corp,* [2007] SCJ No 30. It should be noted, however, that not everyone agrees that this case represents an example of judicial–legislative dialogue. Some suggest that Parliament merely adopted what the Supreme Court dictated in its prior decision.

58. Janet L Hiebert, *Charter Conflicts: What Is Parliament's Role?* (Montreal: McGill-Queen's University Press, 2002); Roach, *supra* note 54.

59. Brian Slattery, "A Theory of the Charter" (1987) 25 Osgoode Hall LJ 701.

60. Petter, *supra* note 47 at 39; Ian Brodie, *Friends of the Court: The Privileging of Interest Group Litigants in Canada* (New York: State University of New York Press, 2002) at xiii–xiv.

61. Frederick Lee Morton & Reiner Knopff, *The Charter Revolution and the Court Party* (Toronto: Broadview Press, 2000).

62. Petter, *supra* note 47; Brodie, *supra* note 60 at 39; McIvor, *supra* note 50 at 198–99. See also analyses of corporate *Charter* litigation: Andrew Petter, "The Politics of the Charter" (1986) 8 Supreme Court L Rev 473 at 490–93; C Tollefson, "Corporate Constitutional Rights and the Supreme Court of Canada" (1993) 19 Queen's LJ 309.

63. Roach, *supra* note 49.

64. Diana Majury, "The Charter, Equality Rights, and Women: Equivocation and Celebration" (2002) 40 Osgoode Hall LJ 297 at para 62–70.

65. *R v Stinchcombe,* [1991] 3 SCR 326.

66. Edward Greenspan & Michael Lavy, "Charter Guarantees to Those Charged with a Criminal Offence—Section 11" in Ryder Gillilard, ed, *The Charter at Thirty* (Toronto: Canada Law Book, 2012); Honourable Marc Rosenberg, "Twenty-five Years Later: The Impact of the Canadian Charter of Rights and Freedoms on the Criminal Law" in B Adell, ed, *The Canadian Charter of Rights and Freedoms after Twenty-five Years* (LexisNexis, 2009) 233.

67. In *Askov,* the court outlined factors to be considered in determining whether a delay is unreasonable, including its length, reasons for the delay, and prejudice to the accused. The court recognized that delay may have very serious implications, causing much anxiety to the accused as well as restrictions on liberty due to pretrial bail conditions. The decision in *R v Morin,* [1992] 1 SCR 771, provided further clarification on assessment of delay.

68. Alan Young, "Adversarial Justice and the *Charter of Rights*: Stunting the Growth of the 'Living Tree" (1997) 39 Crim LQ 362 at 373.

69. *Ibid.*

Chapter 7
Administrative Law

Learning Objectives

After reading this chapter, you should be able to:

■ Name and explain four main principles of administrative law.

■ Explain the content of the duty of fairness.

■ Explain two main avenues of oversight of administrative decision making.

■ Name and describe two standards of judicial review.

■ Name five remedies that can be ordered on judicial review.

Chapter Outline

Introduction

The state exercises its functions through a multiplicity of departments, agencies, boards, commissions, and tribunals. (For the purposes of discussion in this chapter, we will use the term "government agency" to refer to all of these institutions.) These various state institutions are parts of the executive branch, established, appointed, and paid by the executive. They perform a variety of functions, including making decisions on various applications, providing advice, regulating various subject matters, setting and monitoring standards, resolving disputes, and so on. Importantly, in the course of their activities, they make decisions that impact many vital aspects of our lives. For example, all of the following involve administrative decision making: deciding on an application for social assistance or employment insurance; resolving a dispute between a landlord and a tenant before a specialized tribunal; resolving a complaint of discrimination under a provincial human rights code; deciding on a Canadian citizenship application; issuing or refusing to issue a license or a permit; and responding to an access to information request.

It is important to ensure that administrative agencies work expediently and efficiently. Further, given the significant impact that their decisions may have on our lives, they must be subject to certain standards and scrutiny. Administrative law serves these two purposes: it helps promote efficiency in government work and also ensures its fairness.[1] It sets out how administrative decision makers are to make their decisions and allows affected individuals to challenge those decisions. The underlying consideration is that parties who are affected by the government agency's decision must be treated fairly. Administrative law helps us determine what is fair in a given context, and also provides for a number of remedies if a government agency failed to comply with the standards of fairness. Or, as some authors put it, "[t]he goal of administrative law is to ensure the rule of law by providing to those subject to state authority with protection against the unfair, arbitrary or invalid exercise of that authority."[2] See Box 7.1 for an example of an abuse of power against an individual.

This chapter is divided into five sections. Section 1 explains the main features of administrative decision making and principles of administrative law. Section 2 discusses the content of the duty to act fairly. Section 3 reviews the main elements of fair procedure before tribunals. Section 4 explains avenues for review of administrative decisions, and section 5 discusses remedies available.

Box 7.1

Administrative Agencies and Abuse of Power: *Roncarelli v Duplessis*, [1959] SCR 121

To illustrate issues discussed in this chapter, it is useful to start with the following example. Frank Roncarelli operated a restaurant in Montreal. He was a Jehovah's Witness and on many occasions posted bail for other Jehovah's Witnesses who were imprisoned for distributing religious pamphlets in violation of a municipal bylaw. At the time, Quebec authorities considered activities of Jehovah's Witnesses harmful and imposed various restrictions on them. The premier of Quebec, Maurice Duplessis, publicly warned Roncarelli to stop posting bail. When the latter did not stop, Duplessis ordered the Quebec Liquor Commission to cancel Roncarelli's liquor licence. This forced Roncarelli to close the restaurant. Do you see anything problematic in the actions of Duplessis?

In order to answer this question, we need to consider the following:

■ What is the proper process for cancelling a liquor licence, and which government agency or official has the power to make such a decision? Under *An Act Respecting Alcoholic Liquor*, such decisions are to be made by the Quebec Liquor Commission. Premier Duplessis did not have the authority to order the Commission to cancel Roncarelli's liquor licence.

■ What are the prescribed grounds on which a liquor licence can be cancelled? Of course, being a Jehovah's Witness and posting bail for fellow Jehovah's Witnesses was not a valid reason to cancel a licence.

Roncarelli sued Duplessis for damages and the Supreme Court, not surprisingly, found Duplessis' order invalid and upheld the award of damages. It was clear that Premier Duplessis abused his power in order to punish Roncarelli for his activities.

As you can see from this example, actions of public authorities can have a profound impact on individuals. In some circumstances, this power may be abused and, hence, it is necessary to protect citizens against such abuse using safeguards such as the principle of the rule of law discussed in Chapters 1 and 3. In this chapter, we will familiarize ourselves with the other safeguard—administrative law. Administrative law sets the limits of administrative authorities' powers and provides for mechanisms to check and remedy situations where the power is exercised improperly. In connection with the overarching themes of this book (liberty, justice, and limited government), administrative law can be viewed as one of the mechanisms to implement the principles of justice and limited government.

1. ADMINISTRATIVE AGENCIES AND DECISION MAKING: AN OVERVIEW

1.1 Administrative Agencies

Among the variety of federal and provincial agencies, some investigate and advise on various matters; others monitor and regulate certain types of activities; and yet others resolve disputes between individuals or between individuals and government or hear appeals on certain decisions.[3] Some agencies combine several functions, including advisory, investigative, and policy making (see Tables 7.1 and 7.2 for examples). Administrative tribunals occupy a particular place within the system of administrative agencies and much of administrative law is dedicated to tribunal procedure and decision making. Thus, they will be discussed separately in greater detail in section 3.

Administrative agencies do not have inherent powers. The scope of their authority is prescribed by legislation, and agencies must not overstep these prescribed boundaries. Legislation may also set out the decision making procedure that is to be followed by a given agency. In addition, regulations, rules, and guidelines of a particular agency may provide further details.

It is important to keep in mind that each administrative agency is unique. Therefore, its specific powers and decision making procedure will differ from other agencies. While this chapter will provide an overview of the general principles of fairness and most common procedural designs of administrative decision making, no two agencies work in exactly the same way. Thus, if you want to understand the specific procedure of a given agency, you need to examine its enabling statute and other relevant documents.

Table 7.1 Examples of Administrative Agencies, Boards, and Tribunals in British Columbia

Board/Tribunal	Enabling Legislation	Description
BC Human Rights Tribunal	*BC Human Rights Code*, RSBC 1996, c 210	Administrative tribunal that adjudicates complaints of discrimination under the *BC Human Rights Code*
BC Oil and Gas Commission	*Oil and Gas Activities Act*, SBC 2008, c 36	Regulatory agency that oversees oil and gas exploration
BC Review Board	*Criminal Code*, RSC 1985, c C-46	Administrative tribunal that makes decisions regarding custody and conditions of release of persons found to be not criminally responsible
British Columbia Securities Commission	*Securities Act*, RSBC 1996, c 418	Independent government agency responsible for regulating securities trading in BC

Board/Tribunal	Enabling Legislation	Description
British Columbia Utilities Commission	*Utilities Commission Act*, RSBC 1996, c 473	Independent regulatory agency that oversees provision of energy services at fair rates
Building Code Appeal Board	*Local Government Act*, RSBC 1996, c 323	Administrative tribunal that adjudicates disputes regarding application of the BC *Building Code*
Community Care and Assisted Living Appeal Board	*Community Care and Assisted Living Act*, SBC 2002, c 75	Administrative tribunal that hears appeals regarding licensing, registration, and certification of community care and assisted living facilities
Employment Standards Tribunal of BC	*Employment Standards Act*, RSBC 1996, c 113	Administrative tribunal that hears appeals on decisions regarding employment standards
Environmental Appeal Board	*Environmental Management Act*, SBC 2003, c 53	Administrative tribunal that hears appeals on decisions made by government officials on various environmental issues
BC Farm Industry Review Board	*Natural Products Marketing (BC) Act*, RSBC 1996, c 330; *Agricultural Produce Grading Act*, RSBC 1996, c 11; *Prevention of Cruelty to Animals Act*, RSBC 1996, c 372; *Farm Practices Protection (Right to Farm) Act*, RSBC 1996, c 131	Administrative tribunal that hears appeals regarding agricultural grading licences, animal custody decisions, and decisions of commodity boards; it also hears complaints from persons aggrieved by odour, noise, dust, or other disturbances arising from agriculture or certain aquaculture operations
Financial Institutions Commission	*Financial Institutions Act*, RSBC 1996, c 141	Government agency responsible for administering nine statutes that regulate the pension, financial services, and real estate sectors in British Columbia
Financial Services Tribunal	*Financial Institutions Act*, RSBC 1996, c 141	Administrative tribunal that hears appeals on decisions made by the Insurance Council of British Columbia, the Real Estate Council of British Columbia, the Superintendent of Real Estate, the Superintendent of Pensions, and the Registrar of Mortgage Brokers

(continued)

Table 7.1 *(continued)*

Board/Tribunal	Enabling Legislation	Description
Forest Appeals Commission	*Forest Practices Code of British Columbia Act,* RSBC 1996, c 159; *Forest and Range Practices Act,* SBC 2002, c 69	Administrative tribunal that hears appeals on decisions made by government agencies regarding the use and management of forest and range resources
Forest Practices Board	*Forest Practices Code of British Columbia Act,* RSBC 1996, c 159; *Forest and Range Practices Act,* SBC 2002, c 69	Independent agency, at arm's length from the government, that audits government and industry forestry practices and deals with complaints from the public regarding forest practices and government enforcement
Health Professional Review Board	*Health Professions Act,* RSBC 1996, c 183	Administrative tribunal that reviews decisions made by the self-governing colleges of designated health professions regarding investigation and disposition of complaints against their members
Hospital Appeal Board	*Hospital Act,* RSBC 1996, c 200	Administrative tribunal that hears appeals on decisions made by hospital boards
Industry Training Appeal Board	*Industry Training Authority Act,* SBC 2003, c 34	Administrative tribunal that hears appeals on decisions regarding industry training credentials
Labour Relations Board of British Columbia	*Labour Relations Code,* RSBC 1996, c 244	Administrative tribunal that mediates and settles employment and labour relations disputes in unionized workplaces
Mental Health Review Board	*Mental Health Act,* RSBC 1996, c 288	Administrative tribunal that decides on involuntary committal of persons to mental health facilities in BC
Oil and Gas Appeal Tribunal	*Oil and Gas Activities Act,* SBC 2008, c 36	Administrative tribunal that hears appeals on decisions by the Oil and Gas Commission
Passenger Transportation Board	*Passenger Transportation Act,* SBC 2004, c 39	Administrative tribunal that decides on applications relating to the licensing of passenger vehicles (e.g., taxis) and inter-city buses in BC and hears appeals regarding administrative penalties

Board/Tribunal	Enabling Legislation	Description
Property Assessment Appeal Board	*Assessment Act*, RSBC 1996, c 20	Administrative tribunal that hears appeals on property assessments
Real Estate Council of BC	*Real Estate Services Act*, SBC 2004, c 42	Regulatory agency responsible for licensing of real estate brokers and overseeing their conduct
Safety Standards Appeal Board	*Safety Standards Act*, SBC 2003, c 39	Administrative tribunal that hears appeals on decisions of safety officers and managers
Surface Rights Board of British Columbia	*Petroleum and Natural Gas Act*, RSBC 1996, c 361	Administrative tribunal that helps resolve conflicts between holders of surface rights and companies or individuals that seek to explore subsurface resources (e.g., oil, minerals)
Workers' Compensation Appeal Tribunal	*Workers Compensation Act*, RSBC 1996, c 492	Administrative tribunal that hears appeals on decisions concerning compensation, assessments, and occupational health and safety

Note: This table contains information provided at <http://www.adminlawbc.ca/tribunals>, a website developed by the Justice Education Society and the British Columbia Council of Administrative Tribunals (BCCAT), with support from the Administrative Justice Office, Justice Services Branch, BC Ministry of the Justice.

Table 7.2 Examples of Federal Agencies, Boards, and Tribunals

Board/Tribunal/ Agency	Enabling Legislation	Description
Canada Industrial Relations Board	*Canada Labour Code*, RSC 1985, c L-2	Administrative tribunal that deals with labour relations issues
Canadian Cultural Property Export Review Board	*Cultural Property Export and Import Act*, RSC 1985, c C-5	Administrative tribunal that certifies cultural property for income tax purposes and reviews appeals of refused export permits
Military Grievances External Review Committee	*National Defence Act*, RSC 1985, c N-5	Quasi-judicial body that conducts independent external review of military grievances
Canadian Grain Commission	*Canada Grain Act*, RSC 1985, c G-10	Agency responsible for regulating grain handling industry

(continued)

Table 7.2 *(continued)*

Board/Tribunal/ Agency	Enabling Legislation	Description
Canadian Human Rights Commission	*Canadian Human Rights Act*, RSC 1985, c H-6	Independent body that promotes human rights and reviews complaints of discrimination
Canadian Human Rights Tribunal	*Canadian Human Rights Act*, RSC 1985, c H-6	Administrative tribunal that adjudicates complaints of discrimination under the *Canadian Human Rights Act*
Canadian International Trade Tribunal	*Canadian International Trade Tribunal Act*, RSC 1985, c 47	Administrative tribunal that hears appeals from decisions under the *Customs Act*, the *Special Import Measures Act*, and the *Excise Tax Act*
Copyright Board of Canada	*Copyright Act*, RSC 1985, c C-42	Regulatory body that deals with issues of copyright, royalties, licensing, and related issues
Immigration and Refugee Board of Canada	*Immigration and Refugee Protection Act*, SC 2002, c 27	Administrative tribunal that adjudicates various immigration and refugee matters
National Energy Board	*National Energy Board Act*, RSC 1985, c N-7	Independent agency that regulates international and interprovincial aspects of the oil, gas, and electric utility industries
Office of the Information Commissioner	*Access to Information Act*, RSC 1985, c A-1	Independent agency that investigates complaints about federal institutions' handling of access to information requests
Office of the Privacy Commissioner of Canada	*Privacy Act*, RSC 1985, c P-21	Independent agency that promotes awareness of privacy issues and deals with complaints regarding privacy and information handling practices
Parole Board of Canada	*Corrections and Conditional Release Act*, SC 1992, c 20	Administrative tribunal that decides on grant, denial, or cancellation of day or full parole
Patented Medicine Prices Review Board	*Patent Act*, RSC 1985, c P-4	Independent quasi-judicial body that reviews prices of patented drugs in Canada
Transportation Appeal Tribunal of Canada	*Transportation Appeal Tribunal of Canada Act*, SC 2001, c 29	Quasi-judicial body that holds review and appeal hearings originating from the aviation, marine, rail, and bridges and tunnels sectors
Veterans Review and Appeal Board	*Veterans Review and Appeal Board Act*, SC 1995, c 18	Administrative tribunal that hears appeals on decisions made by Veterans Affairs Canada

1.2 Administrative Decision Making

There are two key aspects to administrative decision making: substantive (What is the scope of the decision maker's authority?) and procedural (What decision making procedure is to be followed?). The content of both substantive and procedural aspects is usually found in **enabling legislation**—that is, a statute that mandates the creation of an agency in question. Thus, administrative law does not come from one single statute, but is contained in a variety of federal and provincial statutes that establish agencies, boards, departments, and tribunals. In addition, common law rules are applicable to the determination of fairness of procedure.

1.2.1 Powers of the Decision Maker

The powers of decision makers are outlined in enabling legislation. In some cases, legislation will specifically prescribe action to be taken by an official in specific circumstances. However, it is also recognized that legislation cannot foresee all circumstances that may come before decision makers. Thus, legislation usually accords them discretion in how they perform their functions—that is, allows decision makers the exercise of "a choice from among options."[4] The availability of discretion is usually indicated by the word "may" in applicable legislative provisions. For example, the *Employment Insurance Act* provides that the Canada Employment Insurance Commission "may at any time require a claimant to provide additional information about their claim for benefits."[5] This denotes the Commission's discretion to ask or not to ask the applicant for additional information, depending on the circumstances of the case.

The exercise of discretion is one of the key issues in administrative law: how are we to ensure that it is exercised properly? Discretion allows for flexibility, but it does not allow decision makers to do anything they like. Discretion must be exercised within the parameters prescribed by legislation and consistently with the objectives of that legislation.

Administrative agencies usually develop various policies and guidelines to help their decision makers in the exercise of discretion. Such policies and guidelines are not binding, but they are to be kept in mind by decision makers. Policies and guidelines seek to strike a balance that does not fetter the discretion of individual decision makers, while helping promote a consistent approach to resolution of cases within the agency.

1.2.2 Decision Making Procedure

The decision making procedure may be prescribed in enabling legislation, or an agency may be given the power by a statute to devise the procedure on its own. Procedure includes such things as whether and how parties are given notice of an impending hearing or decision, whether and how relevant information is disclosed to the parties, whether parties have an opportunity to give evidence and cross-examine witnesses, whether a party has a right to be represented by counsel, whether a decision maker has to hold an oral hearing or provide written reasons, and so on.

Some provinces (e.g., British Columbia, Alberta, Ontario, Quebec) enacted general statutes that apply to most provincial tribunals and establish minimum procedural rules for them. For example, Alberta's *Administrative Procedures and Jurisdiction Act* and Ontario's *Statutory Powers Procedure Act* prescribe minimum requirements with respect to notice to the parties, disclosure, the right to make representations, and the duty to provide written reasons. British Columbia's *Administrative Tribunals Act* sets out basic requirements for the operation of provincial tribunals, but it also gives them broad powers to control their own proceedings, including prescribing rules of notice and disclosure, extensions, adjournments, and other issues.

The choice of procedural design for a given agency depends on the context: subject matter, interests at stake, volume of cases, and nature of the parties appearing before the agency. Procedure is devised with these multiple considerations in mind, seeking to balance efficiency, cost, thoroughness, and fairness.

1.3 Key Principles of Administrative Law

Given that administrative decisions can significantly affect individual interests, it is important that they be made fairly and that there are avenues for oversight of administrative decision making. These ideas are reflected in key principles of administrative law:

- Decision makers must act within the limits of the authority granted to them by enabling legislation;
- Decision makers must exercise discretion reasonably;
- Decision makers must follow a fair procedure; and
- Courts have the power to review administrative decision making and order remedies.[6]

2. FAIRNESS OF DECISION MAKING

One of the central questions in administrative law is the duty of decision makers to follow a fair procedure. A fair decision is one that has been made in accordance with a fair process. Procedural fairness includes two key components:

- A right to be heard; and
- A right to have a decision made by an independent and impartial decision maker.

2.1 The Right to be Heard

At a minimum, the right to be heard includes that an individual is notified of the case to be met and is given an opportunity to respond.[7] At the heart of these requirements is the idea of participatory rights of the person affected. As expressed by the Supreme Court:

> ... the purpose of the participatory rights contained within the duty of procedural fairness is to ensure that administrative decisions are made using a fair and open procedure, appropriate to the decision being made and its statutory, institutional, and social context, with an opportunity for those affected by the decision to put forward their views and evidence fully and have them considered by the decision maker.[8]

This allows a concerned individual to present information that might influence the agency's decision, thereby assisting the decision maker to make an informed and rational decision.[9] However, the opportunity to be heard does not mean that an individual receives the outcome she wishes for; it merely allows the individual's input into the process.

What does a fair procedure look like? For example, does it require holding an oral hearing, or is it sufficient for an individual to make written submissions? Should parties have a right to counsel? Should they have a right to call and cross-examine witnesses? There is no one universal format of what is fair; rather, it is determined contextually. In some cases, nothing less than an oral hearing is required, while in others a written submission may be enough. The determination of a duty of fairness in a specific context requires balancing the rights of affected individuals, on the one hand, and considerations of cost, efficiency, volume, and complexity of cases, on the other. Depending on the context, the duty of fairness may give rise to such entitlements as the right to counsel, an oral hearing, disclosure, the right to cross-examination, and more. For example, an oral hearing is the highest form of fairness and would usually be necessary in cases where the most important interests of the individual are affected. A right to an oral hearing may often also create a related entitlement to legal representation to ensure that a person is effectively able to present his case.

The Supreme Court decision in *Baker v Canada* provided some guidance on the factors to be considered in determining what is fair in a given context:

- The nature of the decision;
- The nature of the statutory scheme;
- The importance of the decision to the individual affected;
- The legitimate expectations of the parties; and
- The procedure chosen by the agency.[10]

2.1.1 The Nature of the Decision

The nature of a decision can be classified in various ways:

- *Political versus administrative decisions.* While administrative decisions are subject to the duty of fairness, political or legislative decisions are not.[11]

- *Decisions made in the course of regular activity versus decisions made in the circumstances of an emergency.* Decision making in emergency circumstances may not have to comply with fairness requirements. For example, an emergency decision to transfer an inmate who posed a persistent and serious risk to others (following a knife fight), without giving him an opportunity to obtain legal counsel and without providing him with a report containing a detailed outline of the incident, does not breach the duty of fairness.[12] Where an emergency decision is made, there is often a right to a hearing at a later date which allows for follow-up on the emergency order.[13]

- *Whether an agency has only the power to investigate and report or the power to decide.* If an agency has the authority merely to investigate a certain matter and report on it, it is subject to the more limited duty of fairness, unless the report may adversely impact some individuals. In the latter case, concerned individuals should be allowed to make representations to the investigator.

- *Whether an agency decides on a dispute between two parties or whether a decision is made entirely on the material submitted by the sole interested party.* (For example, in a case of application for benefits, there is only information from the applicant outlining eligibility for the benefit.) Where a decision is made on the basis of the material submitted solely by the interested party and there is an opportunity to reapply, the scope of the duty of fairness is more limited (e.g., there is no need to notify the individual before an adverse decision is made).[14] If a decision is made about a dispute between two parties, the decision maker must allow both parties an equal right to present their case.

- *Whether the process and functions of the decision making body resemble judicial decision making.* The closer the resemblance, the closer the procedural protections should be to a trial model.[15]

2.1.2 The Nature of the Statutory Scheme

This factor considers the following issues: whether enabling legislation prescribes a particular procedure; the nature of the powers assigned to the decision maker (e.g., adjudication of disputes, policy development); and whether there is a possibility of an appeal. For example, if there is no appeal, greater procedural protections may be required.[16]

2.1.3 The Importance of the Decision to the Individual Affected

Individuals may have different interests at stake, some of them more compelling, others less so. The more compelling the interest is, the higher the degree of procedural fairness. For example, if an individual may be deprived of liberty or if an individual's livelihood is at stake, an oral hearing is required.[17]

2.1.4 Legitimate Expectations of the Parties

Decision makers must apply the same procedure consistently to all cases. This creates a **legitimate expectation** that an agency or tribunal would follow the same procedure as it did in the past.[18]

2.1.5 Procedure Chosen by the Agency

Some government agencies are given latitude in designing their own procedure. This allows them to find the best way to deal with cases in an efficient, speedy, and fair manner. It is therefore necessary to consider whether the procedure properly balances the rights of individuals concerned and other considerations related to efficiency, cost, and speed. Courts usually respect the agency's choice of procedure and would not interfere, especially if enabling legislation allows the agency such discretion and if the decision maker possesses specialized expertise.

2.2 The Right to Have a Decision Made by an Independent and Impartial Decision Maker

An impartial decision maker is disinterested in the outcome and does not favour either of the parties. Impartiality requires that a decision maker approach the case with independence and an open mind.[19] *Independence* means freedom from influence by others and freedom to make decisions without interference.[20] It is guaranteed by such factors as security of tenure of decision makers, financial security, and an agency's structural and other independence from the parties.

Impartiality is violated when a decision maker appears to be biased. Bias is "an attitude of mind unique to an individual"[21] that favours one side. Bias may stem from individual or institutional factors. Individual bias may come, for example, from a decision maker's having a financial or personal interest in the outcome. The expression of bias may be found in, for instance, the decision maker's comments or opinions, her persistent interventions in a hearing that favour one party, or her personal connections or past business dealings with any of the parties appearing before her.[22]

Institutional bias may stem from the structure or operation of a decision making body rather than from words, actions, or relationships of an individual decision maker. For example, if an agency does not possess sufficient independence from the parties and does not permit decision makers to make decisions freely, this may give rise to concerns over institutional bias.

In administrative law, the test is not whether the decision maker was actually biased or whether the bias resulted in prejudice to one party, but whether there is a reasonable apprehension of bias: would a reasonable and well informed observer conclude that the decision maker was likely biased? If reasonable apprehension of bias is established, a resulting decision cannot be considered fair and will be overturned.

3. ADMINISTRATIVE TRIBUNALS AND FAIR PROCESS

A variety of provincial and federal tribunals usually either hear appeals on administrative decisions or adjudicate disputes between private parties or between individuals/corporations and the government. Unlike judges, tribunal members do not have to be lawyers, and they come from a variety of backgrounds. In fact, some enabling legislation specifically mandates that they be laypersons with particular expertise in areas that are being adjudicated. Since a large section of administrative law is dedicated to tribunals, we are going to review them in some detail.

Of course, tribunals are subject to the same principles of administrative law as other administrative agencies. However, their decision making procedure is often more elaborate. In fact, tribunals are often characterized by their similarities to and differences from courts. For example, like courts, tribunals can conduct a hearing and have special rules related to notice, disclosure, evidence, questioning of witnesses, adjournments, and submissions by the parties.

Tribunals usually have the power to determine their own procedure and, thus, some of them may have more formal, adversarial, and courtlike processes, while others may be more informal and inquisitorial. As you recall from Chapter 4, in an adversarial system, the burden is on the parties to collect and present evidence, while the decision maker acts as an impartial arbiter. In an inquisitorial model, the decision maker is involved in investigating and questioning witnesses, as well as controlling the proceedings. Overall, tribunals are characterized by more flexible procedure and more permissive rules of evidence than courts. This flexibility is necessary in order to address the peculiarities of cases and claimants dealt with by tribunals. For example, they often deal with unrepresented applicants, very high volumes of claims, and issues that involve access to a benefit or entitlement. Due to this, some commentators have argued that the inquisitorial/adversarial dichotomy is inadequate to describe the work of tribunals. They characterize tribunal work as "active adjudication" that lies between the inquisitorial and adversarial models.[23] While there is no single definition of *active adjudication*, it can include the tribunal focusing issues for determination, adapting to the needs of the parties to ensure their meaningful access and participation, helping parties elicit evidence, and testing the evidence of the parties at the hearing.[24] These functions allow tribunals to assist parties, especially unrepresented ones, and participate in the exploration of issues at stake, but without raising concerns of bias. Further, tribunals differ from courts in that they are not bound by the principles of precedent and stare decisis. Although tribunal members can take note of past decisions on similar issues, they are not required to follow them.

Regardless of the specific adjudication model followed, all tribunal procedures usually include the following key elements:

■ *Notice*. A tribunal needs to give notice to the parties that a decision affecting their interests may be made. A notice must explain the nature of issues involved and give sufficient time to the parties to prepare for the hearing. For example, if one party complained to a human rights tribunal about alleged discrimination, a notice must be given to the other party about such a complaint and that party should be given an opportunity to respond to the complaint.

■ *Disclosure*. Disclosure allows a party to be informed of all relevant information in the possession of the other party. The rules and scope of disclosure in administrative processes are not the same as for civil and criminal process. While in some circumstances extensive disclosure may be necessary, in others a summary of the material may suffice.

■ *Participatory rights*. These rights include the right to be present at the hearing, the right to legal representation, the right to an interpreter, the right to present evidence, and the right to cross-examine witnesses.

Where an oral hearing is held, the parties have the right to be present when evidence is presented and submissions are made to the tribunal.[25] If no oral hearing is held, the party does not have a right to be present during the review of written materials, but it must be shown the evidence considered and must be given a chance to respond.[26]

Section 10 of the *Charter* guarantees a right to counsel but only in limited circumstances such as arrest or detention. Nevertheless, enabling legislation for various tribunals often provides for the right to counsel for persons appearing before them. Counsel before tribunals do not have to be lawyers, and can include other individuals such as union members, consultants, or NGO representatives. For example, individuals who appear before the federal Immigration and Refugee Board (IRB, described in Box 7.2) can be represented by a lawyer, an immigration consultant, or anyone authorized by the claimant (e.g., an NGO worker as long as the latter is not acting for a fee). Allowing representation by both lawyers and nonlawyers is considered to better fit the nature of tribunal work as well as the needs of individuals appearing before it.[27] Given that the majority of individuals appearing before the IRB are immigrants, involvement of nonlawyers may be of great help as they often speak the claimant's language and are familiar with their culture. Representation by nonlawyers also serves the objective of "establishing an informal, accessible (in financial, cultural, and linguistic terms), and expeditious process, peculiar to administrative tribunals."[28]

Section 14 of the *Charter* guarantees the right to an interpreter in "any proceeding" to a person who does not understand or speak the language in which the proceeding is conducted. For example, the IRB provides interpreters for individuals appearing before it.

The right to present evidence includes an opportunity to submit relevant documentation to a tribunal and call witnesses. The rules of evidence in an administrative context are not the same as in civil or criminal trials and are usually less restrictive. For example, hearsay evidence may be admitted as long as it is reliable and relevant.

- *Decision and reasons.* At least two major requirements must be satisfied: (1) a tribunal member who heard the case must decide it; and (2) that tribunal member must give reasons for the decision. A person who participates in the decision should not be absent from the hearing or any part or it. The decision must be made on the evidence presented at the hearing and not on any extraneous information. A decision can be made orally or in writing, although some statutes may require a decision to be made in writing. The reasons for a decision must be communicated to the parties and must be sufficiently detailed in order to explain why a particular conclusion has been reached.

Box 7.2

Example of an Administrative Tribunal: The Immigration and Refugee Board

The Immigration and Refugee Board (IRB) is a federal administrative tribunal that deals with various immigration and refugee issues. For example, the IRB hears appeals on refusal of applications by Canadians to sponsor their family members for immigration to Canada; determines whether a noncitizen should be removed from Canada; and decides whether a person fleeing danger in their country of origin should be given refugee protection in Canada.

The powers and the structure of the IRB are set out in federal legislation—the *Immigration and Refugee Protection Act (IRPA)*—which is the enabling legislation for the IRB. The IRB comprises four divisions: the Immigration Division, the Immigration Appeal Division, the Refugee Protection Division, and the Refugee Appeal Division. Each division deals with a particular set of matters, which influence the requirements of fairness and its corresponding procedure.

Appointment of IRB members

The *IRPA* provides that members of the Immigration Appeal Division and of the Refugee Appeal Division be appointed by the governor in council for a term of up to seven years.[29] Members of the other two divisions are appointed in accordance with the *Public Service Employment Act*—that is, they are public servants. As discussed earlier, the appointment process and security of tenure are among the factors relevant to independence of decision makers. Governor in council appointees can be considered to

(continued)

Box 7.2 *(continued)*

possess a greater degree of independence and impartiality than civil servants who are expected to follow the direction of the government.

Adjudicative model and procedure

The *IRPA* sets out some minimum requirements for the IRB procedure but also leaves the tribunal significant discretion to design its other aspects. For example, the *IRPA* outlines the following minimum requirements: an individual appearing before the IRB has a right to be represented by counsel;[30] the decision maker must give reasons for a decision;[31] and the divisions are not bound by any legal or technical rules of evidence. At the same time, the IRB also has the authority to develop procedural rules, guidelines, policies, and instructions to help guide decision makers' work. Each division is to deal with cases "as informally and quickly as the circumstances and the considerations of fairness and natural justice permit."[32] Thus, the IRB needs to balance multiple objectives: fairness, efficiency, and informality. In fact, as we will see below, there are some differences in procedure among the four divisions. To illustrate the point, let us contrast the procedures of three IRB divisions.

Refugee Protection Division (RPD)

The RPD is tasked with determining whether a person's claim for refugee protection in Canada should be granted. A person can be granted refugee protection if he fears persecution, risk to life, or risk of torture in his country of origin. In this context, the main objective is to find out what has happened to the claimant in the past, what her fears are, and whether her country of origin is able to protect the claimant.

The design of the refugee determination process reflects the peculiarities of refugee claimants' situations. First, refugee claimants constitute a vulnerable population: many of them lived through torture, persecution, and displacement; they are new to Canada and may be uncertain about their rights and the refugee determination process; and

they often do not speak English or French. Second, documentary evidence to support their claims is often unavailable or nonexistent. For example, if a refugee claimant's state has illegally detained or tortured her, there will be no record of such illegal behaviour and the occurrence cannot be proven documentarily. In other cases, documentary evidence may be destroyed as a result of war or other factors. Thus, the claimant's testimony becomes the main source of information and must be found credible by the decision maker in order to be accepted. Most importantly, much is at stake for the claimant: if her claim is denied, she may be sent back to a potentially life-threatening situation. The compelling nature of the claimant's interests along with the other above mentioned considerations favours a high level of duty of fairness. In fact, an oral hearing is required.

But what kind of a hearing should it be: inquisitorial or adversarial? The nonadversarial approach has been adopted for the following reasons. First, claimants are often unrepresented and hence the inquisitorial process may be less intimidating and may allow the tribunal to assist the claimant.[33] Second, no one is opposing the applicant's claim because both the Canadian state and the claimant are guided by the shared goal of protection of human rights.[34] Third, given the large volume of claims, an inquisitorial process that gives decision makers active control over the proceeding can be more efficient.[35]

Refugee Appeal Division (RAD)

The RAD hears appeals on RPD decisions. Unlike the RPD, the RAD normally would not hold a hearing and would decide an appeal on the basis of documentation, written arguments of the parties, and the record from the RPD. The absence of a mandatory oral hearing may be explained by the statutory scheme: a person has already had an oral hearing at the first stage of refugee determination at the RPD.

Immigration Division

The Immigration Division decides whether a person should be held in immigration detention and/or removed from Canada. There is no universal requirement to hold a hearing, but the *IRPA* specifies that the division "must, where practicable, hold a hearing."[36] The nature of the cases before the Immigration Division is different from those before the RPD. When an individual is ordered detained or deported, this means that state authorities consider him dangerous or suspicious. Thus, we have two competing interests at stake: the interest of protecting Canada and Canadians, versus the interest of the individual concerned to be released and/or to remain in Canada. This is reflected in the nature of hearings, which follow an adversarial rather than an inquisitorial model. The individual is, of course, accorded various procedural rights such as notice, disclosure, the right to call witnesses and cross-examine, and the right to counsel.

The example of the IRB illustrates that the determination of what constitutes a fair procedure depends on the context: the nature of issues, interests at stake, volume of claims, and other factors. Even within the same tribunal, different procedures may be used in order to respond to the different nature of cases that various tribunal divisions hear.

4. OVERSIGHT OF ADMINISTRATIVE DECISION MAKING: APPEAL AND JUDICIAL REVIEW

The oversight of executive decision making can be carried out through a number of channels.[37] First, oversight may be conducted internally, within an agency: a higher official within the same agency may be able to review and reconsider a case. Second, the decisions of the top of the executive are subject to parliamentary oversight through such mechanisms as the no confidence vote, daily question period in the House of Commons, and others (recall Chapter 3). Third, the oversight may be carried out by courts through judicial and constitutional review, appeal, and action for damages. **Judicial review** examines whether a given administrative decision was authorized by a statute. **Constitutional review** examines whether actions and decisions of the executive are compliant with the *Constitution* (recall Chapter 6). An appeal allows courts to reconsider an administrative decision. Action for damages allows aggrieved parties to sue for compensation for the harm suffered as a result of an improper administrative decision (recall *Roncarelli v Duplessis*, Box 7.1).[38] In this section, we will focus on judicial review and appeal.

Among the most common grounds on which administrative decisions can be challenged are: decision maker acted outside her jurisdiction; decision maker improperly exercised (or failed to exercise) discretion; decision maker misinterpreted the law; decision maker did not follow a fair procedure; and decision maker acted in bad faith.[39]

The avenues of review that exist in a given case are determined by enabling legislation. In some cases, a person may have a right to an administrative appeal and then that appeal decision may be further judicially reviewed. In other cases, only judicial review may be available.

4.1 Appeal

An appeal may be made within an administrative body itself (to a higher decision making authority) or to an administrative tribunal or to a court; which one it is depends on the enabling statute. The scope of appeal also depends on the statute. Some statutes may permit a complete rehearing, in which case the appellate authority can decide the case anew. Parties may be allowed to provide additional evidence on appeal but usually only if the evidence could not have been obtained and presented earlier, when the first-instance decision was made. Other types of appeals may be heard exclusively on the record and consider only narrow issues of law. The record includes the administrative decision itself, the reasons for the decision, and submitted documentary evidence, as well as a transcript of a hearing (if one is available).

An appellate body usually has the power to substitute the reviewed decision with its own or to send the case back for redetermination.

4.2 Judicial Review

Judicial review is conducted by courts, specifically provincial superior courts and the Federal Court. Which court has the power to review an agency's decision depends on the statutory scheme. For example, decisions of federal tribunals and boards are reviewed by the Federal Court, while decisions of provincial tribunals are reviewed by superior courts. In some cases, parties may have an automatic right to judicial review, while in others they may require a leave to appeal.

4.2.1 Scope of Judicial Review

The scope of judicial review is narrower than an administrative appeal. The court does not rehear the case anew, but rather determines whether the original decision maker made a reviewable error. This error can be with respect to facts, law, or mixed law and facts. Usually only evidence that was before the administrative decision maker can be considered and no new evidence can be adduced.

An important consideration on judicial review is the concept of **deference**, which expresses the court's respect for the administrative agency's decision. Deference does not mean that a court will accept any and all decisions of administrative agencies without subjecting them to any scrutiny. Rather, it shows that the court will pay attention to the reasons that were or could be offered to support the agency's decision.[40] The concept of deference recognizes the special expertise of administrative decision makers and mandates courts to interfere as little as possible into the substance of those decisions. For example, decisions on credibility are accorded deference as the original decision maker is the one who has heard the witness and thus would be in the best position to assess her credibility. Questions of fact and discretion as well as issues where an agency has developed particular expertise are also usually accorded deference.

4.2.2 Standard of Review

The **standard of review** is the "degree of rigour with which a court will scrutinize an agency's decision, and the degree of error or the level of uncertainty about the reasonableness or correctness of an agency's decision that a court will tolerate in deciding whether to accept or overturn the decision."[41] Or, as others put it: "How big an error must the tribunal make before the court will get involved?"[42]

When reviewing the substance of a decision, courts employ one of two standards:[43]

- *Correctness.* According to this standard, there is only one correct answer to a given question. This approach allows no deference: the original decision maker got it either right or wrong. This standard usually applies with respect to questions of general law. For example, if the tribunal's interpretation of the law was incorrect, this is a reviewable error. A court will determine which interpretation of a given legal provision is correct.

- *Reasonableness.* This standard is concerned both with the process of articulating reasons and with the outcomes.[44] It questions whether there is a logical connection between the evidence and the agency's conclusion; whether there is sufficient justification for the decision; and whether the decision making process is transparent and intelligible. It also considers whether an agency's decision falls within the range of defensible outcomes. This standard gives some deference to the original decision maker. Questions of fact, discretion, and policy are usually judged on the standard of reasonableness.

As you can see, the standards of review correspond to the level of deference—high or low—that a court would accord in a given case. The reasonableness standard allows for some deference, but the correctness standard does not. The choice between the two standards indicates the level of intensity with which courts will review a given decision.

How are judges to decide which standard of review is to be applied to the case at hand? Similarly to the duty of fairness, the approach is contextual. Courts identified a set of factors that need to be considered in order to decide which standard of review applies to a given situation. According to the Supreme Court decision in *Dunsmuir*, the test comprises the following. First, courts are to look at previous decisions: whether the standard of review has already been determined with respect to a category of questions at hand. Second, if such a standard has not been determined in past decisions, then a court is to look at the following factors:

- The presence or absence of a privative clause (a **privative clause** restricts or prevents review of an administrative agency's decisions by courts);
- The purpose of the agency as set out in the enabling legislation;
- The nature of the question at issue: law, fact, or mixed law and fact; and
- The expertise of the agency.[45]

The above factors have to be considered as a whole and contextually; it is possible that not all of them will be relevant to every single case.[46] The following factors will point to the reasonableness standard: presence of a privative clause (it indicates that an administrative decision maker should be given greater deference and that intervention by courts should be minimized); special expertise of the decision maker; and questions of law that are within the specialized expertise of the decision maker.[47] The correctness standard would be employed in relation to the following: constitutional issues; issues of law that fall outside of the specialized expertise of the administrative decision maker; and questions of jurisdiction. See Box 7.3 for an example of how the court chose between the two standards.

Choosing between the Two Standards of Review: *Canada (Citizenship and Immigration) v Khosa*, [2009] 1 SCR 339

Sukhvir Khosa, an immigrant to Canada, was convicted of criminal negligence causing death in a street race. As a result of the conviction, removal proceedings were started against him. He appealed the removal order to the Immigration Appeal Division (IAD) of the IRB. The IAD has the discretion to grant special relief (e.g., halt a removal order) on humanitarian and compassionate grounds. In Khosa's case, however, the IAD concluded that there were insufficient humanitarian and compassionate considerations to allow him to remain in Canada. Khosa applied for judicial review of the IAD decision and the case ultimately ended up before the Supreme Court of Canada. One of the issues before the Court was the proper standard of review: should the IAD's decision be reviewed on the standard of reasonableness or correctness? The Court concluded that reasonableness was the proper standard. First, past decisions tended to review IAD decisions on the standard of reasonableness. Second, the four factors pointed toward reasonableness as well:

■ *Presence or absence of a privative clause.* There is no automatic right to appeal and judicial review

of an IAD decision is possible only if the Federal Court grants a leave. This indicates a certain degree of deference to the IAD and protection of its decisions from active judicial intervention.

■ *The purpose of the agency as set out in the enabling legislation.* The IAD deals with various appeals under the *IRPA*, including those from deportation orders. The legislation leaves it to the IAD to determine what constitutes humanitarian and compassionate considerations and whether they are sufficient in a given case to grant stay of removal.

■ *The nature of the question at issue.* The stay of removal is a discretionary privilege. The IAD makes a decision based on facts and policy considerations. In Khosa's case, the IAD conducted a hearing and heard from Khosa himself. As a rule, courts are wary to interfere in fact findings of decision makers who had firsthand opportunity to examine all evidence.

■ *The expertise of the agency.* IAD members have considerable expertise in determining appeals under the *IRPA*.

5. REMEDIES

On judicial review, courts may order a number of different remedies:

■ Quash a decision—This usually will result in the case being sent back to the original decision maker for redetermination. A court may also give directions to the decision maker to be followed on reconsideration. However, such directions do not mean that a particular result must be achieved (e.g., that an application must be decided positively).

■ Issue an order of mandamus—**Mandamus** requires an administrative authority to perform an existing duty. Most commonly, mandamus is used where an agency does not give a decision on the matter within a reasonable time. For example, in *Keybakhi v Canada*,[48] Keybakhi faced a 20-year delay in decision making on his permanent resident application and eventually sought an order of mandamus from the Federal Court. The court ordered Citizenship and Immigration Canada to make a decision within 90 days. The order of mandamus does not mean that a decision on the application must be positive, however; it only requires that a decision be made.

- Declare that a decision maker's or agency's action was contrary to the law.
- Prohibit a decision maker or agency from taking actions they are not authorized by law to take.
- Require a decision maker to follow a fair procedure.

Box 7.4 provides an example.

Box 7.4

Judicial Review of Administrative Decisions and Remedies: *Johnstone v Canada (Border Services)* [2014] FCJ No 455

Johnstone had been employed by the Canada Border Services Agency (CBSA) since 1998. Her husband also worked for the CBSA. They had two children. CBSA employees work on a rotating shift basis, meaning that they are scheduled at different start times and work on different days of the week with no predictable pattern. This made it very difficult for Johnstone to arrange for childcare. She asked the CBSA to provide her with fixed work shifts. The CBSA did offer her fixed work shifts, but only for 34 hours per week, which resulted in her being considered a part-time employee with fewer employment benefits. The CBSA argued that it had no legal duty to accommodate employees with childcare obligations.

Under the *Canadian Human Rights Act*, an individual who feels discriminated against on one of the enumerated grounds can launch a complaint to the Canadian Human Rights Commission (for more on the *Canadian Human Rights Act*, see Chapter 12). The *Act* applies to federal departments and agencies and hence would also be

applicable to the CBSA's actions. Resolution of complaints under the *Act* is an example of administrative decision making. Like other administrative decisions, they can be subject to judicial review.

Johnstone filed a complaint with the Canadian Human Rights Commission, alleging discrimination on the basis of family status contrary to the *Canadian Human Rights Act*. The Commission referred the complaint to the Human Rights Tribunal, which found in favour of Johnstone. It ordered the CBSA to cease its discriminatory practice against employees with childcare responsibilities; to develop a policy, in consultation with Johnstone, for accommodation of such requests; and to compensate Johnstone for the wages lost since the time she was transferred to part-time employment. The Tribunal also awarded Johnstone damages for pain and suffering as well as special compensation for the CBSA's willful and reckless conduct in refusing even to acknowledge the duty to accommodate employees with childcare obligations.[49]

(continued)

Box 7.4   (continued)

The Attorney General of Canada applied for judicial review of the Tribunal's decision. The Federal Court upheld the decision for the most part, but found that the Tribunal exceeded its jurisdiction when it ordered the CBSA to consult with Johnstone when developing new policies.[50] The Court found that the *Canadian Human Rights Act* did not provide that a victim may have such a role. The Court also found that there was some ambiguity in the Tribunal's calculation of the amount of lost wages and referred this issue back to the Tribunal for reconsideration.

The Attorney General appealed the Federal Court decision to the Federal Court of Appeal. The appeal was allowed in part, but the major parts of the lower court's decision were upheld.[51] The Court of Appeal found no error in the determination that the CBSA engaged in discriminatory practices or in the order for the CBSA to develop new policies of accommodation.

This case illustrates several issues discussed in this chapter. First, it provides an example of an administrative tribunal (the Canadian Human Rights Tribunal) that hears cases of alleged discrimination brought by individuals against federal agencies. Second, it demonstrates the oversight mechanism (judicial review by the Federal Court) that is available to check whether the Tribunal made correct and reasonable decisions. Third, it shows the types of errors that may warrant judicial intervention and ways to remedy them. The Court found that the Tribunal exceeded its jurisdiction when it ordered the CBSA to consult with Johnstone on new policies (hence, this order of the Tribunal will not stand). The Court also found ambiguity in the calculation of lost wages and ordered the Tribunal to reconsider the issue.

SUMMARY

Administrative agencies can have significant impact on various aspects of our lives: they make decisions on applications for benefits, issue permits and licences, adjudicate disputes, and perform a variety of other functions. Such agencies do not have inherent powers and their authority (and, in some cases decision making procedure) is determined by enabling legislation. There are multiple federal and provincial statutes that establish various agencies, tribunals, and boards. Hence, administrative law consists of a large number of such statutes as well as common law principles that help determine issues of fairness.

Administrative law seeks to achieve two objectives: facilitate efficiency of administrative decision making, and ensure that it is done fairly. The duty of fairness requires that an individual be allowed an opportunity to be heard, and that the decision be made by an independent and impartial decision maker. What amounts to a fair process is determined contextually: in some cases, notice, disclosure, an oral hearing, and a right to representation may be required, while in others a paper-based process without disclosure or notice would be sufficient.

The oversight of administrative decision making is done through two major channels: appeal and judicial review. An appeal can be made within an administrative agency itself (to a higher level decision maker) or to a tribunal or court, depending on what is provided for by the enabling legislation. Judicial review is conducted by courts. In conducting the review, courts utilize one of two standards of review (depending on the nature of the issue): reasonableness or correctness. If a court finds a reviewable error, it can order a number of remedies, including quashing a decision, requiring a decision maker to follow a proper procedure, declaring actions of a decision maker to be contrary to the law, and prohibiting a decision maker from taking unauthorized actions.

Critical Thinking Questions

1. Why is the duty of fairness important?

2. In what circumstances, in your opinion, would it be necessary to provide an applicant with an oral hearing (rather than to decide a case merely on the basis of documentary evidence and written submissions)?

3. Think of any experience with administrative decision making that you might have had (e.g., if you applied for a government benefit or a licence/permit, or had a dispute heard before a tribunal). Apply the information in this chapter to the analysis of that experience. In what way were you provided with an opportunity to be heard? What evidence could you submit? If your case was before a tribunal, did the tribunal use an inquisitorial or adversarial model of adjudication? Did you have a right to counsel? Was there a possibility to appeal a negative decision?

Further Readings and Resources

1. David Elliott, *Introduction to Public Law: Readings on the State, the Administrative Process, and Basic Values*, 6th ed (Concord: Captus Press, 2007).

2. Laverne Jacobs and Sasha Baglay, eds, *The Nature of Inquisitorial Processes in Administrative Regimes: Global Perspectives* (Surrey: Ashgate, 2013).

3. John Swaigen, *Administrative Law: Principles and Advocacy*, 2nd ed (Toronto: Emond Montgomery Publications, 2010).

Endnotes

1. David Elliott, *Introduction to Public Law: Readings on the State, the Administrative Process, and Basic Values*, 6th ed (Concord: Captus Press, 2007).
2. Michael Bryant & Lorne Sossin, *Public Law* (Toronto: Carswell, 2002) at 151.
3. John Swaigen, *Administrative Law: Principles and Advocacy*, 2nd ed (Toronto: Emond Montgomery Publications, 2010) at 27.
4. Sara Blake, *Administrative Law in Canada*, 4th ed (Toronto: LexisNexis Butterworths, 2006) at 95.
5. *Employment Insurance Act*, SC 1996, c 23, s 50(5).
6. Swaigen, *supra* note 3 at 48–49.
7. Blake, *supra* note 4 at 11.
8. *Baker v Canada*, [1999] 2 SCR 817 at para 22.
9. Blake, *supra* note 4 at 11.
10. *Baker, supra* note 8.
11. Blake, *supra* note 4 at 13–14.
12. *Williams v Canada (Correctional Service, Regional Transfer Board, Prairie Region)* [1991] 1 FC 251.
13. Blake, *supra* note 4 at 15.

14. *Ibid* at 17.
15. *Baker, supra* note 8 at 838.
16. *Ibid.*
17. Blake, *supra* note 4 at 20.
18. *Ibid* at 22.
19. Swaigen, *supra* note 3 at 66.
20. Blake, *supra* note 4 at 101.
21. *Ibid* at 101.
22. Swaigen, *supra* note 4 at 148.
23. Samantha Green & Lorne Sossin, "Administrative Justice and Innovation: Beyond the Adversarial/ Inquisitorial Dichotomy" in Laverne Jacobs and Sasha Baglay, eds, *The Nature of Inquisitorial Processes in Administrative Regimes: Global Perspectives* (Surrey: Ashgate, 2013) 71.
24. *Ibid* at 72.
25. Blake, *supra* note 4 at 47.
26. *Ibid* at 48.
27. *Law Society of British Columbia v Mangat*, [2001] 3 SCR 113 at para 60.
28. *Ibid* at para 72.
29. *Immigration and Refugee Protection Act*, SC 2001, c 27, s 153(1) [IRPA].
30. *Ibid*, s 167(1).
31. *Ibid*, s 169. In case of the Refugee Appeal Division, it must be in writing.
32. *Ibid*, s 162(2).
33. Gerald Heckman, "Inquisitorial Approaches to Refugee Protection Decision-Making: The Australian Experience and Possible Lessons for Canada" in Laverne Jacobs and Sasha Baglay, eds, *The Nature of Inquisitorial Processes in Administrative Regimes: Global Perspectives* (Surrey: Ashgate, 2013) 125 at 126.
34. *Ibid* at 127.
35. *Ibid.*
36. IRPA, *supra* note 29, s 173.
37. Elliott, *supra* note 1 at 50–54.
38. *Ibid* at 53–54.
39. Swaigen, *supra* note 3 at 348–349.
40. *Dunsmuir v New Brunswick*, [2008] 1 SCR 190 at para 48.
41. Swaigen, *supra* note 3 at 358.
42. Colleen M Flood & Jennifer Dolling, "An Introduction to Administrative Law: Some History and a Few Signposts for a Twisted Path" in Colleen M Flood & Lorne Sossin, eds, *Administrative Law in Context*, 2nd ed (Toronto: Emond Montgomery, 2013) at 29.
43. *Dunsmuir, supra* note 40.
44. *Ibid* at para 47.
45. *Ibid.*
46. *Canada (Citizenship and Immigration) v Khosa* [2009] 1 SCR 339 at para 54.
47. *Ibid* at para 55.
48. [2006] FCJ No 674.
49. *Johnstone v Canada Border Services*, [2010] CHRD No 20.
50. *Johnstone v Canada (Border Services)*, [2013] FCJ No 92.
51. *Johnstone v Canada (Border Services)*, [2014] FCJ No 455.

Chapter 8

Criminal Law

Learning Objectives

After reading this chapter, you should be able to:

- Describe two elements of an offence.

- Identify at least five rights guaranteed to an accused person.

- Compare and contrast summary conviction, indictable, and hybrid offences.

- Describe four ways in which an individual can take part in an offence.

- Describe nine defences that exempt an offender from liability.

- Compare and contrast six sentencing options.

- Identify six objectives and five principles of sentencing.

Chapter Outline

Introduction

We often think of criminal law as a means of social control: it deals with injurious conduct by imposing sanctions on offenders and thereby promoting specific and general deterrence. **Specific deterrence** refers to deterring the offender in question from committing offences in the future. **General deterrence** seeks to deter the public at large from committing offences: an example of a punished offender is expected to send a message of general deterrence. While this description is accurate, it provides only a partial picture. Criminal law is not only about deterrence, protection of the public, and imposition of responsibility; it also needs to consider issues of rehabilitation of offenders and restorative justice. To illustrate issues discussed in this chapter, let us look at the real-life case in Box 8.1.

Box 8.1

Determining Principles of Criminal Liability: The Case of Vince Li

Vince Li boarded a Greyhound bus and sat next to Tim McLean. The two had never met before. Suddenly, Li pulled out a knife and killed McLean. He later claimed that he believed McLean to be an alien who had to be killed in order to protect humankind. Medical experts determined that Li

Part I of this chapter outlines the basics of criminal law: main elements and classifications of offences, defences, and sentencing options. Part II focuses on two issues—criminalization of sex work, and sentencing of offenders from disadvantaged backgrounds—that are intended to illustrate some of the critical dimensions of criminal law. Using the recent Supreme Court case *Bedford v Canada*, the first example questions why certain activities are criminalized and what the implications of such criminalization are. The second example is based on the case of *R v Hamilton* (examined in Chapter 2). It illustrates the complex considerations involved in determining appropriate sentences for offenders of disadvantaged backgrounds and raises broader issues of how social context should inform judicial decisions.

Part I. Substantive Law

1. THE BASICS OF CRIMINAL LAW

In order to understand the logic of criminal law, one needs to start with its basics.

- What are the sources of criminal law?
- How are offences defined (that is, what are their required elements)?
- What are the safeguards to ensure a fair criminal process?

1.1 Jurisdiction Over Criminal Law and Sources of Criminal Law

Under the *Constitution Act, 1867*, the federal government has exclusive jurisdiction over criminal law. Importantly, the *Criminal Code* prohibits creation of new common law offences, meaning that only the legislature has the power to prescribe new offences (not the courts). Thus, federal statutes are the main sources of criminal law (e.g., the *Criminal Code*, the *Controlled Drugs and Substances Act*, the *Youth Criminal Justice Act*).

Although provinces do not have the power to make criminal law, they can legislate in areas of their jurisdiction, including setting out penalties for noncompliance with provincial rules. For example, regulation of highways is within provincial jurisdiction and penalties for speeding or other related violations are prescribed by provincial statutes. Such provincial offences are considered quasi-criminal law.

1.2 Elements of an Offence

The *Criminal Code* contains dozens of offences, each defined in its own particular way. However, despite their different formulations, they have similar structure, being composed of two elements: the actus reus and the mens rea. The **actus reus** refers to the physical act (or omission), while the **mens rea** denotes the mental element. In order to achieve conviction, both the mens rea and the actus reus must be proven beyond a reasonable doubt.

1.2.1 Actus Reus

Depending on the offence, the actus reus may be defined in any of the following ways:

- As a specified physical act (e.g., application of force in the case of assault);
- As a physical act accompanied by a specific consequence (e.g., for offences such as murder where the consequence of death is required);
- As being in a certain state (e.g., being in care or control of a vehicle while intoxicated);
- As an omission, that is, where there is a legal duty to act and an individual fails to fulfill this duty. For example, s. 215 of the *Criminal Code* imposes a legal duty to provide necessaries of life (e.g., food, clothing, shelter) in certain types of relationships (e.g., by parents to a dependent child). Failure to do so would constitute an actus reus of an offence.

1.2.2 Mens Rea

Our criminal law recognizes that, as a rule, the commission of a particular prohibited act is not sufficient to convict: the act must be accompanied by moral blameworthiness, a certain mental state of the accused—the mens rea. The requirement of mens rea serves to ensure that morally innocent individuals (e.g., those who did not understand or intend the consequences of their actions) are not convicted. For example, a person who takes someone else's coat, honestly mistaking it for her own, will lack the mental element for the offence of theft and, as a result, should not be convicted.

Further, we need to account for the fact that people may be acting with different degrees of blameworthiness. For example, there is a difference between (1) intentionally running someone over with a car, and (2) dangerous driving without the intention to harm anyone that results in an accident and someone's death. Should liability be the same in both cases? If not, how should the law reflect these differences? Criminal law addresses these questions by distinguishing four types of mens rea, each connoting a different degree of culpability:

1. *Intent.* Intent is the highest degree of blameworthiness, and refers to situations where an individual wished to bring about a certain wrongful consequence. For example, the charge of murder requires proof that the accused intended the victim's death. Importantly, intent is different from motive. While intent conveys the accused's desire for a certain consequence, *motive* explains the reasons for committing a given offence. Motive is not an element of an offence and is not relevant to determining the guilt or innocence of the accused. However, the existence of a motive may help establish a case against the accused. Box 8.2 helps to demonstrate the difference between intent and motive.

Box 8.2

Intent versus Motive: *R v Latimer*, [2001] 1 SCR 3

Robert Latimer had a daughter—Tracy—who was born with a severe form of cerebral palsy. She was said to have the mental capacity of a four-month-old, was bedridden most of the time, and was completely dependent on others for care. She had five to six seizures a day and was believed to experience a great deal of pain, which could not be relieved by medication. Despite this, it was also known that Tracy could enjoy certain activities such as being with her family and listening to music. Over the years, Tracy underwent numerous surgeries and was scheduled for more surgeries in the future. Faced with the prospect of future surgeries (which Latimer considered to be mutilation), Latimer decided that his daughter's life was not worth living and suffocated her with carbon monoxide. He was prosecuted and found guilty of second degree murder. In this case, Latimer's mens rea was intent to kill, but his motive was to relieve Tracy from pain. Although his actions were motivated by compassion, this did not negate the fact that he intended to kill Tracy and, therefore, possessed the mens rea for murder.

2. *Knowledge.* Some offences require that a person has done something "knowingly." For example, the offence of perjury requires that an accused has made a false statement "knowing that the statement is false."[1]

3. *Recklessness.* Unlike intent, **recklessness** refers to situations where a person does not desire to bring about a particular wrongful consequence, but is nevertheless taking an unjustifiable risk, foreseeing that a wrongful consequence might occur. For example, a person who is driving at an excessive speed and running red lights can be considered reckless. While he does not desire to injure anyone, he realizes that someone may end up getting injured.

4. *Willful blindness.* **Willful blindness** is a state of mind in which a wrongdoer chooses to remain ignorant of suspicious circumstances. For example, consider a shop owner who is approached by an individual offering to sell her some merchandise off the back of a truck, at an extremely low price and without any information on the origin of the goods. The circumstances look suspicious: it is possible that the merchandise has been stolen. If the shop owner proceeds with the deal and chooses not to ask any questions, she may be considered willfully blind and may subsequently face a charge of possession of stolen property. Her decision to remain ignorant would not relieve her of criminal responsibility.

How exactly the actus reus and the mens rea are defined will depend on the specific offence in question. For example, s. 265 of the *Criminal Code* defines assault in the following terms:

(1) A person commits an assault when

(a) without the consent of another person, he applies force intentionally to that other person, directly or indirectly . . .

Thus, the actus reus of assault is the application of force (directly or indirectly) and without the consent of the victim. The mens rea is the intent to apply force.

1.3 Safeguards to Ensure a Fair Criminal Process

Offences are viewed as wrongs not only against the victim, but also against the state and society. Reflecting this idea, criminal prosecutions are carried out by the state and there exists a whole state apparatus (the police, the office of the Crown prosecutor, corrections) that investigates and prosecutes offences as well as enforces sentences. Thus, in the criminal justice system, there may be an imbalance of power between the state and its extensive resources, on the one hand, and the accused, on the other. Given that the accused has crucial interests—liberty, reputation, and future—at stake in the process, ensuring fairness is of fundamental importance. After all, the goal of the criminal justice system is not to convict suspects at all costs, but to ensure that justice is done.

Both common law and subsequently the *Charter*[2] outlined a number of safeguards seeking to protect the rights of the accused and ensure fairness of the criminal process. Among the key safeguards are:

- *Presumption of innocence*. The accused is presumed to be innocent until proven guilty in court, according to law. This means, for example, that the accused does not need to reply to a charge and that his failure to testify in court cannot be used to draw a negative inference about his guilt.

- *The right to counsel*. Upon arrest and detention, an individual has a right to counsel (recall Chapter 6, Part I, section 4.1).[3]

- *The right to remain silent*. The accused has the right to remain silent[4] and cannot be compelled to incriminate herself.

- *Proof beyond a reasonable doubt*. The prosecution bears the burden of proving the elements of an offence **beyond a reasonable doubt**. There is no strict definition of this standard, but it may be useful to think of it as located on a spectrum between a balance of probabilities (more likely than not) and absolute certainty; it lies closer to the latter. It also means that a decision maker's assessment of the guilt or innocence of the accused cannot be based on a "gut" feeling, sympathy, or prejudice. It must be based on evidence presented.

- *Other important rights* of the accused include: protection against unreasonable search and seizure; the right to be informed without unreasonable delay of the specific offence; the right to be tried within a reasonable time; prohibition of arbitrary detention; and the right not to be denied reasonable bail.[5]

2. TYPES OF OFFENCES

There are reportedly close to 100 000 offences contained in various federal and provincial statutes.[6] They can be classified in several ways.

2.1 Summary Conviction, Indictable, and Hybrid Offences

This classification is important as it determines how a given case will be dealt with, including which court will hear the case and what sentences may be imposed.

Summary conviction offences are considered less serious and are tried through a simpler procedure. For example, causing a disturbance is a summary conviction offence. Under the *Criminal Code*, the penalties for summary offences are usually up to six months' imprisonment and/or a fine of up to $2000.

Indictable offences are considered more serious and usually involve more complex procedures. Offences such as murder, kidnapping, and robbery are indictable. The maximum penalties for indictable offences vary, but they can be as long as life imprisonment.

Hybrid offences are those that, on the election of the prosecution, can be tried either on a summary conviction or by way of indictment. For example, theft under $5000 is a hybrid offence. In making the election, the prosecution usually considers such factors as the circumstances involving the offence and whether the accused has a prior criminal record.

Summary conviction offences are tried before provincial courts by a single judge. Some indictable offences (e.g., murder, treason) must be tried in a superior court, and others in provincial courts; with respect to still others, the accused may choose either a trial by judge alone or a trial by judge and jury.

2.2 True Crimes and Regulatory Offences

The distinction between true crimes and regulatory offences determines what elements of the offence must be proven in order to achieve a conviction. *True crimes* are acts that are considered inherently wrong both morally and legally (e.g., murder, assault); both the actus reus and the mens rea must be proven in order to achieve a conviction. In contrast, *regulatory offences* (considered quasi-criminal) deal with activities that we generally consider desirable (e.g., driving, construction), yet recognize that, if they were carried out without proper standards and care, they could result in injury to individuals or the public at large. Hence, regulatory offences exist not in order to prohibit particular conduct, but to facilitate responsible behaviour and compliance with established standards. For example, occupational health and safety acts contain regulatory offences penalizing noncompliance with health and safety standards. Regulatory offences are also distinct from true crimes due to the fact that only the actus reus of an offence must be proven in order to obtain a conviction.

2.3 Incomplete Offences

Certain conduct may be an offence even though the intended wrongful act has not been carried out. There are two main types of incomplete offences: attempt and conspiracy.

An *attempt* to commit an offence is an offence in itself. The actus reus of an attempt can be considered accomplished once the accused has gone beyond mere preparation and has come sufficiently close to the commission of a completed offence (essentially, the commission of an offence would have been the next step). For example, determining the location of a future robbery and acquiring a gun for the robbery constitutes mere preparation, while actually coming to the location and walking into the building may be sufficiently close as to constitute attempted robbery. Individuals can be charged with attempts related to any offence in the *Criminal Code* as well as other federal offences.[7]

Conspiracy is an agreement between two or more people to carry out a criminal offence. The reaching of such an agreement alone, even before any actions have been taken to implement it, is sufficient to establish conspiracy. This charge is often used in relation to organized crime activities.

3. PARTIES TO AN OFFENCE

As demonstrated in Box 8.3, an individual can take part in an offence in a number of ways:

- As a *principal offender*, that is, a person who has carried out the wrongful act (e.g., in case of a murder, a person who has delivered the fatal shot).

- By *aiding and abetting* the principal offender. *Aiding* refers to providing assistance either prior to or in the course of an offence (e.g., supplying the gun; holding the victim down). *Abetting* means encouraging an offence. For both aiding and abetting, it must be proven that the accused had an intent to assist or to encourage the principal offender and a general knowledge of the offence to be committed. Mere presence at the scene of an offence does not amount to aiding or abetting.[8]

- By *counselling an offence*—that is, procuring, soliciting, or inciting someone to commit an offence. A person who counsels commission of an offence can be held criminally responsible even if the counselled offence has not been committed or has been committed in a way different from that counselled.

- By being an *accessory after the fact*—that is, by knowingly providing assistance to an offender after the commission of an offence. The assistance can include provision of shelter, food, or information that could help the offender escape the authorities.

Box 8.3

Practical Application: Parties to an Offence

Marc had a grudge against Roberto and decided to kill him. He shared his thoughts with Johann and asked him for assistance in obtaining a gun and a getaway car. Johann agreed to help and supplied the gun as well as drove Marc to and from the victim's house on the day of the murder. Marc shot and killed Roberto. In order to escape from the police, Marc went to his other friend, Dan, told him what happened, and asked to hide in his house. Dan agreed.

This scenario illustrates the following:

- Parties to an offence: Marc is the principal offender; Johann can be considered an aidor; Dan is an accessory after the fact.

- Classification of offences: murder is a true crime and, thus, requires proof of both mens rea and actus reus. It is also an indictable offence that is punishable by life imprisonment.

- Elements of an offence: the *Criminal Code* defines murder in the following way:

229. Culpable homicide is murder

(a) where the person who causes the death of a human being

  (i) means to cause his death, or

  (ii) means to cause him bodily harm that he knows is likely to cause his death, and is reckless whether death ensues or not . . . .

In order to convict Marc, the prosecution must prove beyond a reasonable doubt that he took action that resulted in the victim's death and that he had the intent to cause death. For conviction of Johann and Dan as parties to murder, the prosecution must prove that they had general knowledge of the intended offence, intended to assist Marc, and in fact provided the assistance.

4. DEFENCES

Canadian criminal law recognizes a number of *defences*—the circumstances that may exempt the offender from liability. Defences can be full or partial, codified in the *Criminal Code* or existing in the form of common law rules. A full defence leads to acquittal, while a partial defence only to a reduction of the charge from a more to a less serious one. Let us briefly review the most common defences.

4.1 Self-Defence

This defence recognizes that when a person's life or bodily integrity is at risk, she may be justified in using force against the attacker. In order to establish self-defence, an accused must demonstrate that:

- She believed on reasonable grounds that force, or a threat of force, was being used against her;
- Her actions were taken in order to defend herself; and
- The actions committed were reasonable in the circumstances.[9]

4.2 Defence of Property

Our law also recognizes that a person may be justified in using force to defend his property. In order to establish this defence, an accused must demonstrate that:

- He believed on reasonable grounds that he was in uncontested possession of given property;
- He believed on reasonable grounds that another person:
  - was about to enter, was entering, or had entered the property without being entitled by law to do so,
  - was about to take the property, was doing so, or had just done so, or
  - was about to damage or destroy the property or was doing so; and
- His actions were taken in order to defend the property and were reasonable in the circumstances.[10]

4.3 Not Criminally Responsible (NCR)

Under section 16 of the *Criminal Code*, a person shall not be held criminally responsible if she had a mental disorder that made her "incapable of appreciating the nature and quality of the act or omission" or of knowing that her actions were wrong.

Finding that a person is not criminally responsible (NCR) is not the same as acquitting a person. An acquittal allows the person to go free in the community. When a person is found NCR, a disposition hearing is held in which a court or a review board can make one of three orders against the accused: (1) absolute discharge (release in the community without conditions); (2) conditional discharge (release on conditions); or (3) confinement to a treatment facility. In deciding on a disposition, decision makers must take into consideration such factors as the need to protect the public, the mental condition of the accused, and reintegration of the accused into society. If conditional discharge or custody in a treatment facility is ordered, the case is reviewed every 12 months to determine whether the same conditions are to be continued or whether they can be lifted or altered.

Recall the case of Vince Li (Box 8.1). Li was examined by medical specialists, who determined that he had paranoid schizophrenia. At trial, he was recognized to be NCR and was ordered detained in a treatment facility. Although he has remained there since 2008, the conditions of his custody have been gradually relaxed to reflect that he has responded positively to treatment. For example, initially, Li was not allowed to be outside of the facility, but as a result of periodic reviews he can now go on supervised walks outside.

4.4 Automatism

Automatism refers to situations when a person is in a state of impaired consciousness and, as a result, has no voluntary control over his actions. Automatism may be of two types: (1) caused by a mental disorder (in such a case, an NCR defence will be used); or (2) produced by nonmental disorder conditions (e.g., sleepwalking). In the latter case, if the defence of automatism is successful, it will lead to acquittal.

The defence of nonmental disorder automatism was successful in the infamous *Parks* case.[11] Parks was charged with the murder of his mother-in-law and attempted murder of his father-in-law. He had good relations with his in-laws and did not seem to have any motive to harm them. Parks had a history of sleepwalking and attacked his in-laws while he was in that state. The Supreme Court concluded that sleepwalking was not a mental disorder and upheld the accused's acquittal on the basis of the automatism defence.

4.5 Provocation

Provocation is different from other defences in at least two respects. First, it is only applicable to the charge of murder. Second, it is a partial defence. Thus, if successful, it does not lead to acquittal, but only to a reduction of the charge from murder to manslaughter.

In order to establish the defence of provocation, the following requirements must be met:

- An accused must have been provoked by an insult or a wrongful act that is "sufficient to deprive an ordinary person of the power of self-control";
- Provocation must have been sudden and unexpected; and
- The accused must have acted in the heat of the moment, before regaining self-control.[12]

4.6 Duress

The defence of **duress** recognizes that a person may be forced by someone else to commit an offence. In Canada, this defence is complicated because it exists in two forms: statutory (s. 17 of the *Criminal Code*) and common law. Both provide that this defence is available only to an accused who was under the threat of death or serious bodily harm, believed that the threat would be carried out, and had no safe avenue of escape.[13] However, there are also two important differences. First, s. 17 of the *Criminal Code* can be invoked only by a principal offender. In contrast, the common law defence of duress can be used by other parties to an offence (e.g., an aidor or abettor). Second, s. 17 cannot be used in relation to 22 listed offences, including murder, sexual assault, and robbery.[14] Common law defence of duress may be invoked in relation to any offence.

4.7 Necessity

Similarly to duress, *necessity* refers to situations where a person is forced to commit a wrongful act. However, while duress deals with situations where an accused is forced by a person, necessity addresses cases where an accused is forced by an emergency circumstance. For example, Amir, who is lost in the woods and faces the possibility of dying from cold and hunger, comes across a locked cabin. He breaks into the cabin in order to save his life. If he were charged with mischief, he could invoke the defence of necessity.

In order to establish this defence, an accused must demonstrate that:

- He was in a situation of direct and imminent peril;
- There was no other reasonable alternative to breaking the law; and
- There was proportionality between the harm inflicted and harm avoided.[15]

4.8 Mistake of Fact

This defence covers situations where an individual was mistaken about the circumstances at hand and had no reason to believe that she was committing an offence. For example, if Nina took someone else's jacket under the mistaken belief that it was hers, she could raise the defence of mistake of fact, arguing that she had no mens rea for the offence of theft.

4.9 Consent

The absence of consent is explicitly included as a required element of actus reus of some offences. For example, assault is defined in the *Criminal Code* as "intentional application of force *without the consent of the complainant*" (emphasis added).[16] Thus, where consent is present, the actus reus of an offence cannot be established and an accused cannot be convicted.

While the above rule seems rather simple, it can raise many challenging questions. For example, can someone consent to being killed? Can this defence be used in consensual fights? What if the victim's consent was not freely given, was uninformed, or was obtained by fraud or threats? Our law has addressed these questions by establishing the following rules:

- A person cannot consent to have death inflicted on her; even if such consent is given, it does not absolve of criminal responsibility the person who inflicts the death.[17]

- Consent cannot be used as a defence in fights where there is an intention to inflict serious bodily harm.[18]

- In contact sports, players are considered to have given implied consent to a certain degree of contact and possible application of force to their bodies. Thus, accidental infliction of bodily harm within the rules of fair play would not constitute assault. However, intentional injury that falls outside the rules of fair play is not shielded by implied consent and constitutes assault. For example, during an NHL hockey game, Todd Bertuzzi engaged in a verbal altercation with a member of the opposing team and then struck him in the right temple, causing serious injury. Bertuzzi's actions fell outside the rules of fair play. He was charged with assault causing bodily harm and pleaded guilty.[19]

- No consent is considered obtained where the complainant submits by reason of application of force, threats of force, fraud, or exercise of authority.[20]

- Additional limitations exist in the context of sexual assault. No consent is considered obtained where: the consent is expressed by a person other than the complainant; the complainant is incapable of consenting; the accused induced the complainant to engage in the activity by abusing a position of trust, power, or authority; or the complainant expresses, by words or conduct, a lack of agreement.[21]

4.10 Intoxication

Intoxication is governed by a combination of common law rules and *Criminal Code* provisions. They can be summarized as follows:

- With respect to general intent offences[22] involving violence or the threat of violence, self-induced intoxication can never be a defence (s. 33.1 of the *Criminal Code*)

- With respect to general intent offences that do not involve violence or threat of violence (e.g., property offences), an accused may benefit from the intoxication defence, but only if intoxication was so extreme as to lead to a state akin to automatism or insanity (as per *Daviault*—see Box 8.4); and

- With respect to specific intent offences, intoxication may be a defence (common law rule).

Box 8.4

The Defence of Intoxication: *R v Daviault*, [1994] 3 SCR 63

Daviault was charged with sexual assault. However, he claimed to have no recollection of what happened and denied the charge. An expert who examined Daviault estimated that, at the time in question, the concentration of alcohol in Daviault's blood was so high that it would likely cause death or a coma. In Daviault's case, such a high concentration of alcohol caused a blackout. Thus, it is possible that, due to such extreme intoxication, Daviault was incapable of forming the intent to commit sexual assault. Should intoxication be a defence in this case?

At the time when the case unfolded, the common law rules dictated that the defence of intoxication could be raised with respect to a specific intent offence, but never to a general intent offence. Sexual assault is a general intent offence and, hence, intoxication could not be invoked in Daviault's case. However, this raised a significant concern: Daviault would have to be convicted despite a reasonable doubt regarding the voluntariness of his actions. Such conviction would go against one of the most fundamental principles of criminal law: not punishing persons who had no ability to know or understand their actions.

The majority of the Supreme Court altered the existing common law rules on the defence of intoxication, holding that where intoxication was so extreme as to lead to a state akin to automatism or insanity, it could be a defence even to a general intent offence. Although such a defence was likely to be successful only in rare situations, the decision provoked strong reaction from various interest groups and the public. It was criticized, for example, for ignoring the issues of violence against women and victims' rights generally.[23] In response to public concerns, Parliament added a new provision to the *Criminal Code* to effectively override the decision of the Supreme Court. It provided that self-induced intoxication, no matter how extreme, cannot be a defence to a charge of any general intent offence that "includes as an element an assault or any other interference or threat of interference by a person with the bodily integrity of another person." This is how our approach to the defence of intoxication ended up as a combination of common law and statutory rules.

Table 8.1 presents a comparison of defences.

Table 8.1 Comparison of Defences

Defence	Full	Partial	Common Law	Codified in *Criminal Code*
Self-defence	✓			✓
Defence of property	✓			✓
Automatism	✓		✓	
Intoxication	✓		✓	✓
Mistake of fact	✓		✓	

(continued)

Table 8.1 *(continued)*				
Defence	**Full**	**Partial**	**Common Law**	**Codified in** *Criminal Code*
Consent	✓			✓
Necessity	✓		✓	
Duress	✓		✓	✓
Provocation		✓		✓
NCR	Special dispositions: ■ absolute discharge ■ conditional discharge ■ custody in a treatment facility			✓

5. SENTENCING

If the accused is found guilty or pleads guilty, a sentencing hearing follows, where a judge determines what sentence should be imposed.

5.1 Sentencing Options

The commonly available sentencing options are:

■ *Absolute or conditional discharge*, which leaves a person without a conviction and allows for release with or without conditions. It is available only for offences without a minimum sentence and is usually applied to trivial violations of the *Criminal Code*.

■ *Imprisonment*, which is usually reserved for more serious crimes.

■ **Conditional sentence**, a form of imprisonment that is served in a community under conditions that may include house arrest, curfew, and enrollment in a treatment program.

■ *Fine*.

■ *Restitution*, which intends to compensate the victim for the injury.

■ *Restorative justice* initiatives (see chapter on Alternative Dispute Resolution on Companion Website).

See Table 8.2 for a summary of how adults found guilty in Canadian criminal courts were sentenced, from 2007 to 2012.

Table 8.2 Adult Criminal Courts, Guilty Cases by Type of Sentence					
Type of Sentence	**2007–2008**	**2008–2009**	**2009–2010**	**2010–2011**	**2011–2012**
Total guilty cases, sentences	255 487	263 948	266 430	261 325	246 984
Custody	89 597	91 045	88 982	87 770	86 661

Type of Sentence	2007–2008	2008–2009	2009–2010	2010–2011	2011–2012
Conditional sentence	11 219	11 735	11 955	12 128	11 483
Probation	113 813	118 701	120 370	116 409	110 885
Fine	76 794	78 965	80 757	80 421	72 204
Restitution	7 209	7 100	7 050	6 999	6 270
Other sentences	126 941	133 445	138 828	137 022	126 114

Source: Statistics Canada, online: <http://www5.statcan.gc.ca/cansim/a05?lang=eng&id=2520056>.

5.2 Objectives and Principles of Sentencing

A sentence for a given offence is usually specified in the *Criminal Code* or other statute that has prescribed that offence. However, when you read statutory provisions, you notice that they often prescribe only a maximum or minimum penalty and therefore leave judges significant discretion in tailoring specific sentences. For example, s. 266 of the *Criminal Code* states that assault (when prosecuted by indictment) is punishable by "imprisonment for a term not exceeding five years."

In order to assist judges in determining what sentence would be appropriate in a given case, the *Criminal Code* outlines objectives, purposes, and principles of sentencing. According to s. 718 of the *Criminal Code*, the fundamental purpose of sentencing is "to contribute, along with crime prevention initiatives, to respect for the law and the maintenance of a just, peaceful and safe society by imposing just sanctions . . . ."[24] Section 718 also sets out the objectives of sentencing:

(a) to denounce unlawful conduct;

(b) to deter the offender and other persons from committing offences;

(c) to separate offenders from society, where necessary;

(d) to assist in rehabilitating offenders;

(e) to provide reparations for harm done to victims or to the community; and

(f) to promote a sense of responsibility in offenders, and acknowledgment of the harm done to victims and to the community.

In addition, courts are to consider the following principles of sentencing:

- A sentence must be proportionate to the gravity of the offence and the degree of responsibility of the offender;

- Similar sentences should be imposed on similar offenders for similar offences committed in similar circumstances;

- All available sanctions other than imprisonment that are reasonable in the circumstances should be considered for all offenders, with particular attention to the circumstances of Aboriginal offenders;

- Aggravating or mitigating circumstances must be taken into account;[25] and
- Where consecutive sentences are imposed, the combined sentence should not be unduly long or harsh.

Part II. Critical Perspectives

Criminal law is a powerful tool. When certain activity is criminalized, large numbers of individuals may be subject to sanctions and, stemming from the sanctions, to social stigma. We usually think of criminal law as existing for the benefit of the whole society and for protection of individuals from violence or other disruptive behaviour. While this is true, we should not forget that, in some cases, it has been used as a tool of oppression and marginalization. For example, as you recall from Chapter 2, traditional First Nations ceremonies were criminalized in the twentieth century. The criminalization of opium in the early twentieth century was also racially motivated, as opium use was associated with the Chinese population, which at the time was seen as a highly undesirable group in Canada. Even when criminal laws are not designed to target particular marginalized groups, they may have differential impact on various populations. In this section, we question the impact of criminal laws on two selected groups—sex workers and offenders from disadvantaged backgrounds—and consider how the knowledge of racism and social inequalities should inform judicial decisions.

1. *BEDFORD V CANADA:* SHOULD SEX WORK BE CRIMINALIZED?

Sex work has long been a controversial topic, and different countries have taken various approaches to this issue. For example, most states in the United States criminalize both selling and buying of sex services; in the Netherlands, Germany, and New Zealand, prostitution and the operation of brothels have been decriminalized. In Sweden, the sale of sex is lawful, while buying sexual services is criminalized. In Canada, the selling of sex was not criminalized but some prostitution-related activities constituted criminal offences, namely: keeping a bawdy house (s. 210 of the *Criminal Code*), living on the avails of prostitution (s. 212(1)(j)), and communicating for the purpose of prostitution (s. 213(1)(c)). These provisions reflected a view that prostitution was a social evil due to its immorality and connection to exploitation and disease.[26] The past few decades have seen renewed attention to antiprostitution laws in Canada, including questioning whether consensual adult prostitution should be criminalized. For example, public opinion surveys since 2000 have demonstrated lower levels of support for criminalization, as compared to similar surveys of the 1980s and 1990s.[27] Several government committees examined the issue but were unable to agree on how the laws should be changed.[28] In the absence of change through legislative channels, some activists turned to the courts.

In 2009, three former/current sex workers—Terri-Jean Bedford, Amy Leibovitch, and Valerie Scott—challenged the constitutionality of ss. 210, 212(1)(j), and 213(1)(c) of the *Criminal Code*.[29] They argued that the current law, while allowing sex work, does not allow for it to be carried out safely. The prohibition on bawdy houses prevents sex workers from working indoors; the "living on the avails of prostitution" provision means that sex workers cannot hire security staff, drivers, and managers; and the prohibition on communication forces sex workers to make hasty decisions without properly screening clients. All of these prohibitions increase the dangers of sex work. The Crown, in response, argued the laws were justified since prostitution causes harm to society. It also contended that prostitution was inherently dangerous no matter when, where, or how it occurred.

The arguments of plaintiffs and defendants were rather closely aligned with two dominant feminist perspectives on sex work: (1) sex work as an individual choice; and (2) sex work as inherently dangerous and exploitative.[30] Both parties called academic experts as witnesses at trial in order to inform the court of these respective perspectives.[31] In fact, this case is an excellent example of the relevance of academic research to practice, including litigation before courts.

Proponents of the first approach view sex work as an expression of women's autonomy, recognizing that an individual can make a free choice to engage in sex work.[32] They argue that sex work should be considered a legitimate type of employment and should receive the same protections (health, safety, wages, and working conditions) as other occupations.[33] It is considered that prohibition of sex work makes sex workers more vulnerable to abuse. Proponents of the "sex works as an individual choice" approach advocate for decriminalization and regulation of sex work that, in turn, would allow for enforcement of work and safety standards.

Proponents of the second approach consider prostitution as an expression of patriarchal power relations and a form of violence against women.[34] Prostitution is viewed as inherently exploitative. Truly free and voluntary consent in this context is considered impossible. Thus, they call for decriminalization of sex workers, but object to the decriminalization of clients and third-parties involved in prostitution activities.

In 2013, the Supreme Court upheld the finding that the three provisions in question were unconstitutional as they infringed s. 7 rights of sex workers and were not in accordance with the principles of fundamental justice.[35] The *Criminal Code* prohibitions not only heightened the risks of sex work, but in fact imposed dangerous conditions on prostitution. These provisions effectively prevented sex workers from operating from fixed safer locations, from hiring personnel (such as bodyguards), and from screening potential clients. All of these measures were grossly disproportionate to the objective of preventing the public nuisance that may result from prostitution. The Supreme Court has suspended the declaration of invalidity for one year, allowing Parliament to implement a new regime for regulation of sex work.

In 2014, Parliament amended respective Criminal Code provisions in a number of ways, including: (1) introducing new offences for purchasing and advertising of sexual services; (2) narrowing down the scope of provisions regarding

Photo 8.1 Terri-Jean Bedford flashes a victory sign after the Supreme Court struck down prostitution-related provisions of the *Criminal Code*

Nathan Dennette/Canadian Press/AP Images

communication for the purpose of prostitution (now such communication is not criminalized unless it happens in a public place, or near a school, playground or daycare centre); (3) providing exceptions to the offence of receiving a material benefit from prostitution for persons such as bodyguards and family of sex workers. Although the new law is said to target the demand for sex work and to protect sex workers, some commentators expressed concerns that it does not help make sex work safer and does not significantly change the previously invalidated regime.[36]

2. *R V HAMILTON:* HOW SHOULD THE DISADVANTAGED BACKGROUND OF AN ACCUSED FACTOR INTO SENTENCING?

Recall the case of *R v Hamilton*, discussed in Chapter 2. Hamilton and Mason pleaded guilty to drug importation. Both were black single mothers with limited employable skills and limited income. Hamilton, in particular, said that she committed the offence due to financial need. The judge of the Superior Court concluded that systemic factors of racism, gender discrimination, poverty, and single motherhood contributed to the offenders' decision to commit the offence. He then used these factors to mitigate the sentence.[37] Hamilton and Mason received conditional sentences of 20 and 24 months, respectively. This is a more lenient sentence than is usually applied for drug importation.[38] The Crown appealed, and the Court of Appeal found that the sentences were unfit as they did not appropriately reflect the gravity of the offence.[39] The Court of Appeal concluded that imprisonment was a more appropriate sentence, corresponding to the seriousness of the offence. In its opinion, a conditional sentence did not sufficiently denounce and deter such serious crime.

Although in a strictly legal sense the case is settled by the decision of the Court of Appeal, it raises broader questions about sentencing of accused of marginalized backgrounds. For example, how should judges properly take into consideration social context (e.g., the existence of racism and inequality) in sentencing? Should the social disadvantage of the offender be a factor mitigating criminal liability? Did both the trial and appeal courts take a proper approach to sentencing in *R v Hamilton*?

Critical scholarship has recognized that, in order to achieve substantive equality, we need to be aware of the differences along race, gender, and class lines. Treating everyone the same would not always result in equality, and "blind" justice may reproduce inequality.[40] Canadian courts have recognized that judicial decision making does not occur in a vacuum and should be informed by social context.[41] For example, the evidence at trial can be illuminated by understanding that race and gender bias may be among factors contributing to the offender's dire financial need and motivating the commission of an offence. For instance, in the case of female offenders, past experience of abuse and poverty (including in connection with poor education, few employable skills, dependence on welfare, and sole responsibility for children) are common factors playing a role in the types of crimes committed.[42]

If historic and other background differences of offenders are not recognized, they may be even further marginalized by punishment. The Supreme Court decision in *Gladue*[43] expressly recognized this in relation to Aboriginal offenders. Section 718 of the *Criminal*

Code specifically mandates consideration of sanctions other than imprisonment for all offenders, "with particular attention to the circumstances of Aboriginal offenders." The reference to Aboriginal offenders was included in recognition that racism and discrimination had had a significant impact on the treatment of the First Nations in the criminal justice system.[44] Drawing on *Gladue*, it can be argued that a similar approach should be taken in relation to other groups that have been and continue to be marginalized in the justice system.[45] For example, the Ontario Royal Commission on Systemic Racism in the Criminal Justice System (1995) found that black people were imprisoned at a higher rate, and that direct and indirect discrimination appeared to have had an impact.

The decision in *R v Hamilton* directly engaged some of the above issues and provoked significant academic debate.[46] This debate provides useful vantage points for assessing and appreciating the complex issues raised by the case. Some commentators noted that the lower court's judgment can be viewed as reflecting a progressive view that offenders must be seen in their social context.[47] This context puts into perspective a range of appropriate sentences, although it does not necessarily mandate a mitigated sentence.[48] In contrast, the Court of Appeal was ambivalent on the use of social context. On the one hand, it said that such context is important, but on the other, it denied its relevance in the case at hand.[49] Some suggested that the Court of Appeal decision is a step in a wrong direction that discourages the use of social context and sensitivity to realities of inequality.[50] Others pointed out that both courts drew some questionable links between women, poverty, and drugs, assuming that poor black women with children are prone to being drug couriers.[51] There is a concern that the two decisions may reinforce the idea that drug importation is identified with racialized communities.[52]

None of the above discussion should be seen as suggesting that socially disadvantaged offenders should automatically be treated more leniently. Systemic factors may mitigate a sentence of a socially disadvantaged offender, but for this to happen the disadvantage must be serious enough to impact the offender's ability to comply with the law.[53] In the case of serious and violent crimes, priority is given to the objectives of denunciation and deterrence, and social disadvantage likely will be given less weight.[54] However, in the absence of relevant evidence, it is improper to assume that a person from a disadvantaged background is acting out of financial need.[55] For example, in *R v Hamilton*, it was inappropriate for the lower court to generalize that offenders were conscripted and paid minimal compensation in the absence of direct evidence to that effect.[56]

SUMMARY

Criminal law is an important tool of social control, but it can also play a role in rehabilitation of offenders and promotion of restorative justice. Criminal matters fall within the exclusive jurisdiction of the federal government. Most offences have been codified in a single source—the *Criminal Code*. As a rule, an offence has two elements: the actus reus and the mens rea. The prosecution bears the burden of proving both elements of an offence beyond a reasonable doubt.

Offences can be classified in several ways: (1) summary conviction, indictable, and hybrid offences; (2) true crimes and regulatory offences; and (3) complete and incomplete offences.

Criminal law also provides for a number of defences, the most common of which include self-defence, defence of property, NCR, automatism, provocation, duress, necessity, mistake of fact, consent, and intoxication. If an individual is convicted or pleads guilty, a judge will determine an appropriate sentence. Among sentencing options are absolute and conditional discharge, conditional sentence, imprisonment, fine, restitution, and restorative justice initiatives. In determining a proper sentence, judges are guided by objectives and principles of sentencing outlined in the *Criminal Code*.

While criminal law is seen as serving the good of the whole society, we also need to be aware of the fact that it may have differential impact on various populations. It is increasingly recognized that social context (such as the existence of racism and inequality) can usefully inform assessments of offenders' culpability and appropriate sentencing options. The case of *R v Hamilton* vividly illustrated the challenging nature of determining appropriate sentences for offenders from marginalized backgrounds, and *Bedford v Canada* demonstrated the ability of criminal law to make certain activities (in this case, sex work) more dangerous, to the point of violating rights to liberty and security under the *Charter*.

Critical Thinking Questions

1. Imagine the following scenario: James consumes several beers at a bar. As he is leaving, he sees a man assaulting a woman. James intervenes and, as a result, sustains a severe, deep cut to his arm; the cut is bleeding profusely. James feels that he needs immediate medical attention. He asks his friend to drive him to a hospital, but the friend is too drunk to drive. He tries to look for a cab, but none is available. He wants to call a cab, but he does not have a cell phone and a pay phone at a bar is being used by other patrons. James decides to drive himself to a hospital. He is charged with impaired driving. Is any defence available to him? If yes, is this defence likely to be successful?

2. In your opinion, should the possession, use, and distribution of marijuana be fully decriminalized and regulated? Why? Explain your answer in reference to the principles of criminal responsibility and other relevant considerations discussed in this chapter.

3. Why is the protection of the rights of the accused important? Identify the rights that are protected and analyze their importance for the criminal process.

4. In your opinion, should intoxication be allowed as a defence under Canadian law? Explain your answer in reference to the principles of criminal responsibility.

5. In February 2013, the government introduced Bill C-54, which proposes to make public safety the paramount consideration in decisions on NCR cases, and to provide for mandatory custody of high-risk NCR accused, which could be ended only by a court order. What is your opinion of this proposal? What is going to be its likely effect? Explain.

Further Readings and Resources

1. Joel Pink & David Perrier, eds, *From Crime to Punishment* (Toronto: Carswell Thompson, 2003).
2. Kent Roach, *Criminal Law*, 5th ed (Toronto: Irwin Law, 2012).
3. Simon Verdun-Jones, *Criminal Law in Canada: Cases, Questions, and the Code*, 5th ed (Scarborough: Thomson-Nelson, 2011).

Endnotes

1. *Criminal Code*, RSC 1985, c C-46, s 131(1).
2. See *Charter of Rights and Freedoms*, 1982, c 11 (UK), Schedule B, ss 7–12.
3. *R v Brydges*, [1990] 1 SCR 190; *R v Sinclair*, [2010] 2 SCR 310.
4. *R v Hebert*, (1990) 57 CCC (3d) 1.
5. *Charter, supra* note 2, ss 8–11.
6. Simon Verdun-Jones, *Criminal Law in Canada: Cases, Questions, and the Code*, 5th ed (Scarborough: Thomson-Nelson, 2011) at 8.
7. Don Stuart, *Canadian Criminal Law* (Toronto: Carswell, 2001) at 674.
8. In *Dunlop and Sylvester*, [1979] 2 SCR 881, the Supreme Court examined whether the two accused who observed sexual assault but did not participate in or encourage it could be considered parties to the crime. The Court determined that mere presence at the scene did not make them aiders or abettors.
9. *Criminal Code, supra* note 1, s 34. In deciding what is "reasonable in the circumstances," courts are to consider various factors, including the extent to which the threat was imminent; the size, age, gender, and physical capacities of the parties to the incident; and other factors.
10. *Ibid*, s 35.
11. *R v Parks* [1992] 2 SCR 871.
12. *Criminal Code, supra* note 1, s 232.
13. *R v Ryan* [2013] 1 SCR 14.
14. The full list of offences is as follows: high treason or treason, murder, piracy, attempted murder, sexual assault, sexual assault with a weapon, threats to a third party or causing bodily harm, aggravated sexual assault, forcible abduction, hostage taking, robbery, assault with a weapon or causing bodily harm, aggravated assault, unlawfully causing bodily harm, arson, or an offence under sections 280 to 283 (abduction and detention of young persons).
15. *R v Perka*, [1984] 2 SCR 232.
16. *Criminal Code, supra* note 1, s 265.
17. *Ibid*, s 14.
18. *R v Jobidon*, [1991] 2 SCR 714.
19. *R v Bertuzzi*, [2004] BCJ No 2692.
20. *Criminal Code, supra* note 1, s 265 (3).
21. *Ibid*, s 273.1(2).
22. The *Criminal Code* does not specify which offences are to be considered of general intent and which ones of specific intent. Thus, the task falls on courts. As a rule, a general intent offence seeks to achieve a certain immediate objective and requires only a conscious performance of a given prohibited act (e.g., a basic intent to apply force in the offence of assault). In contrast, specific intent offences possess a further ulterior intent that goes beyond performance of an immediate act at hand (e.g., murder contains not only a general intent to, for example, fire a gun, but also an ulterior intent to do so in order to cause another person's death).
23. Elizabeth Sheehy, "A Brief on Bill C-72" (Ottawa: National Association of Women and the Law, 1995); Randha Jhappan, "The Equality Pit or the Rehabilitation of Justice?" in Randha Jhappan, ed, *Women's Legal Strategies in Canada* (Toronto: University of Toronto Press, 2002) 175 at 212; Tu Thanh Ha, "Men's Defence of Drunkenness Sparks Plans to Change Law," *The Globe and Mail* (November 2, 1994); Debra Black, "A Licence to Rape? Women Fear That a Supreme Court Ruling Tells Men Sexual Assault Is Okay as Long as They're Drunk," *The Toronto Star* (October 27, 1994) E1.

24. *Criminal Code*, *supra* note 1, s 718.
25. *Ibid*, s 718.2. Mitigating factors can include: accused's good character, age, remorse, early guilty plea, or provocation. Aggravating circumstances include:

- evidence that the offence was motivated by bias, prejudice, or hate based on race, national or ethnic origin, language, colour, religion, sex, age, mental or physical disability, sexual orientation, or any other similar factor

- evidence that the offender, in committing the offence, abused the offender's spouse or common-law partner

- evidence that the offender, in committing the offence, abused a person under the age of 18 years

- evidence that the offender, in committing the offence, abused a position of trust or authority in relation to the victim

- evidence that the offence had a significant impact on the victim, considering their age and other personal circumstances, including their health and financial situation

- evidence that the offence was committed for the benefit of, at the direction of, or in association with a criminal organization, or

- evidence that the offence was a terrorism offence.

26. John McLaren, "Recalculating the Wages of Sin: The Social and Legal Construction of Prostitution, 1850–1920" (1996) 23 Man LJ 524.
27. John Lowman & Christine Louie, "Public Opinion on Prostitution Law Reform in Canada" (2012) Canadian Journal of Criminology and Criminal Justice 245; John Lowman, "Deadly Inertia: A History of Constitutional Challenges to Canada's Criminal Code Sections on Prostitution" (2011) 2 Beijing L Rev 33.
28. Lowman, *ibid* at 34.
29. *Bedford v Canada (Attorney General)*, [2010] OJ No 4057.
30. For an overview of various feminist perspectives on sex work, see Lacey Sloan & Stephanie Wahab, "Feminist Voices on Sex Work: Implications for Social Work" (2000) 15 Affilia 457.
31. The plaintiffs, for example, called Dr. Barbara Sullivan as one of their expert witnesses. Her studies concluded that indoor prostitution reduces the risk of violence to sex workers and that decriminalization does not result in the growth of the sex industry. See Leslie Ann Jeffrey and Barbara Sullivan, "Canadian Sex Work Policy for the 21st Century: Enhancing Rights and Safety, Lessons from Australia" (2009) 3:1 Canadian Political Science Review 57; Barbara Sullivan, "Feminist Approaches to the Sex Industry" (1992), online: <http://www.aic.gov.au/media_library/publications/proceedings/14/sullivan.pdf>.

    The defendants called witnesses who supported an abolitionist position on prostitution (for example, Dr. Janice Raymond and Dr. Mary Lucille Sullivan, who were actively involved with the Coalition Against Trafficking in Women (CATW), a nongovernmental organization that seeks to abolish prostitution and advocates against decriminalization of prostitution). Dr. Raymond's work argued that prostitution is a form of violence against women and suggested that there is a connection between decriminalization of the sex industry and human trafficking. Dr. Sullivan asserted that prostitution is inherently dangerous regardless of where it takes place. See, e.g., Mary Lucille Sullivan, *Making Sex Work: A Failed Experiment With Legalised Prostitution* (Melbourne: Spinifex Press, 2007).
32. Holly B Fechner, "Three Stories of Prostitution in the West: Prostitutes' Groups, Law and Feminist 'Truth'" (1994) 4 Colum J Gender & Law 26.

33. Valerie Jenness, *Making It Work: The Prostitutes' Rights Movement in Perspective* (New York: Aldine De Gruyter, 1993); Jo Bindman & Jo Doezema, *Redefining Prostitution as Sex Work on the International Agenda* (London: Anti-Slavery International, 1997).

34. Catherine MacKinnon, *Feminism Unmodified: Discourses on Law and Life* (Cambridge: Harvard University Press, 1987); Kathleen Barry, *The Prostitution of Sexuality* (New York: New York University Press, 1995).

35. *Canada (Attorney General) v Bedford*, 2013 SCC 7.

36. Globe and Mail, "Tory Prostitution Bill Gets Senate Approval" (November 4, 2014), online: <http://www.theglobeandmail.com/news/politics/tory-prostitution-bill-gets-senate-approval/article21450839/>; Richard Brennan, "Sex Workers Want Ontario to Delay Applying Prostitution Bill" (Toronto Star; December 16, 2014), online: <http://www.thestar.com/news/canada/2014/12/16/sex_workers_want_ontario_to_delay_applying_prostitution_bill.html>; Rachel Browne, "Roundup: Canadians Respond to the New Prostitution Law" (Maclean's; December 13, 2014), online: <http://www.macleans.ca/news/canada/roundup-canadians-respond-to-the-new-prostitution-law/>

37. *R v Hamilton* [2003] OJ No 532.

38. [2004] OJ No 3252. According to the guideline set out by the Ontario Court of Appeal in *Cunningham v Madden*, a sentence for drug importation would usually be in the range of two to five years of imprisonment.

39. However, given that by the time the appeal was decided the two women had served most of their sentences, it was determined that they should be allowed to finish their conditional sentences.

40. Elizabeth Comack, "Theoretical Approaches in the Sociology of Law: Theoretical Excursions" in Elizabeth Comack, ed, *Locating Law: Race/Class/Gender/Sexuality Connections*, 2nd ed (Halifax: Fernwood Publishing, 2006) 18 at 20–24.

41. Honourable Lynn Smith, "Judicial Education on Context" (2005) 39 UBC L Rev 569.

42. See, for example, Diane L Martin, "Punishing Female Offenders and Perpetuating Gender Stereotypes" in Julianne Roberts and David Cole, eds, *Making Sense of Sentencing* (Toronto: University of Toronto Press, 1999) at 186–198.

43. [1999] 1 SCR 688.

44. National Council of Welfare, "Justice and the Poor" (Ottawa: Minister of Public Works and Government Services Canada, 2000) at 60–62.

45. Richard F Devlin & Matthew Sherrard, "The Big Chill?: Contextual Judgment after *R. v. Hamilton and Mason*" (2005) 28 Dalhousie LJ 409 at 423.

46. See, e.g., Devlin & Sherrard, *ibid*; Sonia N Lawrence & Toni Williams, "Swallowed Up: Drug Couriers at the Borders of Canadian Sentencing" (2006) 56 U f T LJ 285; Dale Ives, "Inequality, Crime and Sentencing: *Borde, Hamilton* and the Relevance of Social Disadvantage in Canadian Sentencing Law" (2004) 30 Queen's LJ 114.

47. Devlin & Sherrard, *supra* note 45.

48. *Ibid*.

49. *Ibid*.

50. *Ibid*.

51. Lawrence & Williams, *supra* note 46.

52. *Ibid*.

53. Ives, supra note 46 at para 83–86.

54. *Ibid*.

55. *R v Hamilton*, *supra* note 38 (Court of Appeal); Ives, *ibid*.

56. *R v Hamilton*, supra note 38 (Court of Appeal); see also Devlin and Sherrard, *supra* note 45.

Chapter 9
Contract Law

Learning Objectives

After reading this chapter, you should be able to:

- Name seven main principles of contract law.

- Describe how a contract is formed.

- Explain what privity of contract is.

- Explain five ways in which a contract can be discharged.

- Describe five main remedies in contract law.

- Explain tension between the respect for individual autonomy and the protection of weaker parties in contract law.

Chapter Outline

Introduction

We enter into contracts on a daily basis, often without even realizing it. For example, buying a cup of coffee at a café or groceries at the store or a ticket on a bus is a contract. As a university student, you have entered into a contract with a university, under which you pay tuition fees and the university provides you with instruction on a given subject matter. If you work, your relationship with the employer is governed by a contract (as well as applicable labour and employment legislation). Thus, the knowledge of the basics of contract law is not only interesting in theory, but also of great practical use.

Part I of this chapter discusses the fundamentals of contract law: how a contract is formed; what criteria must be satisfied for it to be enforceable by courts; who can enter into contracts; how a contract comes to an end; and what remedies are available for contract breach or defects in contract formation. Part II discusses one of the central tensions in contract law: the respect for autonomy and choice of contracting individuals versus the need to protect vulnerable parties from being taken advantage of. This tension permeates both past and current rules of contract law and is integral to our understanding of the main objectives and principles of this area of law.

Part I. Substantive Law

1. MAIN PRINCIPLES OF CONTRACT LAW

Broadly speaking, a **contract** is an agreement between two or more parties that outlines their rights and obligations and is enforceable by courts. In order for an agreement to be considered a contract, the following requirements must be met:

- Parties have reached an agreement on the subject in question;
- Parties intend to create legally binding relations;
- Parties have legal capacity to enter into contracts;
- Parties entered into a contract voluntarily (e.g., neither party is forced or deceived into a contract);
- A contract has a consideration (that is, it involves something of value for both parties);
- Legal formalities are met (e.g., a contract is in writing or witnessed);
- A contract is not illegal (that is, not prohibited by law or not performed in an illegal manner).

Each of the above requirements is discussed in more detail below.

1.1 Formation of a Contract

The two parts in the formation of a contract are offer and acceptance. An *offer* is an expression of the willingness of one party (the *offeror*) to enter into a contract with another party on certain terms.[1] *Acceptance* demonstrates the willingness of the other prospective party (the *offeree*) to enter into a contract on the terms specified by the offeror.

An offer can be made orally, in writing, or by conduct. An offer does not remain in force forever. It lapses (that is, is no longer valid and cannot be accepted) in the following circumstances: (a) upon the death of the offeror; (b) if the offer has not been accepted within a reasonable time; or (c) if an offeror revoked the offer before it has been accepted.

An offer may outline the time period within which it must be accepted as well as how acceptance is to be communicated to the offeror. If an offer specified a particular mode of acceptance (e.g., in writing) and the deadline for acceptance, the acceptance must be communicated to the offeror in that form and by the specified date. If acceptance is communicated by mail, the acceptance is effective when it is mailed (this is called the *postal acceptance rule*). If acceptance can be communicated electronically, it becomes effective when the message enters the electronic system and can be retrieved.

The offeree's acceptance must be unconditional—that is, accepting the terms of the offer without modification. If the offeree responds with modification of the terms of the offer, she is making a *counter-offer*. This means that the original offer was rejected and a new offer has been made. Now it is up to the original offeror to decide whether to accept the counter-offer.

Once an offer is made and accepted, a contract is formed. A contract creates rights and obligations for parties to it (and, in some cases, for third parties). On the one hand, a contract is an expression of the will and choice of the two parties. On the other hand, by creating certain obligations, it compels particular behaviour or constrains action of the parties in a particular way.

Contracts can be for a one-time transaction (e.g., sale of a particular object) or ongoing (e.g., supply of goods over extended periods of time). A contract can be performed immediately upon reaching an agreement: goods/services and money are exchanged at the same time (e.g., when you buy a cup of coffee). They can also be executory. In an *executory contract*, an agreement is reached at one point, but its actual performance takes place at a later date. For example, on Monday, William concludes a contract for the purchase of certain goods, and those goods are delivered and payment is made on Thursday of the following week.

An offer must be differentiated from an *invitation to treat*, which is a request for offers. For example, merchandise advertising is an invitation to treat, which invites shoppers to make offers to purchase goods at the advertised price.

1.2 Agreement

An agreement must be clearly manifested either by written or verbal exchange between the parties or by their conduct. In some cases, the existence of an agreement may be easily established (for example, when there is a written document where all terms are clearly spelled out). In other cases, courts may have to examine the circumstances to determine if there is an agreement. For example, in *Pickett v Love*,[2] the plaintiff and defendant were romantically involved and Pickett offered to do some renovations on Love's house as he wanted to please her. He did a significant amount of work, but never discussed the estimates or method of payment with Love. She told him that she could not pay for the work. However, when Love ended the relationship, Pickett argued that there was a contract for the renovation work. The court rejected the plaintiff's claim, finding that there was no mutually contemplated obligation to pay for the work done.

1.3 Intention to Create a Legally Binding Relationship

Both parties must have an intention to be bound by the promises they make. In deciding whether parties have had such an intention, courts can inquire into their subjective perceptions as well as into what a "reasonable person" under the circumstances would have perceived.

Not every promise automatically makes a contract. Social agreements and moral vows are not considered contracts and cannot be enforced by courts. For example, a promise to show up at a friend's dinner party is a social—but not a contractual—promise.

1.4 Consideration

A contract must involve a **consideration**—that is, something of value. It can be a payment of money, receipt of goods or services, etc. The requirement of consideration reflects the idea that a contract is a bargain between the parties. It is about an exchange of promises or acts where each side gives and receives something of value.[3] Consideration must be a present or a future act. A past act does not constitute valid consideration. For example, if Jack shovels his neighbour's driveway without discussing this with him and then presents the neighbour with a bill for the services rendered, the payment cannot be enforced. In this case, consideration takes the form of already completed work (a past act) and is no consideration at all.

A promise to do something for free, without a return from the other party, is considered a **gratuitous promise**. In case of a gratuitous promise, there is no contract and such a promise cannot be enforced. The above mentioned case of *Pickett v Love* dealt with precisely such a situation where the plaintiff made a gratuitous promise to the defendant to make some renovations.

Individuals may conclude contracts on a variety of subject matters, including those related to family law (for more, see Chapter 11, Part I, section 6). See Box 9.1 for an interesting example of such use of contract law.

Box 9.1

An Agreement to Obtain a *Get* (Jewish Divorce): *Bruker v Marcovitz*, [2007] SCJ No 54

In *Bruker v Marcovitz*, the parties concluded an agreement settling their matrimonial dispute, including a commitment of both to go to a rabbinical court to obtain a *get* (a divorce document). Under Jewish law, only a husband can give a *get*. If he does not give one, a wife is unable to remarry and have legitimate children under the Jewish law. The defendant refused to give a *get* for 15 years. The wife, in fact, never remarried and had no children. She sued the husband for damages stemming from his noncompliance with the agreement. The husband argued that the award of damages would constitute violation of his freedom of religion.

The majority of the Supreme Court recognized that their agreement created binding contractual obligations. It upheld the decision of the trial court that the husband breached the contract by failing to promptly provide a *get* and the award of damages to the wife. The majority concluded that the husband could not rely on freedom of religion to avoid the consequences of noncompliance with the agreement. It wrote: "public interest in protecting equality rights, the dignity of Jewish women in their independent ability to divorce and remarry, as well as the public benefit in enforcing valid and binding contractual obligations, are among the interests and values that outweigh Marcovitz's claim that enforcing [the agreement] would interfere with his religious freedom."

1.5 Terms of a Contract

Statements in a contract that outline various parameters of the agreement are called *terms of the contract*. The terms of the contract can be classified into two types:

a. *Conditions*—essential terms that strike to the very heart of a contract

b. *Warranties*—other terms of a contract that are less significant

The distinction between conditions and warranties is of great practical importance as it leads to different consequences in case of their breach. A breach of a condition may lead to termination of a contract and may release an innocent party from its obligation to perform under the contract. In contrast, breach of a warranty, while allowing an innocent party to pursue some remedies, would usually not lead to the end of a contract.

The terms of the agreement must be sufficiently clear in order to be enforceable. In the absence of certainty, courts may refuse to recognize that a contract exists.[4]

1.6 Legal Formalities

A contract can be formed in writing or verbally. In some cases, a contract must be in writing, witnessed, and sealed. What formalities are required depends on the contract type. Some contracts must always be in writing in order to be enforceable. These include, for example, contracts for the sale of land, marriage and separation agreements, and guarantees (a promise by one person to pay the debt of another if that other person defaults). With the development of technology, contracts are increasingly taking electronic form and do not necessarily have to be in hard copy. Given the growing popularity of electronic commerce and communication, all Canadian provinces and territories adopted special legislation outlining the rules of econtract formation and other related issues.[5]

1.7 A Contract Must Not be Illegal

Contract law distinguishes two situations of illegality:

a. *Illegality as to contractual formation.* A contract may be illegal if it is made to commit an act prohibited by a statute. For example, some statutes provide that certain activities may be performed only by licensed individuals (e.g., selling vehicles, acting as a mortgage broker). If an individual without a required licence entered into specified contracts, such contracts would be considered illegal.[6] A contract can also be considered illegal for reasons of public policy. For example, one well established public policy rule is that a criminal should not be permitted to profit from a crime.[7]

b. *Illegality as to performance of a contract.* This means that a party is intending to perform a contract in an illegal manner (for example, a business has legally leased the premises but is occupying them without a valid occupancy permit as required by a local bylaw).[8]

A contract that is illegal is void and cannot be enforced. However, there are two exceptions to this rule: (a) where the parties to a contract are not equally guilty (e.g., if one party is either less blameworthy or is a victim of fraud, duress, or oppression); and (b) where the plaintiff repents before the illegal contract has been performed.[9]

For example, in *Buda v Plyplatis*,[10] the plaintiffs invested in an investment club with a promise by the defendants to return the investment within weeks of it having been made. When the defendants did not return the investment, the plaintiffs sued for breach of contract. The court refused relief, finding that the plaintiffs were parties to an illegal pyramid scheme and hence could not recover funds paid under such an illegal contract. In contrast, in *Ouston v Zurowski*,[11] recovery of money was permitted as the plaintiff repented: before the pyramid scheme was put into place, he abandoned any involvement in it and sought to recover the money given to the defendant.

1.8 Consequences of Not Fulfilling Essential Elements of a Contract

If one or more essential requirements for a contract are not met, a contract will be considered void or voidable (depending on the type of deficiency in the contract's formation). If a contract is considered **void**, this means that it has no legal effect. If a contract is void from the start, it is as if it never happened. A **voidable** contract means that a party may choose to **repudiate** (end) a contract without being considered in breach of it. In addition, remedies such as rescission or rectification may be appropriate in some cases (for explanation of remedies, see section 6).

2. CAPACITY TO ENTER INTO CONTRACTS

As mentioned above, parties must have the capacity to enter into a contract. *Capacity* refers to the ability of the person to understand the nature and terms of a transaction and to make an informed decision about it. Contract law identifies three categories of individuals in relation to which issues of capacity may arise:

- minors;
- persons with mental disorders or disabilities;
- highly intoxicated individuals.

Depending on the circumstances, a contract entered into by a person who lacked capacity to do so may be void. In this respect, contract law acts in a protective manner, seeking to ensure that persons lacking capacity are not taken advantage of.

2.1 Minors

Minors are persons under 18 years of age. The law historically recognized the need to protect minors, as it is considered that they can be taken advantage of due to their naivety or inexperience. This does not mean, however, that a minor can never enter into a valid contract. Contract law provides for three regimes in relation to contracts made by minors:

- Some contracts concluded by minors are recognized as valid (e.g., contracts for necessaries of life).

- Some contracts are considered void from the start. This is so when a contract is harmful or prejudicial to a minor.[12]

- Some contracts are voidable on the option of a minor. If a minor chooses not to repudiate a contract, the contract will have its usual, full effect. If a minor repudiates, he is relieved of all future responsibilities under the contract. Importantly, even though a minor may have an option to void a contract, the adult party is always bound by a contract and the contract is enforceable against her.

Which of the above mentioned regimes is applicable depends on at least two factors:

- whether a contract is for necessaries of life or nonnecessaries of life;
- whether the contract has been fully executed or not.

2.1.1 Contracts for Necessaries of Life

Necessaries of life are such things as clothing, food, shelter, and medication.[13] Contracts for necessaries of life concluded by minors are binding on minors and are enforceable. A minor is liable to pay but only a reasonable price for such goods. Under various provincial *Sale of Goods Acts*, a minor is liable only for goods that have been sold and delivered.[14] However, in the case of an executory contract, a minor may be able to repudiate a contract before the goods have been delivered.[15]

2.1.2 Contracts for Nonnecessaries of Life

In contracts for nonnecessaries of life, a minor may repudiate a contract if he has not derived any real advantage under it. However, this is so only for contracts that have not been fully executed. If the contract has been fully executed, courts usually would not set it aside.

For example, in *Staples v Varga*,[16] a 14-year-old bought vintage comic books from the defendant. He used his parents' credit cards without permission to pay for the purchase. When the parents discovered this, they sought to return the books, but the defendant refused to refund the money. The parents sued and argued that the contract with a minor for nonnecessaries of life was voidable and they were entitled to a refund. The court found that the contract was not voidable as the minor received some real benefit from it— namely, he resold some of the acquired comic books. Further, due to having resold some books, he could no longer restore the defendant to the precontract position.

2.2 Persons with Mental Disorders and Disabilities

Persons who have a mental disorder or disability may void a contract they have entered into. Two main factors are usually considered: (a) whether the other party knew of the mental disability (actual knowledge or willful blindness to the facts), and (b) whether a contract was fair.[17] However, in contracts for necessaries of life, persons with disabilities are liable to pay a reasonable price, regardless of the other party's knowledge of disability.[18]

For instance, in *Grapko-Buba*,[19] the plaintiff signed an agreement to purchase a condo without understanding the nature or importance of the document. The plaintiff sought to recover her deposit, but the vendor refused. The court allowed the application. It found that it was not necessary for the vendor to know about the purchaser's incapacity in order for relief to be granted, and that the agreement could be undone without injustice to either party.[20]

2.3 Intoxicated Individuals

An intoxicated individual may be able to void a contract that she entered into while intoxicated. Three conditions must be met:

- due to intoxication, she was unable to understand what she was doing;
- another party to a contract was aware of intoxication; and
- the intoxicated party promptly moved to rescind the contract.

3. PRIVITY OF CONTRACT

Privity of contract refers to the idea that only parties to a contract have rights and obligations under it. Correspondingly, a person who is not a party to a contract (also called a third party) cannot claim benefits or incur liability under that contract. The issue of privity of contract becomes important in the context of enforcing contracts and obtaining remedies for their breach.

Despite the rule of privity of contract, there are several situations in which a third party may assert rights under a contract:

a. *Novation*. It takes place when a third party replaces one of the original parties to an existing contract. Novation effectively terminates the original contract and substitutes it with a new one, possibly on different terms.

b. *Assignment*. Assignment involves a transfer of contractual rights to a third party. Unlike novation, it does not change or replace the original contract. Then, in case of breach, the third party (assignee) is able to sue the other party under the original contract. For example, Seamus lends money to John, but assigns his right to collect the debt to Kalpana. Due to such an assignment, Kalpana can sue John if he does not repay on the due date.

c. *Third-party beneficiary*. Some contracts provide for benefits to be conferred on third parties. For example, a life insurance contract is between a policyholder and an insurance company, but it provides for a payment to a third party—the beneficiary. A beneficiary may sue to enforce a contract for his own benefit.[21]

Parties may also subcontract performance of their obligations to third parties (as long as the contract does not require personal performance). This is called *vicarious performance.* For example, Malik hires Julian to repair his house. Julian subcontracts Bob to perform the work. Thus, there are there two contracts in place: one between Malik and Julian, and the other one between Julian and Bob. If Malik is not satisfied with the quality of the work, he can sue Julian, but not Bob. Julian, in turn, may choose to sue Bob.

4. CIRCUMSTANCES PUTTING INTO QUESTION VALIDITY OF A CONTRACT

A contract is based on voluntary agreement of the parties, which represents the meeting of their minds. However, there may be circumstances that put these features of a contract into question. For example, if one or both parties were acting under a mistake with respect to a contract-related matter, it is uncertain whether a resulting contract truly reflects the parties' meeting of the minds. Or if one of the parties was forced or induced into a contract, the voluntariness of their consent will be in question. This section discusses mistakes, misrepresentation, duress, undue influence, and unconscionability, and their consequences for validity of contracts.

4.1 Mistakes

What happens if both or one of the parties acted under a mistake with respect to a contract-related matter? Can the resulting contract still be considered an expression of their agreement and be valid? The answer to this question depends on the type of mistake that was made. The remedies, depending on the circumstances, may include recognizing a contract as void or voidable, or ordering rescission of a contract or rectification (see section 6 of the chapter). Courts would not readily void a contract for reasons of mistake and where possible would attempt to rectify it.[22]

Contract law distinguishes several types of mistakes:

a. *Common mistake* occurs when both parties make the same mistake (e.g., both consider that the clothing in question is new, while in reality it is secondhand). A contract involving a common mistake that relates to something fundamental in the contract may lead to the contract's being considered void (under common law) or voidable under the rules of equity.[23]

b. *Mutual mistake* happens when both parties are mistaken, but their mistakes are different (e.g., one party wants to buy secondhand clothing and believes that a contract involves secondhand clothing, while the other party believes that a contract is about the sale and purchase of new clothing). If it can be considered that a mutual mistake precluded the parties from having a real agreement on the issue, the contract may be determined void. In deciding on the issue, courts ask whether an objective, reasonable bystander could conclude that the parties intended to contract, and whether the essential terms of that contract can be determined with a reasonable degree of certainty. If it is impossible to ascertain the parties' respective intentions, then they cannot be said to have been in agreement and the contract is void.

c. *Unilateral mistake* occurs when only one party to a contract makes a mistake. An agreement involving a unilateral mistake may be void or voidable (depending on the significance of the mistake) if the other party knew of the mistake and took advantage of it. For example, in *Stevens v Stevens*,[24] the parties signed a marriage contract. One clause of the contract contained an error: it stated that the wife would give the husband the full value of the house if the marriage broke down. In reality, however, she intended him to receive only half of the value of the house and this intention was known to the husband. At the time when the contract was drafted, the wife was not taking medication for her bipolar disorder and did not notice the mistake. The husband and his lawyer were aware of the mistake but did not seek clarification. When the marriage broke down, the husband sought to enforce the contract. The court found that there was no real agreement on the issue and that the contract was void from the start.

4.2 Misrepresentation

Misrepresentation is a misstatement of fact that may mislead or induce a party into a contract. Misrepresentation must be about a fact rather than just an expression of an opinion. For example, if an owner of a painting tells prospective buyers that the canvas was painted by van Gogh (while the owner knows this not to be true), she is committing misrepresentation. However, if the owner says that she thinks it was painted by van Gogh, this would be an expression of opinion and would not constitute misrepresentation.

The impact of misrepresentation on the validity of a contract will vary, depending on the following factors:

■ *Is misrepresentation innocent or fraudulent?* Innocent misrepresentation occurs when one party makes a false statement but believes it to be true. At common law, there is no remedy for innocent misrepresentation (unless misrepresentation constitutes a term of contract), while the rules of equity allow for rescission (cancellation of the contract and restoration of the parties to their precontract positions). *Fraudulent misrepresentation* occurs when a party knows that information is false and makes such false statement with intent to induce another party into a contract. A contract induced by fraudulent misrepresentation is voidable at the election of the innocent party and a court may grant the defrauded party a rescission.

■ *Was the prospective party induced into a contract due to misrepresentation?* If an innocent party is aware of misrepresentation and has entered into a contract anyway or was not influenced by that misrepresentation, such contract will not be rescinded.

■ *Was the party under an obligation to disclose certain information?* As a rule, silence is not considered misrepresentation. However, in some cases, there is a duty to disclose certain information and failing to do so may amount to misrepresentation. For example, in contracts of life insurance, there is a duty upon an applicant to make true and full representation of facts that are material to the insurance risk. For instance, in *Duong v NN Life Insurance Co*,[25] an insurance policy was declared void because the applicants failed to disclose some information regarding family members' medical condition.

4.3 Coercing a Party into a Contract

Contract law recognizes two types of coercion: duress and undue influence.

4.3.1 Duress

Duress occurs when a person is forced to do something under threat of force against himself, his family, or his property. Such a threat negates the existence of free consent and makes a resulting contract voidable. There need not be actual threats of violence. It is sufficient that one party takes deliberate actions to put such pressure on another party as to make him feel that there is no realistic choice but to submit.[26]

For example, in *Aly v Halal Meat Inc*,[27] court set aside a separation agreement between spouses, recognizing that the wife signed it under duress. During the marriage, the wife did not work outside the home, she had a disability, and the husband controlled all financial matters. The husband told her that, if she did not sign the separation agreement, she would have no place to live. This, coupled with her lack of financial resources, caused the wife to feel that she had no choice but to sign the agreement.

4.3.2 Undue Influence

The concept of undue influence covers situations where a party was put under moral pressure to enter into a contract. Two situations may be distinguished: (a) actual undue influence (e.g., such as being bullied into a contract); and (b) presumed undue influence, which arises from a certain preexisting relationship between the parties. The latter may occur where one party is in a position of trust or authority and therefore may exert influence over the other party (e.g., doctor–patient, solicitor–client, guardian–ward). The concept of undue influence questions the sufficiency of consent in a given case[28] and makes such contracts voidable.

4.4 Unconscionability

Unconscionability applies to situations where there is a significant power imbalance between the parties that results in a weaker party being taken advantage of. The unequal bargaining power of the parties may stem from their different levels of knowledge or experience, financial circumstances, or other factors. In order to establish that a contract is unconscionable, the following must be established:

- inequality in the positions of the parties;
- an unfair bargain.[29]

A court may set aside a contract that it finds unconscionable (Box 9.2).

Unconscionability: *Williams v Condon*, [2007] OJ No 1683

Williams was struck by a car and sustained a knee injury. The driver was insured by State Farm Automobile Insurance Company, which was to pay Williams injury-related expenses and income replacement. The insurance company negotiated a settlement agreement with Williams, according to which he released the insurance company and the driver from all further claims for a consideration of $7700. At the time when Williams signed the settlement, he had not yet completed the course of physiotherapy and had not returned to work. Once he started working, his knee became unstable and was popping out of joint from time to time. He eventually had to undergo surgery, had to take some four months off of work, and was unable to return to work full-time. His earnings went down by 25–30%. Subsequently, he sought to have the settlement agreement set aside as unconscionable.

The court found that both conditions of unconscionability were met:

1. *Unequal bargaining power of Williams versus State Farm.* Prior to his injury, Williams worked as a window cleaner earning $1000 a week. He had no other source of income. When he became unable to work, he ended up in a precarious financial situation and was entirely dependent on income replacement payments made by State Farm. State Farm representatives had much more knowledge in assessing damage than Williams. They also had the power to make a decision on Williams's claim and to withhold the payment of benefits if they considered him ineligible.

2. *An unfair bargain.* When a settlement agreement was signed, much was unknown about Williams's condition: he had not recovered yet, he had not yet been examined by an orthopaedic specialist, and State Farm proceeded on a mistaken assumption that Williams merely had a knee sprain (which later turned out to be an anterior cruciate ligament tear). The $7700 settlement amount was very low and clearly unfair to Williams.

5. DISCHARGE OF A CONTRACT

Discharge of a contract refers to a situation when the obligations under it have come to an end and the contract is no longer in force.

A contract can be discharged by the following means:

- By performance;
- By agreement;
- By frustration;
- By operation of the law;
- By breach.

5.1 By Performance

The parties are expected to perform their obligations according to the terms of the contract. Once obligations of both parties are performed, a contract comes to an end.

5.2 By Agreement

In some circumstances, parties may be unable or choose not to perform a contract as originally agreed, yet they do not want to be in breach of it either. Then, they may try to end the existing contract by agreement. This can take several forms:

a. Before a contract is fully executed, parties can agree not to proceed with the contract and conclude a *waiver*, according to which neither party can assert rights under the contract.

b. Parties may conclude a new agreement which replaces the old one, releasing each other from the original contract.

c. Parties can agree to *accord and satisfaction*, which is essentially a "purchase of a release from an obligation arising under contract."[30] This happens when one party is unable or unwilling to perform obligations and makes the other party an offer to terminate the contract for some compensation. For example, if a supplier is unable to provide the goods specified in a contract, she may offer the purchaser substitute goods at a discount. If the purchaser agrees, then this will constitute accord and satisfaction.

5.3 By Frustration

Frustration occurs when, due to some unforeseen circumstances, it is no longer possible to perform obligations under a contract. The impossibility can be physical (e.g., because the subject matter of a contract has been destroyed) or may result from a legal development that has made performance legally impossible. The case of *Cowie v Great Blue Heron Charity Casino*[31] is a good illustration of the latter. Cowie was employed as a security guard. At a certain point, new legislation came into force that required all security guards to be licensed. Cowie was ineligible for such a licence because he did not have a clean criminal record (he had a conviction for which he had never sought a pardon). Without a licence, it was illegal to continue Cowie's employment as a security guard and, as a result, his contract was discharged by frustration.

5.4 By Operation of the Law

The *discharge by operation of the law* means that the law either prescribes that obligations are discharged in certain situations (e.g., a bankrupt is absolved from liability upon an order for discharge) or changes to the law lead to discharge of certain contracts. The illustration of the latter can be found in *Reilly v The King*.[32] The Federal Appeal Board was abolished by legislation before Reilly's term on the board had expired. As a result, Reilly's contract was considered discharged by operation of the law.

5.5 By Breach

A *breach of contract* occurs when one or both parties have not fulfilled their obligations according to the terms of the contract. There are two main types of contract breach:

a. Failure to perform on a due date.

b. Anticipatory breach, which occurs when one party informs the other prior to the due date that it will not be performing its obligations. If anticipatory breach is accepted by the innocent party, this leads to the termination of the future performance of a contract. An innocent party is free from its obligations and may pursue a remedy against the other party (e.g., sue for damages without waiting for the due date).[33]

Not every breach of contract will end a contract and relieve the innocent party of its obligations. If a breach is fundamental and deprived the innocent party of the whole benefit of the contract, this can lead to the discharge of a contract. An innocent party can treat it as ended and terminate its own obligations. If a breach is less serious, then this does not end the contract, but an innocent party may sue for damages[34] (although it still must perform its obligations under the contract).

6. REMEDIES

Contract law provides for a variety of remedies:

- Damages;
- Rescission;
- Specific performance;
- Injunction;
- Rectification.

Which one will be most suitable depends on the circumstances of a case. For example, some of them are employed to address breaches of contract, while others are used when a contract is set aside due to nonfulfillment of certain essential elements of a contract.

6.1 Damages

Damages seek to restore an innocent party to the position she would have been in had the contract been performed. This is the most common remedy in case of breach of contract.

Contract law, however, places on a plaintiff the duty to *mitigate damages*. This means that the plaintiff must take all reasonable steps to reduce the loss resulting from the breach. For example, in a case of wrongful dismissal, an ex-employee is obligated to take reasonable steps to obtain alternative employment.[35] A plaintiff would not be able to make a claim for damages with respect to any loss that he did not take steps to mitigate.

There are several types of damages:

- *Liquidated.* These damages are usually set out in a contract itself: parties agree to a specified penalty in case of contract breach (for example, a supplier agrees to pay $100 for every day of delay in delivering goods). This allows parties to avoid costly disputes and litigation on the amount of damages in case of contract breach.

- *Consequential.* These are damages resulting from the consequences of breach (e.g., loss of expected profits). For example, in *Nguyen v Tran,*[36] the plaintiff hired the defendant to build a restaurant. According to the contract, the project was to be completed by July 31, 2007. However, due to delays, mainly by the contractor, the restaurant was not ready until December 2007. The restaurant owners sued the contractor for breach of contract and asked for damages. The court found that the contract was breached and awarded liquidated damages (as set out by the contract between the parties) as well as the cost of rent, utilities, and property taxes that the plaintiff had to pay during the 4.5-month delay in construction.

- *Punitive.* Punitive damages seek to punish the defendant for malicious, arbitrary, or highly reprehensible misconduct.[37] For example, in *Ottawa Community Housing Corp v Foustanellas (c.o.b. Argos Carpets),*[38] the court awarded punitive damages along with other damages for breach of contract. Ottawa Community Housing Corporation contracted Argos Carpets to install carpeting in its rental units. Argos Carpets installed substandard carpet, misrepresented the amount of carpet installed, and falsified invoices. The court awarded the plaintiff damages for the breach of contract (the use of substandard carpet and misrepresentation of the amount installed) and punitive damages for fraud. See Box 9.3 for another example of a case involving punitive damages.

Box 9.3

Punitive Damages: *Whiten v Pilot Insurance Co,* [2002] 1 SCR 595

The case illustrates what conduct may be considered so egregious as to warrant the award of punitive damages. The Whiten family's home and its contents were destroyed in a fire. The family had home insurance and submitted a claim to Pilot Insurance. The company initially made some payments, but refused further payments alleging that the family had torched its own house. These allegations were insisted upon despite the fact that the local fire chief and the insurance company's own expert investigator concluded that there was no evidence of arson. At trial, the jury was satisfied that Pilot's denial of the claim was intended to force the Whitens to make an unfair settlement for less than what they were entitled to. The insurance company knew from the outset that the arson allegations were unsustainable. Yet, in a planned and deliberate manner, it continued to refuse the claim for over two years while the Whitens' financial situation grew increasingly desperate. The jury awarded $1 million in punitive damages against the company, and the Supreme Court confirmed the award.

6.2 Rescission

Rescission sets aside a contract and restores the parties back to their original precontract positions. This remedy can be used, for example, where a contract resulted from fraud, misrepresentation, or undue influence (Box 9.4).[39] However, it would not be appropriate where it is no longer possible to return the parties to their precontract position (e.g., the goods received by one party have already been consumed or resold).

6.3 Specific Performance

Specific performance is a court order obligating a party to do what she promised to do under a contract. As a rule, this remedy is used when a contract involves a certain unique object and where damages would not properly compensate for a party's failure to deliver that object. This remedy has traditionally been used with respect to contracts for the purchase of land. Each parcel of land is considered unique and damages are considered an inadequate remedy in case of nonperformance.

6.4 Injunction

An injunction is a court order requiring a defendant to either do or refrain from doing something. For example, an injunction may compel a party to perform an obligation under a contract or to abstain from breaking a contract. Frequent use of such remedy is found in relation to contracts that prohibit former employees from soliciting a company's clients. Where such nonsolicitation agreements are violated, employers usually apply for an injunction to force their former employees to comply with the agreements.[40]

Box 9.4

Rescission and Damages: *Murch v Dan Leonard Auto Sales Ltd*, [2013] SJ No 523

Murch was looking to buy a truck with a 7.3-litre engine. Leonard said that he had such a truck available and that it was in great condition. Murch agreed to buy it for $20 000. A few days after the sale, Murch started having problems with the truck. When he took it to a mechanic, it turned out that the truck had a 6.0-litre engine, not a 7.3-litre engine. Murch wanted to rescind the contract and receive his money back. The court found that Murch was entitled to rescission on the basis of misrepresentation (Leonard stated that the truck had a 7.3-litre engine, while in reality this was not true). In addition, the court awarded the plaintiff damages to compensate him for the initial insurance and registration payments on the truck.

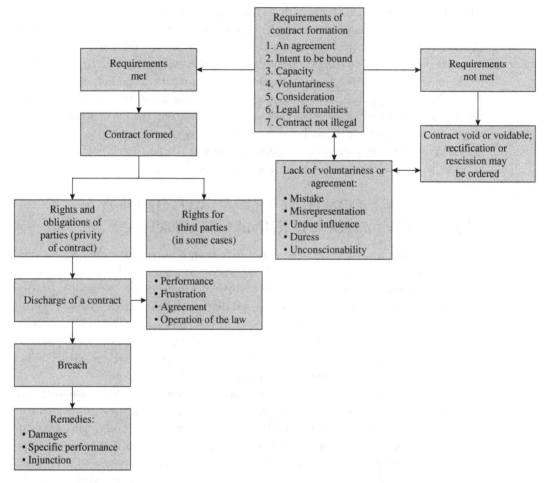

Figure 9.1 Life of a contract

6.5 Rectification

Rectification is an equitable remedy that can be used when parties made a mistake in a contract that distorts their original intention (e.g., a contract specifies a payment of $1000 instead of the $10 000 that was actually agreed upon). Rectification allows a court to amend the terms of the contract in order to reflect the original intention of the parties.

The foregoing characteristics of a contract are summarized in Figure 9.1.

Part II. Critical Perspectives

A contract has traditionally been thought of as an expression of individuals' autonomy, freedom, and choice. At the same time, we also recognize that parties may have unequal bargaining power and that a stronger party may be able to take advantage of a weaker one.

These two statements reflect one of the central tensions in contract law and theory: how do we balance the respect for individual autonomy with the need to protect weaker parties? Should law allow courts to set aside unfair contracts? Or should it take a "hands-off" approach, leaving it up to the parties to ensure that they strike a fair and beneficial deal? These questions are not purely academic, but have great practical significance. If the state takes a hands-off approach, it would respect individual autonomy but, at the same time, allow and implicitly condone unfair contracts. If the state implements multiple measures to protect weaker parties, it may be seen as unduly interfering in individual choices and undermining robust and competitive business behaviour. This section briefly reviews how contract law has attempted to address these competing considerations.

1. CLASSICAL CONTRACT LAW: AUTONOMY, EFFICIENCY, AND A MINIMALIST STATE

Classical contract law of the nineteenth and early twentieth centuries reflected the ideas of the free market prevalent at the time.[41] Individuals were presumed to be independent, informed, rational actors who should be free to exercise their autonomy through contract law. The notion of a rational actor presupposed that individuals have all necessary information to make informed decisions and choose the best course of action.[42] The respect for individual freedom and choice was also supported by efficiency considerations. It was considered that when individuals are free to engage in transactions without state-imposed limitations, they will choose arrangements that are most beneficial for them.[43]

As a result, contract law and scholarship was preoccupied mostly with how to respect and promote individual autonomy and efficiency, rather than with how to protect weaker parties. The parties were expected to look out for themselves and to take responsibility for the choices they made.[44] This approach promoted the idea of individualism, independence, and self-reliance. The main question for classical contract law was whether there was a contract, not whether it was fair. Courts focused on whether the three main elements of contract formation—offer, acceptance, and consideration—were met. If there was a contract, it had to be enforced. It was not for courts to impose obligations that had not been contemplated by the parties or to police whether bargains were fair. While some protections to ensure that parties consented voluntarily (not under duress, fraud, or undue influence) were available, common law provided for no general duty of good faith or disclosure.[45] Overall, it was considered that the state should play a minimal role in regulating contracts or interfering with existing contracts. [46]

The idea of freedom of contract allowed individuals and businesses not only to choose whom to contract with and on what terms, but also to refuse to enter into contracts with certain parties. While at first sight there seems to be nothing wrong with exercising the freedom to refuse to enter into a contract, history shows that such freedom allowed for perpetuation of racial or other bias. In the infamous *Christie v York*[47] case, the defendant, a Montreal tavern, refused to serve beer to a patron who was black. The Supreme Court concluded that the freedom of commerce allowed any business to deal or not to deal with any member of the public. In *Rogers*,[48] the refusal to serve beer to a black person was similarly upheld as an exercise of the freedom of commerce.

2. CONTEMPORARY CONTRACT LAW: BALANCING INDIVIDUAL AUTONOMY AND PROTECTION OF WEAKER PARTIES

Classical contract law was largely unconcerned with the power imbalances between parties to a contract, discrimination, or unfairness of contracts. However, the developments of the second half of the twentieth century—the rise of the welfare state, the promotion of human rights and nondiscrimination, and the growth of critical legal scholarship—provided a new vantage point on contractual relations. They challenged the key presumption of contract law that parties to a contract are always equal, independent, informed, rational actors and recognized the need for some state intervention to protect weaker parties.

Contractual interactions may be impacted by power imbalances, which can either strengthen or undermine a given party's bargaining power. The power imbalances can stem from a variety of factors such as wealth and resources, social status, gender, education level, or language proficiency. For example, the existing distribution of resources determines the person's power to contract and to act as a truly independent rational actor.[49] Some argue that the imbalance of power that underlies contract relations promotes the interests of the advantaged.[50] The more one party owns, the greater is its power. A bargaining power of an already advantaged party is increased every time that party enters into a contract: it reaps more benefits in each contract and over time will end up owning more and more resources.[51] Frequent and powerful participants of the marketplace who have greater legal knowledge can use contract law to their benefit and perpetrate and magnify social inequalities.[52]

As we saw in Part I, common law developed a mechanism to address unequal bargaining power of the parties—the doctrine of unconscionability—that allows courts to set unfair contracts aside. In addition, many countries enacted legislation in selected subject areas, which helps to protect weaker parties. For example, employment laws prescribe some minimum standards (e.g., minimum wage, work hours, vacation time and pay, and the like), thereby limiting the freedom of contract. Due to this legislation, an employment contract cannot offer less than minimum wage, cannot impose unsafe working conditions, cannot obligate employees to work extra hours, and so on. Labour relations legislation does not impose particular minimum standards, but provides for a mechanism for workers to consolidate in unions or associations, which will then have greater bargaining power to negotiate with employers for better work conditions. Federal and provincial human rights codes in Canada directly address situations such as *Christie* and *Rogers* and do not allow businesses or individuals to refuse to enter into contracts with others on discriminatory grounds (see Chapter 12). If individuals face discrimination, they can seek remedies before special provincial commissions and/or tribunals.

Thus, contemporary contract law does incorporate some protections for weaker parties. However, this does not mean that individual freedom and autonomy are no longer important. In fact, they still remain commanding values in most contexts (except where legislation established a special regime such as in the area of employment). Academic debate is divided on the proper balance between individual autonomy and protection of weaker parties. Some scholars, for example, argue that the doctrine of unconscionability infringes on the autonomy of the parties and discourages them from acting responsibly.[53] Further, because courts may set aside unfair bargains, this doctrine is said to create uncertainty and negatively impact business dealings (the more uncertain the enforcement of contracts is, the less likely people are to engage in exchanges).

In contrast, others argue that contemporary contract law does not do enough to address power imbalances. For example, contract law does not consider power imbalances as highly problematic and posits that inequalities can be relatively easily addressed (for example, through the requirements of disclosure). However, the fact that information is disclosed does not necessarily mean that it is properly understood. The language of a contract itself is often rather complex and replete with specialized terms that may not be known to everyone. For example, before reading this chapter, did you understand the concepts of rescission or liquidated damages? Such factors as level of education and language proficiency can play a significant role in a party's ability to understand a contract's technical language and its implications. It has been noted that contracts are better understood by those with a postsecondary degree than those without.[54] In addition, consumers who are not proficient in an official language may be more easily induced into contracts with unfair terms that are not properly translated or explained to them.[55] However, as some noted, a mere inability to read and understand an official language is insufficient to set a contract aside; it is necessary to look at the party's level of sophistication and presence of any other disadvantaging factors such as a party's disability or old age, undue influence, duress, misrepresentation, or fraud.[56]

From the above brief discussion it is clear that contract interactions need to be viewed in the broader context of socioeconomic status of the parties, as such status may impact their ability to make a truly voluntary and informed decision. While contract law does allow for some protection of weaker parties, it continues to struggle with striking a proper balance between freedom of contract and fairness. The current era of neoliberalism places strong emphasis on individual self-reliance, swaying the rules of contract law closer to the freedom of contract side of the spectrum.

SUMMARY

Contract law is an important facilitator of our activities, from daily routines such as buying groceries to activities of major commercial enterprises. It thus needs to create a flexible framework for the exercise of our autonomy and choices, while at the same time ensuring certainty and enforceability of contracts. This is achieved through multiple rules, including requirements for contract formation, various options of discharge of contracts, and remedies to address contract breach and deficiencies in contract formation. In order for a contract to be formed, seven major requirements must be met: (1) an agreement between the parties; (2) an intention to be legally bound; (3) capacity to enter into a contract; (4) voluntariness; (5) presence of a consideration; (6) satisfaction of legal formalities; and (7) that a contract is not illegal. If one or more of these requirements are not met, a contract may be void or voidable. If all requirements are met and a contract is valid, it creates rights and obligations for parties to a contract (this is reflected in the idea of privity of contract). In some cases, a contract may create rights for third parties (beneficiaries). It is also possible for parties to a contract to assign their rights or to subcontract their obligations under that contract to third parties.

Ideally, we expect a contract to be carried out—that is, discharged by performance. However, a contract may also be discharged in other ways: by agreement, frustration, operation of the law, and breach. In the case of breach in particular, an innocent party may apply for various remedies, including damages, specific performance, and injunction.

While historically contract law prioritized individual autonomy and freedom of contract, some common law and statutory rules have also been developed to protect vulnerable parties from being taken advantage of. Power imbalances may lead to unfair contracts and may contribute to further marginalization of disadvantaged groups. However, the debate is still ongoing as to the proper balance between freedom of contract and protection of the vulnerable. So far, compared to some other areas discussed in this book, contract law is an outlier in the sense that it is not considered a primary site for promoting redistribution and social justice objectives.[57]

Critical Thinking Questions

1. Imagine the following situation: Rob purchased life insurance and made Laureen the beneficiary. Rob died while carrying 30 pellets of cocaine in his stomach (one of the pellets had burst). The insurance company refused to pay, saying that Laureen's claim was barred by the public policy principle that a person should not be allowed to insure against his own criminal act. Apply the concepts studied in this chapter and answer the following questions: can Laureen (given that she was not a party to the insurance contract) sue for contract enforcement? Should the insurance contract be considered illegal because Rob was engaging in criminal activity that led to his death? Should Laureen be able to receive the payment under the insurance policy?

   You may find the following decision of the Supreme Court helpful in answering the above questions: *Oldfield v Transamerica Life Insurance Co. of Canada* [2002] 1 SCR 742.

2. In your opinion, how (if at all) should contract law address inequality in bargaining power of parties to a contract?

3. Imagine the following scenario: Nancy is employed as a nurse at a hospital. However, she is found guilty of professional misconduct and her registration as a nurse is revoked. The hospital cannot employ as nurses individuals who do not have the required professional registration. What happens with respect to Nancy's employment contract? Can the contract be considered discharged? If yes, on what basis (e.g., by agreement, by frustration, or something else)?

4. Recall any of the recent contracts that you have entered into and analyze them by applying the concepts studied in this chapter: was the contract in writing or verbal? Was it executory? Were all of the main principles of contract formation observed? Was there any power inequality between you and the other party? If yes, how did it influence the contract?

Further Readings and Resources

1. Jean Fitzgerald and Laurence Olivo, *Fundamentals of Contract Law*, 2nd ed (Toronto: Emond Montgomery, 2005).

2. Paul Michell, "Illiteracy, Sophistication and Contract Law" (2005) 31 Queen's LJ 311.

3. Linda Mulcahy, *Contract Law in Perspective*, 5th ed (Abingdon: Routledge-Cavendish, 2008).

4. Michael Trebilcock, *The Limits of Freedom of Contract* (Cambridge: Harvard University Press, 1993).

Endnotes

1. Gerald Fridman, *The Law of Contracts*, 5th ed (Toronto: Carswell, 2006) at 26.
2. [1982] SJ No 729.
3. Fridman, *supra* note 1 at 83–87.
4. *Ibid* at 19.
5. See, e.g., *Electronic Commerce Act, 2000*, SO 2000, c 17 (Ontario); *Electronic Commerce Act*, SNS 2000, c 26 (Nova Scotia); *Electronic Commerce Act*, RSPEI 1988, c E-4.1 (PEI); *Electronic Transactions Act*, SBC 2001, c 10 (British Columbia).
6. Fridman, *supra* note 1 at 342.
7. *Oldfield v Transamerica Life Insurance Co of Canada*, [2002] 1 SCR 742.
8. Fridman, *supra* note 1 at 352.
9. *Buda v Plyplatis*, [2004] OJ No 5175.
10. *Ibid*.
11. (1985), 63 BCLR 89 (BCCA).
12. Jean Fitzgerald & Laurence Olivo, *Fundamentals of Contract Law*, 2nd ed (Toronto: Emond Montgomery, 2005) at 51.
13. Under the *Sale of Goods Acts*, RSO 1990, c S.1, s 3(2), necessaries of life are defined as "goods suitable to the condition in life." Courts have taken the position that what amounts to necessaries of life for a given individual depends on his way of life. Thus, something that is a luxury for a poor person may be considered a necessary of life for the rich.
14. Fridman, *supra* note 1 at 142.
15. Fitzgerald & Olivo, *supra* note 12 at 47.
16. *Staples (next friend of) v Varga (c.o.b. True Legends Sports Cards and Comics)* [1995] AJ No 200.
17. Fridman, *supra* note 1 at 159–160.
18. *Ibid* at 162.
19. *Grapko-Buba (Litigation guardian of) v Law Cranberry Development Ltd* [2001] OJ No 2562.
20. Reversed on appeal but on a different ground that did not deal with whether the other party must know about mental disability. *Grapko-Buba (Litigation guardian of) v Law Cranberry Development Ltd* [2003] OJ No 2156.
21. See, e.g., *Oldfield, supra* note 7.
22. Fitzgerald & Olivo, *supra* note 12 at 71.
23. Fridman, *supra* note 1 at 256.
24. *Stevens v Stevens*, 109 OR (3d) 421.
25. *Duong v NN Life Insurance Co. of Canada*, [1999] OJ No 2680.
26. *Aly v Halal Meat Inc*, [2013] OJ No 1329 at paras 367–68.
27. *Ibid*.

28. *Morrison v Coast Finance Ltd et al.*, [1965] BCJ No 178.

29. *Ibid* at para 4; *Norberg v Wynrib*, [1992] 2 SCR 226 at para 40.

30. *British Russian Gazette & Trade Outlook Ltd v Associated Newspapers Ltd* [1933] 2 KB 616 at 643–644 cited in Fridman, *supra* note 1 at 572.

31. *Cowie v Great Blue Heron Charity Casino*, [2011] OJ No 5573.

32. *Reilly v The King*, [1934] 1 DLR 434.

33. Fridman, *supra* note 1 at 606.

34. *Ibid* at 580–581.

35. *Ibid* at 781.

36. *Nguyen v Tran*, [2012] OJ No 1762.

37. *Whiten v Pilot Insurance Co*, [2002] 1 SCR 595.

38. [2013] OJ No 765.

39. Fridman, *supra* note 1 at 813.

40. See, e.g., *Precision Fine Papers Inc v Durkin*, [2008] OJ No 703.

41. Linda Mulcahy, *Contract Law in Perspective*, 5th ed (Abingdon: Routledge-Cavendish, 2008) at 28.

42. Danielle Kie Hart, "Contract Law Now—Reality Meets Legal Fictions" (2011) U Balt L Rev 1 at 47.

43. *Ibid* at 235–36.

44. Jay M Feinman, "Critical Approaches to Contract Law" (1983) 30 UCLA L Rev 829 at 840.

45. JA Manwaring, "Unconscionability: Contested Values, Competing Theories and Choice of Rule in Contract law" (1993) 25 Ottawa L Rev 235.

46. Hart, *supra* note 42 at 14–15. However, not everybody agreed that the state indeed took a minimalist role. For example, Cohen argued that contract law is shaped by public policy considerations and that the state intervenes, often in unnoticeable ways, into virtually every aspect of contract law. Morris R Cohen, "The Basis of Contract" (1933) 46 Harv L Rev 553.

47. [1940] SCR 139.

48. *Rogers v Clarence Hotel Co*, [1940] BCJ No 25.

49. Feinman, *supra* note 44 at 842.

50. Hart, *supra* note 42.

51. *Ibid* at 66.

52. Feinman, *supra* note 44 at 845.

53. Manwaring, *supra* note 45.

54. Hart, *supra* note 42 at 49.

55. Julian Lim, "Tongue-tied in the Market: the Relevance of Contract Law to Racial-language Minorities" (2003) 91:2 California L Rev 579 at 604.

56. Paul Michell, "Illiteracy, Sophistication and Contract Law" (2005) 31 Queen's LJ 311.

57. There is, however, some scholarship on the issue. See, for example, Anthony Townsend Kronman, "Contract Law and Distributive Justice" (1980) 89 Yale L Rev 472.

Chapter 10

Tort Law

Learning Objectives

After reading this chapter, you should be able to:

- Name and explain six functions of tort law.

- Explain the difference between intentional torts and torts of negligence.

- Compare and contrast seven types of intentional torts.

- Define the concept of the duty of care.

- Describe defences to intentional torts and torts of negligence.

- Identify and describe two types of damages that can be claimed in tort lawsuits.

- Define the concepts of contributory fault/negligence, joint tortfeasors, and strict liability.

- Explain the impact of class, race, and gender on tort law rules and outcomes.

Chapter Outline

Introduction

What is tort law about? To answer this question, let us have a look at the following example: Kanye enters an intersection on a red light and collides with another car. Christina, the other driver, suffers very serious injuries, spends a month in a hospital, and partially recovers. However, the brain injury has a lasting impact and Christina is unlikely to be able to return to work in the future. Further, she requires ongoing chiropractic sessions and rehabilitation support. Is there a way for Christina to recover the losses suffered?

Yes, a remedy is available under tort law. She can sue Kanye to obtain financial compensation for the harm that she has suffered as a result of the collision. If her case is made out, she could be compensated for past and future medical expenses as well as future loss of income (if she is unable to return to work due to injury). However, how would a court calculate such future losses and expenses? Would Christina's current socioeconomic position impact the court's projection of her future income? These and other questions will be discussed in this chapter.

Tort is derived from the Latin word *tortus*, which means crooked or twisted. In early English, it was used as a synonym for *wrong* and has survived as a technical term to this day.[1] In very general terms, tort law is a body of rules that determines under what circumstances and how victims of wrongdoings may recover compensation for the harm that they have suffered in noncontractual relations.

It is important to see tort law in connection with other areas of law, particularly criminal and contract law. Contract law can provide a remedy for losses resulting from nonfulfillment of a contractual obligation (recall Chapter 9). In contrast, tort law can be used for harms suffered in noncontractual interactions where the parties to a suit are often strangers to each other (as in the case of Kanye and Christina). Therefore, the two areas of law are complementary, ensuring that individuals have recourse against wrongdoings in both contractual and noncontractual contexts.

The conduct that may be considered a tort can also constitute a criminal offence. For example, assault is both a criminal offence and a tort. Thus, a perpetrator may be criminally charged and, in addition, the victim may sue in tort to obtain financial compensation for injuries. It should be noted, however, that there are significant differences between the criminal and tort law processes, including the requirements to be met for establishing that a wrongful act has been committed, the objectives, and the consequences of each process. Importantly, while a crime is considered a public wrong and is prosecuted by the state, a tort is a private wrong and tort action needs to be brought by the individual victim. Tort can be seen as one of the ways to promote justice, namely through imposing an obligation on the wrongdoer to compensate for the victim's injury.

Part I. Substantive Law

1. FUNCTIONS OF TORT LAW

Tort law performs multiple functions:

- *Compensation.* By award of damages, it seeks to compensate victims for the loss they have suffered (e.g., medical costs, emotional distress, loss of income).
- *Deterrence and admonition.* The imposition of liability on the wrongdoer and an obligation to pay damages to victims may help promote more responsible conduct and deter careless acts both by a specific wrongdoer and by the general population. The

possibility of being held liable for not only intentional conduct but also negligence is considered to create incentives for individuals and businesses to take greater care or take reasonable precautions in planning and exercising certain activities.

- *Standard setting.* Linked to the objectives of deterrence and admonition is the ability of tort law to establish certain standards of behaviour. For example, in the context of negligent torts, the concept of a reasonable person (explained below) reflects a minimum standard of conduct for a given activity.

- *Psychological.* The availability of a tort law remedy may help empower victims of wrongdoings and allow for the recognition of the injustice they suffered.

- *Educational.* Tort lawsuits can attract media and scholarly attention, thereby informing the public about certain types of wrongdoings or problems. They can also help generate an impetus for change.

- *Ombudsman.* An **ombudsman** is an impartial and independent officer established to investigate allegations of maladministration and to make recommendations for improvement. Tort law, of course, does not literally involve an officer investigating allegations of maladministration, but tort lawsuits may perform an ombudsman-like function when they expose wrongful or negligent actions of state authorities or private businesses. For example, violations of individual rights by the police may be pursued as a tort action, which, if successful, may promote more responsible conduct by the police. Compensation would likely not be the primary objective in such lawsuits, but rather the plaintiff would seek to bring about change to the practices of a given agency[2] and/or create incentives for government officials to be more attentive to the needs of citizens.[3]

In the nineteenth and early twentieth centuries, admonition and punishment were viewed as the primary functions of tort law.[4] Later in the twentieth century, compensation emerged as one of the key functions, which largely remains the case to date. While it is recognized that tort law may serve ombudsman, psychological, and educational functions, they are considered secondary.

2. TYPES OF TORTS

There are two types of torts: intentional and negligent.

2.1 Intentional Torts

Intentional torts are those where a **tortfeasor** (a person who has committed a tort) wished to produce a certain wrongful result. Among the most common intentional torts are battery, assault, false imprisonment, trespass to land, wrongful interference with chattels, and defamation.[5]

2.1.1 Battery

Battery occurs when a person intentionally causes harmful or offensive contact with another person. For example, hitting, punching, or grabbing somebody constitutes battery.

The contact does not have to cause harm to the victim; its mere offensive or unwanted nature is sufficient to constitute battery. For example, hugging or kissing someone against their will would constitute battery. However, this does not mean that any nonconsensual contact amounts to battery. Contact that constitutes a part of our everyday life (e.g., tapping someone on the shoulder to get their attention) would not be considered battery. Box 10.1 presents an example of the tort of battery.

Battery: *Malette v Shulman et al*, 63 OR (2d) 243 (upheld on appeal: 72 OR (2d) 417 (ONCA))

After a car accident, Malette was rushed to a hospital unconscious. Her injuries were severe and a treating physician determined that a blood transfusion was necessary. As the nurse was preparing Malette for transfusion (Malette was still unconscious), the following message was found on a card she was carrying: "NO BLOOD TRANSFUSION! As one of Jehovah's Witnesses with firm religious convictions, I request that no blood or blood products be administered to me under any circumstances. I fully realize the implications of this position, but I have resolutely decided to obey the Bible command: 'Keep abstaining . . . from blood' (Acts 15:28, 29). However, I have no religious objection to use the nonblood alternatives, such as Dextran, Haemaccel, PVP, Ringer's Lactate or saline solution." Despite being aware of the card, the physician administered a blood transfusion as it was necessary to save Malette's life. Has the doctor committed any tort?

Malette sued Shulman, alleging that by performing a blood transfusion against her wishes, he committed battery. The court agreed and awarded her $20 000 in damages.

One may be puzzled by the decision in *Malette v Shulman*: what can be more important than saving someone's life? Is it fair to hold liable a doctor who was performing his duty?

The trial court found that the doctor had acted "promptly, professionally" and "carried out [the treatment] in a competent, careful and conscientious manner." In its view, the doctor was well aware of the card, but felt in his professional judgement that he had to administer the blood transfusion to save Malette's life. However, by acting contrary to the instructions on the card, Shulman violated the patient's rights to make decisions over her own body. Because Malette did not wish to have a blood transfusion, administration of such treatment, even in order to save her life, constituted unwanted interference with her body—battery by definition. The court stated: "However sacred life may be, fair social comment admits that certain aspects of life are properly held to be more important than life itself. . . . Refusal of medical treatment on religious grounds is such a value."

The decision of the trial court was upheld by the Court of Appeal. The Court of Appeal again emphasized respect for religious freedom: "To transfuse a Jehovah's Witness in the face of her explicit instructions to the contrary would, in my opinion, violate her right to control her own body and show disrespect for the religious values by which she has chosen to live her life."[6]

This case provides a useful illustration not only of the tort of battery, but also of a more far-reaching point about the importance of recognizing the value of one's religious beliefs.

2.1.2 Assault

Assault occurs when a tortfeasor intentionally creates an apprehension of immediate harmful or offensive contact (e.g., Carlene shakes a fist at Jack). In contrast to battery, which requires contact, assault occurs without contact as soon as the victim is under apprehension of immediate harm. In reality, assault and battery usually follow quickly one after the other. The following two examples demonstrate the difference between assault and battery:

■ If Carlene shakes a fist at Jack and then immediately punches Jack, she will have committed both assault and battery.

■ If Carlene shakes a fist at Jack and then immediately proceeds to punch Jack, but Jack ducks and avoids the punch, Carlene will have committed only assault but not battery as no harmful or offensive contact has occurred.

2.1.3 False Imprisonment

False imprisonment occurs when a person intentionally confines another person within certain fixed boundaries. The tort is committed when the confinement is unauthorized and a confined person has no free avenue of escape. A person may be confined by force or threat of use of force or by psychological means if he believes there is no choice but to comply. For example, in *Chopra v Eaton Co*,[7] following an argument with an Eaton's store employee, Chopra was handcuffed and held in the Eaton's security office for over two hours until the police were finally notified. The court concluded that, while the head of security was justified in arresting Chopra,[8] he did not contact the police as soon as was reasonably practicable and therefore was liable for false imprisonment.

2.1.4 Trespass to Land

Trespass to land means entering or being on someone's property without authorization. It may occur when a person enters the property without authorization or when the initial entry was lawful, but then the visitor refuses to leave on the request of the owner.

2.1.5 Wrongful Interference with Chattels

Chattels are movable property. The tort of wrongful interference with chattels covers the following situations: unauthorized touching of one's property (called "trespass to chattels"); interference in ownership of possession of one's personal property ("conversion"); and unlawful retention of someone else's property and refusal to return it ("detinue").

2.1.6 Defamation

Defamation is the making of false statements that can damage a person's reputation and lower him in the estimation of the community. Both individuals and corporations may sue for defamation.[9] Defamation can take two forms: *libel* (written word[10]) and *slander* (spoken word) (see Box 10.8 for an example of defamation).

2.1.7 Defences to Intentional Torts

Like criminal law, tort law recognizes a number of defences—that is, circumstances that may relieve a tortfeasor of liability:

- *Consent.* If a victim consented to a certain act that otherwise would constitute a tort, the tortfeasor will not be held liable. Consent must be freely given (e.g., not under duress or obtained by fraud). In case of medical treatment, consent must also be informed, meaning that the patient has been provided with information concerning the proposed treatment. For example, in the above case of Malette, had she given free and informed consent to the blood transfusion, that consent could have been used as a defence against any subsequent lawsuit for battery.

- *Self-defence.* When a person is under a threat from someone, she may be justified in using force in order to protect herself. However, the force used must be proportionate to the threat and must be employed only to repel the attack, not to retaliate against the offender.

- *Defence of others.* The law recognizes that we may need to use force to protect not only ourselves against an attack but also others (e.g., a parent protecting a child against assault).[11]

- *Defence of property.* A person may use force to defend his personal and real property (e.g., expelling a trespasser from his land if she refuses to leave), but the force used must be reasonable.

- *Necessity.* This defence may be raised when a person finds himself in imminent danger from a certain external source (in contrast to self-defence, where danger emanates from a person). Necessities can be private and public. A private necessity occurs when one is seeking to protect a private interest (e.g., a person trespassed on private property in order to find shelter from a violent typhoon). However, the defence of private necessity covers only situations where no actual damage was caused.[12] A public necessity refers to situations where some private rights are interfered with for the purpose of protecting the community at large (e.g., the police trespass on private property in order to apprehend an offender).[13]

2.2 Negligence

Recall the example from the chapter's introduction: Kanye did not intend to harm anyone, but by failing to follow the traffic rules he fell below the standard that we expect of prudent drivers and caused an accident that led to Christina's injury. It is this failure to exercise reasonable care that gives rise to liability in torts of **negligence**. Thus, in contrast to intentional torts, which reflect the tortfeasor's desire to bring about a certain wrongful consequence, torts of negligence impose liability for failure to take proper care.

The tort of negligence rests on several key concepts: the duty of care, the standard of care, causation, and proximity (each of them is explained below). In order to succeed in action for negligence, a plaintiff must satisfy the court that: (a) a duty of care exists; (b) this duty has been breached; and (c) damage was caused by the breach.

2.2.1 Duty of Care

The definition of the duty of care was articulated in the 1932 UK case of *Donohue v Stevenson*.[14] Donohue bought a bottle of ginger beer and, upon consuming some of it, discovered the remains of a decomposed snail in the bottle. She became sick. Donohue could not sue the manufacturer under contract law as she did not buy the drink directly from it. She sued in tort, but at the time, there was no recognized duty of manufacturers toward consumers. In a groundbreaking decision, the UK House of Lords found that the manufacturer owed a duty of care to consumers. It wrote:

> The rule that you are to love your neighbour becomes in law, you must not injure your neighbour . . . You must take reasonable care to avoid acts or omissions which you can reasonably foresee would be likely to injure your neighbour. Who, then, in law is my neighbour? The answer seems to be—persons who are so closely and directly affected by my act that I ought reasonably to have them in contemplation as being so affected when I am directing my mind to the acts or omissions . . . in question.

In other words, the notion of the **duty of care** means that a person or a corporation has a responsibility to avoid actions that can be reasonably foreseen to cause harm to others. This implies that a human being or corporation has to keep in mind others that may be affected by its actions.

2.2.2 How Do We Know When a Duty of Care Exists?

While there are multiple situations when a duty of care may arise, this does not mean that we owe it to everyone at all times. Then, how do we know when such a duty exists? There is no statute that exhaustively outlines all circumstances under which a duty of care may exist and the issue is left for courts to decide. For example, case law recognized that doctors owe a duty of care to their patients; motorists, to other motorists and pedestrians; and manufacturers, to consumers. The list of these recognized duties developed over time and is not closed; new ones may be added in the future.

When a court is called to decide on a specific lawsuit, it will first check whether a duty of care in a similar situation has already been recognized. If it has been, then the court will proceed to the next stage, namely establishing whether a duty of care in the case at hand has been breached. However, where a court is faced with a new situation, in which no duty of care has been established yet, it will have to decide whether such novel duty should be recognized. In order to decide on this, courts employ the following test:

1. Whether the circumstances disclose reasonably foreseeable harm and proximity sufficient to establish a prima facie duty of care (**prima facie** means at first sight, upon initial observation); and

2. If so, whether there exist residual policy considerations, outside the relationship of the parties, which justify denying the imposition of the duty of care.[15]

This test recognizes that tort law can be an important tool to promote more responsible conduct, but it also considers the broad social implications of establishing new duties of care. When a new duty of care is recognized, it expands the scope of liability, thereby indirectly imposing new limitations on individual, business, and/or government activities. In some cases, such limitations may be well justified, while in others they may raise serious concerns about societal costs of expanded liability. The case in Box 10.2 demonstrates complex considerations involved in determining novel duties of care.

Box 10.2

Dobson (Litigation Guardian of) v Dobson, [1999] 2 SCR 753: Does a Mother Owe a Duty of Care to Her Fetus?

Dobson was 27 weeks pregnant. She was driving in a snowstorm, lost control of her vehicle, and collided with another car. As a result of the collision, the fetus suffered injuries and was born prematurely with permanent mental and physical impairment. The child's guardian (acting on behalf of the child) brought an action for damages against the mother, alleging that the collision was caused by her negligent driving. Canadian law had not previously recognized the duty of care for mothers in relation to their fetuses and, thus, it was for the court to decide whether this novel duty of care should be established. What would you decide: recognize a new duty or not? Why?

In Dobson (Litigation Guardian of) v Dobson, the majority of the Supreme Court held that a mother does not owe a duty of care to her fetus. There were strong policy considerations against recognizing such a duty. First, such a duty would impose significant limitations on women's lifestyle decisions and therefore interfere with their autonomy. Second, it would be difficult to determine a proper standard of conduct for pregnant women.

The Court noted that everything a pregnant woman does—what she eats or drinks, whether and where she works, and any physical activity she undertakes—has the potential to impact the fetus. If a mother were to be held liable for prenatal negligence, her most mundane daily activities could come under the scrutiny of courts. This would restrict a pregnant woman's activities and reduce her autonomy to make decisions concerning many aspects of her life. The Court also expressed concerns about the articulation of a "reasonable pregnant woman" standard. Had the duty been recognized, decision makers would be able to dictate, according to their own notions, proper conduct for pregnant women. In addition, the disparities in the financial situations, education, access to health services, and other life circumstances of pregnant women could lead to an unfair application of a uniform reasonable pregnant woman standard to disadvantaged groups.

This case demonstrates that, in considering a novel duty of care, courts have to keep in mind not only parties to a case, but also broader implications of recognizing a novel duty for society at large.

2.2.3 Breach of the Duty of Care and the Standard of a "Reasonable Person"

If the duty of care exists, then the court will proceed to determine whether the defendant has breached the duty. The conduct of a defendant is measured against a **"reasonable person" standard** that seeks to represent an objective general standard of behaviour for a given activity. The underlying question is: did the defendant fail to do what a reasonable person would have done under the same circumstances? If the defendant is determined to have fallen below the standard of a reasonable person, she is considered to have breached the duty of care.

A "reasonable person" is a legal construct, projecting assumptions about acceptable standards of behaviour. A reasonable person is considered to have an average level of intelligence and to know common things such as that fire burns, knives cut, and so on. In the context of professional activities (e.g., in relation to lawyers, doctors, or architects), the conduct of a defendant is measured against a standard of a "reasonable practitioner" in a given occupation that possesses specialized knowledge and skills.

2.2.4 Causation and Proximity

There must be a connection between the defendant's conduct and damage (that is, causation). In order to establish causation, courts use the "but for" test: if the harm would not have occurred but for the negligence of the defendant, there is causation. In some cases, establishment of causation can be rather straightforward (e.g., in the example of careless driving mentioned at the beginning of the chapter), but in other cases, it may be complicated (see Box 10.3).

Importantly, not only does there have to be a causal link between the actions of the defendant and the plaintiff's loss, but such causation must be proximate. The requirement of proximity does not speak of physical nearness, but rather reflects the idea that persons should be held liable only for usual and foreseeable rather than freakish consequences of their

---

Box 10.3

Causation: *Cottrelle v Gerrard*, [2003] OJ No 4194

Cottrelle developed a sore on her foot. She visited her family physician, Gerrard, on a number of occasions but did not receive proper medical attention. As a result, the sore became infected, she developed gangrene, and her leg had to be amputated below the knee. Cottrelle was diabetic and it is known that diabetics are at risk for developing gangrene on their feet. Cottrelle brought a lawsuit against Gerrard, alleging that he was negligent in the treatment.

In order to succeed in her action, Cottrelle needed to establish that: (1) Gerrard owed her a duty of care; (2) he breached that duty; and (3) the damage to Cottrelle was caused by that breach.

1. *Duty of care.* Courts have long recognized that physicians owe a duty of care to their patients. Thus, Gerard owed a duty of care to Cottrelle.

2. *Breach of the duty of care.* Gerrard's conduct is to be assessed according to the standard of a reasonable practitioner equipped with the necessary knowledge. In order to establish

what this standard is and whether Gerrard has lived up to it, the court has to hear from medical experts. During the trial it was determined that, by failing to examine Cottrelle's foot and to monitor her condition, Gerrard fell below the standard of a reasonable physician. Medical experts testified that, had Cottrelle received aggressive treatment, she might not have lost her leg. Thus, Gerrard was in breach of the duty of care to Cottrelle.

3. *Causation.* Although medical experts agreed that a more aggressive treatment might have saved Cottrelle's leg, they also acknowledged that given Cottrelle's preexisting medical condition—diabetes and atherosclerosis—she likely would have lost her leg anyway. There was insufficient evidence that *but for* Gerrard's negligence, Cottrelle would not have lost her leg. Thus, causation was not established. Correspondingly, Cottrelle's lawsuit could not succeed.

Proximity: *Palsgraf v Long Island Railway Co,* 162 NE 99 (1928)

The plaintiff was standing at one side of a railway platform beside a set of scales. Many metres away, a passenger was trying to board a train. As the passenger was running late, a railway guard gave him a boost to help him onto the train. As a result, the passenger dropped a package, which as it turned out contained fireworks. The fireworks exploded. The explosion knocked over the scales, which fell on top of the plaintiff and caused injury. Even though the guard caused the chain of events, it could not have been foreseen that boosting a passenger onto a train would cause harm to the plaintiff standing many metres away. Thus, despite the causal link, it was considered too remote and no liability was imposed in this case.

wrongful acts.[16] Or, as others have put it, the main question is: ". . . is the harm too unrelated to the wrongful conduct to hold the defendant fairly liable?"[17] See Box 10.4 for an illustration.

2.2.5 Defences to Torts of Negligence

There are two main defence to torts of negligence:

- *Voluntary assumption of risk*. This defence may be invoked when the plaintiff had knowledge of the risk of injury involved in a given activity and voluntarily assumed that risk. This is, for example, the case in sports where participants are considered to have accepted the risks inherent to a game (e.g., that a hockey player may be hit by other players in the course of a game). This defence will not cover situations where an injury was inflicted outside of the rules of fair play, however.

- *Illegality*. A plaintiff who was harmed while participating in an illegal activity cannot recover damages for the harm suffered in the course of that activity. For example, a person who gets accidentally injured by his criminal associate during a robbery would not be able to recover compensation. However, the Supreme Court decision in *Hall v Hebert* has imposed a notable limitation on this defence, stating that it would not generally apply in cases of personal injuries.[18]

3. SPECIAL CATEGORIES OF LIABILITY

In addition to the above described general rules for intentional torts and torts of negligence, there exist several other categories of liability with their peculiar rules. While we cannot review all of them, the following will be discussed:

- Strict liability;
- Nuisance;
- Occupier's liability; and
- Crown liability.

3.1 Strict Liability

Tort law usually imposes liability where a tortfeasor was at fault—either in a form of intent or negligence. However, in certain circumstances a defendant may be held liable even in the absence of intent or negligence; this is known as **strict liability**. Strict liability (along with intentional and negligent torts) is the third basis on which liability in tort may be imposed. Given that we would usually consider it unfair to hold a person liable in the absence of fault or negligence on their part, strict liability is applicable only in limited cases and, as a rule, where a certain activity is inherently dangerous to others.

Strict liability may be found where there was a nonnatural use of land and where a certain substance has escaped. The origins of the concept of strict liability can be found in the case of *Rylands v Fletcher*.[19] The defendant built a water reservoir for his textile factory. The reservoir was located above the mine owned by the plaintiff. Although the reservoir was properly constructed, one day water broke into the mine and flooded it. The trial court found the defendant liable and the decision was upheld on appeal. The House of Lords summed up the main principle of strict liability as follows: "If a person brings, or accumulates, on his land anything which, if it should escape, may cause damage to his neighbour, he does so at his peril. If it does escape and cause damage, he is responsible, however careful he may have been, and whatever precautions he may have taken to prevent the damage."[20]

Some defences to strict liability are available, including (a) an act of God (if an escape was a result of an unforeseen natural event); (b) consent of the plaintiff to the presence of the dangerous thing; and (c) deliberate act of a third party causing the escape.

3.2 Nuisance

Nuisance is ". . . an activity which results in an unreasonable and substantial interference with the use and enjoyment of land."[21] It may result from negligent, intentional, or no-fault conduct. The nature of the tort of nuisance is well summarized in *Smith v Inco*:

> People do not live in splendid isolation from one another. One person's lawful and reasonable use of his or her property may indirectly harm the property of another or interfere with that person's ability to fully use and enjoy his or her property. The common law of nuisance developed as a means by which those competing interests could be addressed, and one given legal priority over the other. Under the common law of nuisance, sometimes the person whose property suffered the adverse effects is expected to tolerate those effects as the price of membership in the larger community. Sometimes, however, the party causing the adverse effect can be compelled, even if his or her conduct is lawful and reasonable, to desist from engaging in that conduct and to compensate the other party for any harm caused to that person's property. In essence, the common law of nuisance decided which party's interest must give way. That determination is made by asking whether in all the circumstances the harm caused or the interference done to one person's property by the other person's use of his or her property is unreasonable.[22]

Nuisance can take public and private forms. A public nuisance interferes with public convenience and welfare, while private nuisance is about unreasonable interference with the use and enjoyment of one's land.

Nuisance can result from, for example, environmental, noise, or odour pollution. In contrast to trespass to land, where a tortfeasor is found on someone else's property, in case of nuisance, a tortfeasor uses her own land in a way that negatively affects her neighbours. For example, the emission of strong odours by a tobacco factory near a residential area was determined to be a nuisance.[23] So was the operation of a training school and airfield for motorized hang-gliders that produced much noise in a quiet rural area.[24] Seemingly innocuous activities such as installing a noisy air conditioning unit on one's property may create a nuisance and lead to liability. For example, in *Suzuki v Munroe*,[25] the Monroes installed an air conditioner a couple of metres from their neighbours' bedroom window. The air conditioner was so noisy that the neighbours were unable to sleep and experienced a significant degree of stress. The court found that the operation of an air conditioner that exceeded accepted noise levels constituted a nuisance. Effectively, the tort of nuisance protects landowners' rights by imposing restrictions on actions taken on neighbouring lands.

3.3 Occupier's Liability

The issue of occupier's liability is concerned with the question of whether an occupier of certain premises owes a duty of care to the entrants. Such a question has practical significance in our everyday lives: for example, if a shopper slips and falls on a wet floor in a shopping mall, is the mall owner responsible for the injury? If a person invites friends to his home and one of the invitees is injured on the premises, is the host responsible?

An occupier is a person who is in control of given premises but does not have to be the owner. Common law rules on occupier's liability were complex and varied the extent of the duty of care, depending on whether an entrant was unwanted (e.g., a trespasser) or given permission to be on the premises. In the past, it was considered that the occupier had a duty to protect lawful entrants from danger, but little duty was owed to trespassers. Most provinces have now adopted legislation that replaced common law rules of occupier's liability. As a result, there is generally a duty of care owed to all entrants to ensure that premises are reasonably safe.[26] In practical terms, this means, for example, that landlords must maintain and repair the premises to ensure that their tenants are safe; hosts owe a duty of care to their invitees; shopping malls and other businesses owe a duty to shoppers or other people on the premises.

3.4 Crown Liability

The **Crown** refers to the monarch (currently Queen Elizabeth II) along with representatives in Canada (governor general and lieutenant governors), and can also refer to federal and provincial governments as well as their subordinate agencies and personnel. Can an individual sue the Crown just like any other tortfeasor? Historically, the Crown could not be sued in tort. The rationale was that the "Crown could do no wrong" and that as the creator of courts and laws the Crown could not also be a litigant before those courts.[27] However, over time it was accepted that the Crown should not be immune from suits in tort. Nevertheless, the issue of Crown liability is challenging: on the one hand, imposition

Policy versus Operational Decisions: *Just v British Columbia*, [1989] 2 SCR 1228

The plaintiff, Just, and his daughter were driving for a day of skiing at Whistler Mountain. While they were waiting for the traffic to move forward, a large rock weighing more than a tonne came loose above the highway and crashed down upon the plaintiff's car. His daughter was killed and he was seriously injured. Just sued the authorities of British Columbia for negligence in maintaining the highway properly. The trial court determined that the issue of how and when to conduct road inspections was a policy decision and therefore immune from tort action. However, on appeal the Supreme Court found such decisions to be operational, thereby opening them to scrutiny.

of liability on the Crown may achieve important objectives such as promoting government accountability, but on the other hand, the Crown should have sufficient freedom to take various actions for the benefit of the public without being preoccupied about issues of liability. These two sets of duties may sometimes be in conflict and require courts to carefully weigh the approach to liability.

One of the factors that helps courts decide on the issue is the distinction between the Crown's policy and operational decisions. It is generally considered that policy decisions (that is, decisions as to which activity to undertake and how to carry it out) should not attract liability. Policy decisions are viewed as an exercise of the Crown's discretion to consider various political, social, and economic factors for the benefit of society. In contrast, operational decisions—that is, decisions that are taken in implementation of policy—may attract liability. See an example in Box 10.5.

Although courts are wary of expanding the scope of the Crown's liability, several notable cases recognized that the authorities are not immune from liability. For example, in *Hill*,[28] the majority of the Supreme Court recognized that the tort of negligent investigation exists in Canada and that the police owe a duty of care to an individualized suspect. In *Odhavji*, it was determined that the chief of police owes a duty to a family of a suspect killed by the police to ensure that proper investigation of the incident is carried out.[29]

See Figure 10.1 for a summary of the information about torts.

4. CONTRIBUTORY FAULT OR NEGLIGENCE

Tort law recognizes that in some cases the plaintiff's conduct or lack of care may have contributed to his loss and will reflect this contributory fault or negligence in apportionment of damages. Essentially, the concept of *contributory negligence* recognizes the shared responsibility of the plaintiff and defendant for losses. For example, a plaintiff who was 20% at fault would not be able to recover 100% of losses, but only the 80% that is

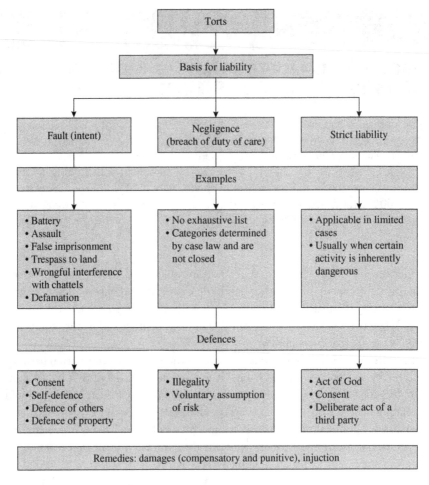

Figure 10.1 Overview of torts

attributed to the defendant. Courts will determine the apportioning of fault and liability, based on individual circumstance of a given case. A common example of contributory negligence is intoxication (see Boxes 10.6 and 10.7).

5. JOINT TORTFEASORS

In some cases, several persons may have been involved in a wrongdoing. Such individuals will be considered *joint tortfeasors*. The liability for damages will be apportioned among joint tortfeasors according to the degree of their responsibility (e.g., if one tortfeasor is 30% at fault and the other is 70% at fault, they will be responsible to pay the plaintiff 30% and 70% of damages, respectively).

Box 10.6

Duty of Care, Voluntary Assumption of Risk, and Contributory Negligence: *Crocker v Sundance Northwest Resorts Ltd*, [1988] SCJ No 60

Sundance Northwest Resorts Ltd, an operator of a ski resort, held a "tubing" competition that involved two-person teams sliding down a steep hill in oversized tubes. Crocker and his friend entered the competition. Crocker signed the waiver form without reading it and did not even appreciate that it was a waiver. Prior to the competition, Crocker consumed large quantities of alcohol. As he was visibly drunk, the owner and the manager of the resort asked Crocker if he was in any condition to participate in the competition. Crocker replied that he was and neither the manager nor the owner did anything to dissuade or stop him from participating. During the competition, Crocker injured his neck and became quadriplegic. He sued Sundance for negligence.

The case raised the following questions:

- Did Sundance owe a duty of care to Crocker?
- Did Crocker voluntarily assume the risk involved?
- Was Crocker contributorily negligent (due to becoming voluntarily intoxicated prior to the competition)?

Prior to reading the rest of the discussion, please try to answer the above questions on your own. Would you hold Sundance liable for Crocker's injury? Why or why not?

Did Sundance owe a duty of care to Crocker? The duty of care requires an individual or a corporation to keep in mind those who may be affected by their actions. Historically, the duty

of care has been framed more as requiring noninterference or abstinence from certain dangerous activities than as imposing an affirmative duty to act. However, over time, it has been recognized that in some situations such an affirmative duty may exist. In the case of Sundance, the central question was whether Sundance had the duty to take certain steps to prevent a visibly intoxicated Crocker from competing in the dangerous tubing competition. The Supreme Court concluded that such a duty existed and found that Sundance failed to carry out the duty.

Did Crocker voluntarily assume the risk involved?

As a general rule, persons participating in sporting activities, including those involving high risks (e.g., cliff climbing), are considered to have voluntarily assumed the risks involved and cannot hold anyone else responsible for their injuries. In our case, however, the Supreme Court concluded that Crocker had not voluntarily assumed the risk. First, his intoxication at the time of the competition likely prevented him from understanding the risks involved. Second, although he had signed the waiver form, he had not read it and was not even aware that he was signing a waiver. Hence, the signature did not represent Crocker's true intention.

Was Crocker contributorily negligent?

Crocker was recognized as being contributorily negligent as his voluntary intoxication did contribute to the accident. Liability was apportioned with 25% to Crocker and 75% to Sundance.

Box 10.7

Contributory Negligence and Damages: *Jacobsen v Nike Canada Ltd*, [1996] BCJ No 363

Jacobsen worked for Nike Canada as a warehouseman. On the day in question, he was working off site at a trade show, where Jacobsen's supervisor provided workers with food and free beer. The plaintiff had consumed at least eight beers and then had gone to two clubs and drunk more beer. On the way home, he lost control of his car, drove into a ditch, and was thrown out of the car. He suffered a spinal cord fracture, which made him a quadriplegic. When Jacobsen sued the employer for damages, the court recognized that the employer was negligent because it failed to monitor the consumption of alcohol by the plaintiff, and took no steps to determine if the plaintiff was impaired and to prevent him from driving. However, the plaintiff was also partially responsible for his injuries as he continued drinking after leaving work. Liability was apportioned 75% to the defendant and 25% to the plaintiff.

The plaintiff was 19 at the time of the accident and had a grade 12 education. He had wanted to become a fireman or a policeman but, as a result of the accident, he was confined to a wheelchair and had limited arm and leg function. He also would require personal attendant care and homemaker services for the rest of his life. The court awarded the following damages:

- general damages;
- special damages;
- past wage loss;
- cost of future care;
- expense for the plaintiff's specially adapted vehicle;
- expense to adapt the house;
- loss of earning capacity; and
- compensation for the cost of care the plaintiff's brother gave him for the four years before the trial.

6. REMEDIES

6.1 Damages

Let's again recall the example from the beginning of the chapter. Christina suffered multiple injuries, which left her unable to work as well as requiring various support services in the future. Thus, her losses include: (1) costs of medical care shortly after the injury; (2) cost of future care (e.g., chiropractic sessions); (3) loss of income for the period while Christina was recovering; and (4) loss of future income due to inability to rejoin the workforce after the accident. Could Christina sue Kanye for recovery of all these losses? Yes, she could. Tort law recognizes the wide-ranging nature of losses and allows for their compensation through damage awards. Damages are supposed to bring the plaintiff into the position that she would have been in *but for* the tort that has been committed.

There are two main types of damages:

1. *Compensatory*. This type of damages seeks to compensate various losses by the plaintiff and is divided into:

   ◼ *Special damages*—to compensate plaintiffs for actual monetary losses and out-of-pocket expenses incurred prior to the judgment in the case (e.g., medical expenses).

   ◼ *General damages*—to compensate plaintiffs for anticipated future expenses such as loss of future income or future medical expenses. General damages may also be claimed for nonmonetary losses such as pain and suffering.

   ◼ *Aggravated damages*—can be claimed when the tortfeasor's particularly outrageous conduct has exacerbated the plaintiff's injuries and brought about additional mental distress or humiliation.

2. *Punitive*. Punitive damages serve to punish the defendant for outrageous conduct and deter others from committing similar acts. As the Supreme Court stated in *Hill v Church of Scientology of Toronto*, "[p]unitive damages may be awarded in situations where the defendant's misconduct is so malicious, oppressive and high-handed that it offends the court's sense of decency."[30] In the case described in Box 10.8, both punitive and aggravated damages were awarded.

6.1.1 How do Courts Calculate the Amount of Damages to be Awarded?

Theoretically, the description of the above damages appears simple, but how do courts calculate the amount of awards? In the case of special damages, it may be relatively easy based on receipts of actual expenses incurred. However, what about calculation of general

Box 10.8

Defamation and Punitive Damages: *Reichmann v Berlin*, [2002] OJ No 2732

The court awarded both aggravated and punitive damages in a defamation case in which the defendants, Cohen and Berlin, for over three and a half years repeatedly threatened to publish and eventually published on the Internet false allegations that the victim cheated a man out of his inheritance. They published false statements on at least seven websites and distributed cards to the plaintiff's neighbours alerting them to the existence of these websites. The underlying motive for this defamation campaign was extortion. At some point in the past, the two defendants had lost a lawsuit in relation to inheritance and believed that the plaintiff assisted their opponent on the case. Cohen and Berlin then wrote to the victim demanding compensation and threatened to publish their allegations if the money was not paid. The victim refused and then the defamation campaign followed.

damages such as the loss of future income? How are courts to determine the amount that the plaintiff would have earned in the future?

To determine the loss of future income in Christina's case, the court would look at what Christina was earning at the time of the accident and what her projected earnings would have been over her working lifetime. National statistics and actuarial tables may be used for the purpose of such calculations. In addition to looking at the plaintiff's earnings at the time of the accident, the court would also consider whether the earnings were likely to remain the same or increase due, for example, to promotions, the plaintiff's career profile, and other factors.[31] The court would also consider any *contingency deductions*—that is, factors other than the injury that could have reduced the plaintiff's capacity to earn.

6.2 Other Remedies

In addition to damages, plaintiffs may seek other remedies such as an injunction. As described in Chapter 1, an injunction is a court order that requires a defendant to stop doing something that damages the plaintiff, or to do something that benefits the plaintiff. For example, in the case of *Suzuki v Monroe* discussed in section 3.2, merely awarding damages to the plaintiffs would not fully meet their needs: if the defendants could continue operating their very noisy air conditioner, the plaintiffs would continue suffering from this nuisance. Hence, the court not only awarded damages, but also issued an injunction prohibiting operation of the air conditioner at night when it was most disruptive.

Part II. Critical Perspectives
1. THEORETICAL PERSPECTIVES ON TORT LAW: AN OVERVIEW

Over the past century, the following three schools of thought have been particularly prominent in the analysis of tort law:

- Economic approach;
- Corrective justice approach; and
- Critical approach: critical legal studies, feminist studies, and critical race theory.

Each of these perspectives offers a unique view on tort law, advancing a particular idea as to what its main functions are and how tort law rules should be interpreted and applied.

The **economic approach** focuses on the efficient allocation of resources and views deterrence as the main rationale for tort law liability. It suggests that the fear of liability would create incentives for individuals and businesses to make their activities safer. This scholarship discussed which regime—strict liability, negligence, or contributory negligence—would allow for greater deterrence of accidents and should be used as the primary standard of liability in tort. Tort law rules are, thus, viewed as ways to determine cost-spreading, risk, and cost avoidance in society.

In contrast, the **corrective justice approach** analyzes tort law from the perspective of a moral theory. It considers tort law as a mechanism to correct the harm suffered by the victim and emphasizes the moral obligation of the wrongdoer to rectify the victim's injury.[32] Thus, it views compensation to the victim as one of the main functions of tort law. Unlike the economic approach, which considers broad societal interests, the corrective justice perspective is focused on the relationship between the parties and the restoration of justice between them. Correspondingly, it argues that the factors that apply to one party only (e.g., the plaintiff's vulnerable position) or policy considerations external to the parties' relationship are not relevant and would interfere with fair determination of liability.[33]

During the twentieth century, these two schools of thought became dominant in debates on tort law, but they are not without limitations. For example, not every type of injury can be properly assessed merely by efficiency analysis of the economic approach. The corrective justice approach does not give sufficient consideration to policy issues. Further, neither the economic nor the corrective justice approach considers the gender, race, and class impact of tort law rules. The corrective justice approach seeks merely to restore the plaintiff to the status he would have obtained if not for the injuries and therefore it would reproduce the existing disparities along gender, race, and class lines in the amount of damages awarded.[34]

In the late 1980s, new **critical scholarship** on tort law started to emerge. This scholarship seeks to question the neutrality of tort law rules and expose their differential impact on various groups based on race, gender, class, and other characteristics. For example, it pointed out that tort law reflects the class structure of a capitalist society: "You are what you own, what you earn, and what you do."[35] Feminist scholarship on tort law has drawn attention to the gender bias in the assessment of damages as well as the nonrecognition of certain types of harm that are perceived as largely feminine. Scholars such as Chamallas and Wriggins argue that tort law is part of the power structure that disadvantages women and minority groups.[36] Race also prominently figured in tort law's assessment of damages. For instance, early twentieth century cases from the United States demonstrate a significant difference in amounts of damages awarded to white and black plaintiffs in comparable situations. In *Griffin v Brady*,[37] a judge reduced the amount of award because he considered that the harm sustained by an African American for being falsely accused of stealing was less than the harm a white man would have suffered in the same circumstance.[38] The application of critical perspectives to analysis of tort law is illustrated below, in the discussion of two issues: what harm is recognized as compensable, and what is the impact of race/class/gender factors on calculation of future loss of income?

2. WHAT HARM IS RECOGNIZED AS COMPENSABLE?

In the case of intentional torts, harm is presumed once the wrongful conduct has been proven. However, in the case of negligence, the plaintiff must establish that real harm was caused by the defendant. Correspondingly, a question arises as to what tort law would recognize as harm. Generally, harm has to be to a legally recognized interest (e.g., damage to person, damage to property, damage to reputation).[39]

Feminist scholarship critiqued tort law's lack of understanding of injuries to females.[40] For example, in the early twentieth century a distinction was drawn between physical and emotional injuries, with the latter not being recognized as harm that could be compensated in tort law. Thus, physical and property interests usually associated with the male world were recognized as valuable and compensable, while emotional and psychological interests (which were perceived as largely feminine) were not.[41] A series of US cases from the late nineteenth and early twentieth centuries denied recovery to women who suffered miscarriages due to nervous shock resulting from the defendant's negligent actions because their injuries were classified as largely emotional.[42]

Certain types of losses were not even recognized as a woman's own. For example, the loss of capacity to provide household services was actionable only by the woman's husband, thereby construing such injury not as a woman's personal loss, but rather as a loss to her husband.[43]

While, over time, tort law rules have moved away from the restrictive approaches described above, the differentiation along gender lines can still be found in contemporary tort law. For example, concerns are raised about undervaluation of the seriousness of women's injuries in sexual battery and discrimination cases, as well as in cases involving damage to women's reproductive systems.[44]

3. WHAT IS THE IMPACT OF GENDER/RACE/CLASS FACTORS ON THE CALCULATION OF FUTURE LOSS OF INCOME?

Damages are supposed to put the plaintiff in the position she would have been in *but for* the injury. Thus, traditionally, tort law assesses loss by reference to what a plaintiff would have earned in the labour market. Critical scholarship on tort law has identified several concerns with this approach.

3.1 Reliance on Gendered and Race-Specific Income Tables

To calculate plaintiffs' future earnings, courts usually referred to gendered and race-specific actuarial tables, which reflected wage differences between men and women, Aboriginal and non-Aboriginal groups, and racial minorities and nonminority groups. By relying on such tables, tort law reproduced existing disparities and undercompensated marginalized groups. For example, in the case of a car accident as described at the beginning of the chapter, the amount of award for the loss of future income could differ, depending on whether the injured person was a man or a woman. In the case of First Nations plaintiffs, reliance on statistical indicators of workplace participation, life expectancy, and health outcomes (which are lower for First Nations than for non-Aboriginal groups) has also led to lower awards.[45]

3.2 Presumptions about Women's Lifestyles

Courts can apply contingency deductions to damage awards to account for factors that would have reduced a plaintiff's earning capacity. In the case of female plaintiffs, courts often adopted a patriarchal view of women's lifestyles, presuming that a woman would get married, have children, and (at least temporarily) leave the labour force. A woman leaving the labour force in order to care for the children is considered a contingency and hence leads to a lower amount of damages awarded.[46] This does not take into account the current realities that women do not necessarily leave the labour force when they start a family and that there exist income replacement schemes such as parental leave. At the same time, the same contingency deductions are usually not applied to males who get married.[47]

3.3 Reliance on Family Background as a Predictor of Future Education and Career Achievement

Imagine a young plaintiff who has not yet made any firm decisions about a future career path or education (e.g., a secondary school student who was injured in a car accident and, as a result, suffered serious brain damage, leaving her unemployable). How are we to determine the amount of her future income loss? In such cases, courts tended to rely on the plaintiff's family background to project whether she would be likely to obtain a college or a university education and which career path she would likely take.[48] For example, courts tended to conclude that if the plaintiff's parents were university educated, the plaintiff was more likely to go to a university, too. Conversely, if a plaintiff came from a less advantaged background, he was projected to likely end up with a lower level of education and a lower-paying job. Such an approach reproduces class distinctions, leads to reduced awards for plaintiffs of disadvantaged backgrounds, and fails to recognize that a child's future is not automatically predetermined by his family background.

The reliance on family background as a predictor of a plaintiff's income often leads to consideration of information not only about the general socioeconomic position of a given family, but also about tragic experiences such as alcohol abuse, suicide rates, unemployment, and others. This tends to put plaintiffs themselves on trial and, if factored into the assessment of damages, may lead to further disadvantage.[49]

As a result of the above rules, tort law may produce different outcomes for plaintiffs from different groups in society based on race, gender, and class, and contribute to marginalization of disadvantaged groups. Some plaintiffs may experience cumulative disadvantage due to the compound impact of race, gender, and class factors. For example, women may be doubly undercompensated in damage awards: first, the use of gender-specific tables produces a lower estimation of future income and then this amount is further reduced due to contingency deductions.

Critical scholarship not only highlighted the gender/race/class dynamics of tort law, but also urged courts to be attentive to these issues.[50] Some suggested that one of tort law's goals should be to reduce the imbalance in wealth, status, and power and to empower the disadvantaged. Others note the importance of legal education in sensitizing the public to critical issues of tort law.[51] Yet others make various proposals that would help decision makers better understand the nature of plaintiffs' injuries and be more sensitive in their assessment of harm and damages. For example, Kate Sutherland, writing in the context of sexual assault cases, suggests developing a tradition of legal storytelling as a way to enable decision makers to better understand the nature of injuries suffered by the plaintiffs and empathize with them.[52] Narratives may help decision makers put themselves into the plaintiffs' shoes and experience the injuries from their perspective. Cooper-Stevenson suggests that the damages for female plaintiffs should be calculated based on actuarial tables for men with similar education and skills.[53] He also argues that calculation of future loss of income should be based on the notion of one's earning capacity rather than a prediction of what the plaintiff would have earned. In fact, courts are taking some steps in the proposed directions by, for instance, starting to use male or blended earnings statistics in assessment of future income for female plaintiffs.[54]

SUMMARY

Tort law prescribes rules under which victims of wrongdoings can obtain redress for the harm suffered in noncontractual relations. It performs a number of functions: compensation to victims, deterrence of wrongful conduct, standard setting, and psychological, educational, and ombudsman functions. Torts fall into two major categories: intentional and negligent. While an intentional tort represents willful conduct on the part of the tortfeasor, negligence refers to situations when a person fell below the expected standard of care, causing harm to others. There are also some special cases where liability may be imposed even in the absence of negligence or fault (strict liability). A tortfeasor may be able to advance various defences in order to avoid liability. Tort law also recognizes that in some cases the plaintiff may have contributed to his own injury (contributory fault or negligence).

Among the most common intentional torts are: battery, assault, defamation, false imprisonment, and trespass. In torts of negligence, there is no specifically prescribed list, but rather they develop incrementally through case law. In order to succeed in action for negligence, a plaintiff must satisfy the court that: (a) a duty of care exists; (b) this duty has been breached; and (c) damage was caused by the breach. For example, it has been recognized that the duty of care exists in the following relations: doctors to their patients; drivers to pedestrians and other drivers; and manufacturers to consumers.

Damages are the main remedy in tort law. They seek to put the plaintiff in the position she would have been in *but for* the injury. Damages can be compensatory and punitive. If the plaintiff contributed to her injuries, the amount of damages is reduced proportionately to her fault/negligence.

Critical Thinking Questions

1. Review the case of *Ross (Guardian ad litem of) v Watts* [1997] BCJ No 1998. How did the court assess the plaintiff's employability and loss of future income? Do you agree with the way the court used the plaintiff's family background and earnings statistics for Aboriginal workers to assess the loss of future income? Discuss in light of the critical perspectives provided in this chapter.

2. Consider the following scenario: Ann and Derrick were introduced to each other by family members and started dating. Ann lives in Canada and Derrick lives in Fiji. Derrick wrote passionate love letters to Ann; the two discussed future plans, including the desire to have children and live in Canada. Ann travelled back and forth a few times and the two eventually got married. Ann paid for everything and arranged for Derrick's immigration to Canada. Once Derrick arrived, he stayed with Ann for only a few days, filed for divorce, and then disappeared. It was also discovered that he had an affair with another woman while he was in the relationship with Ann. Ann was devastated. She suffered a nervous breakdown and for a period of time was unable to work.

   a. In your opinion, would tort law provide a remedy for Ann? If yes, what kinds of losses could she claim and what types of damages could she recover? If not, why not?

   b. Research case law to find out how courts have dealt with cases similar to Ann and Derrick's. Does the position reflected in case law coincide with your initial response to questions in part (a)?

3. In your opinion, what objectives of tort law are the most important? Why?

4. In your opinion, should tort law be used as a tool for promoting social equality, or should it merely restore individuals to the position they would have been in if not for the injury? Explain your answer in reference to critical perspectives discussed in this chapter.

Further Readings and Useful Resources

1. Martha Chamallas & Jennifer B Wiggins, *The Measure of Injury: Race, Gender, and Tort Law* (New York: New York University Press, 2010).

2. Ken Cooper-Stephenson and Elaine Gibson, eds, *Tort Theory* (North York: Captus Press, 1993).

3. Margaret Kerr et al., *Canadian Tort Law in a Nutshell*, 3rd ed (Toronto: Carswell, 2009)

4. Allen M Linden & Bruce Feldthusen, *Canadian Tort Law*, 8th ed (Toronto: LexisNexis, 2006).

5. Sherilyn J Pickering, "Feminism and Tort Law: Scholarship and Practice" (2010) 29 WRLSI 227.

Endnotes

1. Allen M Linden & Bruce Feldthusen, *Canadian Tort Law*, 8th ed (Toronto: LexisNexis, 2006) at 1.
2. Linden & Feldthusen, *supra* note 1 at 23–24.
3. Philip Osborne, *The Law of Torts*, 2nd ed (Toronto: Irwin law, 2003) at 12–18; Allen M Linden, *Canadian Tort Law*, 7th ed (Toronto: Butterworths, 2001) at 25.
4. G Edward While, *Tort Law in America: An Intellectual History* (Oxford University Press, 2003) at 62.

5. There are also other intentional torts such as deceit, abuse of process, and malicious prosecution, but they will not be discussed in this chapter.

6. Malette v Shulman, 72 OR (2d) 417 at para 25.

7. [1999] AJ No 277.

8. The court noted that when Chopra pushed the head of security to free himself, he committed an assault, and the head of security was justified in arresting him.

9. Linden & Feldthusen, *supra* note 1 at 772.

10. Libel encompasses not only written statements, but also pictures, films, television, and recorded phone messages. Linden & Feldthusen, *supra* note 1 at 774.

11. Linden & Feldthusen, *supra* note 1 at 92.

12. *Ibid* at 95.

13. *Ibid* at 94–95.

14. [1932] AC 562.

15. *Anns v Merton London Borough Council*, [1978] AC 728 as restated in *Cooper v Hobart*, [2001] 3 SCR 537.

16. Donald Harris, *Remedies in Contract and Tort* (Weidenfeld and Nicolson, 1988) at 206.

17. Linden & Feldthusen, *supra* note 1 at 360.

18. [1993] 2 SCR 159. In this case, both the defendant and the plaintiff were intoxicated and were in a car together. The defendant allowed the plaintiff to roll-start his car downhill, which resulted in an accident and serious head injuries to the plaintiff.

19. Rylands v Fletcher [1861–73] All ER Rep 1, LR 3 HL 330.

20. *Ibid* at 340.

21. Lewis N Klar, *Tort Law*, 4th ed (Toronto: Thomson Carswell, 2008) at 726.

22. *Smith v Inco Ltd*, [2011] OJ No 4386 at para 39.

23. *Appleby v Erie Tobacco Co*, [1910] OJ No 64.

24. *Manitoba v Adventure Flight Centres*, [1983] MJ No 51.

25. [2009] BCJ No 2019.

26. Margaret Kerr et al., *Canadian Tort Law In a Nutshell*, 3rd ed (Carswell, 2009) at 50–53.

27. *Ibid* at 67.

28. *Hill v Hamilton-Wentworth Regional Police Services Board*, [2007] 3 SCR 129. The plaintiff was subject to investigation, criminal prosecution, wrongful conviction, and incarceration for 20 months.

29. *Odhavji Estate v Woodhouse*, [2003] SCJ No 74. The lawsuit was brought by the family members of Manish Odhavji, who was fatally shot by the Toronto police subsequent to a bank robbery. The family alleged that the officers had breached their duty to fully cooperate with the Special Investigations Unit and that the chief of police was negligent in ensuring that the police officers carried out their duties in accordance with the *Police Services Act*.

30. Hill v Church of Scientology of Toronto, [1995] 2 SCR 1130 at 1208.

31. Harris, *supra* note 16 at 265–266.

32. See various essays on the topic in Ernest J Weinrib, ed, *Tort Law*, (Darthmouth: Ashgate, 2002). For a wider range of perspectives on tort law as well as critiques of economic and corrective justice approaches, see Ken Cooper-Stephenson and Elaine Gibson, eds, *Tort Theory*, (North York: Captus Press, 1993).

33. Ernest Weinrib, "Private Law and Public Right" (2011) U f T LJ 191 at 192.

34. Elizabeth Adjin-Tettey, "Replication and Perpetuating Inequalities in Personal Injury Claims through Female-Specific Contingencies" (2004) 49 McGill LJ 309.

35. Richard L Abel, "A Critique of Torts" (1990) 37 UCLA L Rev 785.
36. Martha Chamallas & Jennifer Wriggins, *The Measure of Injury: Race, Gender, and Tort Law* (New York University Press, 2010).
37. 117 NYS 1136 (1909).
38. Chamallas and Wriggins, *supra* note 36 at 52–62.
39. Kerr et al., *supra* note 26 at 41.
40. E.g., Lucinda Finley, "The Hidden Victims of Tort Reform: Women, Children, and the Elderly" (2004) 53 Emory LJ 1263; Lucinda Finley, "The Priceless–Worthless Dilemma: In Defense of Individualized Non-Economic Damages" in DM Engel & M McCann, eds, *Fault Lines: Tort Law and Practice* (Stanford University Press, 2009); Lucinda Finley, "Female Trouble: The Implications of Tort Reform for Women" (1997) 64 Tennessee L Rev 847; Jamie Cassels, "Damages for Lost Earning Capacity: Women and Children Last" (1992) 71 Can B Rev 447 at 448; Leslie Bender, "An Overview of Feminist Torts Scholarship" (1993) 78 Cornell L Rev 575.
41. Chamallas and Wriggins, *supra* note 36 at 38.
42. *Ibid* at 39–47.
43. Regina Graycar, "Hoovering as a Hobby and Other Stories: Gendered Assessments of Personal Injury Damages" (1997) 31 UBC L Rev 17 at para 20.
44. Finley, *supra* note 40; Bruce Feldthusen, "Discriminatory Damage Qualifications in Civil Actions for Sexual Battery" (1994) 44 U fT LJ 133.
45. Adjin-Tettey, *supra* note 34.
46. See, for example, *Lee v Swan*, [1996] BCJ No 259.
47. Adjin-Tettey, *supra* note 34 at para 30.
48. *Ibid.*
49. *Ibid* at para 44.
50. E.g., feminist scholarship noted the importance of acknowledging the power–dependency–vulnerability relationship. See Jan Cowie, "Evaluating an Issue of Consent in Sexual Battery Cases Difference, Dominance, Dilemma: A Critical Analysis of Norberg v Wynrib" (1994) 58 Sask L Rev 357.
51. Bender, *supra* note 40.
52. Kate Sutherland, "Measuring Pain: Quantifying Damages in Civil Suits for Sexual Assault" in Ken Cooper-Stephenson and Elaine Gibson, eds, *Tort Theory* (North York: Captus Press, 1993) 212.
53. Ken Cooper-Stephenson, "Damages for Loss of Working Capacity for Women" (1978–1979) 43:2 Sask L Rev 7.
54. See, e.g., *Walker v Ritchie* [2003] OJ 18; *Cho v Cho*, [2003] 36 RFL (5th) 79; *Shaw v Arnold*, [1998] BCJ No 2834.

Chapter 11
Family Law

Learning Objectives

After reading this chapter, you should be able to:

- Name and explain six requirements for a valid marriage.
- Outline rights and obligations of parties in cohabitation and marriage.
- Name and explain four types of domestic contracts.
- Name and explain two ways to dissolve a marriage.
- Describe the main rules governing division of property, support, and custody upon relationship breakdown.
- Explain how support obligations can be enforced.
- Describe two main types of measures that can be taken to protect and assist victims of family violence.
- Explain the tension between respect for individual autonomy, fairness, and protection of vulnerable parties in the family context.

Chapter Outline

Introduction

Imagine the following situation: Andrew and Gina were married for 15 years, but their marriage broke down. They have three children. Andrew is a lawyer and is the primary income earner. Gina worked as a teacher prior to marriage as well as during the first three years of marriage, but then quit her job in order to take care of the children. The couple has a house, a car, savings accounts, and other assets, including valuable works of art. Andrew and Gina need to deal with multiple issues: how do they formally end their marriage? Who will have custody of the children? How is the property to be divided? Would Gina be entitled to spousal support? If yes, how is its amount to be determined? Do they have to go to court to get these issues resolved, or can they negotiate their own settlement?

This chapter will examine these as well as other related issues. Further, in connection with discussions in preceding chapters, family law offers useful illustrations of the following themes: (1) public versus private law; (2) law and social change; and (3) critical perspectives.

As you recall from Chapter 1, it is traditional to divide law into public and private. However, family law occupies a special space as it comprises both of these dimensions. On the one hand, the family has traditionally been considered a private sphere where state interference should be minimal. Much of family law indeed concentrates on rights and obligations between private individuals—family members. On the other hand, by defining what relationships are legally recognized, who can marry, and what support obligations family members have, law projects certain societal values and images of "acceptable" relations. By setting out rules for matrimonial property division, as well as child and spousal support, family law plays a distributive role seeking to promote a degree of economic equality between separated spouses/partners. How a family is defined also has implications for other areas of law, such as welfare schemes, survivor's pension benefits, and taxation.

The key definitions and principles of family law have undergone notable changes, especially since the mid-twentieth century. In this chapter, we will notice the transformation in the legal recognition first of opposite-sex common law relationships, then same-sex common law unions, and subsequently same-sex marriages. We will also observe the increasing influence of equality and women's rights discourse that led to, among other things, the recognition of a woman's distinct legal personality within a marriage and then alteration of the rules of division of property and support to ensure more equal distribution of assets between separated spouses. In light of the development of reproductive technologies, family law has started to grapple with new questions (e.g., should a known sperm donor be recognized as a child's legal parent), which will be discussed in Part II.

Many aspects of family law are impacted by issues of gender, race, and class. Despite family law reforms and affirmation of equality between spouses/partners, in reality, *inequality* is often present within and among families. For example, women continue to be worse off than men upon relationship breakdown.[1] The unequal bargaining power between spouses/partners may lead to unfair domestic agreements. In light of such unequal power, should the law intervene to restore fairness? For example, if Andrew and Gina conclude a separation agreement that allows Andrew to keep most of the family property and leaves Gina with few assets, should courts be able to set such an agreement aside and order what they consider to be a more equitable division of property? In Part I, we will see how this question has been answered by courts; then, in Part II, we will analyze these judicial decisions from a critical perspective.

Part I. Substantive Law

Substantively, family law can be divided into the following key components:

- Jurisdiction over family law;
- Formation of marriage and cohabitation;
- Rights and obligations of parties in marriage/cohabitation;
- Division of property upon relationship breakdown;
- Child custody and support;
- Spousal support; and
- Enforcement of support obligations.

Each of these issues is examined below.

1. JURISDICTION OVER FAMILY LAW

First of all, we need to know which level of government has authority over family law. In Canada, the jurisdiction over family matters is divided between the federal and provincial governments. Under s. 91 of the *Constitution Act, 1867*, the federal government has power over issues of marriage and divorce. In realization of this power, it passed such legislation as the *Divorce Act* and the *Civil Marriage Act*. As to provinces, two powers under s. 92 are of relevance to the family context: solemnization of marriage, and property and civil rights. Under these heads of power, provinces have passed their own legislation related to family matters, including cohabitation outside marriage, division of property, and other issues.

As a result of this federal/provincial division of powers, the Canadian family law regime is complex. For example, if a person makes a claim for support and child custody in the context of divorce proceedings, the issues are governed by federal divorce legislation—the *Divorce Act*. However, if the same issues arise independently of divorce, they are regulated by provincial or territorial legislation. In addition, the adjudication of family law issues is divided between two levels of provincial courts. For example, in Ontario, issues of divorce can be heard only in the superior court, while child protection and adoption cases appear only in the provincial court of justice. At the same time, both courts can deal with child and spousal support, child custody, and access. In order to simplify resolution of family matters, Ontario established a number of unified family courts where the split jurisdiction of provincial and superior courts has been brought together under the Family Court branch of the Superior Court.

2. FORMATION OF MARRIAGE AND COHABITATION

The past century saw significant changes in societal and legal views on various forms of cohabitation. Traditionally, marriage was the only recognized framework for sexual relations and child rearing. It was defined as an opposite-sex union with distinct roles for husband and wife. The wife was responsible for taking care of the household and children. She was also expected always to be available to provide sexual services to the husband, and the concept of marital rape was not even recognized in Canadian law until 1983. The husband had decision making authority and also had an obligation to support the family. Once a woman got married, her property and its management was transferred to her husband. A woman could not enter into a contract, sue, or be sued in her own name. The concept of unity of personality dictated that a woman's rights were to be exercised by her husband. Until the 1970s and 1980s, the doctrine of interspousal immunity precluded spouses from suing each other, which meant that women could not sue their husbands for physical or sexual abuse.

A marriage was seen as a relationship of permanence: divorce was difficult to obtain and there was no uniform legislation on divorce in Canada until the 1960s.[2] Cohabitation without marriage not only inspired social disapproval but was also penalized by the legal regime. Cohabiting partners did not have an obligation of mutual support, and children of these relationships were not considered part of a larger family. Until the 1970s, the nature of the parent's relationship defined the status of the child: a legitimate child of marriage or an illegitimate child of cohabitation.[3]

During the 1980s and 1990s, law gradually recognized opposite-sex cohabiting couples for the purposes of spousal support as well as taxation, social assistance, and pensions. However, there remained a significant difference in matrimonial property regimes between married and unmarried couples. In the late 1990s, same-sex common law couples gained the same recognition as opposite-sex common law couples (prompted by the case of M v H).[4] In the early 2000s, as a result of litigation launched by gay rights activists, three provincial courts found that the unavailability of marriage for same-sex couples was unconstitutional.[5] In 2005, Parliament passed legislation that made it possible for same-sex couples to marry in civil ceremonies.

It is interesting to note the roles of courts and legislatures in promoting the above social changes. In the 1970s and 1980s, courts tended to uphold a more conservative view on family and it was the legislators who facilitated recognition of common law relationships. However, in relation to same-sex marriage, the legislators were reluctant to respond, despite opinion polls showing increasing acceptance of such marriages.[6] As a historically marginalized group without much political influence, gays were unable to secure change through the legislative process and had to turn to courts for protection and affirmation of their *Charter* rights[7] (recall our discussion on courts, legislatures, and interest groups in Chapter 6, Part II, section 2).

Despite the variety of currently recognized forms of family, marriage continues to be a privileged type.[8] As shown in Figure 11.1, according to the 2011 census, married couples

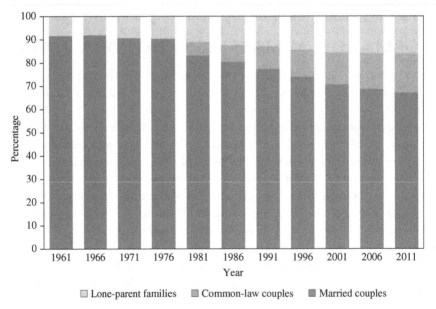

Figure 11.1 Distribution (in percentage) of census families by family structure, Canada, 1961–2011

Note: 1981 was the first year when common law unions were counted in the census. 2001 is the year when same-sex common law couples were first counted. 2006 is the year when same-sex married couples were first counted.

Source: Statistics Canada: http://www12.statcan.ca/census-recensement/2011/as-sa/98-312-x/2011003/fig/fig3_1-1-eng.cfm

remained the predominant family structure and constituted 67% of all couple families; common law unions constituted 16.7%;[9] 0.8% of all couples were same-sex couples.[10]

2.1 Marriage

Section 2 of the federal *Civil Marriage Act* states: "Marriage, for civil purposes, is the lawful union of two persons to the exclusion of all others."[11] Both opposite-sex and same-sex couples have the right to marry. However, as you can see, the definition covers only civil, but not religious marriages. Thus, it is possible for religious officials to refuse to perform same-sex marriages if this is contrary to their religious beliefs.

In order for a marriage to be legally valid, the following requirements must be met:

- Parties must reach the age of consent, which is prescribed by provincial legislation and varies. For example, it is 18 in Ontario and Manitoba; 19 in British Columbia and Newfoundland and Labrador; and 16 in Nova Scotia and PEI.

- Parties must have the mental capacity to understand the nature of marriage and the duties and responsibilities that it creates.

- Parties must give free consent and not be misled or forced into a marriage.

- Parties must not be too closely related to each other. The *Marriage (Prohibited Degrees) Act* states: "No person shall marry another person if they are related lineally, or as brother or sister or half-brother or half-sister, including by adoption."[12]

- All prior marriages of parties must be dissolved. If either party has been previously married, such marriage must be terminated by annulment or divorce. It is also a criminal offence to be in a polygamous marriage, although actual prosecutions are rare.[13]

- Parties must have gone through some form of marriage ceremony (civil or religious). At a minimum, a marriage ceremony must have witnesses and the parties must publicly declare their desire to be married.

2.2 Cohabitation

Cohabitation (also known as common law relationship) arises without parties going through a marriage ceremony. Unlike in the case of marriage, there is no formal marker of the relationship and there may be disputes as to when a couple really entered into a common law relationship. For a common law relationship to be created, the following must be present:

- Agreement between the parties;

- Legal capacity to enter cohabitation (age of consent, mental capacity, voluntariness);

- Parties must be living together;

- Consummation of sexual intercourse; and

- Public and continued recognition of the relationship.[14]

Importantly, for a common law relationship to be considered to exist, it is not enough that two persons merely live together and engage in sexual activity. A certain level of commitment to each other and interdependence needs to be demonstrated.[15]

3. RIGHTS AND OBLIGATIONS IN MARRIAGE AND COHABITATION

While there are some commonalities with respect to rights and obligations of parties in marriage and cohabitation, there are also some differences. Major rights and obligations can be divided into the following categories:

- *Mutual obligation of financial support.* Both married and unmarried couples have such an obligation. However, under provincial/territorial laws, parties in common law relationships usually need to cohabit for a certain minimum period of time (ranging between one and three years) before such an obligation arises.

- *Obligation to support children.* The scope of this obligation is the same for married and unmarried couples.

- *Rights of custody and access.* Both parents in married and unmarried couples have such rights.

- *Division of property.* There is a difference in the way how property is divided for married and unmarried couples. Under provincial legislation, as a general rule, property acquired or an increase in property value during marriage is divided equally between spouses. In contrast, unmarried couples are not always covered by the same provincial legislation and hence are not entitled to equal division of property.

4. DISSOLUTION OF MARRIAGE

There is no special process for dissolution of cohabitation. The parties merely cease their cohabitation and interdependence. However, in the case of marriage, a prescribed process must be followed and it is not enough for a married couple to merely stop cohabiting in order to legally end their marriage. A marriage can be officially dissolved by either divorce or annulment.

4.1 Divorce

The *Divorce Act* provides for one single ground for divorce: marriage breakdown. There are three circumstances when marriage breakdown can be established:

- *Adultery.* Adultery has been traditionally defined as voluntary sexual intercourse of a married person with another person of the opposite sex. However, the change in the definition of marriage to include same-sex couples has also led to a corresponding redefinition of adultery.[16]

- *Cruelty.* The *Divorce Act* does not define cruelty, but case law provides numerous examples of what constitutes cruelty: physical and/or emotional abuse, denial of necessary financial support, neglect of wife and children due to husband's addiction to work, excessive demand for sexual intercourse, and others.[17]

■ *Separation for at least one year immediately prior to the commencement of divorce proceedings.* Separation may be established by a couple living physically apart. However, a couple may be considered separated even if they continue to reside under the same roof but live separate lives (e.g., they eat, do household chores, and socialize separately; they sleep in separate bedrooms and have no sexual relations).[18]

In order to obtain a divorce, one or both parties must petition to court. A court may decide on divorce with or without a hearing. In case of adultery or cruelty, divorce can be granted speedily, without waiting for one year of separation. However, only the innocent party has the right to petition for divorce on those grounds. Figure 11.2 shows Canada's marriage and divorce trends from 1926 to 2008.

4.2 Annulment

While divorce terminates a legally valid marriage, an **annulment** declares that a marriage is legally void. An annulment is granted by court. There are two types of annulments:

■ *Marriage that is void ab initio (that is, from the very beginning).* If one of the requirements for legal validity of marriage (see section 2.1) is not met, such marriage is considered void ab initio. It is as if it never took place.

Figure 11.2 Numbers of marriages and divorces in Canada, 1926–2008

Source: Statistics Canada: http://www.statcan.gc.ca/pub/91-209-x/2013001/article/11788/fig/fig7-eng.htm

- *Marriage that is voidable on the option of one or both parties*. A voidable marriage remains valid, unless one of the parties wishes to annul it. Nonconsummation of marriage makes a marriage voidable.

5. ISSUES UPON BREAKDOWN OF MARRIAGE OR COHABITATION

When a marriage or a common law relationship breaks down, several issues need to be addressed:

- Spousal support;
- Child support;
- Division of property; and
- Custody of children.

The federal *Divorce Act* and provincial family law statutes set out the basic rules on custody, support, and division of property. In the past 30 years, a number of changes have been made to promote greater gender equality between the parties. For example, the equal division of property acquired in marriage gave recognition to the contribution made through unpaid household work by a stay-at-home spouse. The rules of spousal support, while promoting self-sufficiency, also recognize that some may not be able to achieve it if they were out of the workforce for a long period of time and are of older age. The details of all these rules are described in sections 7–9. However, it is possible for the parties to opt out of the statutory regime by devising their own domestic contract (see below), which may resolve property, support, and custody issues differently from the statutory framework.

6. INTERRELATIONSHIP OF FAMILY AND CONTRACT LAW

While we may not think of family matters from the perspective of contract law, there is an important interrelationship between the two. Married and unmarried couples are able to resolve a variety of issues by concluding a domestic contract. The most common kinds of domestic contracts are:

- *Marriage contract*. A marriage contract can be entered into by persons who intend to marry or are already married. It can outline how division of property, child support, and spousal support will be resolved should the marriage end. One issue that such contracts cannot deal with is child custody arrangements.
- *Cohabitation agreement*. A cohabitation agreement can be concluded by individuals in a common law relationship and can address the same issues as a marriage contract.
- *Separation agreement*. A separation agreement can be concluded by married or unmarried couples upon breakdown of their relationship and can address division of

property, child and spousal support, and child custody arrangements. For example, Andrew and Gina's case in the chapter's introduction can negotiate a separation agreement.

■ *Family arbitration agreement.* In this agreement, a couple consent to submit resolution of their family law dispute to arbitration, which outlines the issues in dispute and the design of the arbitration process.

Marriage and cohabitation agreements are forward looking in the sense that they try to anticipate issues that would arise upon relationship breakdown and outline how those issues would be resolved. Separation agreements come about after the relationship has broken down and deal with existing rights, obligations, and disputes. They usually result from parties attempting to resolve the issues through alternative dispute resolution (ADR) techniques such as negotiation, mediation, or arbitration (see chapter on ADR on Companion Website). ADR has the advantage of avoiding the costs, delays, and contentious nature of litigation. At the same time, one needs to be mindful of any potential power imbalance between the parties that may lead to unfair agreements.

Like other contracts, domestic agreements are binding, and if an agreement is breached, an innocent party can turn to courts to seek enforcement. However, as with other contracts, courts may intervene and set a contract aside on the basis of fraud, duress, undue influence, or unconscionability (recall Chapter 9). Importantly, when a domestic contract is set aside, the main objective is not to restore individuals to their precontract position (as in the case of ordinary contracts) but to proceed to a new, post-separation distribution of assets under a family law statute (Box 11.1).[19]

Box 11.1

Hartshorne v Hartshorne, [2004] 1 SCR 550: Should a Marriage Contract Be Set Aside?

Robert and Kathleen Hartshorne were married for nine years and cohabited for two years prior to that. They met at a law firm where Robert was a partner and Kathleen was an associate. They had two children (one child was born prior to the wedding and the other after). Kathleen quit her job after the birth of the first child and was financially dependent on Robert. It was a second marriage for both, and Robert was determined to ensure that he would not have to give half of his hard earned assets to Kathleen upon separation. Robert had approximately $1.6 million in assets and

Kathleen had debts. Robert presented Kathleen with a marriage contract, which stipulated that they would be completely independent of each other with respect to control and administration of all property. Kathleen would not be entitled to equal division of property, but would receive only a 3% interest in the matrimonial home for each year that the parties were married up to a maximum of 49%. Kathleen consulted with a lawyer, who said that the contract was unfair and advised her against signing it. Nevertheless, she signed the

(continued)

Box 11.1 *(continued)*

agreement upon Robert's insistence on the wedding day. Otherwise, the wedding likely would not have happened.

When the couple separated, Kathleen was entitled to property valued at $280 000 under the marriage contract and Robert kept $1.2 million in assets. In your opinion, is the agreement fair or should it be set aside?

Kathleen sought to have the agreement set aside and the case reached the Supreme Court. The Court found that the agreement was not unfair. The majority of the judges noted that the mere fact that the terms of the agreement differ from a statutory regime does not make the agreement unfair. Rather, fairness takes into account "what was within the realistic contemplation of the parties, what attention they gave to changes in circumstances or unrealized implications, then what are their true circumstances, and whether the discrepancy is such . . . that a different apportionment should be made."[20] The judges noted that Kathleen was a well educated woman trained in law who understood the implications of the agreement. She made a conscious choice to sign a contract that was unfair and chose to give away her rights.

Do you agree with this conclusion? Should the court have taken into consideration the power imbalance between Robert and Kathleen? We will come back to these questions in Part II of this chapter and examine them from a critical perspective.

7. SUPPORT PAYMENTS

The resolution of issues of spousal and child support is governed by the federal *Divorce Act* and by provincial/territorial statutes. Whether a federal or a provincial/territorial statute is to be applied is determined as follows:

- If an application for spousal and/or child support is initiated together with divorce proceedings, support issues are decided according to the *Divorce Act*.

- If an application for support is not linked to a divorce (e.g., a couple has not initiated a divorce or has already obtained one), support issues are resolved according to provincial/territorial statutes.

While worded differently, the underlying principles of both the *Divorce Act* and relevant provincial/territorial statutes are substantively similar and are expected to lead to the same outcomes.

7.1 Spousal Support

Both married and unmarried spouses can make a claim for spousal support. However, while a married spouse can make such a claim regardless of the length of marriage (e.g., even if it was a very short one), the definition of unmarried spouses under provincial statutes usually requires a certain period of cohabitation before any entitlement to support may arise. For example, under Ontario's *Family Law Act*, a couple must have cohabited for a period of no less than three years or have been in a relationship of some permanence and have a biological or adopted child together.[21]

Both the *Divorce Act* and relevant provincial/territorial legislation identify the following key objectives of spousal support:

1. *To relieve economic hardship arising from relationship breakdown.* Following relationship breakdown, one spouse may have a significantly lower standard of living than during marriage. Support payments are supposed to alleviate such hardship until the individual achieves self-sufficiency.

2. *To promote self-sufficiency* of each ex-spouse, in so far as is practicable, within a reasonable period of time.

3. *To recognize any economic advantage or disadvantage arising from a relationship.* This objective may be considered particularly relevant to situations where one spouse stayed at home and the other was the primary income earner. Such an arrangement may lead to various advantages/disadvantages for each spouse.[22]

Andrew and Gina's case from the chapter's introduction provides a useful illustration of the objectives of spousal support (Box 11.2).

The above objectives reflect two major rationales behind support orders:

- *Compensatory.* This rationale is reflected in objective 3 and seeks to compensate the stay-at-home spouse for the sacrifice of future earning power. The assessment of this basis for spousal support requires the court to examine what has happened during a relationship, how long it lasted, and what roles the spouses performed during the marriage.

- *Noncompensatory.* This rationale is reflected in objectives 1 and 2. This basis of spousal support requires examination of the current means and needs of the parties.

Courts have broad discretion in determining amounts of support and its duration. In determining such issues, they are to consider a variety of factors. For example, the *Divorce*

Box 11.2

Practical Application: Andrew and Gina's Case

By staying at home, Gina likely enabled Andrew to more fully dedicate himself to his career, thereby contributing to his success and increased earning capacity. However, the longer Gina remained out of the labour force, the more difficult it was for her to subsequently find employment. Upon their relationship breakdown, the two spouses found themselves in different positions of advantage/disadvantage: Andrew has a job and income, while Gina not only does not have an independent source of income, but may not be able to find a job quickly. Support payments are intended to recognize these different positions and compensate the stay-at-home spouse for the disadvantage resulting from this traditional family arrangement. In the absence of independent source of income, Gina is likely to have a significantly lower standard of living than during marriage, so support payments will also seek to alleviate resulting hardship. However, it is expected that Gina would seek self-sufficiency and would make an effort to reenter the labour force.

Act mandates looking at "the condition, means, needs and other circumstances of each spouse."[23] "Condition" includes such factors as spouses' age, health, needs, and position in life; "means" refers to the parties' financial resources and income; "needs" reflects the individual's accustomed lifestyle, subject to the other spouse's ability to pay.[24] There is no single model of support, and no single objective or factor is considered overriding. The underlying rationale is to look at the consequences of marriage for each spouse and seek fair distribution of economic consequences of marriage.[25]

In 2005, the Department of Justice released Spousal Support Advisory Guidelines that contain formulas for calculation of spousal support. They are not binding, but are intended to assist lawyers in negotiating settlements (for example, assessing reasonableness of offers) as well as judges in the exercise of their discretion.

A person who requires spousal support needs to make an application to court. Where a marriage contract or a separation agreement exists, the court will examine that agreement, but is not necessarily bound by its terms. However, an existing agreement should only be cast aside where the applicant shows that the agreement fails to substantially comply with the objectives of the *Divorce Act*.[26] See Box 11.3.

Box 11.3

Gammon v Gammon, [2008] OJ No 603: Should a Separation Agreement Be Set Aside?

Mr. and Mrs. Gammon first cohabited for at least seven years and then were married for another seven. They separated in 2004. The husband was the primary income earner, making over $100 000 per year. The wife worked in various office jobs and her income was approximately $25 000 per year. According to the separation agreement, the wife received a lump sum payment of $130 000 representing her interest in the matrimonial home and a one-time lump sum payment of spousal support. She waived any claim to ongoing spousal support. At the time when the agreement was negotiated, Mrs. Gammon was in a fragile emotional state: she did not want the separation and was devastated. Although she received legal advice on the agreement, in reality she did not understand its terms. In 2005, Mrs. Gammon applied to court to set the separation agreement aside. How is a court to determine if the agreement should be set aside?

The decision of the Supreme Court in *Miglin v Miglin*[27] provided a test to be used to decide on the issue. The test involves two stages:

a. *Examination of the context in which the agreement was negotiated (was it negotiated fairly?).* A court is to consider the following factors: conditions of the parties, including any circumstances of oppression, pressure, or other vulnerabilities; whether parties received independent legal advice; and the extent to which the agreement takes into account the objectives of the *Divorce Act.*

b. *Examination of the circumstances at the time of the application for spousal support:* whether there was a significant and unforeseen change in the parties' circumstances that warrants setting aside the agreement.

Applying the *Miglin* test, the Ontario Superior court set aside the provisions of the Gammons' agreement on spousal support.[28] On the first part of the test, the court was satisfied that Mrs. Gammon was vulnerable as a result of her emotional state as well as her alcohol dependency. Although this in itself did not constitute sufficient grounds to set aside the agreement, other factors played a role: the long-term relationship of the parties; the role of the husband as the main breadwinner; and the economic hardship that the wife suffered as a result of the marriage breakdown. The court concluded that Mrs. Gammon was unlikely to achieve self-sufficiency to enjoy the lifestyle she had had during marriage. The court further found that one lump sum payment of spousal support was insufficient to address the objectives of the *Divorce Act*. It ordered the husband to pay the wife retroactive and ongoing spousal support.

Support orders can be of set or indefinite duration. The duration of spousal support depends on a variety of factors, including the ability of the dependent spouse to achieve self-sufficiency and the basis on which support was awarded (compensatory or noncompensatory). There is no presumed duty on the dependent ex-spouse to achieve self-sufficiency and it may not be possible in some circumstances. Even if an ex-spouse is able to satisfy basic needs, this does not automatically amount to self-sufficiency. Rather, the question is whether the spouse is able to maintain a reasonable standard of living taking into account the lifestyle enjoyed during marriage.[29] If support was ordered entirely on a compensatory basis, then even achievement of self-sufficiency by the dependent spouse does not automatically justify decrease or termination of spousal support.[30]

The terms of support orders can be varied in case of substantial, unforeseen, and continuing change in the "condition, means, needs or other circumstances" of either spouse.[31] A change must be of such nature that, had it been known at the time of the initial award, it would likely have resulted in different terms of the support order.[32]

7.2 Child Support

A parent is obligated to provide support to their child in both marriage and common law relationships. Under the *Divorce Act*, a parent is obligated to provide support until the child turns the age of majority (if the child has not withdrawn from the parent's charge) or if the child is over that age but is unable to self-support. A similar requirement is found under provincial legislation.[33]

There are federal *Child Support Guidelines* that seek to provide some uniformity in the amounts of awards across Canada. Comparable guidelines have also been developed by provinces.

7.3 Enforcement of Support Payments

Enforcement of support obligations has been a significant challenge. For example, in 2012–2013, only 49.7% of cases were in full compliance with child and spousal support payments.[34]

To address this problem, provinces created special structures to monitor and enforce such payments. For example, Ontario established the Family Responsibility Office (FRO), which enforces all support orders made by Ontario courts (unless the order was withdrawn from the FRO system). The payment first goes to the FRO, which then directs it to the recipient of support. If payments are not made, the FRO can take a number of enforcement measures, including: garnishing the payor's bank accounts; reporting the payor to the credit bureau; suspending the payor's driver's licence, passport, and federal licences; issuing a writ for seizure and sale of the payor's property; reporting the payor to professional organizations; seizing the payor's lottery winnings; and commencing a hearing that could lead to imprisonment of up to 180 days for nonpayment. The latter measure can be particularly powerful. While our law has generally departed from the principle of incarceration for debt, in the context of family law, imprisonment for nonpayment is not considered punishment but merely the means to facilitate enforcement.[35] However, imprisonment is a measure of last resort and is to be imposed only where the debtor has the ability to pay.[36] If a debtor is unable to pay, incarceration is inappropriate. For example, in *Ontario (Director, Family Responsibility Office) v De Francesco*,[37] the debtor had a disabling and treatment-resistant condition that made him unable to perform full- or part-time work. He had recently lost a job that he had held for 25 years, had to apply for social assistance, and had to spend his severance pay on legal fees, leaving no money for support payments. The court concluded that incarceration was neither warranted nor appropriate in this case, since there were valid reasons why De Francesco was unable to pay support.

8. CHILD CUSTODY

Susan Boyd provides an enlightening overview of the law's changing approach to child custody in her book *Child Custody, Law, and Women's Work*.[38] In the nineteenth century, fathers had the absolute right to custody; by the twentieth century, more emphasis started being placed on the welfare of children; and by the mid-twentieth century, mothers had a presumption in their favour. By the 1980s, the best interests of the child was established as the main consideration in determining custody and both parents were recognized to have equal right to custody. Finally, the 1990s saw increased emphasis on shared parenting and maximum contact between children and parents, including noncustodial parents.

Currently, each parent has a right to seek custody, but the ultimate arrangement is determined either by a separation agreement or by the court. **Custody** means that a parent has the right and responsibility to make decisions affecting the child's well-being. In contrast to custody, **access** has more limited scope. It means the right to visit children and to be visited by them as well as the right to make inquiries and obtain information about health, education, and welfare of the children.[39] In some cases, *supervised access* may be ordered. It may be appropriate where there are concerns about the visiting parent's drug or alcohol use or where the safety of the custodial parent is an issue. Supervised access can take several forms. For example, it may require that a member of the family be present on the same premises or in the same room as the visiting parent, or that contact between the child and the access parent may be made in specially set up supervised access centres.

Gina and Andrew in our scenario may obtain *joint custody*, or one of them may obtain custody and the other would only have access. Joint custody presupposes cooperation between parents and may not work where they are not able to maintain effective and respectful communication.[40]

The determination of custody issues is guided by the *best interests of the child* (not the wishes or interests of the parents). The concept of the best interests of the child does not have an exact definition, but case law and legislation provided a number of factors that are to be considered. For example, Ontario's *Children's Law Reform Act* includes such factors as: the love, affection, and emotional ties between the child and each parent; the child's views and preferences; the length of time the child has lived in a stable home environment; the ability and willingness of each parent to provide the child with guidance, education, and necessaries of life; the parenting plan of each parent; and the permanence and stability of the family unit where the child is proposed to live.[41] These factors are not exhaustive and neither has priority over the other.

While the above factors seem straightforward, their actual application may be influenced by various assumptions about good and bad parenting and benefits of parental contact for the child. Academic literature points at some problematic trends. For example, historic analysis of case law demonstrates that the image of good motherhood tended to reflect a white, middle-class, nuclear family model, where a mother is available to care for the children full-time.[42] This norm disadvantages women who are unable to fit the definition due to reliance on social assistance, disability, or sexual orientation.[43] For example, a mother with a disability who arranges for others to perform caretaking responsibilities for the children may be seen as not fitting the pattern of expected parenting.[44]

The current emphasis on maximum contact between the child and parents also has produced some problematic trends. For example, analysis of judgments from Ontario and British Columbia revealed that access was ordered in almost all cases, even where the noncustodial parent had a history of violence against the child and/or the former partner, or where the parent had no previous relationship with the child.[45] Maximum contact even in high conflict situations seemed to have been equated with the best interests of the child.[46] However, there is little scientific support for the assertion that in a high conflict situation such contact is beneficial for the child.[47]

When one parent takes the child without having legal custody, or without the permission of the custodial parent, this is considered child abduction. While the child may not be in real physical danger, relocation is considered disruptive to the child's life. Child abduction by a noncustodial parent is a criminal offence.[48] In addition, each province has a central authority that can assist in returning children who were taken from one province to the other. If the child is taken outside of Canada, an international treaty—the *Convention on the Civil Aspects of International Child Abduction*—can facilitate the child's return. If a foreign country where the child was taken is a party to the *Convention*, its authorities are under an obligation to take all appropriate measures to ensure voluntary return of the child to Canada.

9. DIVISION OF PROPERTY

Property and civil rights are the subject matter of provincial jurisdiction and, thus, division of property in case of relationship breakdown is governed by provincial legislation. Especially in the past, this legislation has focused only on married couples, leaving cohabiting couples to the common law property rules. This resulted in different division of property regimes for married and unmarried couples (see below). The Supreme Court decision in *Walsh* concluded that the existence of these different regimes does not violate equality under the *Charter*.[49]

Recently, some provinces started to include unmarried couples under the matrimonial property statutes (e.g., Saskatchewan, Manitoba, Northwest Territories, Nunavut). Once a couple cohabits for a specified period of time, it is covered by the statutory regime. Other provinces such as Nova Scotia and Newfoundland and Labrador allow unmarried couples to register as partners and thus become covered by matrimonial property statutes.

9.1 Married Couples

As a rule, provincial statutes provide that married couples are entitled to equal shares of property that has been acquired in marriage or of the increase in property value during marriage. This division reflects the idea that both spouses equally contribute to the marriage regardless of the actual work they perform (e.g., if one spouse stays at home and the other works outside of the home). Thus, the property acquired by Gina and Andrew during marriage will be divided equally between them. Some items are excluded from being considered family property: for example, insurance payments received by either spouse, or gifts or inheritance received during marriage.

Some property may be physically divided into halves, while other property cannot. Since courts have no power to order transfer of property, equal sharing is achieved by an *equalization payment*. Where one spouse gets to keep certain property, he must make an equalization payment to the other spouse. For example, if Andrew gets to keep the works of art that are worth $50 000, he will have to make a $25 000 equalization payment to Gina to reflect the equal division of property between the spouses.

9.2 Unmarried Couples

Division of property for unmarried couples is usually determined by who holds the title to the property. While most Canadian provinces started to extend marital property regimes to unmarried couples, Quebec draws a sharp distinction between married and common law relationships. Common law spouses are not entitled to either spousal support or division of property. The Supreme Court has recently heard a challenge to this Quebec law.

The case *Quebec v A*[50] involved a common law couple: 32-year-old Eric met 17-year-old Lola in her native Brazil. Lola eventually moved to Quebec, where Eric financially supported her. Lola made a few attempts at a modelling career but otherwise did not work

Table 11.1 Marriage Versus Cohabitation

	Marriage	**Cohabitation**
Formation	■ Marriage ceremony ■ Five basic requirements (age, capacity, consent, not too closely related, not already married)	■ No ceremony ■ Cohabitation and interdependence ■ Five basic requirements (age, capacity, consent, consummation, public recognition of relationship)
Dissolution	■ Divorce or annulment	■ No special process ■ Parties cease cohabitation and interdependence
Child custody	■ Best interests of the child ■ Both parents can claim custody	■ Best interests of the child ■ Both parents can claim custody
Spousal support	■ Can be claimed regardless of the duration of marriage	■ Can be claimed only after a certain period of cohabitation or if parties have a child together
Division of property	■ Property acquired in marriage divided 50/50	■ Regimes differ by province; often different from married spouses

during their relationship. The couple lived together for seven years and had three children. Lola wanted to get married but Eric said that he did not believe in the institution of marriage. Once the couple separated, Lola argued that different regimes for married and unmarried couples in Quebec violated s. 15 (equality) under the *Charter*.

The judges of the Supreme Court were divided on the assessment of various aspects of the claim, but ultimately concluded that the different regimes for married and unmarried couples in Quebec were not discriminatory. The majority focused on the importance of respecting individual autonomy and freedom of couples who choose not to marry. The judges noted that common law partners can protect their interests by entering into a cohabitation agreement that could provide for payment of support and/or division of property upon relationship breakdown. Do you agree with the Court's conclusion, especially in light of the fact that Lola wanted to get married but Eric did not? This case raises issues of fairness, equality, and respect for individual autonomy similar to the *Hartshorne* case, and will be discussed in Part II of the chapter.

Table 11.1 summarizes the characteristics of marriage and cohabitation.

10. FAMILY VIOLENCE

Family violence can come in a variety of forms: spousal abuse, child abuse, and elder abuse. Abuse can be physical, emotional, sexual, and financial. The common characteristic in all forms of abuse is the exercise of domination or power over an individual and the use of that power for oppression.

There are various mechanisms to address family violence and its consequences, but they can be generally divided into public and private law remedies.

10.1 Public Law Remedies

Among the public remedies are various federal and provincial laws and initiatives, including:

- legislation that criminalizes abusive behaviour and provides for various protection options;
- support structures for persons escaping violence (e.g., shelters, transition houses);
- provision of counselling services;
- crime victim compensation schemes; and
- awareness education and initiatives.

The *Criminal Code* contains a number of provisions that can be used to address situations of family violence (with some of them specifically responding to family violence, and others not): assault, aggravated assault, assault with a weapon, sexual assault, criminal harassment, sexual interference with children, sexual exploitation of children, and failure to provide necessaries of life. In addition, provincial family laws provide for other mechanisms to assist victims of domestic violence such as restraining orders, orders for exclusive possession of a matrimonial home, and powers of the police, justices of the peace, and social workers to intervene in family violence situations.

Every province adopted special legislation for the protection of children. While it is best for a child to be raised by the family, in some cases, the family environment may be so disruptive or unhealthy that a child should be removed from it. Special agencies—Children's Aid Societies or Child and Family Services—investigate allegations of abuse and may bring forward applications for removal of children from their families. For example, under Ontario's *Child and Family Services Act*, a child is considered to be in need of protection in the following circumstances:

- the child has suffered physical harm;
- the child has been sexually molested or sexually exploited;
- the child requires medical treatment and the child's parent or caregiver does not provide it;
- the child is under 12 and has killed or seriously injured another person or caused serious damage to another person's property, services or treatment are necessary to prevent a recurrence, and the child's parent or caregiver does not provide or refuses or is unable to consent to those services or treatment;
- the child's parent is unable to care for the child and the child is brought before the court with the parent's consent; and
- other circumstances.[51]

If a child is found to be in need of protection, a judge—guided by the best interests of the child—must determine a further course of action. Three options are available:

- *Supervision order.* A child remains with the parents but child protection agencies periodically visit to check on the situation.

- *Temporary wardship order.* A child is temporarily placed in a group or foster home and parents can visit the child periodically. This order may be appropriate where it is considered that a parent–child relationship may be restored over time and the child may eventually be able to return home.

- *Permanent wardship.* This order terminates parental rights and does not allow natural parents access to the child. The child may be placed for adoption without the natural parents' consent.

10.2 Private Law Remedies: Torts

Issues of domestic violence are most commonly addressed through the public law means discussed above. However, they usually do not address the financial consequences of abuse.[52] For example, victims of domestic violence may incur long-term medical costs of treatment and/or have limited employment options due to past injuries. Hence, they may need to resort to private law remedies, which are available through, for example, tort law (recall Chapter 10) as well as spousal support orders.[53]

A tort lawsuit can seek compensation for the harm suffered, including ongoing expenses and loss of income. However, case law analysis demonstrates that so far plaintiffs have enjoyed only limited success.[54] Such lawsuits are less likely to be successful where there was no prior criminal conviction of the defendant for spousal violence. This creates a significant challenge for plaintiffs given that domestic violence often goes unreported and that even reported cases do not always lead to prosecution and conviction. Further, even successful lawsuits often result in relatively low damage awards.[55] In addition, many victims may not be able to pursue a tort lawsuit due to lack of awareness about this avenue of recourse and/or high costs of litigation.

In addition to tort law, there is some room in family law for obtaining financial compensation for the consequences of spousal abuse.[56] In *Leskun*, the Supreme Court held that while spousal misconduct cannot be a factor considered in spousal support orders, the consequences of misconduct on the innocent spouse may be considered (e.g., if spousal abuse triggered depression which in turn impacted the spouse's employment ability).

Family violence causes wide-ranging damage—physical, psychological, and financial—all of which needs to be addressed by measures of protection and recourse. Currently, public law measures concentrate mostly on victim protection, while private remedies focus on financial compensation, albeit with limited effectiveness. As some authors have noted, it is necessary to develop public remedies that provide more comprehensive financial compensation for victims of family violence.[57]

Part II. Critical Perspectives

The feminist perspective has been one of the most prominent angles of analysis in family law.[58] In order to illustrate some of the critical issues in contemporary family law, we will concentrate on two themes: (1) choice, autonomy, and power imbalance in family law; and (2) assisted conception and definition of parent.

1. CHOICE, AUTONOMY, AND POWER IMBALANCE IN FAMILY LAW

The fact that family law contains both public and private dimensions produces complex tensions. On the one hand, family matters are considered private and hence should not be subject to intrusive state regulation. Individuals' choices to live in common law relationships versus marriage or to conclude domestic contracts on certain terms different from the statutory framework are the expression of their autonomy that should be respected. On the other hand, the principles of equality, fairness, and protection of the vulnerable are also reflected in family law and authorize certain intervention in family matters. For example, the statutory rules on division of property and support play a distributive role and allow for unfair domestic contracts to be set aside. The tension between these two sides of family law is vividly reflected in the cases of *Hartshorne* and *Quebec v A* discussed in Part I.

In the 2013 decision of *Quebec v A*, the Supreme Court concluded that the exclusion of unmarried couples from the spousal support and division of property regime under the Quebec Civil Code was not discriminatory. It arrived at a similar conclusion a decade earlier in *Walsh* with respect to different matrimonial property regimes for married and unmarried couples in Nova Scotia. Both decisions emphasized the respect for the couple's choice not to marry and correspondingly not be covered by the regime for married couples. However, what about the concerns that the decision not to get married was the choice of one rather than both parties? As you might recall, in *Quebec v A*, Lola wanted to get married, while Eric did not. Then, can cohabitation really be viewed as a free choice by both partners?

In *Hartshorne*, the Supreme Court refused to set aside a contract that was significantly unfair to Mrs. Hartshorne. In this case, we find a similar theme of viewing the spouses as equal, rational actors who are free to make their own choices. Mrs. Hartshorne was an educated woman, she obtained independent legal advice, and she understood the consequences of signing the agreement. If she made a bad deal, she should take responsibility for it and courts should not intervene. The decision expresses that individual autonomy should be respected and that it is not the role of the law to protect people against their poor judgments. However, can Mrs. Hartshorne's consent be understood as an expression of choice and autonomy, given that she already had a child with Mr. Hartshorne before the marriage, was financially dependent on him, and realized that the wedding would not happen if she did not sign the marriage contract?

We already know the outcomes of both discussed cases. In resolving the tension between respect for choice and autonomy on the one hand, and fairness and protection of the vulnerable on the other, the Supreme Court gave priority to the former. Our system traditionally places paramount value on liberty and autonomy. Individuals should be able to make their choices freely and to take responsibility for them. There is nothing inherently unfair in upholding these values in the context of family law. On the other hand, the critical perspective encourages us to look at the context in which the choice and autonomy are exercised. For example, we need to acknowledge that the formal equality of spouses/partners does not necessarily translate into their substantive equality. They do not always have equal bargaining power in domestic contracts, which may result in unfair deals.[59] Mrs. Hartshorne's "choice" to sign the contract can be seen as a result of her precarious position. Similarly, Lola did not really choose the common law relationship, but ended up in it because Eric was not open to the idea of marriage. The Court noted that unmarried couples can still protect their interests by entering into a domestic contract (an option open to Lola), but as some academics noted, it is unrealistic to presume that many would do so. From a psychological point of view, people are often not prepared to deal with personal relations by means of a contract.[60] Further, a domestic contract can be concluded only if both partners agree. If Eric was unwilling to get married, what are the reasons to believe that he would be willing to sign a cohabitation agreement that gave Lola a share of his assets and an entitlement to spousal support?

2. LAW AND SOCIAL CHANGE: LESBIAN FAMILIES, ASSISTED CONCEPTION, AND DONOR'S RIGHT TO CUSTODY AND ACCESS

Society is constantly changing and law needs to keep up with those changes. In the family law context, the development of reproductive technologies has posed new and challenging questions. Traditionally, parentage rules were based on a heterosexual family that would conceive a child without the use of reproductive technology. A child could have only two parents (of opposite sex), and the biological parents were also recognized as the legal parents. However, the development of reproductive technology as well as other social developments led to fragmentation of parenthood.[61] For example, a child may have a biological father (whose sperm was used for conception) and a social father (who takes care of the child's welfare and upbringing). The processes of providing an egg, carrying a child, and commissioning the child's conception can be done by different women, each of whom may have a claim to parentage. In this section, we will briefly review whether family law has yet provided an adequate response to these social changes.

Imagine the following scenario: Jane and Nadia are a same-sex couple. They make an arrangement with Mikal to be a sperm donor. As a result, Jane conceives a child. Jane and Nadia want the child to be brought up within their family and without contact with Mikal. While Mikal initially agrees, he later attempts to assert his parental rights. Who are the child's parents: Jane and Nadia? Mikal and Jane (given that biologically the child is theirs)? Or all three of them?

Legislatures were relatively slow to address questions raised by the above scenario and the task often fell on courts.[62] Legal parentage was traditionally determined by biology: the birth mother was considered the mother and the man with whom she cohabited was presumed to be the father. With the advancement of reproductive technologies new presumptions developed, such as the preconception intention of the parties (did the individual intend to bring up the child as their own?). In cases of assisted conception, it allowed a man to whom the woman was married or joined in common law to be declared the child's father. In contrast, lesbian families faced some challenges regarding recognition of lesbian nonbiological mothers (like Nadia) as a second parent.[63] The legislative regulation of this issue is patchwork and incomplete. In certain provinces, a lesbian nonbiological mother could be declared as a coparent but only if the child's father is unknown or refuses to acknowledge the child. Where lesbian couples turned to courts to affirm their parental status, they faced mixed success.[64] In cases with known sperm donors, courts usually relied on biology and refused to exclude the donor from parentage. In the scenario described above, reliance on biology would lead to the conclusion that the donor (Mikal) is the child's parent (along with Jane) but would exclude Nadia from being considered a parent. The recognition of Mikal as a legal parent means that he can claim rights to custody and access and is essentially inserted into a lesbian family without its consent. Thus, on the one hand, the integrity of a lesbian family is disturbed by inclusion of the donor as the father. On the other hand, the nonbiological mother in a lesbian couple is often given no status at all in relation to the child, despite her actual participation in the child's care and upbringing.[65] In 2007, an Ontario court recognized that a child may have three parents where a lesbian couple and a known donor made a three-way coparenting agreement prior to conception.[66] However, this decision is so far the only one of its kind and does not necessarily lead to routine recognition of three-parent families.

So far, the law has not fully and comprehensively addressed parentage in lesbian couples, which results in their facing greater challenges and uncertainty than heterosexual couples using assisted conception. This demonstrates not only the incremental nature of legal change but also that inequalities persist—in this case along the lines of sexual orientation.

SUMMARY

Family law is a complex subject area that comprises both public and private law dimensions as well as a division of various aspects of family matters between federal and provincial jurisdictions. At a practical level, family law outlines rules with respect to formation and dissolution of marriage and cohabitation; rights and obligations of spouses/partners; division of property; spousal and child support; child custody; and protection against family violence. In order for marriage or cohabitation to be formed, such minimum requirements as the age of consent, mental capacity, and voluntariness must be satisfied. In addition, in the case of marriage, parties must go through a ceremony and must dissolve all prior marriages. A marriage can be dissolved by a divorce or an annulment. The rights and obligations of parties in marriage and cohabitation have many similarities, but there are also differences. In both types of relationships, parents have an equal obligation of child support and have a right to seek custody. Spouses/partners also have an obligation of mutual financial support, but for common law couples it arises only after a certain period of cohabitation. With respect to division of property, the regimes differ: in marriage, property acquired during marriage is divided equally between the spouses; in cohabitation, the division is based on who holds the title to given property (although some provinces now provide for opportunities for common law couples to be covered under matrimonial property regimes).

Family law often raises challenging questions about balancing private law objectives of autonomy and choice versus public law concerns for the protection of the vulnerable. We also need to be aware of the potential impact of factors such as understanding of gender roles and notions of good parenting, as well as issues of race and class on the application of family law rules. As society changes, so does family law in its vision of these factors and a proper balance between public and private law values.

Critical Thinking Questions

1. Section 43 of the *Criminal Code* provides that a teacher or a parent may be justified in using force (that is reasonable under the circumstances) against a child for disciplinary purposes. In your opinion, is it ever justifiable to use force against a child? Find out if this provision has been challenged before courts and what courts decided. Do you agree with the court decision?

2. In your opinion, is the existence of different regimes for married and unmarried couples discriminatory? Why?

3. In your opinion, should family law give priority to the values of choice and autonomy, or should it be more interventionist in protecting interests of the vulnerable parties? Explain and give examples.

Further Readings and Resources

1. Maureen Baker, ed, *Families: Changing Trends in Canada*, 6th ed (Toronto: McGraw-Hill Ryerson, 2009).

2. Nicholas Bala et al, eds, *Canadian Child Welfare Law: Children, Families and the State*, 2nd ed (Toronto: Thomson Educational Publishing, 2004).

3. Susan B Boyd, *Child Custody, Law, and Women's Work* (Don Mills: Oxford University Press, 2003).

4. Fiona Kelly, *Transforming Law's Family: The Legal Recognition of Planned Lesbian Motherhood* (Vancouver: UBC Press, 2011).

5. Mary Jane Mossman, *Families and the Law in Canada: Cases and Commentary* (Toronto: Emond Montgomery Publications, 2004).

Endnotes

1. Robert Leckey, "Families in the Eyes of the Law: Contemporary Challenges and the Grip of the Past" (2009) 15:8 *IRPP Choices* at 9.
2. *Ibid* at 6.
3. *Ibid* at 19.
4. M v H, [1999] 2 SCR 3.

5. *Halpern v Canada*, [2002] OJ No 2714; *Hendricks v Canada*, [2002] JQ No 3816; *EGALE v Canada*, [2003] BCJ No 994.

6. Nicholas Bala, "Controversy over Couples in Canada: The Evolution of Marriage and Other Adult Interdependent Relationships (2003) 29 Queen's LJ 41 at para 123–131 (Quicklaw).

7. *Ibid* at para 127.

8. For discussion, see Bala, *ibid*.

9. Statistics Canada, "Portrait of Families and Living Arrangements in Canada," online: <http://www12.statcan.ca/census-recensement/2011/as-sa/98-312-x/98-312-x2011001-eng.cfm>.

10. *Ibid*.

11. *Civil Marriage Act*, SC 2005, c 33, s 2.

12. *Marriage (Prohibited Degrees) Act*, SC 1990, c 46, s 2(2).

13. For discussion of the *Criminal Code* prohibition of polygamy and freedom of religion, see *Reference re: Criminal Code of Canada (BC)*, [2011] BCJ No 2211. The court found that the provision limited the freedom of religion but was justified under s. 1 of the *Charter*.

14. Malcolm C Kronby, *Canadian Family Law*, 10th ed (Mississauga: J Wiley, 2010) at 10.

15. *Soper v Soper* (1985), 67 NSR (2d) 49; *Yakichuk v Oaks*, [2003] SJ No 216.

16. *SEP v DDP*, [2005] BCJ No 1971.

17. Julien D Payne & Marilyn A Payne, *Canadian Family Law*, 4th ed (Toronto: Irwin Law, 2011) at 198–203.

18. *Cooper v Cooper*, (1972) 10 RFL 184.

19. Robert Leckey, "A Common Law of the Family? Reflections on *Rick v Brandsema*" (2009) 25 Can J Fam L 257 at para 25 (Quicklaw).

20. *Ibid* at para 67.

21. *Family Law Act*, RSO 1990, c F.3, s 29.

22. See, e.g., *Divorce Act*, RSC 1985, c 3, s 15.2(6); Ontario's *Family Law Act*, *ibid*, s 33(8).

23. *Divorce Act*, *ibid*, s 15.2(4); see also *Family Law Act*, *ibid*, s 33(9).

24. *Menegaldo v Menegaldo*, [2012] OJ No 2186 at para 40.

25. Payne & Payne, *supra* note 17 at 262.

26. *Miglin v Miglin*, [2003] 1 SCR 303.

27. *Ibid*.

28. *Gammon v Gammon*, [2008] OJ No 603.

29. *Fisher v Fisher*, [2008] OJ No 38 at paras 52–59 (ONCA).

30. *Menegaldo*, *supra* note 24 at para 48.

31. *Divorce Act*, *supra* note 22, s 17(4.1); see also *LMP v LS*, [2011] 3 SCR 775.

32. *Willick v Willick*, [1994] 3 SCR 670.

33. For example, under the Ontario *Family Law Act* (s. 31), *supra* note 21, a parent is under an obligation to provide support to a child under the age of majority as well as to those who are over the age of majority but are full-time students.

34. Statistics Canada, "Child and Spousal Support, by Payment Compliance, by Province and Territory (Canada)," online: <http://www.statcan.gc.ca/tables-tableaux/sum-som/l01/cst01/legal47a-eng.htm>.

35. *Fischer v Ontario (Director, Family Responsibility Office)*, [2008] OJ No 4922; *Ontario (Director, Family Responsibility Office) v Kilpatrick*, [2008] OJ No 3826.

36. *Kilpatrick*, *ibid* at para 35.

37. [2012] OJ No 6338.

38. Susan B Boyd, *Child Custody, Law, and Women's Work* (Don Mills: Oxford University Press, 2003) at 2.
39. Kronby, *supra* note 14 at 70.
40. E.g., *Hurst v Gill*, 2010 NSCA 98.
41. *Children's Law Reform Act*, RSO 1990, c C.12, s 24(2).
42. Boyd, *supra* note 38.
43. *Ibid* at 5.
44. *Ibid* at 16–17.
45. Fiona Kelly, "Enforcing a Parent/Child Relationship at All Costs? Supervised Access Orders in the Canadian Courts" (2011) 49 Osgoode Hall LJ 277.
46. Rachel Birnbaum & Stephanie Chipeur, "Supervised Visitation in Custody and Access Disputes: Finding Legal Solutions for Complex Family Problems" 29 Can Fam L Q 79.
47. Kelly, *supra* note 45; Claire Sturge & Danya Glaser, "Contact and Domestic Violence: The Experts' Court Report" (2000) 30 Fam L 615.
48. *Criminal Code*, RSC 1985, c C-46, ss 282(1), 283(1).
49. *Nova Scotia v Walsh*, [2002] 4 SCR 325.
50. *Quebec (Attorney General) v A*, [2013] 1 SCR 61.
51. *Child and Family Services Act*, RSO 1990, c C.11, s 37(2).
52. While there are some crime victim compensation programs, they usually provide limited financial compensation.
53. See, e.g., *B(P) v B(W)* (1992), 11 OR 3d 161; *Y(AD) v Y(MY)*, [1994] BCJ No 375.
54. Fiona Kelly, "Private Law Responses to Domestic Violence: The Intersection of Family Law and Tort" (2009) 44:2 SCLR 321 at 323.
55. *Ibid*.
56. *Ibid*.
57. *Ibid*.
58. This is not to suggest that women's issues are the only critical issues in the area of family law. In the past decade, certain groups started to express increased concern about fathers' rights, arguing that the changes in law disadvantage fathers. For critical appraisal of these developments see, for example, Robert Menzies, "Virtual Backlash: Representations of Men's 'Right' and Feminist 'Wrong' in Cyberspace" and Susan B Boyd & Claire FL Young, "Feminism, Fathers' Rights, and Family Catastrophes: Parliamentary Discourses on Post-Separation Parenting, 1966–2003" in Susan B Boyd, ed, *Reaction and Resistance: Feminism, Law, and Social Change* (Vancouver: UBC Press, 2007).
59. Carol Rogerson, "*Miglin v Miglin* 2003 SCC 24: They Are Agreements Nonetheless" (2003) 20 Can J Fam L 197.
60. Bala, *supra* note 6 at para 27.
61. Susan B Boyd, "Gendering Legal Parenthood: Bio-genetic Ties, Intentionality and Responsibility" (2007) 25 Windsor YB Access Just 63.
62. Leckey, *supra* note 1 at 20.
63. Fiona Kelly, "Equal Parents, Equal Children: Reforming Canada's Parentage Laws to Recognize the Completeness of Women-led Families" (2013) 64 UNB LJ 253.
64. See generally Fiona Kelly, *Transforming Law's Family: The Legal Recognition of Planned Lesbian Motherhood* (Vancouver: UBC Press, 2011).
65. Kelly, *supra* note 63; see also Kelly, *ibid*.
66. *AA v BB*, [2007] OJ No 2 (CA).

Chapter 12
Human Rights in Canada

Learning Objectives

After reading this chapter, you should be able to:

- Name nine major international human rights treaties and their monitoring bodies.

- Explain four main functions of international treaty bodies.

- Describe an individual complaints and a periodic reporting mechanism.

- Outline three main characteristics of federal and provincial human rights codes.

- Explain the concept of duty to accommodate.

- Describe the structure of the Ontario human rights system.

- Name and explain four main stages of complaints resolution before the Human Rights Tribunal of Ontario.

Chapter Outline

Introduction

We have all heard of human rights, but what does this concept really mean? What rights are considered human rights? What protections do they engender? Is there an international document that contains a list of all human rights? This chapter will provide a very brief overview of the international human rights regime to answer these questions. It will also provide several illustrations of Canada's implementation of its human rights obligations. In particular, Part II of the chapter discusses the *Canadian Human Rights Act* and provincial human rights codes, which provide individuals with an accessible recourse against discrimination and can be seen as one example of implementation of Canada's international obligations.

Part I. International Human Rights

Prior to reading this section, please answer the following questions. How would you define human rights? In your opinion, what rights can be considered human rights? (Give examples)

The idea of human rights is grounded in the notion of human dignity and equal moral worth of all individuals. It reflects minimum standards necessary for a dignified life. On the one hand, human rights protect individuals' liberty from undue state or other interference. On the other hand, they also require states to create certain conditions to enable human flourishing and exercise of liberties. Human rights help empower individuals. They create an opportunity for them to make claims against governments: as some have noted, they can shift the "balance of power from rulers to the ruled."[1] Human rights can also be seen as values and goals that help promote new standards in society and greater accountability of governments.

International human rights law is an area of international law (see the Companion Website). **Public international law** primarily regulates the behaviour of states and international organizations and determines their rights and obligations. Human rights, however, are peculiar in the sense that they not only outline state obligations, but also focus on individuals as bearers of rights.

1. INTERNATIONAL HUMAN RIGHTS TREATIES

International law develops in large part by means of the **treaty**—that is, an international agreement between states that intends to create binding legal obligations. Treaties can be bilateral (between two states) or multilateral (with participation of several states). They can be concluded on a variety of subject matters ranging from trade to military cooperation to human rights. Treaties can appear under a variety of titles, including *convention*, *covenant*, *protocol*, *pact*, *agreement*, and others. Like contracts in domestic law, treaties create binding obligations on states.

Treaties have been the main tool for development of international human rights norms. The post-Second World War period has seen increasing attention to human rights issues, largely prompted by the atrocities of war and the desire not to let them happen again. In 1945, the UN adopted the *Universal Declaration of Human Rights*. It had no binding force, but outlined a list of key human rights and subsequently served as the basis for development of human rights treaties. See Box 12.1 for excerpts from the declaration.

Box 12.1

Excerpts from the *Universal Declaration of Human Rights*

. . . Therefore **THE GENERAL ASSEMBLY** proclaims **THIS UNIVERSAL DECLARATION OF HUMAN RIGHTS** as a common standard of achievement for all peoples and all nations, to the end that every individual and every organ of society, keeping this Declaration constantly in mind, shall strive by teaching and education to promote respect for these rights and freedoms and by progressive measures, national and international, to secure their universal and effective recognition and observance, both among the peoples of Member States themselves and among the peoples of territories under their jurisdiction.

Article 1

■ All human beings are born free and equal in dignity and rights. They are endowed with reason and conscience and should act towards one another in a spirit of brotherhood.

Article 2

■ Everyone is entitled to all the rights and freedoms set forth in this Declaration, without distinction of any kind, such as race, colour, sex, language, religion, political or other opinion, national or social origin, property, birth or other status. Furthermore, no distinction shall be made on the basis of the political, jurisdictional or international status of the country or territory to which a person belongs, whether it be independent, trust, nonself-governing or under any other limitation of sovereignty.

Article 3

■ Everyone has the right to life, liberty and security of person.

Article 4

■ No one shall be held in slavery or servitude; slavery and the slave trade shall be prohibited in all their forms.

Article 5

■ No one shall be subjected to torture or to cruel, inhuman or degrading treatment or punishment.

Article 6

■ Everyone has the right to recognition everywhere as a person before the law.

Article 7

■ All are equal before the law and are entitled without any discrimination to equal protection of the law. All are entitled to equal protection against any discrimination in violation of this Declaration and against any incitement to such discrimination.

Article 8

■ Everyone has the right to an effective remedy by the competent national tribunals for acts violating the fundamental rights granted him by the constitution or by law.

Article 9

■ No one shall be subjected to arbitrary arrest, detention or exile.

Article 10

■ Everyone is entitled in full equality to a fair and public hearing by an independent and impartial tribunal, in the determination of his rights and obligations and of any criminal charge against him.

Article 11

■ (1) Everyone charged with a penal offence has the right to be presumed innocent until proved guilty according to law in a public trial at which he has had all the guarantees necessary for his defence.

■ (2) No one shall be held guilty of any penal offence on account of any act or omission which did not constitute a penal offence, under national or international law, at the time when it was committed. Nor shall a heavier penalty be imposed than the one that was applicable at the time the penal offence was committed.

Article 12

■ No one shall be subjected to arbitrary interference with his privacy, family, home or correspondence, nor to attacks upon his honour and reputation. Everyone has the right to the protection of the law against such interference or attacks.

. . .

Article 18

■ Everyone has the right to freedom of thought, conscience and religion; this right includes freedom to change his religion or belief, and freedom, either alone or in community with others and in public or private, to manifest his religion or belief in teaching, practice, worship and observance.

Article 19

■ Everyone has the right to freedom of opinion and expression; this right includes freedom to hold opinions without interference and to seek, receive and impart information and ideas through any media and regardless of frontiers.

Article 20

■ (1) Everyone has the right to freedom of peaceful assembly and association.

■ (2) No one may be compelled to belong to an association.

Article 21

■ (1) Everyone has the right to take part in the government of his country, directly or through freely chosen representatives.

(continued)

Box 12.1 *(continued)*

- (2) Everyone has the right of equal access to public service in his country.
- (3) The will of the people shall be the basis of the authority of government; this will shall be expressed in periodic and genuine elections which shall be by universal and equal suffrage and shall be held by secret vote or by equivalent free voting procedures.

. . .

Article 23.

- (1) Everyone has the right to work, to free choice of employment, to just and favourable conditions of work and to protection against unemployment.
- (2) Everyone, without any discrimination, has the right to equal pay for equal work.
- (3) Everyone who works has the right to just and favourable remuneration ensuring for himself and his family an existence worthy of human dignity, and supplemented, if necessary, by other means of social protection.
- (4) Everyone has the right to form and to join trade unions for the protection of his interests.

Article 24.

- Everyone has the right to rest and leisure, including reasonable limitation of working hours and periodic holidays with pay.

Article 25.

- (1) Everyone has the right to a standard of living adequate for the health and well-being of himself and of his family, including food, clothing, housing and medical care and necessary social services, and the right to security in the event of unemployment, sickness, disability, widowhood, old age or other lack of livelihood in circumstances beyond his control.

. . .

Article 26.

- (1) Everyone has the right to education. Education shall be free, at least in the elementary and fundamental stages. Elementary education shall be compulsory. . . .

Source: United Nations. http://www.un.org/en/documents/udhr/

Currently, international human rights law comprises multiple documents, but the core of it consists of the *UN Declaration of Human Rights* and nine major human rights treaties:

1. The *Convention on Elimination of All Forms of Racial Discrimination* (CERD) (1965);
2. The *International Covenant on Civil and Political Rights* (ICCPR) (1976);
3. The *International Covenant on Economic, Social and Cultural Rights* (ICESCR) (1976);
4. The *Convention on Elimination of All Forms of Discrimination against Women* (CEDAW) (1979);
5. The *Convention against Torture* (CAT) (1984);
6. The *Convention on the Rights of the Child* (CRC) (1989);
7. The *International Convention on the Protection of the Rights of All Migrant Workers* (1990);
8. The *Convention on the Rights of Persons with Disabilities* (2006); and
9. The *International Convention for the Protection of All Persons from Enforced Disappearance* (2006).

The nine conventions listed above are multilateral treaties, which are open for signature and ratification by all states in the world. In fact, the majority of states are parties to those treaties. These treaties contain a list of the most fundamental rights of individuals and impose obligations on states to ensure those rights. State obligations with respect to human rights have three main dimensions:[2]

a. To *respect* human rights. The state must abstain from interfering in individual rights (e.g., a state must not arbitrarily detain people or subject them to maltreatment).

b. To *protect* human rights. States must protect individuals and groups from human rights violations. For example, if private parties (such as individuals or corporations) are violating human rights, the state must take measures to stop those violations.

c. To *fulfill* human rights. This involves taking positive steps (e.g., allocation of resources) to ensure the exercise of human rights. For example, in order for a person to be able to exercise the right to education, an education system must be in place, including school buildings, teaching staff, school supplies, and so on.

To illustrate the content of human rights treaties, let's have a look at three examples: the *International Covenant on Civil and Political Rights* (ICCPR), the *International Covenant on Economic, Social and Cultural Rights* (ICESCR), and the *Convention against Torture* (CAT).

1.1 The *International Covenant on Civil and Political Rights* (ICCPR)

Both the ICCPR and the ICESCR built on the *Universal Declaration of Human Rights* and sought to translate its nonbinding provisions into a treaty that would create obligations for states. Their texts were adopted in 1966 and they came into force in 1976.

The ICCPR, as the title suggests, focuses on civil and political rights. The bulk of it consists of enumeration of various rights, including the right to life, liberty, and security of person; prohibition of torture and cruel, inhuman, or degrading treatment or punishment; prohibition of slavery; right to equality and nondiscrimination; right to freedom of thought, conscience, and religion; right to freedom of association; and others.

As with other international law treaties, the ICCPR creates obligations for parties. They are to "respect and to ensure to all individuals . . . rights recognized in the present Covenant" as well as "to take the necessary steps" for the implementation of the covenant.[3]

1.2 The *International Covenant on Economic, Social and Cultural Rights* (ICESCR)

The ICESCR incorporates a range of social, economic, and cultural rights, including the right to work, to just and favourable conditions of work, to education, to social security, to equality and nondiscrimination, to an adequate standard of living, to food, to physical and mental health, to cultural life, and others.

The obligations of parties are framed somewhat differently from the *ICCPR*: "Each State Party to the present Covenant undertakes to take steps . . . to the maximum of its available resources, with a view to achieving progressively the full realization of the rights recognized in the present Covenant. . . ."[4] This formulation recognizes that implementation of social, economic, and cultural rights may hinge on the availability of state resources and not all states may be able to ensure implementation of all rights immediately.

1.3 *Convention against Torture (CAT)*

The CAT provides a definition of torture and imposes a number of obligations on states. First, it categorically prohibits torture and prohibits states from removing individuals to other countries where there are grounds to believe substantial risk of torture exists. No exceptional circumstances can justify resorting to torture or removal to a country where an individual may be tortured. Second, states must take legislative, judicial, and other measures in order to prevent and prosecute acts of torture in their territories. Third, states are also to take other measures such as to provide victims of torture access to remedies, educate law enforcement officials, and monitor interrogation and other custody procedures to ensure that torture does not occur.

2. INTERNATIONAL TREATY BODIES

While virtually all states officially proclaim their respect for human rights, in reality, they do not always comply with their human rights obligations. Thus, a number of international bodies have been created in order to monitor and facilitate compliance. Each of the major nine human rights treaties provides for the establishment of a **treaty body** with powers that include monitoring and promotion of states' compliance with their obligations under those treaties. The list of treaty bodies and their functions is outlined in Table 12.1.

Treaty bodies are made up of experts in human rights appointed for a specific term. State parties nominate and elect members of the treaty bodies. However, those members serve in a personal capacity and not as representatives of states—this ensures that they are impartial and are not subject to political pressure from their respective governments. The number of experts varies from 10 to 23, depending on the treaty body (e.g., the Human Rights Committee and the Committee on Elimination of Racial Discrimination have 18 members; the Committee against Torture has 10 members).

Please note that in addition to the treaty bodies, there are other international mechanisms that help monitor state compliance with human rights. For example, there is Universal Periodic Review before the UN Human Rights Council.[5] However, discussion of those other mechanisms is beyond the scope of this chapter.

Table 12.1 Human Rights Treaty Bodies

Treaty	Entry into Force	Treaty Body	Reviewing Periodic Reports	Issuing General Comments	Adjudicating Individual Complaints	Investigating Systemic Human Rights Violations
International Covenant on Civil and Political Rights (ICCPR)	1976	Human Rights Committee	✓	✓	✓	
International Covenant on Economic, Social and Cultural Rights (ICESCR)	1976	Committee on Economic, Social and Cultural Rights	✓	✓	✓	
International Convention on the Elimination of All Forms of Racial Discrimination (CERD)	1969	Committee on the Elimination of Racial Discrimination	✓	✓	✓	
Convention on the Elimination of All Forms of Discrimination against Women (CEDAW)	1981	Committee on the Elimination of Discrimination against Women	✓	✓	✓	✓
Convention against Torture (CAT)	1987	Committee against Torture	✓	✓	✓	✓
Convention on the Rights of the Child (CRC)	1990	Committee on the Rights of the Child	✓	✓	pending	
International Convention on the Protection of the Rights of All Migrant Workers and Members of Their Families (CMW)	2003	Committee on Migrant Workers	✓	✓	✓	
Convention on the Rights of Persons with Disabilities (CRPD)	2008	Committee on the Rights of Persons with Disabilities	✓	✓	✓	
International Convention for the Protection of All Persons from Enforced Disappearance (CED)	2010	Committee on Enforced Disappearances	✓	✓	✓	✓

Treaty bodies usually perform four main functions:

a. *Review of state periodic reports on compliance*. Under each treaty, states parties are required to submit periodic reports (usually every two to five years) to a treaty body, outlining measures taken to implement treaty obligations. A corresponding treaty body reviews state periodic reports as well as other relevant information and issues **concluding observations**. These observations essentially provide an assessment of the state's compliance with a treaty. They usually: (i) acknowledge the state's advancements in compliance; (ii) outline areas of concern that require further action; and (iii) make suggestions and recommendations. The reporting process can be seen as a dialogue between states and treaty bodies with the objective to ultimately improve compliance. It is expected that a state will use these concluding observations in order to address existing areas of concern.

b. *Adjudication of interstate and individual complaints*. This mechanism allows states as well as individuals to make complaints to a treaty body about alleged violations of treaty obligations by a state party. For example, if an individual considers that a state party violates his rights under the ICCPR, he can complain to the Human Rights Committee. The interstate complaints mechanism has not been used, likely due to concerns that such complaints would damage diplomatic and other interstate relations. Thus, the complaints that treaty bodies receive usually come from individuals and/or groups.

An examination of a complaint involves two stages: (i) determining its admissibility (i.e., whether the complaint can be examined by a treaty body); and (ii) consideration on the merits.

A complaint is inadmissible if: it is made anonymously; it is being examined or has been examined by another international body; it is manifestly unfounded or an abuse of process; or domestic remedies have not been exhausted. The last criterion indicates that international complaints are not a substitute for domestic process: an attempt should be made to resolve an issue through national mechanisms first.

If a complaint is admissible, a treaty body will consider its merits. A treaty body does not conduct a hearing with both parties present. Rather, it examines the allegations based on written submissions of the complainant and the response of the government concerned. A treaty body determines whether a violation has occurred or is about to occur and makes a recommendation on an appropriate remedy. If a treaty body finds that a violation has been committed or is about to be committed, it can recommend several types of actions, including that the state in question abstains from a certain action (e.g., does not remove the complainant to another country where she would be at risk of torture), conducts a public investigation, pays compensation, or ensures nonrepetition of the violation. However, the decisions of treaty bodies are not binding and there is no international authority to enforce them. Hence, it remains ultimately up to a given government to decide whether it will comply with the recommendations. The complaints mechanism is often considered to be more of a "naming and shaming" tool rather than an effective practical remedy, but it is hoped that it can generate public pressure in order to force states to comply.

c. *Interpretation of treaty provisions.* While the provisions of human rights treaties appear clear and concise at first sight, multiple questions may arise at the stage of implementation. Treaty bodies have the power to issue general comments that provide interpretation of treaty provisions.

d. *Investigation of systemic violations of human rights.* Some treaty bodies may institute inquiries on allegations of systemic human rights violations. For example, if the Committee against Torture obtains reliable and well founded information on systemic practice of torture in a given state, it can invite that state to cooperate and may set up an inquiry, including a visit to the state party to examine the situation and produce a report.

3. CANADA AND THE INTERNATIONAL HUMAN RIGHTS SYSTEM

Canada is a party to seven major human rights treaties (it is not a party to the *Convention on the Rights of Migrant Workers* and the *Convention on Enforced Disappearances*). Given that Canada takes a transformationist approach to treaties (see the chapter on international law on the Companion Website), they are not automatically parts of domestic law, but have to be implemented through a multitude of laws and policies by various levels of government, depending on the subject matter.[6] In some cases, the existing domestic legislation may already meet treaty obligations and then no changes need to be made.

As a party to major human rights treaties, Canada must provide periodic reports to seven corresponding treaty bodies. With respect to individual complaints, it is subject to review under the *ICCPR, CAT,* and *CEDAW.*

In order to illustrate Canada's interaction with the international human rights system, let us examine the following two examples related to the *CAT*: a periodic report and an individual complaint against Canada. *However, before proceeding to the next section, please pause for a moment to discuss the following question. In your opinion, is Canada a country that respects human rights, and is it usually compliant with human rights obligations? Explain.*

3.1 Canada's Sixth Periodic Report to the Committee Against Torture

In 2010, Canada submitted a periodic report to the Committee against Torture. If you go to the link provided below and look under "CAT" and 6th reporting cycle you will see the following entry for Canada (reproduced in Table 12.2): http://tbinternet.ohchr.org/_layouts/TreatyBodyExternal/countries.aspx?CountryCode=CAN&Lang=EN.

This entry visually exemplifies the interaction between a state party (like Canada) and the international treaty body (the Committee against Torture).

a. The first file on the list is the government report on compliance with the *CAT*. It reflects the Canadian government's position on compliance with obligations under

Table 12.2 Consideration of Canada's Sixth Periodic Report to the Committee Against Torture

Treaty			Signature Date	Ratification Date, Accession(a), Succession(d) Date
CAT - Convention against Torture and Other Cruel Inhuman or Degrading Treatment or Punishment			23 Aug 1985	24 Jun 1987

Reporting Cycle			Session (Year)		
VII			52 (2014)		
VI			48 (2012)		

Document type	Symbol/Title	Due date	Submitted date	Publication Date	Download
State party's report	CAT/C/CAN/6	23 Jul 2008	20 Oct 2010	22 Jun 2011	View document
List of issues	CAT/C/CAN/Q/6			04 Jan 2012	View document
Info from Civil Society Organizations	Amnesty International				View document
Info from Civil Society Organizations	Amnesty International				View document
Info from Civil Society Organizations	Canadian Centre for International Justice				View document
Info from Civil Society Organizations	Canadian Centre for Victims of Torture				View document
Info from Civil Society Organizations	Canadian Civil Liberties Association				View document
Info from Civil Society Organizations	Canadian Federation of University Women (CFUW)				View document
Info from Civil Society Organizations	Glocal Initiative to End All Corporal Punishment of Children				View document
Info from Civil Society Organizations	International Civil Liberties Monitoring Group (ICLMG)				View document
Info from Civil Society Organizations	International Disability Alliance (IDA)				View document
Info from Civil Society Organizations	Lawyers against the War				View document
Info from Civil Society Organizations	Lawyers' Rights Watch Canada and The International Civil Liberties Monitoring Group				View document
Info from Civil Society Organizations	The Center for Constitutional Rights and the Canadian Centre for International Justice				View document
Info from NHRIs	The Canadian Human Rights Commission				View document
Info from other stakeholders	Submission by John McNamer				View document
Statement					View document
List of delegation/participants					View document
Concluding observations	CAT/C/CAN/CO/6			25 Jun 2012	View document
Follow-up issues	Concluding observations CAT/C/CAN/CO/6, paras. 12, 13, 16 & 17			01 Jun 2012	View document
Follow-up State party's report	CAT/C/CAN/CO/6/Add.1	01 Jun 2013	20 Aug 2013	16 Oct 2013	View document
Follow-up information from other sources	Amnesty International		08 May 2015		View documents
Summary records	CAT/C/SR.1076			23 May 2012	View document
Summary records	CAT/C/SR.1079			31 May 2012	View document

		Session (Year)
V		34 (2005)
IV		34 (2005)
III		25 (2000)
II		10 (1993)
I		3 (1989)

Source: United Nations Human Rights. http://tbinternet.ohchr.org/_layouts/TreatyBodyExternal/countries.aspx?
CountryCode=CAN&Lang=EN

the CAT. Given that Canada is a federal state, the report contains a separate section on the actions of the federal government and sections on the activities in each province. The report provides illustrations of various measures taken to implement the CAT obligations: criminalization of torture; prosecution of persons involved in torture; training of consular officials on torture awareness; funding of service providers assisting victims of torture; and other measures.

Task: Please go to the link provided above, download the government report, and review a part of it that outlines federal measures for compliance with the CAT. What impression does the report create? In your opinion, is Canada taking sufficient steps to ensure compliance with the CAT?

b. Alternative reports on Canada's compliance with the CAT by NGOs. There are 12 of them and they are listed under the heading "Info from Civil Society Organizations."

Task: Compare information in the following reports: the government report (paragraphs 15–25, 86–96) versus submissions by Amnesty International (the first file by Amnesty) (pp. 16–19, 23–24) and the Canadian Civil Liberties Association (paragraphs 76–78, 80, 100): do they paint the same picture of Canada's compliance with CAT obligations as the government report?

As you must have noticed, NGO submissions are more critical of Canada's practices than the government report. NGO reports can help provide greater scrutiny and more comprehensive evaluation of a state's practices.

c. Concluding observations of the Committee against Torture on Canada's compliance with the CAT (CAT/C/CAN/CO/6). The committee reviewed the government report as well as NGO submissions and provided its evaluation of Canada's compliance. The committee's concluding observations highlight positive aspects of Canada's practices as well as areas of concern.

It is hoped that Canada will pay due attention to the committee's recommendations and will take appropriate action, which will be reflected in the next periodic report. Unfortunately, however, the reporting process does not always result in changes. For example, the Canadian government maintains that it is already compliant with the CAT, despite the existence of some practices that expressly contradict the CAT. One of the best known issues is Canada's position that removal to torture may be justified in exceptional circumstances[7] (contrast this with Article 3 of the CAT, which imposes an absolute prohibition on removal to torture and provides for no exceptions).

3.2 An Individual Complaint Against Canada to the Committee Against Torture

Mostafa Dadar escaped to Canada from Iran. His life was at risk due to his opposition to Ayatollah Khomeini and strong loyalty to the Shah. Following the installation of Ayatollah Khomeini in power, Dadar was arrested and tortured, including being subject to a mock execution. Eventually he managed to escape and was resettled to Canada as a refugee in 1988. In Canada, Dadar was treated for severe depression, anxiety, and suicidal tendencies. He was diagnosed with chronic post-traumatic stress disorder resulting from past experience of torture. Over the years, he committed and was convicted of theft under $5000, an assault, and an aggravated assault. In 2000, on the basis of those convictions, the authorities declared Dadar to be a danger to the public. This opinion was formed despite the conclusion of the Correctional Services of Canada that Dadar poses a low risk to the general population. In 2001, Dadar was ordered deported to Iran. Dadar argued that he would be at risk of torture there. Canadian authorities, however, concluded that given the passage of time (it has been 17 years since Dadar left Iran), he would be of limited interest to the Iranian authorities. Further, the immigration officer stated that even if he were in error and if Dadar would be at substantial risk of torture, removal would nevertheless be justified. Dadar challenged the removal order before Canadian courts, but the order was upheld. Thus, Dadar exhausted domestic remedies and, as a last resort, turned to international bodies. He made a complaint to the Committee against Torture, arguing that his deportation to Iran would violate Canada's obligations under the CAT.

The committee concluded that there were substantial grounds to believe that Dadar might be at risk of torture in Iran and that his removal would violate Article 3 of the CAT. Despite this decision, Canada deported Dadar to Iran. His fate is unknown, except for the fact that he was briefly detained and questioned upon return.[8]

The two examples above do not intend to suggest that Canada is never compliant with human rights obligations. Rather, they illustrate the inherent difficulties of ensuring compliance with international human rights obligations and the significant power that states hold in the process.

4. DO INTERNATIONAL HUMAN RIGHTS MAKE A DIFFERENCE?

Much debate on international human rights focuses on the following three questions:

- Why do states join human rights treaties?
- Do states comply with their international obligations and what factors impact compliance?
- Do human rights treaties facilitate changes in state practices?

A given state's decision to join human rights treaties is a result of many factors, including the state's current regime (democratic or autocratic), domestic pro-human rights advocacy efforts, and international pressure. For example, it has been noted that democratic states are more likely to ratify human rights treaties than autocratic regimes.[9] Some states join because of genuine commitment to human rights,[10] while others seek merely to create an impression of change and make a small concession to the opposition to keep it at bay.[11]

A mere ratification of a treaty does not necessarily translate into actual and effective change to state practices.[12] Effective implementation of human rights may be impeded, for example, by the lack of resources, limited capacity of state institutions, or civil wars and other widespread violence.[13] Weak and failing states are often unable to adequately pay and supervise state officials in order to ensure enforcement of human rights standards and prevent corruption and impunity. Very strong and centralized power of a state may also have a negative impact on human rights if it is used to oppress dissent and opposition.

Some argue that states abide by human rights only when it is beneficial for them to do so.[14] For instance, national security, economic, or other interests may trump human rights concerns. Others, however, suggest that it is no longer possible for states to disregard human rights if they want to be a part of the international community.[15] States gradually "socialize" into the acceptance of human rights norms through a variety of external and internal influences and initiatives.[16]

So, do human rights really make a difference? A growing number of empirical studies are attempting to answer this question. Some suggest that ratification of human rights treaties does little to actually improve human rights,[17] while others found some positive correlation between the two.[18] The extent to which state practices comply with human rights varies by country, but, in general, human rights do have the potential to impact domestic practices in a number of ways. First, human rights obligations can constrain state action or compel the state to take certain steps. The very idea of state **sovereignty** is transforming under the influence of human rights norms. Increasingly, state sovereignty is viewed not only as a right to regulate internal affairs, but also as a responsibility to the state's population, particularly in regards to protection from such serious human rights abuses as crimes against humanity, war crimes, and genocide.[19] Second, by becoming a party to a human rights treaty, a state opens itself to scrutiny by treaty bodies—a development that not only sheds light on state practices, but may also compel at the very least slow progress toward greater compliance with human rights. Third, international human rights norms can be used to inform and interpret domestic legislation, bringing it closer to compliance with international norms. Finally, international human rights norms can be an important advocacy tool in the hands of local activists attempting to bring about change. Thus, even though international human rights are not backed by coercive power, they can produce change in other ways, such as changing how people think and empowering local communities to lobby their respective governments for a change.

4.1 What is Canada's International Human Rights Record?

The above discussion of various factors affecting state compliance with human rights obligations provides a context for understanding Canada's practices as well. In the immediate post-Second World War period when the United Nations' *Universal Declaration of Human Rights* was drafted, Canada was not prepared to wholeheartedly accept the idea of human rights.[20] Its foreign policy was dictated predominantly by economic and security interests. However, this position started to change in the 1970s as Canada was building its distinct international identity. Humanitarianism, participation in international organizations, compliance with international obligations, peacekeeping, refugee protection, and other foreign policy initiatives targeted at promoting peace and democracy became some of the key features of that identity.[21] While material interests continued to play an important role in Canada's behaviour, Canadian internationalism and promotion of human rights evolved from being merely a matter of foreign policy to being an ethical obligation toward others.[22] This position is reflected in various government statements. For example, the website of the Department of Foreign Affairs, Trade and Development says that "[h]uman rights is a central theme of Canadian foreign policy . . . [because] Canadians expect their government to be a leader in the field of human rights by reflecting and promoting Canadian values."[23] The 2013 Speech from the Throne characterized Canada as follows: "Canada stands for what is right and good in the world. This is the true character of Canadians—honourable in our dealings, faithful to our commitments, loyal to our friends. Confident partners, courageous warriors and compassionate neighbours."[24]

Thus, on the one hand, Canada has a strong tradition of active participation in international human rights initiatives. Compared to some states, it can generally be said to be more committed to rights protections and have stronger domestic institutions (e.g., courts, provincial human rights tribunals) to support human rights. On the other hand, despite official commitment to human rights, concluding observations of various treaty bodies demonstrate that implementation of certain obligations is lacking. Concerns with respect to certain areas (e.g., indigenous peoples' rights, women's rights, rights of refugees and migrants) as well as the lack of implementation of previous recommendations have been highlighted by various treaty bodies.[25] However, the Canadian government has not always taken active steps to remedy the situation.

Amnesty International noted that in the past years (particularly since the Conservative Party came into power in 2006), Canada has seemed to be less active in promoting and joining various human rights initiatives.[26] For example, it has not ratified some recent treaties that provide for individual complaints mechanisms (e.g., the Optional Protocols to the ICESCR, the *Convention on the Rights of the Child*, the *Convention on the Rights of Persons with Disabilities*). Neither has it considered ratifying the *Convention on Migrant Workers*, despite the increasing numbers of such workers in Canada. The current process for domestic monitoring of Canada's implementation of international human rights obligations is also lacking in transparency, effectiveness, and accountability. Thus, there is a certain contradiction between the government rhetoric and the actual state practices that often fall short of international standards. Although Canada has a strong tradition of supporting human rights, continuous effort is required to ensure that it remains in good standing with respect to both accession and compliance with an evolving body of international human rights law.

Part II. *Canadian Human Rights Act* and Provincial Human Rights Codes

As mentioned above, the implementation of Canada's human rights obligations can take place through a multitude of laws, policies, and initiatives by both federal and provincial/territorial governments. This section examines the *Canadian Human Rights Act* and provincial human rights codes as examples of promotion of international human rights principles.[27]

Both the *Canadian Human Rights Act* and provincial human rights codes seek to promote equality and nondiscrimination. Thus, although their titles contain reference to human rights, in reality they do not cover all areas of human rights, but only their one segment— equality and nondiscrimination. The *Canadian Human Rights Act* is a federal statute that applies to federal departments and agencies; Crown corporations; and federally regulated private sector organizations, employers, and providers of goods, services, facilities, and accommodation. Provincial human rights codes apply to provincial government agencies, private businesses, and individuals that act as employers or provide goods, services, and accommodation.[28] Thus, taken together, these pieces of legislation create a mutually complementary regime of nondiscrimination and equality protection at the federal and provincial levels.

The regimes of the *Canadian Human Rights Act* and provincial human rights codes include three key components:

1. An outline of prohibited forms of discriminatory treatment, prohibited grounds of discrimination, and social areas to which the *Act* and provincial codes apply (e.g., provision of services, employment, and the like);

2. A duty to accommodate (it seeks to remove barriers on individuals' access to goods, services, employment, and accommodation);

3. Establishment of special bodies—commissions and/or tribunals—to examine complaints of discrimination and otherwise promote equality and nondiscrimination.

Each of the above components is described in more detail below.

1. SITUATION PRIOR TO THE IMPLEMENTATION OF THE *CANADIAN HUMAN RIGHTS ACT* AND PROVINCIAL CODES

Imagine the following situations: (1) a restaurant owner refuses to serve you because of your race or ethnicity; and (2) you apply for a job and, although you have the required qualifications, the employer refuses to hire you because of your religious beliefs and practices. How can you affirm your rights? Can private individuals and companies refuse to enter into a contract with others on such grounds as, for example, race, religion, or sexual orientation?

In the early twentieth century, the notion of the freedom of contract allowed individuals and businesses to refuse to enter into transactions, including on discriminatory grounds. For example, in the well known case of *Christie v York Corp* (1940),[29] the Supreme Court upheld the tavern's refusal to serve a patron of colour as an exercise of freedom of contract. These types of precedents contributed to the legitimization of discrimination and created limited opportunities for its victims to fight for their rights.[30]

Over time, some legislation was passed to prohibit and penalize certain types of discrimination (e.g., *Ontario Racial Discrimination Act, 1944; Ontario Fair Employment Practices Act, 1951*). However, these statutes did not provide victims of discrimination with effective redress. First, in order to succeed in a lawsuit, they had to prove discrimination beyond a reasonable doubt—a high standard that was difficult to meet. Second, the authorities were often reluctant to deal with cases of discrimination. The human rights codes and the federal counterpart that emerged in the second half of the twentieth century sought to provide a more effective and accessible mechanism for victims of discrimination. Currently, a private party cannot refuse to, for example, enter into a contract on the basis of any of the prohibited grounds outlined in the codes. Victims of discrimination can launch a complaint with a human rights tribunal or commission. The complaints process is supposed to facilitate access to justice, make it easier for persons to advance their cases, and resolve disputes in a more collaborative fashion rather than in an adversarial mode typical of court litigation.

2. KEY ELEMENTS OF HUMAN RIGHTS SYSTEMS

2.1 Types of Discriminatory Treatment and Prohibited Grounds of Discrimination

Discriminatory treatment can take a variety of forms:[31]

a. **Direct discrimination** occurs when an action or a rule on its face discriminates on a prohibited ground (e.g., a restaurant owner refuses to serve a patron because of the patron's ethnicity).

b. **Constructive discrimination** refers to policies or practices that appear neutral, but in reality have a differential impact on groups protected by human rights codes, creating disadvantage or stereotyping (e.g., a rule that nobody is allowed to wear a head covering could lead to constructive discrimination against persons from certain religious groups).

c. _Harassment_ is vexatious comments or conduct based on one of the prohibited grounds that is known or ought to be known to be unwelcome.

d. _Poisoned environment_ develops when an individual is made to feel unwelcome in a certain setting because of insulting or degrading comments or actions that have been made based on a prohibited ground. For example, a supervisor who makes derogatory, insulting, and crude comments in relation to females creates a poisoned environment.[32]

Both the _Canadian Human Rights Act_ and provincial human rights codes contain lists of grounds on which discrimination is prohibited. The lists in federal and provincial legislation are similar, but some provincial human rights codes contain more extensive lists than the _Canadian Human Rights Act_. The _Canadian Human Rights Act_ outlines 11 grounds: race, national or ethnic origin, colour, religion, age, sex, sexual orientation, marital status, family status, disability, and conviction for an offence for which a pardon has been granted or in respect of which a record of suspension has been ordered. In contrast, Ontario's _Human Rights Code_, for example, contains 17 grounds (see section 3 below); British Columbia has 13, and Nova Scotia, 16.

2.2 Duty to Accommodate

The Canadian Human Rights Act and provincial human rights codes create a duty for employers, landlords, and service providers to deliver various types of accommodation in order to ensure equal access to groups protected under the codes. There is an obligation to consider an individual's request for accommodation and explore options for providing such accommodation (Box 12.2). The types of accommodation required will depend on

Box 12.2

How Human Rights Complaints Can Make a Difference: _Lepofsky v Toronto Transit Commission_ (2005 and 2007)

An individual complaint can often have a far-reaching impact prompting systemic changes. For example, several years ago, the Toronto Transit Commission (TTC) implemented an automatic system to announce all stops on buses, streetcars, and subway trains. This change was motivated by two decisions of the Ontario Human Rights Tribunal, which examined two complaints by Lepofsky, who argued that the TTC has a duty under the Ontario _Human Rights Code_ to accommodate the needs of visually impaired persons by clearly and consistently announcing all stops.[33] Lepofsky is blind and in the absence of such announcements faced significant challenges travelling by public transit. He corresponded with the TTC on the issue for a number of years, but in the absence of cooperation from the TTC filed a human rights complaint. The Human Rights Tribunal found that there was a duty to accommodate and ordered the TTC to ensure that all stops are announced in a clear and consistent manner. The implementation of the Tribunal's decision would benefit not only Lepofsky, but also other similarly situated persons as well as anyone travelling by TTC.

the situation at hand. For example, accommodation based on religion may include providing time for prayer or time off work on religious holidays. Accommodation on the basis of disability may involve building a wheelchair ramp or rearranging the workplace.

There is, however, a limit on the duty to accommodate: an employer, service provider, or landlord has an obligation to accommodate only up to the point of undue hardship, which may include extremely high cost of accommodation and/or significant health and safety risks. What constitutes undue hardship will be determined on a case by case basis.

One of the factors that may limit the duty to accommodate is the existence of a **bona fide occupational requirement** (BFOR)—a requirement that is necessary for proper and safe performance of a job. For example, in order to work as a driver, a person must have acceptable vision. Acceptable vision constitutes a BFOR. In order to determine whether a particular occupational requirement is reasonable and justifiable, an employer must demonstrate that the standard:

- Was adopted for a purpose that is rationally connected to the job to be performed;

- Was adopted in good faith; and

- Is reasonably necessary to accomplish a legitimate purpose, namely that it is not possible to accommodate the employee without the employer suffering undue hardship.[34]

However, even if a rule is a BFOR, there is a duty to accommodate to the point of undue hardship. See Box 12.3.

Box 12.3

The Duty to Accommodate: Case Examples

In *Pannu v British Columbia (Workers' Compensation Board)*,[35] the BC Human Rights Tribunal found that the employer validly acted on the basis of a BFOR. Pannu was a recaust operator at a pulp mill and one of his tasks was to stay behind in case of evacuation and shut down the equipment. According to the Workers' Compensation Board regulations, anyone who may be exposed to poisonous gases is required to wear a self-contained breathing apparatus. The regulations also require anyone who might have to wear the apparatus to be clean-shaven as facial hair prevents the mask from sealing properly. Pannu is a Sikh who wears a beard as a tenet of his faith. Following an inspection, the non-compliance with the regulations was discovered and the employer was ordered to take measures to ensure that the regulations are observed. The employer removed Pannu from his position. Pannu filed a complaint, arguing that he was discriminated against on the basis of religion. The Human Rights Tribunal found that providing an exemption for workers like Pannu would constitute an undue hardship as it would undermine the safety of workers. Thus, the complaint was dismissed.

The *Pannu* case can be usefully contrasted with *Loomba v Home Depot Canada*.[36] Loomba was a Sikh security guard who, in observance of his faith, wears a turban. A Home Depot store where he was assigned to work was under construction and hardhats were required under the *Occupational Health and Safety Act*. As Loomba could not wear a hardhat because of the turban, the manager

(continued)

Box 12.3   *(continued)*

refused to allow him to work. The Tribunal found that the requirement of wearing a hardhat was enforced selectively: others were allowed to remain in the area without a hardhat, while Loomba was not. The Human Rights Tribunal of Ontario found that Loomba was treated differently and more stringently because of his creed and, thus, was discriminated against on the basis of creed.

2.3 Human Rights Commissions and/or Tribunals

At the federal level, the Canadian Human Rights Commission and Human Rights Tribunal have been established to ensure compliance with the *Canadian Human Rights Act*. The commission performs a number of functions, including discrimination prevention, dispute resolution, policy and knowledge development, and initial examination of human rights complaints. The Canadian Human Rights Tribunal deals with complaints of discrimination that are referred to it by the commission (applicants do not have direct access to the tribunal).

Human rights tribunals and/or commissions have also been established at the provincial level to promote equality and deal with complaints about discrimination. In some provinces, a similar model to the federal level is used whereby the commission screens cases before they go to the tribunal. In other provinces (e.g., Ontario), individuals have direct access to the tribunal, while the commission is tasked with broad policy and education functions.

3. ONTARIO *HUMAN RIGHTS CODE* AND SYSTEM

Given that it is impossible to review all provincial human rights codes and systems in this chapter, we will use Ontario as an example.

As mentioned above, provincial human rights codes promote equality and nondiscrimination in specific social areas and in relation to specified grounds. For example, under the Ontario *Human Rights Code*, these social areas are:

- Employment;
- Housing;
- Goods;
- Services and facilities;
- Contracts; and
- Membership in trade and vocational associations.

When the Ontario *Human Rights Code* was enacted in 1962, it contained only six prohibited grounds, but has been progressively expanded to include other grounds. They currently include:

- Race;
- Colour;

- Ancestry;
- Place of origin;
- Citizenship;
- Ethnic origin;
- Disability;
- Creed;
- Sex (including sexual harassment and pregnancy);
- Sexual orientation;
- Gender identity;
- Gender expression;
- Family status;
- Marital status;
- Age;
- Receipt of public assistance (applies only to claims about housing); and
- Record of offences (applies only to claims about employment).

In Ontario, the human rights system consists of three agencies:

1. *The Human Rights Tribunal of Ontario (HRTO)*. It hears complaints under the *Human Rights Code* and can order various remedies if a violation is found. The tribunal receives approximately 3000 complaints a year.[37] In 2013–2014, most of them related to employment (74%), and goods, services, and facilities (22%).[38] Disability was the top ground of discrimination (54%), followed by reprisal (27%), sex (25%), and race (22%).[39]

2. *The Human Rights Legal Support Centre*. The tribunal process was designed to enable individuals to navigate and participate in the process even if they have no legal representation. In fact, in 2013–2014, 76% of applicants before the HRTO were self-represented.[40] The Human Rights Legal Support Centre was created to assist applicants by providing legal assistance in filing applications, legal representation at mediations and hearings, as well as related matters.

3. *The Ontario Human Rights Commission*. The work of the Ontario Human Rights Commission is focused on public education, awareness, and promotion of systemic changes. The powers of the commission include: developing public policy on human rights, conducting research, monitoring and reporting on anything related to human rights in the province, and conducting public inquiries; in addition, it can initiate its own application before the HRTO.[41]

An individual who considers that her rights have been violated can file an application with the HRTO. The examination of a complaint consists of the following stages:

1. *Application*. The process is initiated by an individual, a group, or an organization by filing an application with the HRTO. It must clearly identify the area(s) and ground(s) of alleged violations; name the organization and/or person(s) against whom the application is made; describe incidents of discrimination; specify how they

impacted the applicant (e.g., financially, emotionally); and state what remedy the applicant is seeking. An application should be filed within one year of the date on which the alleged discrimination occurred.

2. *Response.* The HRTO sends the respondent a copy of the application and allows him to reply to the allegations. If the respondent does not file a response within the required timeframe, the tribunal may determine that the respondent has violated the *Code* and make an order against him.

3. *Mediation.* The HRTO assists parties in coming to a mutually agreeable solution through mediation. Mediation is voluntary and, thus, can occur only if both parties agree to it. At the mediation stage, an adjudicator meets with both parties, listens to their positions, and asks questions that may assist with resolution of the case. The adjudicator does not make a decision on the case, but gives the parties a chance to find a solution. This is an example of an ADR mechanism built into a dispute resolution process (see the chapter on alternative dispute resolution on the Companion Website). If a settlement cannot be reached, the case proceeds to a hearing.

4. *Hearing.* At the hearing, the applicant and the respondent present evidence and may call witnesses. Upon hearing all information, an adjudicator can either (1) dismiss the case if no violation is established, or (2) find a violation and order a remedy. An example of remedies provided in one case can be found in Box 12.4. Possible remedies are:

   a. monetary compensation (e.g., for lost wages);

   b. nonmonetary remedies, seeking to put the applicant in the position she would have been in had the discrimination not occurred (e.g., reinstatement on the job);

   c. public interest remedies that would have a broader impact and would seek to prevent similar discrimination in the future (e.g., an order to change hiring practices).

Box 12.4

Remedies: *Qureshi v G4S Security Services (Canada) Ltd*, [2009] OHRTD No 428

Qureshi applied for a job as a security guard at G4S Security Services, passed the initial screening, and even commenced job training. However, his job application was rejected as soon as the company found out that he would need approximately one hour off each Friday in order to pray. Qureshi filed a complaint under the Ontario *Human Rights Code*. The HRTO found that discrimination on the basis of creed had occurred.[42] It ordered the following remedies:

a. monetary compensation for lost wages, and for injury to dignity, feelings, and self-respect; and

b. public interest remedy—the company was required to amend its policy with respect to accommodation and disseminate it to all Ontario employees.

SUMMARY

The core of international human rights law consists of the UN's *Universal Declaration of Human Rights* and nine major human rights treaties. These treaties outline the most fundamental rights necessary for a dignified life and state obligations to respect, protect, and fulfill those rights. While most states officially proclaim their respect for human rights, in reality, their practices are not always compliant with the human rights norms. In order to facilitate compliance, each of the nine major human rights treaties (or their optional protocols) established a treaty body with the powers to review states' periodic reports, adjudicate individual and interstate complaints, and issue interpretations of treaty provisions. Although decisions and recommendations of treaty bodies do not have binding force, it is hoped that they can help change state practices by drawing attention to issues of concern, informing interpretation of domestic laws and inspiring domestic advocacy efforts.

Canada is a party to seven major human rights treaties and its laws and policies have been directly and indirectly impacted by international human rights law. The *Canadian Human Rights Act* and provincial human rights codes are among the avenues that help advance the rights to equality and nondiscrimination. The *Act* and provincial codes prohibit discrimination in specific social areas and in relation to specified grounds, as well as impose a duty on employers, landlords, and service providers to accommodate individuals up to the point of undue hardship. The *Act* and codes also provide for establishment of specialized bodies (such as human rights commissions and/or tribunals) to resolve individual complaints of discrimination, promote public awareness and systemic change, and otherwise assist individuals in knowing and affirming their rights under the *Act* and provincial codes.

Critical Thinking Questions

1. Singh is Sikh and wears a turban as a tenet of his faith. He rides a motorcycle to work, but does not wear a helmet because of his turban. One day, he is stopped by the police and fined for not wearing a helmet. Singh considers that, under the provincial human rights code, there is a duty to accommodate and that he should be allowed to ride a motorcycle without a helmet. Assess the situation by applying concepts from this chapter. Is there a duty to accommodate Singh?

2. An owner of a taxi company refuses to hire women as drivers. He says that being a man is a BFOR because: (a) men are better drivers; (b) men can better deal with unruly or drunk customers; and (c) it is not safe for women to be taxi drivers as they are more likely to be attacked by customers. Assess the situation by applying concepts from this chapter.

3. In your opinion, do international human rights treaties make a difference? If yes, how? If not, why? Give concrete examples from the Canadian context to support your opinion.

4. In your opinion, do any groups within the Canadian population face issues of food insecurity? Is food insecurity a violation of human rights?

   You may find useful to examine the report of UN Special Rapporteur on the Right to Food following his visit to Canada: <http://www.srfood.org/images/stories/pdf/officialreports/20121224_canadafinal_en.pdf>. Does the report provide new information about Canada that you had not been aware of?

5. Discuss the following scenario: Marvan, a Sri Lankan citizen of Tamil descent, immigrated to Canada in 1997. Several years later, the Canadian Security Intelligence Service concluded that he was a member of an organization considered terrorist by the Canadian government. As a result, the authorities are seeking to deport Marvan back to Sri Lanka. However, Marvan is claiming that he should not be removed because his life would be in danger: Sri Lankan authorities are known to detain and torture persons suspected of membership in terrorist organizations.

Analyze the situation from the human rights perspective and particularly in relation to Canada's obligations under the *Convention against Torture*. Does international human rights law allow deportation in cases such as Marvan's? Can Marvan turn to any international treaty bodies to prevent his removal from Canada?

Further Readings and Resources

1. Michael Goodhart, ed, *Human Rights: Politics and Practice* (Oxford University Press, 2009).

2. Jack Donnelly, *Universal Human Rights in Theory and Practice*, 2nd ed (Ithaca: Cornell University Press, 2003).

3. Laura K Egendorf, ed, *Human Rights: Opposing Viewpoints* (Farmington Hills: Greenhaven Press, 2003).

4. Andrew Lui, *Why Canada Cares: Human Rights and Foreign Policy in Theory and Practice* (McGill-Queen's University Press, 2012).

5. Andrew S Thompson, *In Defence of Principles: NGOs and Human Rights in Canada* (Vancouver: UBC Press, 2010).

6. The website of the UN High Commissioner for Human Rights contains links to treaty bodies, texts, and status of ratification of major human rights treaties: <http://www.ohchr.org>.

7. Amnesty International is a well known NGO that works on a variety of human rights issues. It produces an annual report with information on human rights situations in countries around the world: <www.amnesty.org>.

8. Bayefsky.com is a website that provides an accessible way to search for decisions of treaty bodies, periodic reports, and other information on human rights treaties and state compliance with them: <www.bayefsky.com>.

Endnotes

1. Wade Cole, "Sovereignty Relinquished? Explaining Commitment to the International Human Rights Covenants, 1966–1999" in Beth Simmons, ed, *International Law* (London: Sage, 2008), volume VI at 89.

2. Office of the UN High Commissioner for Human Rights, "What are Human Rights?", online: <http://www.ohchr.org/en/issues/Pages/WhatareHumanRights.aspx>. The notion of the three dimensions of human rights is also reflected in various general comments by international treaty bodies. See, for example, Committee on Economic, Social, Cultural Rights, General Comment No 19 "The Right to Social Security", online: <http://daccess-dds-ny.un.org/doc/UNDOC/GEN/G08/403/97/PDF/G0840397.pdf?OpenElement>.

3. *International Covenant on Civil and Political Rights*, [1976] CanTS No 47, Art 2.

4. *International Covenant on Economic, Social and Cultural Rights*, CanTS No 46, Art 2(1).
5. Office of the UN High Commissioner for Human Rights, "Basic Facts about the UPR," online: <http://www.ohchr.org/en/hrbodies/upr/pages/BasicFacts.aspx>.
6. Canadian Heritage, "Core Document Forming Part of the Reports of States Parties" (October 1997) at para 138, online: <http://www.pch.gc.ca/pgm/pdp-hrp/docs/core-eng.cfm#a4>.
7. In 2002, the Supreme Court decision in *Suresh v Canada* [2002] 1 SCR 3, held that, as a rule, Canada should not deport individuals to torture, but, in exceptional circumstances, such removal may be justified.
8. There was a follow-up by Amnesty International, but no further information after 2006 is available. See online: <http://amnesty.org.14feb-youth.com/en/library/asset/AMR20/002/2006/en/7508984f-fa09-11dd-b1b0-c961f7df9c35/amr200022006en.pdf>.

    In its communication to the *Committee against Torture* in 2006, the Canadian government stated that a Canadian representative spoke with the complainant's nephew who said that Dadar arrived in Tehran without incident, and has been staying with his family. See online: <http://www.bayefsky.com/html/canada_cat_follow_juris.php>.
9. Cole, *supra* note 1.
10. Beth Simmons, *Mobilizing for Human Rights: International Law in Domestic Politics* (Cambridge: Cambridge University Press, 2009) at 65.
11. Emilie Hafner-Burton & K Tsutsui, "Human Rights in a Globalizing World: The Paradox of Empty Promises" (2005) 110:5 Am J Sociol 1373
12. For a detailed discussion of the impact of human rights treaties, see Oona Hathaway, "Do Human Rights Treaties Make a Difference?" in Beth Simmons, ed, *International Law* (London: Sage, 2008), volume VI, 123.
13. Emilie M Hafner-Burton, "A Social Science of Human Rights" (2014) 51 J Pease Res 273 at 276; Emilie Hafner-Burton, *Making Human Rights a Reality* (Princeton, New Jersey: Princeton University Press, 2013), ch 6.
14. See generally David P Forsythe, *Human Rights in International Relations* (New York: Cambridge University Press, 2000); Jack Donnelly, *Realism and International Relations* (New York: Cambridge University Press, 2000); Jack L Goldsmith & Eric A Posner, *The Limits of International Law* (Oxford: Oxford University Press, 2005).
15. Christian Reus-Smit, "Human Rights and the Social Construction of Sovereignty" (2001) 27:4 Review of International Studies 519; Thomas Risse, "International Norms and Domestic Change: Arguing and Communicative Behaviour in the Human Rights Area" (1999) 27:4 Politics Society 529.
16. Thomas Risse & Kathryn Sikkink, "The Socialization of International Human Rights Norms into Domestic Practices: Introduction" in Beth Simmons, ed, *International Law* (London: Sage, 2008), volume VI, 187; Risse, *supra* note 15.
17. L Keith, "The United Nations International Covenant on Civil and Political Rights: Does It Make a Difference in Human Rights Behaviour?" (1999) 36:1 J Peace Res 95; Oona Hathaway, "Do Human Rights Treaties Make a Difference?" (2002) 111 Yale LJ 1935;
18. T Landman, "The Politic Science of Human Rights" (2005) 35:3 Brit J Polit Sci 549.
19. Francis Deng, *Sovereignty as Responsibility: Conflict Management in Africa* (Brookings Institution Press, 1996).
20. Andrew Lui, *Why Canada Cares: Human Rights and Foreign Policy in Theory and Practice* (McGill-Queen's University Press, 2012) at 49–51.

21. Don Munton & Tom Keating, "Internationalism and the Canadian Public" (2001) 34:3 Canadian J Pol Sci 517 at 532.

22. *Ibid* at 533.

23. Foreign Affairs, Trade and Development Canada, "Canada's International Human Rights Policy," online: <http://www.international.gc.ca/rights-droits/policy-politique.aspx>.

24. Speech from the Throne to open the second session of the forty-first Canadian Parliament (16 October 2013), online: <http://www.speech.gc.ca/eng>.

25. For example, Committee on the Rights of the Child, "Concluding Observations on the Combined Third and Fourth Periodic Report of Canada, Adopted by the Committee at its Sixty-first Session (17 September–5 October 2012)", online: <http://tbinternet.ohchr.org/_layouts/treatybodyexternal/Download.aspx?symbolno=CRC%2fC%2fCAN%2fCO%2f3-4&Lang=en>; Concluding Observations of the Committee on Economic, Social and Cultural Rights (2006), online: <http://tbinternet.ohchr.org/_layouts/odyexternal/.aspx?symbolno=E%2fC.12%2fCAN%2fCO%2f4&Lang=en>; Concluding Observations of the Committee on the Elimination of Discrimination against Women, online: <http://tbinternet.ohchr.org/_layouts/treatybodyexternal/Download.aspx?symbolno=CEDAW%2fC%2fCAN%2fCO%2f7&Lang=en>.

26. Amnesty International, "Matching International Commitments with National Action: A Human Rights Agenda for Canada" (2012), online: <http://www.amnesty.ca/sites/default/files/canadaaihra19december12.pdf>.

27. The preambles of some provincial human rights codes contain references to the *Universal Declaration of Human Rights*. However, none of them specifically state that they are implementing Canada's international obligations.

28. Although the *Canadian Human Rights Act* and provincial human rights codes are not parts of the *Constitution*, due to their important subject matter they are considered to have a quasi-constitutional status.

29. [1940] 92 SCR 139.

30. Carol A Aylward, *Canadian Critical Race Theory: Racism and the Law* (Halifax: Fernwood Publishing, 1999) at 79.

31. There are some differences in the language used by the *Canadian Human Rights Act* and provincial human rights codes, but they generally seek to combat similar forms of discriminatory treatment. The *Canadian Human Right Act* outlines the following prohibited discriminatory practices:

   - Denying someone goods, services, facilities, or accommodation;
   - Providing someone goods, services, facilities, or accommodation in a way that treats them adversely and differently;
   - Refusing to employ or continue to employ someone, or treating them unfairly in the workplace;
   - Following policies or practices that deprive people of employment opportunities;
   - Paying men and women differently when they are doing work of the same value;
   - Retaliating against a person who has filed a complaint with the commission or against someone who has filed a complaint for them; and
   - Harassing someone.

32. See, for example, findings in *Harriott v National Money Mart*, 2010 HRTO 353.

33. The first complaint was with respect to the lack of consistent announcements on subways (*Lepofsky v Toronto Transit Commission*, 2005 HRTO 36); the second was with respect to the lack of announcements on buses and streetcars (*Lepofsky v Toronto Transit Commission*, [2007] OHRTD No 23).

34. *British Columbia (Public Service Employee Relations Commission) v BCGSEU*, [1999] 3 SCR 3.

35. *Pannu v Skeena Cellulose Inc*, [2000] BCHRTD No 56.

36. *Loomba v Home Depot Canada Inc*, [2010] OHRTD No 1422.

37. HRTO, "HRTO Statistics," online: <http://hrto.ca/hrto/?q=en/node/128>.

38. HRTO, "Fiscal Year 2013-2014," online: <http://hrto.ca/hrto/?q=en/node/197>.

39. *Ibid*.

40. *Ibid*.

41. Ontario Human Rights Commission, "About the Commission," online: <http://www.ohrc.on.ca/en/about-commission>.

42. *Qureshi v G4S Security Services (Canada) Ltd*, [2009] OHRTD No 428.

Glossary

Aboriginal title Aboriginal communities' right to land and to the use of that land for a variety of activities—whether connected to distinct Aboriginal traditions or not

access in the child custody context, a parent's right to visit children and to be visited by them as well as the right to make inquiries and obtain information about health, education, and welfare of the children

access to justice effective right and ability of individuals to advance legal claims to protect their interests and to defend themselves against claims by others

actus reus in criminal law, the element of an offence that refers to the physical act (or omission)

adversarial system system of adjudication where the primary responsibility for collection and presentation of evidence lies with the parties to a case; a judge acts as an impartial arbiter who makes a decision on the basis of the evidence and the arguments presented by the parties

alternative dispute resolution (ADR) a set of mechanisms that seek to help parties resolve disputes outside courts; includes negotiation, mediation, arbitration, and other techniques

annulment cancellation of a marriage; declaration that it is legally void

appellant a party that lost a case at the trial level and initiates an appeal to a higher court

beyond a reasonable doubt in criminal law, a standard of proof that lies in between a balance of probabilities and absolute certainty, closer to the latter

bona fide occupational requirement a requirement that is necessary for proper and safe performance of a job; it is one of the factors that may limit the duty to accommodate under provincial and federal human rights acts

case law (or common law) a body of judicial decisions produced by courts of a particular country

checks and balances a mechanism that helps ensure that no one branch of government can dominate the other two; each branch has certain powers in relation to the other branches that allow it to "check" against possible abuses of power

civil law system a system of law that relies on legislation (particularly in the form of codes) as the main source of law

common law system a system of law that relies on precedents (judicial decisions) as the primary method of law creation

concluding observations comments and recommendations that a treaty body makes upon review of states' periodic reports on their compliance with a given human rights treaty

conditional sentence a form of imprisonment that is served in a community under conditions that may include house arrest, curfew, and enrollment in a treatment program

consideration in contract law, something of value that forms a subject matter of a contract

constitutionalism a principle dictating that all government action must be compliant with the *Constitution*

constitutional review review by courts of actions and decisions of the executive and legislature for compliance with the *Constitution*

contract an agreement between two or more parties that outlines their rights and obligations and is enforceable by courts

contributory negligence in tort law, a defence against torts of negligence that claims that the plaintiff is partially responsible for injuries

corrective justice a theory of justice that focuses on correcting inequality that results from wrongdoings or unfair dealings between individual parties; the inequality may be corrected, for example by means of financial compensation

critical legal studies a theory that questions objectivity and neutrality of the law; it focuses on the impact of politics, power, and other factors on the content of laws

critical race theory a theory that exposes racial inequalities and highlights law's role in marginalizing minorities

Crown the monarch (currently Queen Elizabeth II) along with representatives in Canada (governor general and lieutenant governors); it also can refer to federal and provincial governments as well as their subordinate agencies and personnel

custody in family law, means that a parent has the right and responsibility to make decisions affecting the child's well-being

damages financial compensation that seeks to bring a plaintiff into the position that she would have been in but for the wrongdoing

defamation making of false statements that can damage a person's reputation and lower him in the estimation of the community

deference recognizes the special expertise of administrative decision makers and mandates courts to interfere as little as possible into the substance of those decisions

direct democracy a form of democracy that allows people to be directly involved in government decision making; in contemporary societies, direct democracy is exercised through referendum, recall, and initiative

discharge of a contract ending of obligations under a contract; the contract is no longer in force

distinguishing a precedent arguing that there is a significant difference between the precedent and the case at bar and that, as a result, the precedent is inapplicable

distributive justice a theory of justice that examines how resources and entitlements are and should be allocated in society

duress forcing a person to do something (including violating the law) under threat of harm against the person and/or their family

duty of care in tort law, an obligation to avoid actions that can be reasonably foreseen to cause harm to others

enabling legislation legislation that authorizes the creation of an agency in question and outlines its powers

executive federalism a form of federalism where the executive plays a central role in interactions between the two levels of government

feminist theory a theory that exposes law and social institutions as profoundly male-centred

general deterrence an objective of legal rules that seeks to deter the general public from certain types of conduct; for instance, an example of a punished offender is expected to send a message of general deterrence

gratuitous promise in contract law, a promise to do something for free, without a return from the other party

hybrid offences offences that, on the election of the prosecution, can be tried either on a summary conviction or by way of indictment

indictable offences offences that are considered more serious and are usually tried by more complex procedures

inherent right to self-government a right of First Nations communities that exists by virtue of their original settlement in Canada; it cannot be granted or taken away by dominant Euro-Canadian institutions

injunction a court order requiring a person to either do or refrain from doing something

inquisitorial system a system of adjudication where a judge participates in investigating a case, collecting evidence, and questioning witnesses

interest groups groups of individuals or organizations that share a common set of goals and have joined together to persuade a government authority to adopt a policy, law, or decision that will help protect or advance the interest of a given group

intervener an individual, agency, or organization that is not a party to a given case, but that has a substantial and direct interest in the case and is allowed to make submissions on the issue to a court hearing the case

judicial review examination by courts of whether a given administrative decision was authorized by a statute

jurisdiction specific powers and/or subject areas assigned to a given authority (e.g., a court or a level of government)

leave to appeal permission from a court to have a case heard before that court

legitimate expectation an expectation that an agency or tribunal would follow the same procedure as it did in the past

legal aid a system funded by the government that seeks to promote access to justice for low-income individuals

legal pluralism a theory that argues that law can be produced by various actors (state and non-state) and at different sites (local, national, international); these multiple legal regimes exist at the same time within a given territory

legal realism a theory that acknowledges the impact of nonlegal factors such as values and backgrounds of judges on outcomes of cases

lobbying a form of direct or indirect communication of an interest group or individual with government for the purpose of influencing law and/or policy

majority government a situation when a given party holds the majority of seats in the House of Commons or in a provincial legislative assembly

mandamus a court order requiring an administrative authority to perform an existing duty

mens rea in criminal law, the element of an offence that denotes the mental aspect of given wrongful conduct

minority government a situation when a given party has more seats in the House of Commons or a legislative assembly than any other party, but falls short of 50% plus one seat

natural law a theory that considers that man-made laws must be reflective of higher "natural" values

negligence a type of tort that imposes liability for tortfeasor's failure to take proper care

notwithstanding clause section 33 of the *Charter* that allows federal Parliament and provincial legislatures to enact laws that infringe upon *Charter* rights and declare that those laws will operate notwithstanding the provisions of the *Charter*

Oakes **test** a test set out in the case of *R v Oakes* that courts use in order to determine whether an infringement of a *Charter* right is justified under s. 1 of the *Charter*

obiter dicta "other things" said in a given decision

ombudsman an impartial and independent officer established to investigate allegations of maladministration and to make recommendations for improvement

parliamentary supremacy a doctrine that Parliament is the supreme law maker; it has the power to enact, amend, and repeal laws, including overriding or modifying common law rules

positivism a theory that, in contrast to natural law, does not draw a close link between law and morality; validity of a law is determined by

whether it was enacted according to an established procedure, not whether it is consistent with a higher "natural" law

precedent a judicial decision in an earlier case that governs resolution of future similar disputes

prima facie at first sight; upon initial observation

principle of responsible government a principle mandating that a given government can remain in power only for as long as it enjoys the support of the legislature

principles of fundamental justice in the context of s. 7 of the *Charter*, these are legal principles that are reflective of society's core notions of justice; they are used to determine whether a limitation on a s. 7 right is allowable (e.g., the right to know a case against oneself and to respond to that case is a fundamental principle of justice)

privative clause a statutory provision that restricts or prevents review of an administrative agency's decisions by courts

privity of contract in contract law, an idea that only parties to a contract have rights and obligations under it

public international law an area of international law that regulates interactions *among* states as well as international organizations and defines their rights and duties

ratio decidendi reasons for a court's decision

"reasonable person" standard in tort law, an objective general standard of behaviour for a given activity; it is applied in the context of torts of negligence

recklessness a concept in criminal law that refers to situations where a person does not desire to bring about a particular wrongful consequence, but is nevertheless taking an unjustifiable risk, foreseeing that a wrongful consequence might occur

rectification in contract law, a remedy that allows a court to amend the terms of the contract in order to reflect the original intention of the parties

representative democracy a form of democracy where the population elects representatives who act on its behalf

repudiate to end a contract without being considered in breach of it

rescission in contract law, a remedy that allows a contract to be set aside and restores the parties back to their original precontract positions

restorative justice a theory of justice that views an offence as an event that ruins the relationship between a wrongdoer and a victim as well as those within a community; restorative justice initiatives focus on re-establishing the harmony in these relations through problem solving, dialogue, reconciliation, and forgiveness

retributive justice a theory of justice dictating that a wrongdoer should be subject to punishment proportionate to the degree of their blameworthiness

rule of law a principle that no one—whether private individual or public official—is above the law; all government action must be authorized by law and exercised within the limits prescribed by it

rules of equity rules developed by the courts of chancery in Britain to provide relief from rigid common law procedures; they purported to reflect spiritual ideas of fairness

separation of powers a principle dictating that no official can be a member of more than one branch of government

single member plurality electoral system a system under which the candidate who gains the most votes in a given riding (even if it is less than 50% of votes) wins the seat in the legislature

social change modifications in how individuals interact with each other and the state, how they govern themselves, what values they consider important, and how they organize various activities in public and private spheres

sources of law authorities, documents, and principles from which legal rules originate

sovereignty exclusive authority of the state over individuals in its territory and the power to regulate matters within its territory

specific deterrence measures targeted at deterring an offender in question from committing wrongdoings in the future

standard of review a degree of rigour with which a court will scrutinize an administrative agency's decision

stare decisis a principle in common law that requires lower courts to follow decisions of higher courts

strict liability an approach that allows imposition of liability in the absence of fault or negligence; it is often employed in relation to activities that are inherently dangerous

strict party discipline a mechanism of party control that requires members of legislature to vote in support of their party's position

subordinate legislation legislation that is passed not by elected legislatures, but by the executive (e.g., ministries, departments, agencies, boards) under enabling statutes; subordinate legislation takes the form of regulations, rules, and bylaws

summary conviction offences offences that are considered less serious and are tried by simpler procedures

system of law a set of historically rooted beliefs and practices with respect to how the law is formed, its nature and role in society, and organization of the legal system

tortfeasor a person who has committed a tort

treaty an international agreement between states that intends to create binding legal obligations

treaty body in international human rights, a body established under one of nine major human rights treaties that has the power to monitor state parties' compliance with their obligations under those treaties

trespass a tort of unlawful interference with someone else's property; can be with respect to land as well as personal property

ultra vires outside of the jurisdiction of a given agency/level of government

unconscionability in contract law, a situation where there is a significant power imbalance between the parties to a contract that results in a weaker party being taken advantage of

void having no legal effect

voidable in contract law, a contract that a party may choose to end without being considered in breach of contract

willful blindness a state of mind in which a wrongdoer chooses to remain ignorant of suspicious circumstances

Index

R. v. Hamilton, 32–36, 181, 196–197
R. v. Hamilton and Mason, 36
R. v. J.A., 61
R. v. Latimer, 183
R. v. Morgentaler, 127–128, 141, 148
R. v. N.S., 137–138
R. v. Quong-Wing, 145
R. v. Stinchcombe, 149
R. v. Tessling, 136
R. v. Van der Peet, 27
R. v. White, 36
race, 110, 196, 245, 246–248
race-specific income tables, 246
radical feminism, 110
radical feminists, 116
ratio decidendi, 30, 33–34, 34
reading down, 142
reading in, 142
"reasonable person" standard, 234–235
reasonableness, 173
recall, 45
recklessness, 183
rectification, 219
reference cases, 77
Reference re Senate Reform, 77
referendum, 45
Refugee Appeal Division (RAD), 170
Refugee Protection Division (RPD), 170
refugee reform legislation, 53
regulation, 4–5, 29
regulatory offences, 185
Reichmann v. Berlin, 243
Reilly v. The King, 215
religious-based systems of law, 19–20
remedies
    see also specific remedies
    administrative law, 174–175
    "appropriate and just" remedy, 141
    under the Charter, 141–143
    under common law, 22
    contract law, 216–219
    family violence, 270–271
    public law remedies, 270–271
    tort law, 242–244, 271
reporting of decisions, 32–33
representative democracy, 44, 106–107
reproductive technology, 273–274
The Republic (Plato), 103
republics, 45
repudiation, 208
rescission, 212, 218
residential schools, 63, 110
residual power, 126
respondent, 79
responsible government, 50
restitution, 192
restorative justice, 6, 192
retributive justice, 6
right to be heard, 164–166
right to counsel, 135–136, 168, 184
right to remain silent, 184
RJR-MacDonald Inc. v. Canada (Attorney General), 55
Rodriguez, Sue, 104

Rogers case, 221
Roman Catholic Church, 117
Roman law, 21, 22
Roncarelli v. Duplessis, 157, 171
royal assent, 50
Royal Commission on Aboriginal Peoples, 62–63, 64
Royal Proclamation of 1763, 25
rule of law, 10–13, 47, 56, 107
rules of equity, 22
Rylands v. Fletcher, 237

S

Safe Streets and Communities Act (Bill C-10), 52
Sale of Goods Acts, 209
same-sex couples, 256–257
same-sex marriage, 256
Sauvé v. Canada (Chief Electoral Officer), 108–109, 143–144
Scott, Valerie, 194
search and seizure, unreasonable, 136
second reading, 49
second wave feminism, 116
security of the person, 134–135
self-administration, 64
self-defence, 187, 232
self-government. See Aboriginal self-government
self-management, 64
Senate, 47, 48, 48f, 49, 50, 53, 54, 77, 113, 129
Senate reform, 77, 130
sentencing, 192–193t, 192–194, 196–197
separation, 259
separation agreement, 260–261, 264–265
separation of powers, 45, 107
severing offending provisions, 141
sex work, 194–196
sexual assault, 190
shari'a, 20
single member plurality electoral system, 47
Small Claims Court, 78, 81
social agreements, 206
social change, 6–7, 273–274
social contract, 107
socialist systems, 20–21
sources of law, 8
    in Canada, 27–36
    case law, 30–36
    criminal law, 181
    legislation, 27–29
South America, 24
sovereignty, 64, 290
Soviet Bloc, 20
Soviet Union, 123
Spain, 24
special damages, 243
specialized courts, 82–83
specific deterrence, 180
specific performance, 218
Speech from the Throne, 57, 291

spousal abuse, 269–271
spousal support, 262–265
Spousal Support Advisory Guidelines, 264
standard of review, 172–173, 174
standard setting, 229
standing committees, 49–50
Staples v. Varga, 209
stare decisis, 31
Statute of Westminster, 124
statutes, 28
statutory enactment process, 48–50, 51f
statutory jurisdiction, 81
Statutory Powers Procedure Act (Ontario), 163–164
Stevens v. Stevens, 212
Stinchcombe case, 149
storytelling, 110–111
strategic litigation against public participation (SLAPP), 62
strict liability, 237
strict party discipline, 48
striking down legislation, 141
structure of government. See government structure
subject matter areas, 14
subordinate legislation, 28
substantive law, 14
Summa Theologica (Aquinas), 3
summary conviction offences, 184–185
sunna, 20
Superior Court of Justice, 80, 81
supervised access, 266–267
supervision order, 271
support payments, 262–266
Supreme Court of Canada, 53, 80, 83–85, 84t, 88, 108
Sutherland, Kate, 248
Suzuki v. Munroe, 238, 244
system of checks and balances, 45
system of courts, 79–80, 79f
system of law, 8, 24f
    bi-juridicial system, 27
    in Canada, 24–27
    chthonic legal tradition, 19
    civil law system, 22–23
    common law system, 21–22
    mixed systems, 24
    overview of selected systems, 18–24
    pluralist system, 27
    religious-based systems of law, 19–20
    socialist systems, 20–21
systemic violations of human rights, 287
systems of government, 44–46

T

the Talmud, 20
Talmudic legal tradition, 20
Tax Court, 83, 87
temporary wardship order, 271
terms of a contract, 207
Tessling case, 136
theoretical perspectives
    critical legal studies, 109–110